POPOVA

DMITRI V. SARABIANOV AND NATALIA L. ADASKINA

POPOVA

Translated from the Russian by Marian Schwartz

HARRY N. ABRAMS, INC., PUBLISHERS, NEW YORK

In many instances, the orientation of Popova's works cannot be established
with certainty. The editors have tried to adhere to the most recent
judgments by scholars of her work.

Editor, English-language edition: Phyllis Freeman

Library of Congress Cataloging-in-Publication Data

Sarab'ianov. Dmitriĭ Vladimirovich.
Popova / by Dmitri V. Sarabianov and Natalia L. Adaskina; translated
from the Russian by Marian Schwartz.
p. 396 cm.
Translation of: Lioubov Popova
ISBN 0-8109-3701-8
1. Popova, Liubov. 2. Artists—Russian S.F.S.R.—Biography.
3. Constructivism (Art)—Russian S.F.S.R.   I. Adaskina, N. L.
(Natal'ia L'vovna)   II. Title.
N6999.P67S27   1989
709'.2'4—dc19   89-242
[B]   CIP

Originally published in French under the title *Lioubov Popova*
by Philippe Sers Editeur, Paris, 1989

English translation copyright © 1990 Harry N. Abrams, Inc.

Published in 1990 by Harry N. Abrams, Incorporated, New York
A Times Mirror Company

Printed and bound in Italy

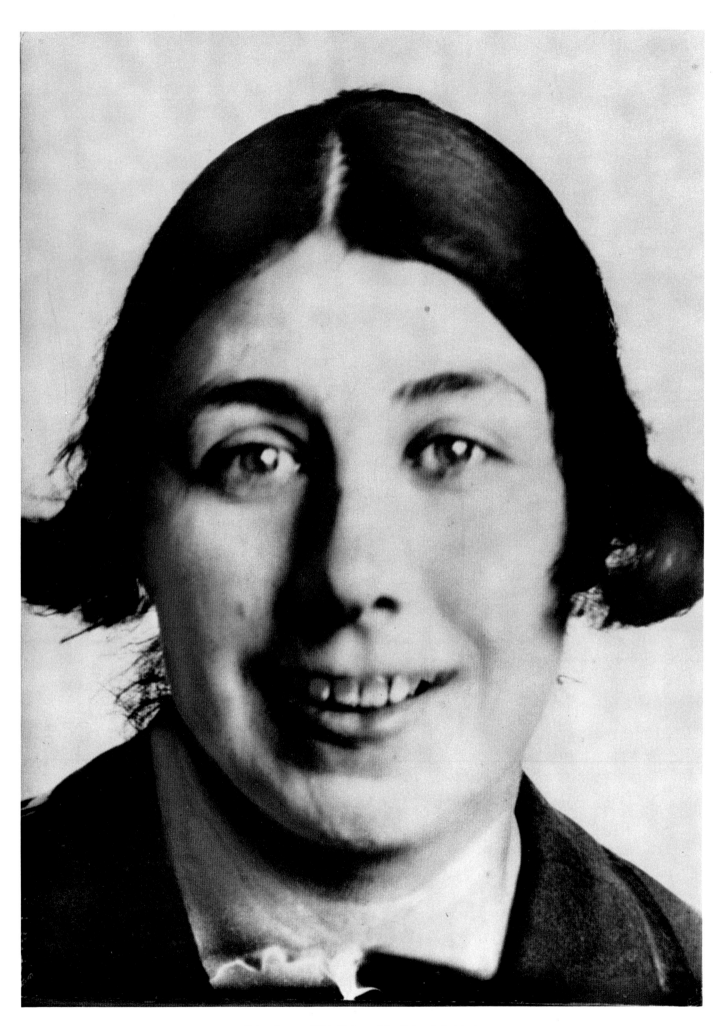

Liubov Popova. 1924. Photograph by Aleksandr Rodchenko

CONTENTS

PART ONE: PAINTING
DMITRI V. SARABIANOV

Painter or Designer?   12
The Early Work   12
The Early 1910s: Female Models, Apples, Trees   14
Moscow—Paris—Moscow   41
The Paintings of 1913   42
Cubo-Futurism   57
The Paintings of 1914—15: Genres, Subjects, Motifs   58
Musical Instruments   60
"Objects"   62
Reliefs   64
Faces, Figures   65
The Last Landscapes   68
Popova and Suprematism   109
Reminiscences of Reality   111
Painterly Architectonics: Meaning, Principle, Evolution   133
The Paintings of 1920   137
Spatial Force Constructions   139

Notes to Part One   145

PART TWO: THEORY, TEACHING, THEATER, AND DESIGN
NATALIA L. ADASKINA

A Time of Changes   190
Popova's Creative Evolution in the Early 1920s   191
A First Appeal to the Formal Method   191
Inkhuk: The Ideas of Objective Analysis   193
Objective and Nonobjective: The Modern Style?   194
"From Representation to Construction"   196
Vkhutemas: "The Essence of the Disciplines"   198
Vkhutemas: "Discipline No. 1—Color"   212
The Search for a New Creative Object   213
GVYTM: "Theater as Production"   213
GVYTM: "The Construction of Form and Space"   214
GVYTM: "The Material Element of the Play"   215
Vkhutemas: The Plan for a
   "Production Studio in the Basic Department"   216
The Paradoxes of Popova's Theatrical Work   217
The First Experiment: The Chamber Theater—
   Romeo and Juliet   217
The Second Experiment: The Children's Theater—
   The Tale of the Priest and Balda, His Helper   219
The Third Experiment: The Comedy Theater—
   The Locksmith and the Chancellor   219
Collaboration with Meierkhold: First Episode—
   A Mass Festival on Khodinskoe Field   249
Collaboration with Meierkhold: Second Episode—
   The Magnanimous Cuckold   250
The Priest of Tarquinia: "A Production Not in
   Keeping with Its Concept"   254

Expediency!   255
Collaboration with Meierkhold: Third Episode—
   Earth on End   255
"Production Work": Studies for Verbovka   273
The Experiment in Monumental Design: Mossovet—
   The Poets Club   274
Popova's Graphic Design: The Traditions of the
   "Futurist" Book   274
The "Ornamental" Side of Popova's Graphic Design   275
The Book Cover as a Spatial Organism   275
The Poster: Representation in Popova's Late Work   276
Graphic Design: The "Montage Style"   277
Production Art   299
The Teacup Design   299
At the Textile Print Factory   299
Popova and Constructivism in the Textile Industry   300
Fashioning Clothing   303
A Place in the Ranks—A Place in History   304

Notes to Part Two   305

APPENDIXES
Writings by Popova   345
Chronology   387
Glossary   390
Index   391

PART ONE: PAINTING

PAINTER OR DESIGNER?

In 1921 Liubov Popova, along with her colleagues at the Institute of Artistic Culture, proclaimed the death warrant of easel painting: they resolved to renounce it forever. Only Popova managed to keep that promise. Dead in 1924, she did not live to see the former Constructivists once again take up the brush, begin to work from nature, paint landscapes and still lifes. Possibly Popova too would have had to backtrack eventually. Fate, though, had its own plans: her creative activity was cut short at the crest of her enthusiasm for textile and costume design.

In fact, all but the last two or three years of her regrettably brief artistic life had been bound up with painting, and she had created sublime, polished works; she had revealed her brilliant talent swiftly and fully. Her evolution as a painter proved exceptionally logical and purposeful.

Whichever position we take—whether we reject painting and find the greatest scope for artistic development in the twentieth century in the field of design, or we affirm the inalienably intrinsic worth of fine art—we cannot fail to recognize Popova's accomplishments in painting. From the latter perspective, the painting speaks for itself; from the former, the painting cannot be forgotten, for it functioned as a creative laboratory, fueling her great successes in the field of theater and in textile and graphic design. Even if we consider Popova's last years, as a designer, the culmination of her artistic path, we still must recognize that her painting was a necessary precondition.

THE EARLY WORK

The milieu that produced Popova at the beginning of this century was actively involved with culture; many of the people in it were interested in art, collected works of art, tested their own powers as artists.

The family into which Liubov Sergeevna was born on April 24, 1889, were merchants.[1] Liubov's great-grandfather had been a miller, and her grandfather became a prominent textile manufacturer. Although her father, Sergei Maksimovich, devoted his energies to augmenting his wealth and to his business, he was also a well-known philanthropist and devotee of music and theater. Popova's relatives on her mother's side were also music lovers.

Her mother, Liubov Vasilievna Zubova, belonged to an equally fast-rising branch of the Russian third estate, the bourgeoisie. Her father had been a serf, but the very next generation not only displayed a passion for education and culture but also participated at the highest cultural levels. Liubov Vasilievna's brother was a prominent collector who later, under the Soviets, gave the government two Stradivarius violins. Liubov

Vasilievna's nephew, Vasilii Pavlovich Zubov, became a well-known Soviet cultural historian, an expert on the Italian Renaissance.

Liubov Sergeevna had two brothers and a sister: Sergei was the eldest, then Liubov, Pavel, and Olga.[2] Pavel, who became the guardian of his sister's artistic legacy, was the most outstanding of the children, except for Liubov. He earned a law degree from Moscow University; studied philosophy, psychology (as a disciple of the renowned Georgii Chelpanov, an exponent of "experimental introspection"), and classical literature; translated Aristotle and Hegel, and in his later years taught in and eventually chaired the Department of Logic at Moscow University. He was married to Tolstoy's granddaughter, Anna Ilinichna. Liubov's cousin Vera Aleksandrovna Popova was a well-known sculptor. On her mother's side, Vera Popova was a direct descendant of the architect Fedor Shechtel and his son, the artist Lev Zhegin. These people, only a representative few, indicate the breadth and quality of the cultural achievements of Popova's relatives.

The future artist passed her childhood outside Moscow at Krasnovidovo, an estate not far from the village of Ivanovskoe, where there was a factory and workers' houses. The children were tutored at home by teachers from the factory school. Their drawing teacher was a professional artist, K. M. Orlov, a friend of their father. The sole remaining trace of Liubov's artistic activity in those years is an entry in a list of works by the artist (compiled after her death by Aleksandr Vesnin, Ivan Aksionov, and others) for the watercolor *Forest*, roughly dated by the compilers 1902 or 1904. Although we do not know the work itself, we can nonetheless make a few deductions about it: since Popova kept this childhood drawing in her studio, she must have valued it, and one can assume that it was a landscape from nature.

In 1902 the entire family moved to Yalta, a resort town in the Crimea on the Black Sea, where the future artist attended Gymnasium. Then—in 1906—the family went back to Moscow, to a house on Novinsky Boulevard, where the artist lived until the end of her life. She finished Gymnasium, then A. S. Alferov's two-year course, which was similar to the program of the literature department of the university. This is a fact of some importance; a serious education in the humanities was rarely available to Russian painters. Popova undoubtedly put that education to good use both in her elaboration of theoretical problems of art and in her work on theatrical sets and costumes. In her notes (page 344) we come across lists of books with references not only to the works of Goethe, Shelley, Pushkin, and nineteenth-century French lyric poets, but to the journal *Logos* and Paul Deussen's *Vedanta, Plato, and Kant: Culture and Wisdom of the Ancient Indians*. The young artist's interests should not surprise us in light of the cultural environment that surrounded her.

About the development of Popova's artistic talent during her Gymnasium years we know practically nothing. We have no information on any of her Yalta experiences, and we have only meager information about the first years after her return to Moscow in the form of one pencil drawing labeled *View from My Window onto Houses* (1906; page 28).[3] That drawing remains puzzling in Popova's artistic career—possibly because we know no other compositions from that period. Depicting timbered walls and roofs with chimneys, it attests to a certain degree of influence from World of Art graphics—which often tended to look to the past—above all, those of Mstislav Dobuzhinsky.

In 1907 Popova entered the studio of Stanislav Zhukovsky, later switching to the school of Konstantin Yuon and Ivan Dudin. In the latter, instruction was conducted on a very advanced level; many Russian painters attended Yuon's school (Yuon himself was a prominent Impressionist). Here Popova found her first friend and comrade-in-arms, Liudmila Prudkovskaia—the sister of another artist, Nadezhda Udaltsova. In the summers of 1908 and 1909 the friends worked together at the Popov family's country home, Krasnovidovo, dreaming of establishing their own studio.

The earliest works by Popova on the Vesnin-Aksionov list are dated 1908. Popova's own list dates only from 1913;[4] evidently she considered everything prior to that merely prehistory. For us, however, that prehistory possesses definite interest. It demonstrates the artist's swift journey from nature studies in the tradition of Russian realistic landscape, slightly influenced by Impressionism, to the latest word in French Cubism. Like many other Russian painters of the early twentieth century, in half a decade Popova completed a journey that should have taken several generations.

The works from the end of the first decade of this century were inspired above all by her teachers. Both Zhukovsky and Yuon, like the other masters of the Union of Russian Artists, preached a form of Impressionism, dealing most often with landscape, and chose simple motifs characteristic of the everyday condition of Russian nature, the Russian countryside, the Russian provinces.

The motifs of Popova's pictures fit in well with the spirit of that group. Barns, haystacks (page 35, left), landscapes with a bridge (page 29), with a church, with a washerwoman rinsing linen on the banks of a river (page 30)—all dating from 1908—for these subjects chosen by Popova there are many similar scenes by Yuon and Zhukovsky, by Igor Grabar and Konstantin Korovin, even by Valentin Serov, who divided his work between typical Moscow Impressionism and Petersburg Modernism. The compositional devices Popova employed also lie within the confines of the system elaborated by the Moscow Impressionists. As the work of these masters suggests, Popova's approach to nature was free of any doctrinaire viewpoint. She picked

some realistic scene and worked within the boundaries of her deliberately chosen "chance" compositions.

True, occasionally Popova's compositions reflect considered selection and placement, and several works reveal an interest in decorativeness and expressiveness.

The modifications that the young Popova introduced into the Union of Russian Artists' conception of landscape were altogether natural. At exhibitions in Moscow she more than likely would have encountered the Symbolist works of Nikolai Krimov, Nikolai Sapunov, and Sergei Sudeikin. We do know that at her request her father subscribed to *Zolotoe runo* (Golden Fleece), the most progressive Russian art journal of the day, the organ of the Symbolist Blue Rose artists of Moscow.

The year 1908 was especially rich in new exhibitions from which Popova received new stimuli: in January, "Wreath-Stephanos" in Moscow; in April, "Wreath" in Petersburg and "Salon of the *Golden Fleece*" in Moscow; in May, "Modern Trends" in Petersburg; in the fall, "Link" in Kiev and the exhibition of the Moscow Association of Artists in Moscow; in the winter, the sixth exhibition of the Union of Russian Artists in Moscow and the "Salon" in Petersburg. Naturally, Popova could not have seen all of these: she did not get to Kiev until the summer of 1909 and to Petersburg until 1911. Nevertheless, there is every reason to believe that she attended the Moscow shows, and she may have heard or read about the others.

Popova's works of 1908 reveal the impression the compositions of Natalia Goncharova made on her. In 1908 at the "Salon of the *Golden Fleece*" Goncharova exhibited her painting *Petrovsky Park*, in which the Neoprimitivist conception of painting is clearly evident. Goncharova's methods—generalized painting of the trunks and leaves of trees surrounded by a dark outline, stylized figures of people presented in their most typical, refined manifestations, the tension generated by patches of color—all this Popova echoed in diluted form in her paintings of 1908.

Of course, the experiments of the novice artist cannot be explained solely by Russian sources. In a questionnaire compiled by Tatiana Pakhomova shortly after Popova's death, there is a reference to the "brief imitation of Van Gogh," which was followed by the influence of Gauguin (equally short-lived, by the way) and Cézanne. Nearly all the landscapes mentioned above are marked by an enthusiasm for Van Gogh, which revealed itself in an energetic use of color, a vigorous brushstroke, and even the employment of certain motifs: for example, green rows on pink ground that seem to hurtle forward from the deep background in *Landscape with Female Figures* (page 31). This early enthusiasm for Van Gogh and Cézanne also prompted Popova's desire to visit Paris.

While landscape composition was one focus of the beginning artist's attention, so too were the still life and the portrait. In the painting *Still Life. Milk Pitcher. Plein Air* (1908; page 35, left),[5] one is aware of specific deficiencies in artistry: the subjects are not very firmly "placed"; they slip. However, the brushwork is more decisive than in the landscapes. This composition reveals clearly the influence of the Union of Artists: the motif of a table covered with objects and set in a garden or on a veranda was widespread among the Moscow Impressionists—for instance, Korovin and Grabar, the Union's leading artists. Popova resolved her own *plein air* still life with restraint and caution. She did not succeed in integrating the complex color relationships and occasionally resorted to unmodulated colors (in the red of the napkin); but she did attempt complex treatment of the color white, taking reflections into account.

In the somewhat later *Portrait of a Girl Against a Tile Stove* (ca. 1909; page 34), Popova remained entirely within the traditional understanding of the portrait, fixing the viewer's attention on the particularities of the model—the sharpness of her gaze, the angularity of her figure. At the same time she achieved some success in her interpretation of the form itself: the overall structure improves, volume condenses somewhat, the contours of the figure become more intense and vigorous.

THE EARLY 1910s: FEMALE MODELS, APPLES, TREES

Too few compositions have survived from the early 1910s to enable us to form an adequate picture of that stage in Popova's development,[6] and we have only a few facts from her biography of that time—an important one being her trip to Kiev in the summer of 1909, where she had a chance to see much ancient Russian painting and as well as work by the Symbolist Mikhail Vrubel.

The following months were marked by a great deal of travel. In the spring of 1910 the entire Popov family took a short trip to Italy, where Liubov, while still a long way off from her Futurist enthusiasms, took great delight in the works of the masters of the fourteenth and fifteenth centuries, especially Giotto and Pinturicchio. In June, she traveled to Pskov and Novgorod, in the summer of 1911 to Petersburg, where she visited the Hermitage for the first time, in the fall to the ancient cities of Rostov the Great, Yaroslavl, Suzdal, Yuriev Polsky, Pereslavl, and once more, Kiev. The old masters and, again, ancient Russian painters were the focus of Popova's attention. Their art thrilled her; she had no thought of destroying classical traditions or making a fundamental revision in painting.

Ancient Russian enthusiasms are especially typical of the early 1900s. It was then that the first efforts were made to exhibit, collect, and clean icons; for the first time art experts could inspect the Russian icon in its primordial splendor. The icon was coming to be recognized as the primary source of the national tradition. Kuzma Petrov-Vodkin and Pavel Kuznetsov, Mikhail Larionov and Natalia Goncharova, Vladimir Tatlin and Kazimir Malevich, Aleksandr Shevchenko and Aleksei

Grishchenko—each of these artists in his or her own way mastered that legacy. The young Popova's enthusiasm was symptomatic, but it was not manifested immediately in her compositions. It functioned, rather, as "potential," reverberating later, at the onset of the mature period in her artistic career.

Vrubel had a particularly strong influence on Popova. The very look of the master, vividly expressed in his wall paintings at the Church of Saint Cyril and in the many paintings and drawings found in Kiev, had to have impressed her. Vrubel's incinerating passion, his honesty and candidness before the world, vanquished Popova, even shattered her equilibrium.

In his article on Popova's posthumous exhibition, Aksionov, a close friend who knew her well, strongly emphasized the crisis atmosphere of that period. He spoke of her "departure from Symbolist mysticism (very torturous and difficult, nearly costing L. S. her reason),"[7] and linked the artist's attendant moods to the impact of Vrubel's art. Aksionov wrote: "Vrubel's Gothic coincided with L. S.'s personal attraction to the Gothic style, to its voluminous structures, to the sharply defined edges of its intersecting planes—it is no wonder she was especially interested during that period 1911–12, which was for her also a time of great change, in the pencil drawings of Vrubel, then already very ill."[8] Aksionov writes that evidences of Popova's interest in Vrubel were discovered in her studio after her death: the catalog from a 1912 exhibition and newspaper clippings with marginal notes in her handwriting. The artist concealed this passion of hers from her friends, who would scarcely have looked favorably on such admiration for the father of Russian Symbolism.[9] As for "Symbolist mysticism," no trace of it was ever revealed in her painting or graphics. However, her poems and prose sketches from the years 1907–11 are permeated by mystical moods, full of Symbolism, written under the obvious influence of Symbolist poetry.

Popova's works that we know from the end of the first and beginning of the second decade of this century can be divided into three groups: female models, still lifes, and studies of trees. To judge by the Vesnin-Aksionov list, yet another group could be added: portraits, but these have not survived. Nevertheless, from the female models and still lifes, it is evident that she was making a systematic study of the human body, its anatomy and its proportions. In the 1908 series of landscapes the human figure had been, perhaps, Popova's weakest area, as the artist herself could not help but see. Now she was filling in the gaps in her schooling. In the years around 1910 Popova did much drawing. The drawings dated 1909–10 include, besides models, copies of frescoes and icons (possibly impressions from her trips to Kiev and other ancient cities). A number of sketchbooks, comprising over five hundred drawings from the year 1911, are devoted wholly to male and female models. These, as a rule, are quick pencil sketches that fix the structure of the human body, a pose, occasionally the volume. Most often they are outlines; only rarely are hatchstrokes added. The poses of the male and female models in this series of drawings are quite diverse. The figures stand, lie, sit, kneel with their hands resting on the floor; the arms are sometimes folded across the chest, or raised overhead, or spread out to the side or in opposite directions: one up, the other down. It is as if the artist were verifying her ability to construct a form faultlessly.

In this new phase of Popova's career she shared studio space with fellow artists at several locations. In the fall of 1911, after returning from Kiev, evidently dissatisfied with the boring, unchallenging work at Yuon and Dudin's school, Popova and Liudmila Prudkovskaia set up a studio on Antipievsky Street in Moscow. According to contemporaries' accounts, the work done at this studio was not particularly successful. Very soon after, Popova and Prudkovskaia were joined by S. Karetnikova; Liudmila's sister, Nadezhda Udaltsova; and, later, Vera Pestel. In the fall of 1912 work began in a collective studio on Kuznetsky Bridge, in the so-called Tower, where Popova found herself alongside Vladimir Tatlin, Udaltsova, Viktor Bart, N. E. Rogovin, Anna Troianovskaia, and Aleksandr Vesnin. Evidently the drawings that have been preserved were done in all these studios, but most of them date from the studio on Antipievsky Street.

In contrast to most other artists of the Russian avant-garde during those years, Popova and Tatlin assigned great importance to life drawing. Tatlin's influence, which could be seen in Popova's work immediately after her return from abroad in 1913, may to some extent have been prefigured by her intense study of the structural characteristics of the human body. Even her posing of the model brings Tatlin to mind. Tatlin loved the same turns of the figure, fixed poses—less everyday than constructed (page 33).

Popova's paintings of models were done mostly in 1911–12. One of them, *Male Model (Semi-Reclining Old Man),* on a green ground (page 32, top), corresponds exactly to a series of pencil drawings depicting the same figure in the same pose (page 33, right). This study, executed hurriedly and expressively, accentuated by Gauguinesque outlining done with a dark line and an open, energetic stroke, still harks back to the landscapes of 1909. *Seated Male Model (The George Costakis Collection,* fig. 731) was drawn with only slightly more restraint and with more attention given to modeling the form and conveying the space. The artist's acquaintance with Cézanne's painting is evident, which should come as no surprise. Cézanne was already well known in Russia, and especially in Moscow, where he was represented by first-class works in the collections of Ivan Morozov and Sergei Shchukin. The Moscow artists who formed the Jack of Diamonds[10] group soon were nicknamed the Moscow Cézannists. Cézanne's legacy became the ground from which new directions in Russian painting were to spring. Popova was quite sympathetic to these new trends. As she developed in the early 1910s, so too, gradually, did the Cézannesque qualities of her compositions. We can already note them to a significant extent in *Female Model* (1911–12; page 46), which depicts a model sitting on a chair, with drapery based directly on Cézanne's example. The painting of the figure itself becomes more concentrated, more plastic, a fairly typical example of the modified Cézannism that was widespread particularly among Moscow artists.

One of the still lifes that has survived from that time—*Apples and Drapery* (1911–12; page 32)—also follows the manner of the early Jack of Diamonds. Nearly square in its format (28⅛ × 28"), this still life consists of several very simple elements: four apples, gray and blue drapery, a table leg. The gray drapery "flows" from the top and the blue "rises" up. In the center they interact quite vigorously, while the apples, calmly and confidently occupying their place on the plane and in space, neutralize those dynamics and reinforce the idea of the square. Unlike Popova's previous paintings, in which unmediated expression predominated, *Apples and Drapery* is much more rational and tends toward structural precision and careful composition.

Also from the pre-Paris period (1911–12) are the studies of trees (pages 36, 37, 38, right, and 39), of which she completed at least ten. (One is in the Omsk Regional Museum of Art; we have some idea of yet another from a photograph of Popova's studio taken after her death. We can assume that all these studies were similar, as is indicated as well by the large collection of tree drawings in the Costakis collection, the Irkutsk Regional Museum of Art, and several private collections in Moscow.) Within the series—in India ink or pencil—the manner and character of Popova's artistic thinking undergo almost no change. Unquestionably she is striving to reveal their construction but never bares it intentionally. Rather, she is studying, generalizing.

Aksionov had this to say about these compositions: "We can assume with good cause that the Cézannism of her own drawings [the trees] from the summer of 1912 was still to a significant extent permeated by a Gothic perception of nature."[11] This statement from a specialist on Popova who witnessed her work in progress is doubly interesting for us. It gives us justification for dating the depictions of trees 1912—or at the outside, 1911–12. In addition, the author unambiguously identifies the Cézannism and the Vrubelism in Popova's compositions. Indeed, the keenness of her angular rhythms and the parallel movement of her hatchstrokes give all the signs of the artist having assimilated her Vrubelist "Gothic" beginning. On the other hand, Popova's trees recall some of Cézanne's, especially in his graphics. It is difficult to say with complete assurance that Popova saw, if not the originals, then at least reproductions of similar drawings or watercolors by Cézanne. She may have been proceeding to her structural thinking from his oil paintings.

15

In the painting *Trees* (1911–12; page 45) we can catch the echoes not only of Cézannism but also of Cubism—weak Cubism, to be sure, without any organized, finished system functioning as a basis or goal. The object's structure is dismantled on Popova's canvas not in space but on the plane. Despite the fact that *Trees* is classified as a study, the canvas seems complete, finished. The artist reveals the constructive principle in the tree-organism. *Trees*—exactly like the male and female models—is constructed from nature according to the eternal laws of architectonics. Compositional fragmentation turns out to be mere outward appearance. It is absolutely irrelevant that clumps of foliage are cut off by the frame or that the ends of the trunks go beyond the borders of the painting plane. Popova does not let the pictorial energy escape the bounds of the canvas. The green, green-blue, and yellow spots together create a certain balance that heralds the system of arrangement of spots and planes in her later *Painterly Architectonics*. Popova follows a relatively direct path to her goal—even if that goal is still out of sight. She is led by the originality of her talent, which was destined for a painterly-architectural system of thought. It was as if she were waiting for her moment to come.

Naturally, mature Cubism would bring her even closer to her goal, allowing her to create not only general postulates for her own original pictorial conception but also its forms. On the way to her goal stood Paris.

Liubov Popova. 1891

The house at Krasnovidovo, near the village of Ivanovskoe, where the artist spent her childhood

Liubov Vasilievna Popova (Zubova) and Sergei Maksimovich Popov,
Liubov Popova's parents

Liubov Popova and her older brother, Sergei. 1891

Liubov, her younger brother, Pavel, and Sergei Popov

On the veranda of the house at Krasnovidovo. Liubov Popova is the second from the left

The Popov children (left to right): Olga, Pavel, and Liubov. The older women
are probably governesses; Adda Dege may be the second from the right

Liubov Popova (on the left in front) in the family circle

Sergei, Pavel, and Liubov Popov in Yalta. Adda Dege may be on the right

Liubov Popova as a Gymnasium student in Yalta. ca. 1902

Liubov Popova (at her father's left), with her brothers, Sergei and Pavel

View from My Window onto Houses. 1906. Pencil on paper, 3 × 6⅛" (7.4 × 15.7 cm.). Costakis Collection, Athens

Ivanovskoe, Bridge. 1908. Oil on canvas, 19⅛ × 15⅛" (48.5 × 38.5 cm.). Private collection, Moscow

Landscape with a Red House and a Woman Washing. 1908. Oil on canvas, 15⅛ × 19″ (38.5 × 48 cm.). Private collection, Moscow

Landscape with Female Figures. 1908. Oil on canvas, 13⅝ × 17⅛" (34.5 × 43.5 cm.). Private collection, Moscow

Male Model (Semi-Reclining Old Man). ca. 1911. Oil on canvas, 28⅛ × 28″ (71.5 × 71 cm.).
Private collection, Moscow

Apples and Drapery. 1911–12. Oil on canvas, 28⅛ × 28″ (71.5 × 71 cm.).
Private collection, Moscow

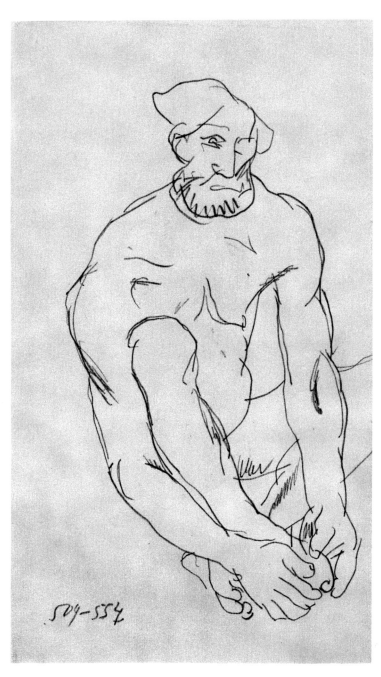

Male Model. ca. 1911. Pencil on paper, 13¾ × 8⅝" (35 × 22 cm.).
Private collection, Moscow

Male Model. ca. 1911. Pencil on paper, 14⅛ × 8¼" (36 × 21 cm.).
Private collection, Moscow

Portrait of a Girl Against a Tile Stove. ca. 1909. Oil on canvas,
24¼ × 16¾″ (61.5 × 44.5 cm.). Tretiakov Gallery.
Gift of George Costakis

Still Life: Milk Pitcher. Plein Air. 1908. Oil on canvas, 27¾ × 21⅛" (70.6 × 53.7 cm.).
Costakis Collection, Athens

Haystacks. 1908. Oil on canvas, 17⅜ × 13¾" (44 × 35 cm.).
Private collection, United States

Trees. 1911–12. Pencil on paper, 7⅞ × 10⅝″ (20 × 27 cm.). Private collection, Moscow

Trees. 1911–12. Pencil on paper, 10⅝ × 7⅞″ (27 × 20 cm.). Private collection, Moscow

Female Model. ca. 1911. India ink on paper, 14 × 8⅝″ (35.5 × 22 cm.).
Private collection, Moscow

Trees. 1911–12. Ink on paper, 17⅜ × 14⅛″ (44 × 35.9 cm.).
Costakis Collection, Athens

Tree. 1911–12. India ink on paper, 13¾ × 8⅝″ (35 × 22 cm.).
Irkutsk Regional Museum of Art

Tree. 1911–12. Ink on paper, 14 × 8⅞″ (35.5 × 22.5 cm.).
Costakis Collection, Athens

Nadezhda Udaltsova, her sister Varvara Nikolskaia, and Liubov Popova (the man is unidentified)

MOSCOW—PARIS—MOSCOW

The thought of visiting Paris, of working in one of the Paris *académies*, did not come to Popova out of the blue. After having become close to several masters of the Russian avant-garde, having seen many works by French painters at Moscow exhibitions, and finally, having taken her fill of the French in Shchukin's collection, which was available for viewing, Popova clearly felt the need for a thoroughgoing revitalization of her own art with the help of Paris air and the French *maîtres*. In the fall of 1912 Popova set out for Paris along with her old governess, Adelaide Robertovna (Adda) Dege, and her friends Udaltsova (whose younger sister, Prudkovskaia, stayed home due to illness), Karetnikova, and Pestel. The latter two quickly returned to Moscow, however, but Popova and Udaltsova stayed in Paris for a long time, taking rooms with Dege at the quiet pension of Madame Jeanne (home to many Russian artists studying in Paris). After getting acquainted with the city's museums and other tourist attractions, the friends began to look for a suitable *académie*. On the advice of Aleksandra Exter[12] (a fellow Russian artist who had been in Paris for some time), they decided on the then well-known studio La Palette, where Jean Metzinger, Henri Le Fauconnier, and André Dunoyer de Segonzac—representatives of the "second wave" of French Cubism—taught. Joint study and prolonged residence in the same pension drew Popova and Udaltsova very close. This was more than a friendship; it was a creative intimacy.

Aleksandra Exter was by no means the first Russian artist of her generation to study with French masters. Just a year before Popova arrived, Aristarkh Lentulov had come to Paris, where he had been friendly with Albert Gleizes, Metzinger, Le Fauconnier, Robert Delaunay, Roger de La Fresnaye, and others. Before that a Jack of Diamonds colleague of Lentulov's—Piotr Konchalovsky—had spent several years in France. Many representatives of the Russian avant-garde went there in the 1910s—Tatlin, Goncharova, Larionov, Vladimir Baranov-Rossiné, Natan Altman, David Shterenberg, Georgii Yakulov, Olga Rozanova. In contrast to their precursors—the artists of the World of Art, Viktor Borisov-Musatov, the masters of the Blue Rose—their interests shifted away from the Nabis group, even from Van Gogh and Gauguin, to the Cubists. At the beginning of this century the Russian artist Maria Vasilieva settled in Paris and in 1909 founded her own academy.

Russian sculptors as well as painters formed a special colony in Paris: Boris Ternovets, Iza Burmeister, Aleksandr Vertepov, all of whom studied with Antoine Bourdelle at the Académie de la Grande Chaumière. There were also Hungarian masters, led by the famous Jozsef Csáky.

One of the Russian sculptors, Vera Mukhina, had a friendship with Popova that dated back to Moscow and the Yuon-Dudin studio, and Mukhina was a loyal admirer of hers. Together they went to museums, exhibition halls, and studios. A significant visit took place in 1913, when they went to the studio of Aleksandr Archipenko, by then a very popular sculptor, who had been born in Russia but had settled permanently in Paris.

Popova's teachers Metzinger and Le Fauconnier were artists famous not only in Paris but also in Russia. Their works had been exhibited during the 1909–10 season at the international salon arranged by Vladimir Izdebsky and at the first exhibitions of the Jack of Diamonds group, in the years 1910–12. Popova was almost certainly acquainted with their work even before she arrived in Paris.

In one of Nadezhda Udaltsova's journal entries from the time she and Popova were studying at La Palette, we read: "Liubov Sergeevna understood little of what Le Fauconnier was saying. Everything is broken down into a thousand lines; she has no feel for the plane."[13] Judging from this entry, the Moscow "proto-Cubism" that Popova brought to Paris with her was not a strong enough basis from which to attain the latest heights in French Cubism. The talented artist managed to overcome these difficulties soon enough, however.

At present it is impossible to determine precisely which of Popova's works were done in Paris or whether any of them have survived to our day. Some compositions do have a specific date—1913. But they are probably from the post-Paris period, when the artist was working in the studios of Tatlin and Aleksei Morgunov. As for the paintings of 1912, all we can do is speculate on the basis of the existing drawings to determine whether these works were done during her studies at the Tower or at La Palette. We can make some judgments about these puzzling works from the Vesnin-Aksionov list, which includes only six pictorial works for 1912—cityscapes with buildings (two with smokestacks). There were no works from 1912 at her posthumous exhibition—nor were there any at the exhibitions of the mid-1910s.

We have only one source from which to re-create at least in general terms the look of those works—the artist's drawings, which include sketches of cityscapes (pages 50–53).[14] These drawings are executed in the Cubist manner, they are cousins of the female-model sketches of 1913, and in their subject matter correspond to the compositions mentioned by Vesnin and Aksionov. All of them are cityscapes, all of them depict buildings, and some have large smokestacks (pages 50–53). These last, in their very motif and manner of drawing, recall the famous painting by Picasso in the Shchukin collection—*Factory at Horta de Ebro* (1909). The buildings' crystalline surfaces, the obelisk-like smokestack, the spheres of the trees (Picasso has palms), the high perspective, which makes the foreground seem to float away under the viewer's feet—all these devices and motifs are completely in keeping with the landscape works not only of Picasso but of Gleizes, Delaunay, and Le Fauconnier. Therefore, it is natural to assume that those works of Popova's were done in Paris, especially since the motifs give us no reason to identify them with any Russian cities. The arcaded walls, the bridges linking the buildings, the turrets on the roofs—all these motifs would be incongruous for a Russian city. The composition and the choice of perspective also seem unusual. In one of these drawings the artist overturns the building cubes, juxtaposing their slanting lines, which go off in various directions. The buildings start to rock, as often happens in Delaunay's land-scapes. Popova uses a rather limited group of stereometric forms. The parallelepiped and sphere dominate: on the surface the lines most often form rectangles, triangles, and semicircles. Here we have in the making the forms she will use in the *Male Models* of 1913—works of full-fledged Cubism.

The only painting we have to compare with the city land-scape drawings is a landscape in oil with several motifs that coincide with those of the drawings.[15] Evidently it was used for her *Composition with Figures* of 1913 (page 56, left), where the upper left-hand corner is repeated almost in its entirety. This confirms an early date (1912) and discredits the date 1915 assigned to the landscape by a gallery that exhibited it in 1979.

The "landscape episode" was but a brief interlude in Popova's early Cubist period. Two years later she was no longer drawing landscapes, returning to them only in the years 1915–16, when her figurative work was on the wane. Having started with the most "natural" sort of painting, the landscape, Popova consciously set it aside for a time: the most organic way to "overcome nature" was in the still life, the portrait, and the single-figure composition—more static, more object-oriented genres, even if Popova did treat them expressively and dynamically.

Despite the small number of works from 1912 that have survived, it is clear that Popova's stay in Paris bore its fruits. She spent her Paris months in sustained work. Only toward the end, in May of 1913, did she allow herself to relax a little. She and her friends Mukhina and Ternovets went to Brittany, where Madame Jeanne, their landlady at the Paris pension, had a small house. Immediately thereafter Popova returned to Moscow.

THE PAINTINGS OF 1913

As we have mentioned, Popova began enumerating her works with a painting from 1913. In her archives is her statement that "by 1914, I was working completely independently."[16] Perhaps she had postponed her independent work longer than neces-sary. Be that as it may, her return from Paris marked a new stage in her development, and in this respect the works of 1913 are most revealing. They show how Popova herself saw her independence. Obviously it was not a question of her freeing herself of contemporary art's influences altogether but rather of her ending her apprenticeship period. She had left behind the

stages of development that mirrored the passage of Russian art "through old territory," territory her predecessors had already covered. Popova, along with the other masters of Russian art, had emerged at the leading edge of artistic inquiry. Here, too, there was no question of getting along without any influences. Rather, they came from various directions—French Cubists, Italian Futurists, Tatlin and other Russian masters of the early 1910s. Popova's art was born at the crossroads of these trends, after she had come into her mature and independent period. Thus, we can understand why her personal log begins in 1913.[17]

The single-figure compositions—the *Female Models* (pages 47 and 48)—bring to mind numerous drawings from the years 1912–13 (pages 54 and 55). This would seem to be the same full-length figure—standing or sitting in a distinctive, although relatively typical, movement or positioning of the feet and the head. But in her drawings the artist was seeking, apart from architectonics, uniqueness of gesture and pose. In the paintings a plastic formula is elaborated, often repeating the same motif. The *Female Model (Standing)* on page 47 is almost identical to the figure of the woman on the right in *Composition with Figures* (page 56, left). As for the seated female model, it is reproduced in all the variations we already know—with only a few changes. These changes involve the sizes, the color scheme, a few details, but least of all—the figure itself. Popova has finished her "homework" and gone on to intensified Cubist "investigations" to research into form.

In comparing the *Female Model (Seated)* (page 48) in any of its versions with Popova's later Cubist paintings—for example, with the 1915 compositions *Portrait of a Philosopher* (page 92) and *Traveling Woman* (pages 96 and 97)—a difference is immediately apparent: the *Female Models* deal much more with spatial development and the later works with the plane. True, even in the *Female Models* the idea of the organization of the canvas, of the balance of forms on the painting surface, makes itself felt through the volume. Yet the principle of the harmonious distribution of volumes in space, however shallow, predomi-nates. The figure is surrounded by cubes, parallelepipeds, and cylinders—not squares, rectangles, or circles, as later.

An important quality that is present in the best of the *Female Models* is their architectonic tendency. It is no accident that Popova devoted this kind of attention precisely to her seated-figure compositions, all of which are very similar. One shows a brown figure on a green ground, another on a dark blue ground, a third includes varicolored Cubist elements—red, yellow, green, crimson, brown. Juxtaposing the versions makes it clear that Popova was seeking the harmony of the integral organism, placing forms around the figure, striving for bal-ance, making adjustments, securing the various parts, tucking them into each other as if she were tightening nuts, inserting the bones on which the legs, arms, and neck of the model turn, as on hinges. The process by which she made these paintings must be called construction.

Composition with Figures demonstrates a multiobject variation on the same theme. The very complement of the "objects" depicted is broader: a second figure is added, there is a still life in the foreground, and the work is set in a landscape. The construction is filled with real objects, whereas the surroundings of the single-figure *Female Models* consisted of nothing but abstract stereometric forms, objects more contrived than real. We can assume that work on the single- and on the double-figure compositions went on at the same time. *Composition with Figures* and *Person + Air + Space (Seated Female Model)* (page 49) demonstrate to an equal extent the marks of that transitional moment when two paths can be discerned: one toward the affirmation of the surface of the canvas and the flattening of the subject's volume; the other toward the shift from decorative three-dimensionality to real three-dimensionality. This clarification would actually come about in 1915, but in 1913 each of her works—especially *Composition with Figures*—contains the beginnings of both paths. In the lower half of the canvas, depth and surface clash sharply. The diagonal lines of the foreground, the very placement of objects, accentuate the depth of the work. The tilted guitar, the metal pitcher, the vase with fruit, are purposely angled to draw the viewer's eyes into the work. But that direction is neutralized by two sections of grillwork that seem to have been hung parallel to the surface of the canvas, creating a rhythm of squares. This balance between the illusion of volume and the plane is a key concept of the entire work. The figure seated on the left is depicted in a complicated pose; her head seems to be carved out of wood and, with its protuberances, emphasizes real space. In addition, long straight lines are scattered over the surface, uniting the figures and objects in an overall contour and "tying" them to the surface. In the complexity of the relations of its various volumes and lines, *Composition with Figures* is quite similar to Malevich's *Knife Sharpener*, done the previous year. On the other hand, Popova's painting directly expresses the Cubist ideas formulated in the 1912 book *Du Cubisme* (On Cubism), by Gleizes and Metzinger: a pictorial composition must be built on the correlations of straight lines and curves.[18] She selects objects with straight and curved outlines, combining them with each other; often, moreover, she seems to place straight lines and curves arbitrarily right on the surface. The few long straight lines stretching almost the entire length of the canvas seem to mark the major forms, and despite the staccato of the color patches, it is clear that she favors large overall color planes.

Still Life with Tin Dish (page 56, right), which we know only from a contemporary photograph, shows affinities with both *Composition with Figures* and the general tendencies in the development of Popova's art. The cylindrical forms of the objects depicted in the still life are ready to step out beyond the limits of the plane and be transformed into a relief. But in contrast, they are counterbalanced by the rectangular planes and straight lines lying on the surface. Clearly the still life played a supporting role in her work on *Composition with Figures*. We find in both works the same objects—for example, the metal pitcher with the raised lid. But this is not the only point. The pitcher itself becomes an analogy for the female figures, the forms of which are treated as if they were clad in armor and would make a metallic ring on contact with each other. Perhaps uniting a figure or figures with a still life was a special task Popova had set herself.[19]

Popova's paintings of 1913 were done in the wake of her Paris classes and under the direct influence of the compositions of her Russian friends. At that time Tatlin was probably the most authoritative figure in her orbit. It was during these years that he was creating his best paintings, as he approached the frontier beyond which painting ended and a new type of art—sculpto-painting—began. His works of 1912–13 embodied the ideas of painterly "Pre-Constructivism." He was looking for a constructive foundation for the object or the figure, and he was constructing these subjects according to the laws of architecture. Although in 1913 Popova could have been called his follower, her experience of foreign art continued to be extremely compelling. She came into direct contact with it again during her third trip abroad.

This trip abroad was not so long as her second, but it was rich in impressions and complicated in itinerary. Late in 1914 Popova set out for Paris, and by mid-April 1915, she, Mukhina, and Burmeister were leaving Paris for Italy. While still in France their route took them through Lyons and to Menton, situated along the Italian border. After they crossed the border, the first large city they came to was Genoa. From there they took a steamer via Livorno to Naples. En route they managed to see Pisa with its renowned tower and baptistry. Naples itself and neighboring Amalfi, Salerno, Pompeii, Herculaneum, and Capri were historic sites not only for Italians but for Russians as well: Russian artists of the first half of the nineteenth century had been very fond of spending time there. For two weeks Popova and her friends stayed in Rome, where they visited the museums and ancient buildings. Judging from Mukhina's stories, their behavior abroad was free and unfettered, not like shy schoolgirls' at all.

Paestum, with its early, nearly archaic classicism, made a great impression on the women. Popova also saw the Gothic cathedrals of Milan, Siena, and Orvieto (in the restrained Italian version of the Gothic, of course, strikingly distinct from the French with which she was familiar from Paris), the Roman and Renaissance architecture of Florence, fairy-tale Venice, and Ravenna with its famous Tomb of Theodoric. The architecture of antiquity, the Gothic, and the Renaissance, like the architecture of ancient Rus before and that of Central Asia later, left perhaps the strongest mark on Popova's artistic consciousness. The "sense of architectonics" that stood her in such good stead in the late 1910s was a gift of nature, but it was strengthened by all that she had seen. Her Italian impressions during these two months of 1915 were particularly important in this regard, especially since by the time of her last trip the artist had already learned to "build," to "construct."

Italian painters posed a special interest for Popova. Once again she encountered Giotto at the churches of Saint Francis in Assisi and in the Arena Chapel in Padua. Carpaccio, Tintoretto, and especially Guido da Siena impressed her deeply.[20] It is interesting that the names of the greatest artists of the Italian Renaissance—da Vinci, Raphael, and Michelangelo—are nowhere to be found in Popova's notes or in the testimonies of her companions or biographers. Perhaps her attention was directed primarily at what had heretofore been little known, at what had not yet crystallized in her memory. Moreover, Popova undertook this trip as an artist with her own ideas, desirous of finding confirmation for them in the history of art. This is how Mukhina recalls her friend:

"Popova's reaction to Italy was very intense, impassioned. If she is bothered by a particular question, for example, the relationship of colors, she fixes all her attention on that, looks for that everywhere. If she doesn't find the answer to that question in a great artist, she passes him by. While she was dashing around over the relationship of colors, she was simultaneously determining the intensity of the color, the weight of the color."[21] Probably the principal heroes of the High Renaissance did not deal with all the questions that so concerned Popova during this period of her foreign travel.

But certainly her Italian and, especially, her Renaissance impressions were of major importance in her development. To the Gothic interests noted by Aksionov, therefore, we have to add the Renaissance. After all, we find Renaissance associations both in the lofty utopianism of Popova's mature painterly work and in the harmoniousness of her architectonic constructions. As regards Popova's personality, her appearance, there too we can easily and rightly discern Renaissance traits.

The discussion of Popova's personality follows immediately upon the description of her travels because one of her greatest admirers was one of her traveling companions, the sculptor Vera Mukhina, who later became very well known. For many years Mukhina was strongly influenced by Popova, under the spell of her personality, and after the artist's death Mukhina reminisced about her many times. Here is another of her recollections of Liubov Sergeevna:

L. S. was tall; she had a good figure, marvelous eyes and luxuriant hair. Despite all her femininity, she had an incredibly sharp eye for life and art. . . . She had a marvelous feeling for color and was all in all

very talented. She was the first to begin to unveil the essence of art for me. Until then I had conveyed only what I saw. But if an artist conveys only what he sees, then he's a naturalist. You have to convey what you feel and know. She made me understand that. She taught me how to look at color, at the treatment of colors in the Russian icon, for example. She was excited by everything new. She loved to express her opinions on works of art. I was beginning to see.[22]

A statement like this is completely in order. Liubov Popova did indeed possess some kind of magical magnetic power. She was always surrounded by admirers and worshipers—men and women. Friends found in her a loyal support. She was capable of gathering around her people of like mind, capable of attracting followers. She was by nature straightforward, courageous, and outspoken. There were situations when her pride scared people off, as happened with Aleksandr Rodchenko and Varvara Stepanova when they first met her[23]—which did not, however, keep them from becoming loyal friends later. But usually Popova was enchanting, to the point of making more than one man fall in love with her. To the end of her days she maintained her loyalty to her "faithful admirer" Aleksandr Vesnin. In the early 1920s Sergei Bobrov dedicated poems to her. Ivan Aksionov was her devoted friend until her last breath.

Popova did everything decisively and boldly. She easily let go of the old—habits, attachments, ways of life, styles of painting—and even boasted of how free and easy she was. She was intent on the future; any dissatisfaction with herself spurred her on to find something new, to keep moving all the time, moving toward new frontiers. This sense of purpose determined the role she played in Moscow in the years 1914–15, when painters and art theoreticians gathered around her, when a weekly gathering was organized at her home on Novinsky Boulevard for papers to be read (by Udaltsova, Vesnin, and others). The famous artist, critic, and theoretician Aleksei Grishchenko came; art historians M. S. Sergeev, Boris R. Vipper, and Boris von Eding (Popova's future husband), and the philosopher Pavel Florensky attended from time to time. The circle that formed around Popova was a natural extension of the collaborative activity that Moscow artists had carried on first in the Tower on Kuznetsky Bridge and later in the studios of Tatlin and Morgunov on Ostozhenka Street. These groups were not exhibiting associations, although many of the artists around Popova participated in the "Jack of Diamonds," "Donkey's Tail," and "Union of Youth" exhibitions. Popova herself, being younger than her friends, first began exhibiting in 1914, in the fourth "Jack of Diamonds" exhibition, where she showed her *Composition with Figures* and *Still Life with Tin Dish*. There she was bidding farewell to her timid past rather than heralding her future. Udaltsova wrote in *Moi vospominaniia* (My Reminiscences): "Popova and I, we go everywhere together. Our first things were drawn under the powerful influence of Metzinger's *L'Oiseau bleu*—later we went on to our Cubist things."[24]

Trees. 1911–12. Oil on canvas, 23⅞ × 18¾" (60.5 × 47.5 cm.). Private collection, Moscow

Female Model. ca. 1912. Oil on canvas, 49 × 28½″ (124.5 × 72.5 cm.). Private collection, Moscow

Female Model (Standing). 1913. Oil on canvas, 41⅜ × 27⅜" (105 × 69.5 cm.). Tretiakov Gallery. Gift of George Costakis

Person + Air + Space (Seated Female Model). 1913. Oil on canvas, 49¼ × 42⅛″
(125 × 107 cm.). Russian Museum

Female Model (Seated). 1913. Oil on canvas, 24 × 19⅝″ (61 × 50 cm.). Private collection, West Germany

Cityscape with Smokestack. 1912. Pencil on paper, 9¼ × 12¼" (23.5 × 31 cm.). Private collection, Moscow

Cityscape with Smokestack. 1912. Pencil on paper, 9¼ × 12¼" (23.5 × 31 cm.). Private collection, Moscow

Houses. 1912. Pencil on paper, 9¼ × 12¼" (23.5 × 31 cm.). Private collection, Moscow

Cityscape. 1912. Pencil on paper, 12¼ × 9¼" (31 × 23.5 cm.). Private collection, Moscow

Houses. 1912. Pencil on paper, 9¼ × 12¼" (23.5 × 31 cm.). Private collection, Moscow

Female Model. ca. 1913. Pencil on paper, 10½ × 8⅛" (26.7 × 20.6 cm.). Private collection, Moscow

Above: Female Model. ca. 1913. Pencil on paper, 12¼ × 9¼" (31 × 23.5 cm.).
Private collection, Moscow

Above right: Female Model. ca. 1913. Pencil on paper, 10⅜ × 8" (26.5 × 20.5 cm.).
Irkutsk Regional Museum of Art

Woman and Child. ca. 1913. Pencil on paper, 12¼ × 9¼" (31 × 23.5 cm.).
Private collection, Moscow

Composition with Figures. 1913. Oil on canvas, 61¾ × 48¾" (157 × 123 cm.). Tretiakov Gallery. Gift of George Costakis

Still Life with Tin Dish. 1913. Location unknown. Contemporary photograph

CUBO-FUTURISM

In the years 1915–16, Popova probably exhibited at more shows than in any other period of her life. They were predominantly shows of a Futurist tendency: in March 1915 in Petrograd, "Tramway V" (with Malevich, Tatlin, Ivan Puni, Rozanova, Udaltsova, Exter, and others); at the turn of 1916 in Petrograd, "The Last Futurist Exhibition: 0.10" (with the same participants, joined by Mikhail Menkov, Pestel, Ksenia Boguslavskaia, Altman, Vasilieva, and others); in March 1916 in Moscow, "The Store," in which many of those already cited participated. After this, they were joined by Rodchenko and Lev Bruni: in November 1916 in Moscow, "Jack of Diamonds," which by the time of that exhibition had lost many of its leaders but had been enriched by Malevich, Marc Chagall, Ivan Kliun, Puni, Rozanova, and Udaltsova; in December in Petrograd, "Modern Russian Painting" at Nadezhda Dobychina's art gallery, where Popova exhibited along with Chagall, Wassily Kandinsky, Lentulov, Robert Falk, Puni, Nikolai Kulbin, and others. With rare exceptions, Popova showed pictures of a Cubo-Futurist nature at these exhibitions.

Cubo-Futurism, whose orbit Popova entered in 1914–15, was by that time some years old and enjoyed considerable fame—albeit rather scandalous. One might even say that at that time it was already nearing its termination, after which artistic discoveries would have to follow, leading art off in new directions. It was in the teens that these new directions were being engendered—through the efforts of Malevich, Tatlin, and other Russian avant-gardists. Popova found herself in the very thick of these new inquiries. She too would make the leap into this new unknown area of artistic discovery. In fact, this did not happen until 1916. In 1914–15, her work remained within the bounds of the current general style, although unique and original features of Popova's artistic personality did show through.

The Cubo-Futurism we speak of was not an integral, finished stylistic tendency in Russian art. It arose through the efforts of Futurist poets and painters, who, entering into intimate contact with one another, testing their powers in mixed art forms, advanced a program that blasted previous trends. In their poetry and painting, they asserted the principle of innovation. Disputes, brash declarations, sharp polemics, unrelenting efforts to shock a public oriented toward the usual artistic norms—all these were characteristic of Cubo-Futurism, but there was no real stylistic unity of any kind to their work.

Everything that breached traditional conceptions and everything headed for that breach was called Cubo-Futurism. Larionov proved to have been one of the fathers of Cubo-Futurism back in his Primitivist period, to say nothing of his Rayism, which opened up new perspectives for sympathetic contemporaries. The Cubo-Futurist book *A Slap in the Face of Public Taste* was published in 1912 by the Burliuk brothers,

David and Vladimir, Vladimir Mayakovsky, Velimir Khlebnikov, and Aleksei Kruchenykh.

However, the artists whose work best fits the label Cubo-Futurism were Malevich, Tatlin, Goncharova (in some manifestations), Rozanova, Udaltsova, Puni, Morgunov, and Kliun. But even within this group no Cubo-Futurist stylistic unity was ever worked out. This is largely explained by the fact that two distinct trends propagating different principles and programs lay at the base of Cubo-Futurism. French Cubism, which had been quite well known in Russia since the early 1910s and had taken firm root in Russian soil, was in many ways fundamentally opposed to Italian Futurism. In Russia, Cubism was well known not only from exhibitions and collections but also because many artists had studied in Paris. Italian Futurism reached Russia primarily in the form of manifestos, which were translated into Russian, and from various articles in the press. In 1914 the leader of Italian Futurism, Filippo Marinetti, went to Russia, where he received a decidedly cool reception. The organizers of his meetings with Russian poets and artists were hard pressed to avert what seemed like an inevitable scandal. Nevertheless, the Russians did not turn their backs on Futurism itself; they simply felt that it took on special aspects in their own country. Although for the poets, the concept of Cubo-Futurism was altogether natural and coincided with their creative principles (they borrowed several devices from contemporary Cubist painting), for the painters, combining the two concepts posed significant problems. The principle of persistence, the Cubists' notion that an object or figure was a static construction, stood in opposition to the Futurists' "plastic dynamism." True, a few French Cubists took a serious interest in Futurism and tried to meet it halfway. Among them were Marcel Duchamp, Jacques Villon, La Fresnaye, Fernand Léger, Gleizes, and Metzinger, who formed the group known as the Section d'Or; they criticized "classical" Cubism for being colorless and static. The critic Marcel Boulanger once called this version of French painting Cubo-Futurism,[25] but the term did not catch on in France, although it did at the time have a certain justification in fact. After the famous exhibition of Italian Futurists in Paris in February 1912 at the Bernheim-Jeune Gallery, the debate between the Italians and French slacked off somewhat, and they began to look for points of similarity. Of course, this compromise could be only minor and relative at best, for their principles remained largely mutually contradictory.

In Russia, Cubo-Futurism began to be cultivated with particular intensity as a historical-artistic concept after this famous reconciliation between Cubism and Futurism had already taken place. Russian artists tried to capitalize on the fruits of various tendencies, to incorporate not only Cubism and Futurism but also Fauvism and Expressionism. In the mid-teens, though, it was Cubism and Futurism that aroused the greatest interest among artists, and the experiments of Russian painters at the end of the first decade of the century and the beginning of the second had begun to indicate that these trends might converge.[26]

What resulted from this were highly original variations on the basic Western European tendencies. Cubism did in fact borrow several dynamic features from Futurism, and Futurism, for its part, did "progress" toward the static, to say nothing of the fact that in its Russian version it did not acquire the emphasis on machines, pandynamism, and panurbanism characteristic of "pure" Futurism as it had arisen in Italy. In its "pure" form Futurism achieved only minor development on Russian soil.[27] Goncharova did a few "programmatically Futuristic" compositions. She introduced new industrial themes (*Factory,* 1912), tried to juxtapose new forms of movement and speed (*Airplane over Train,* 1913), and used the motif of electricity several times. However, despite the Futurist devices of multiple depiction of one object in order to express dynamic movement, in her *Bicyclist,* for example, the composition is ultimately subordinate to the symmetry, and the dynamism, as a result, is limited.

Malevich's famous *Knife Sharpener* (1912), done with an obvious nod to the experiments of Futurism, carries in it the idea of persistence. The diagonal movement of the various objects and their development in space seem to neutralize the central placement of the figure: the persistence Malevich sought is not destroyed by the abundance of arms and legs: their contours seek stability and tend toward greater persistence.

A similar example is Popova's 1913 *Seated Female Model* (page 49), which took its alternate title, *Person + Air + Space,* as well as certain details such as the cone and the cylinder, from Umberto Boccioni. The Cubist idea, however, predominated in this picture, although it posed certain problems that were not at all typical of French Cubism: the balance between depth and surface, and decorativeness, which the masters of "orthodox" French Cubism rejected. It is in this treatment of specific problems that the traditional national style comes through.

Among the artists of the Russian avant-garde, probably Rozanova in 1913–14 rendered the most consistent version of Futurist painting. It is no mere coincidence that she (along with Exter and Kulbin) were participants in the international exhibition of Futurists held in Rome in the spring of 1914. Her *Ports* and *Factories,* dynamic posters and lithographed illustrations, proved more than adequate to the principles of dynamic plasticity.

Thus we can say with confidence that in this movement, which in Russia was given the name "Cubo-Futurism," the Cubist tendencies predominated, whereas Futurism in its "pure" form was not explored very consistently. Popova's work is graphic confirmation of this situation.

THE PAINTINGS OF 1914–15: GENRES, SUBJECTS, MOTIFS

The two or three years Popova spent in the Cubo-Futurist orbit were unusually fruitful. She exhibited at all the shows listed above, with several pictures in each, more often than not with new works. A good third of the easel paintings shown at her posthumous exhibition in 1924 were from these years.

Popova's successes at this time were determined by a whole set of circumstances. First of all, her study in Paris, which continued to bear fruit long after her return, played a major role: these lessons were supplemented by her subsequent travels and by the broad contacts between Russian and French art, which increased until the outbreak of the war. Second, her Italian journey drew her closer to Futurism, but simultaneously it developed and strengthened her sympathies for classical art. Third—and this is probably the most important—were the times. Popova found herself in an environment of incredible creative inquiry. Her colleagues in the Futurist exhibitions were working with extraordinary intensity during those years. Many—especially Malevich and Tatlin—were discovering new principles or were at the brink of new discoveries. Others were ready to rush after the leaders as soon as the new discoveries were accepted and published. For many masters of Russian "leftist" painting, these years were especially productive. And this was the case for Popova.

At this time Popova chiefly focused on two genres, the still life and the portrait. We have already spoken of the temporary disappearance of the landscape—a tendency typical among the Cubo-Futurists. If the Cézannist Cubists of the Jack of Diamonds, led by Konchalovsky, Ilya Mashkov, Falk, and Lentulov, not only maintained the landscape as their chief genre throughout the 1910s but also frequently realized their stylistic aspirations in it, then artists such as Malevich, Tatlin, Udaltsova, Kliun, and Puni resorted extremely rarely to the more or less traditional landscape, or abandoned it in their evolution altogether (Malevich), or else transformed the landscape into a theoretical composition, a special kind of rebus demanding a solution and leaving no place for real space or objects (*Landscape Running Past* by Kliun). In the process of shifting from painting what is seen to painting what is known, the landscape genre had the most difficulty; more than the others, its prestige suffered. Both in early Cubism in France and in the works of the founders of the Jack of Diamonds, however, landscape still retained its position, at the cost of a special "objectification of space." Later stages of Cubism, which demanded the dismantling of the object and its subsequent synthesis on the canvas, did not work well with landscape.

It is easy to explain how still life moved to the fore as a genre in early and late Cubism. In Russian painting it underwent intense development about 1905–9. At first the Impressionists

(Grabar and Korovin) and later several masters of Russian Modernism—Aleksandr Golovin from the World of Art; Sapunov, Sudeikin, Martiros Saryan, Kuznetsov of the Blue Rose; and, finally, the painters of the Jack of Diamonds—inaugurated still life's triumphal march in Russian painting, which until that time had resorted to that genre only very infrequently.

Still life's stock rose especially because artists were then striving more and more to make their paintings "objects." To the extent to which a painting lost its mimetic quality, ceased to be a depiction, an illusion of any kind of real-world phenomenon, it itself turned into a thing. In the still life the subject as object, as motif, and the painting as thing seemed to be converging. The painting was taking on its own "weight," its own volume; the paint layer was moving increasingly toward a third dimension, and the paint itself was becoming autonomous, "objectified."

Popova's art was developing in complete harmony with this general notion. Still life became the predominant genre in her art of the mid-1910s. But along with still life, the single-figure portrait composition and genre had proved themselves amenable to Cubism. Of course, the portrait and genre aspects of these compositions are only a departure point for the artist since Cubist paintings give only an abstract conception of either an actual face or a specific event. Nevertheless, the human figure was a subject from the very start of the Cubist movement. After Les Demoiselles d'Avignon, Picasso quickly shifted over to single-figure compositions, executed under the influence of African sculpture, and then turned to the portrait, to toreadors and harlequins. At the very beginning of his Cubist journey Braque drew his famous Large Nude (1908). Gleizes, Metzinger, Léger, La Fresnaye, and Juan Gris depicted dancers, swimmers, smokers, pianists, men and women in cafés. In these works the human figure at first resembled the subject, then was dismantled and gathered into a synthetic composition. The figure was turning out to be an object quite well suited to all these experiments.

The subjects and motifs used in the painting of Cubism suggest a different sort of thinking. Cubism seemingly freed itself from the direct movement toward nature, granting the artist freedom to interpret the world of objects. From this one might conclude that there was no limit to the motifs on which the artist might focus. What we see, however, is the exact opposite. The circle of subjects narrows, iconographic images appear that migrate from picture to picture, borrowed by many artists from the work of the originators. What Cubist didn't draw a violin or a guitar after Braque and Picasso had done so? Nearly every Cubist after Cézanne did a still life of a dish of fruit. This repetition of motifs may seem to contradict the new attitude toward nature. In fact, it does not. Generally speaking, painting's progression toward the new principles of Cubism was the final stage in a more or less continuous contact with reality. The

way into art for this reality was no wider than the narrow neck of a bottle through which liquid drips in. It should come as no surprise that only select motifs and objects, those that best fitted the specifics of Cubism, its interests, passed through that neck. True, within the limits of this iconography there were some individual and national manifestations. The things artists chose were either evidence of a nation's daily life, or they permitted the development of those painterly-plastic qualities that the artists of this school embodied. It is easy to explain, for example, the prevalence of the violin in French Cubism. The amazing cohesiveness of its form, the traces of high craftsmanship left by human hands on the curved surfaces, the sharp, repetitive rhythm of the line of pegs—all this accentuates the "thingness" of the violin and simultaneously provides a basis for the soaring of that artistic intellectualism characteristic of the French. It is another matter that later the violin, as a proprietary object of Cubist painting, passed into the art of other schools, especially the Russian.

We can also explain the presence of other objects in the works of the French Cubists—books, newspaper clippings, pipes, playing cards. And just as easily understand the frequent use of the motifs of the dance, the café table with one or two people, the figure of the musician, the swimmer. These motifs are quite traditional in French painting. Many of them traverse much of the nineteenth century, having first appeared in Impressionism and Post-Impressionism and from there, as a rightful legacy, passing into Cubism.

In the art of the Russian Cubo-Futurists, including Popova, we find the same subjects and motifs as in French art. Udaltsova's and Popova's Violins came to their art directly from Braque and Picasso. Single-figure compositions depicting smokers, pianists, women with guitars, and so forth were done under the influence of Metzinger, Le Fauconnier, Gleizes, Gris, Villon, and Léger. Gris's Le Lavabo brings to mind Udaltsova's "kitchen still lifes." While much of the iconography of Russian Cubism is taken from the French, at the same time uncommon objects do invade the iconography in given instances. In Popova we frequently encounter the traditional Russian tray (pages 74 and 75), which was an almost obligatory feature of the still lifes of her predecessors in the Jack of Diamonds—Konchalovsky, Mashkov, Aleksandr Kuprin. This "purely Russian" object came into art both as a symbol of national life and as a device for enhancing the decorativeness of the pictorial composition. In Popova it also is accompanied by the Russian word for tea (chai) written on the canvas, thereby suggesting, in conjunction with the tray, the traditional Russian practice of tea drinking. If we recall here the popularity of the samovar in Russian still life of that era (from Konchalovsky and Lentulov to Malevich), the motif of the tray becomes perfectly logical, for it combines traditional national and aesthetic qualities.

Let us turn our attention to the abundance of compositions

that depict clocks, among which are several Popovas (page 73). If we recall pictures such as Rozanova's *Metronome,* Goncharova's *Dynamo Machine,* or her *Weaver,* which depicts a machine with numerous wheels and cogs, then we can view this interest of Russian artists in simple mechanisms as normal but, simultaneously, distinctive. *Metronome* and Popova's *Clocks* are stimulated not by the symbolic idea of time passing but by a rather primitive curiosity about moving mechanisms, about pendulums and springs. All these details are dispersed over the surface, presented to the viewer in their purified, stripped-down form.

Topical compositions of the Russian Cubo-Futurists fall almost entirely within the iconographic code created by French Cubism. As we see, Russian Cubo-Futurism's originality was expressed only to a small degree in the iconography, but to a much greater degree in the realm of style. We shall attempt later to demonstrate this originality. For now we will see only that Russian Cubism did not divide into developmental stages as in French Cubism, where the synthetic stage was followed by the analytic. Insofar as Russian Cubism was received from French hands, virtually ready-made, Russian Cubo-Futurists combined both these stages into one. In the work of one artist or another at one time or another there appear both Cubist still lifes that retain the objective form of the things and convey their more or less real existence in space, as well as compositions in which the objective form is "dispersed" over the picture's surface, forcing the viewer to assemble them in his imagination.

MUSICAL INSTRUMENTS

Popova's still lifes from the years 1913–14—*Tin Dish* (page 56, right), which depicts all the objects in their entirety, as well as the compositions with dismantled musical instruments, done most likely in 1914, after her return from Italy—demonstrate a similar conjunction of disparate principles. The most famous example of this kind of composition is the so-called *Italian Still Life* (page 79).[28]

We know, in addition, at least three other compositions very similar to *Italian Still Life*.[29] This abundance of variations on a single theme is characteristic for Popova not only during the period of her Cubo-Futurist experiments but in later years as well. At the base of all these compositions is the silhouette of a violin standing vertically or leaning slightly, which is echoed several times. In a few versions the sounding board is displaced with respect to the fingerboard; in *Italian Still Life* these parts of the instrument are almost completely detached from one another.

With rare exception, almost all the versions include text written in French, Italian, or English in Roman letters ("des canons," "Roma," "les ateliers" [page 71], "wallpaper" [page 72]). Moreover, usually the word is incomplete, and sometimes

we get only endings or unintelligible combinations of letters. This use of inscriptions comes from Cubism's originators— Picasso and Braque. Words or letters served various functions: they revealed or, the reverse, muddled the meaning of what was depicted, they hinted, they made the viewer guess by adding letters to the process of synthesizing the image's meaning, which was now supposed to be the viewer's job. We observe the same devices in Popova. The word "canons" makes the viewer look in the abstract forms for silhouettes of weapons. "Roma" and "Italia" provide a rather precise address for the stimulus of her impressions. "Wallpaper" engenders a more oblique association: at that time the Cubists—including Popova—were eagerly turning to pasted clippings from newspapers and wallpaper (even if there is no "wallpaper" collage in the version of the picture where the word is written on the canvas).

But this mental game does not exhaust the inscriptions' functions. They also have a spatial-plastic importance. In *Italian Still Life* the word "canons" is written volumetrically; each letter has a white outline, which, like a distinctive countershadow, adds dimension to the depiction. The inscription seems to hang from the foreground, and behind it the object world of the still life unfolds; it looks as if it were written on a glass surface through which the objects show. Sometimes the inscriptions have letters solidly painted in and interspersed with letters designated merely by a contour. This device creates the unique effect of an abyss running through the foreground and middle ground.

Of course, the depiction of the instrument plays the leading role in the still lifes—the curved contour of the sounding board, the split objects, or simply the color planes overlapping or partially blocking out one another. In the future Popova would call this compositional device "interleaving." Comparing Popova's still lifes with the works of the French Cubists, it is easy to observe that it was she who expressed this interleaving most definitively, although we do find some manifestations of it in Picasso, Braque, and Gris as well. In the 1910–11 paintings by Picasso and Braque, planes form the vibrating surface of the object, and the vibration is realized within the limits of a shallow space. Each of the planes, however, is not confirmed as a stable spatial depth. In Popova the planes are broader, more like solid objects. In the later pictures of Braque and Picasso (1912–14) interleaving makes itself felt to a greater extent. Particularly illustrative is Picasso's canvas *Ma jolie*—the nearest thing to a prototype for Popova's *Italian Still Life*. But in Picasso, textural interests dominate over spatial. Popova also expressed an interest in textural effects in her use of collage and of various powders to vary the surface of spatial relief, and of contrasts between adjacent surfaces. More important for her, however, was finding a logic to the interaction between the planes. Therefore these planes are most often painted opaquely, so that no light comes through, in order to avoid the impression of translucency, which Picasso succumbed to. But they intersect in an extremely shallow space. Sometimes one of the planes that is placed under another and partially covered with a third seems to switch places with an adjacent plane and be covered, when it itself was supposed to have been covering the adjacent one. Moreover, the viewer perceives the combination as natural. This stacking of planes (reminiscent of M. C. Escher's optical illusions) accentuates again the minor role of depth. The levels accumulate on top of one another, almost canceling out depth entirely. Some forms seem to break up this "stratification" and draw the depiction out to the surface of the canvas. Most often it is abstract forms or lines lacking any association with concrete objects that take on this function.

The role of these nonobjective forms gradually increases. In one version of this composition (page 72), Popova repeats the instrument's silhouette three times and then constructs an entire system of lines—mostly vertical, but set at an angle. Here again the "Gothic" attachments of the artist creating an "arched" composition make themselves felt. But there is yet another unique quality that distinguishes this particular version from analogous works by French masters: Popova's attempt to construct a decorative whole by using beautiful linear curves, rhythmic repetitions, and soft combinations of red, dark blue, and yellow.

In all the still lifes with musical instruments we have examined, the composition seems to be born out of chaos—sometimes laboriously, as in Italian Still Life, where the forms overcome motion of various kinds with great effort; sometimes this occurs more easily, more freely, without tension. It is especially important to underscore the skill the artist must have to contain the energy of the movement within the limits of the canvas. This concentration of forms requires great effort on the part of the painter, an ability to rule the frequently fantastic world that she herself has created.

The version of Musical Instruments that we called decorative above actually is a transitional step between Italian Still Life and Violin (1915; page 79).[30] Unlike the preceding works, Violin is in the oval shape common for Cubist compositions of the early teens (for example, in Braque and Picasso). In some versions of Musical Instruments Popova seemed to be working toward the oval form already: rounding the angles of the composition, following the outline of the instrument, and filling the remaining space with neutral forms ready to vanish the moment the oval appeared. In its very format Violin proved to be a synthesis of her previous investigations, although this was not the only point, of course. Violin might well be called the most integrated and elaborated of all the still lifes of Popova's Cubo-Futurist period. It combines curved and straight lines, segments of circles and angles, planes and edges, subtly and precisely, in a unified composition. We can accurately read and

recognize all the objects placed on the successive planes. The picture is apprehended as a beautifully executed Cubist exercise; it includes all the essential elements of a Cubist still life: inscriptions, broken volumes, a restrained color scheme, a lively painterly texture.

The inclusion of so many "typical" elements diminishes the individual qualities of the work, although we must admit that Popova passed the examination with flying colors. Violin is similar to many compositions of French Cubism—as well as being closely related to Udaltsova's painting by the same name. Here we can firmly establish the important similarity between Popova and Udaltsova, although on the whole the latter applied the principles of French Cubism much more consistently.

Despite its unique classicism Violin did not exhaust Popova's interest in musical instruments. She created several works entitled Guitar during the years 1914–15.[31] We can assume that work on the Guitars was going on at the same time as the other Musical Instruments were being done. But the actual nature of the Guitars proved somewhat different from the compositions examined above. First of all, the Guitars are simpler—both in their complement of objects and their placement, and in the interrelationship of adjacent or overlapping planes. The development within this group testifies to Popova's desire for economy, to be rid of superfluous details, to arrive at a precise and "pure" resolution. In one of the sketches (page 71, right) and in the final version (page 78) the objects are restricted to half a guitar with a broken fingerboard, a notebook, a table on which the guitar "stands," and a bottle reminiscent of Juan Gris's. In the upper portion of the canvas the word "VALS[E]" is written. There is no puzzle, no faltering of any kind here. The inclusion of half a guitar along with the other objects has more of an enumerative than a compositional purpose.

In one version (page 77) the artist's desire for maximum simplicity leads her to a degree of economy not to be found in her work before or after. The composition contains only half a guitar (without a fingerboard) in an oval and placed partly on a gray background and partly on a black plane. The left part of the oval is "colored" a milky white. Here there is no allusion to volume: all the objects are deployed on a single plane. Perhaps this is why Popova's textural investigations intensified. In places the gray background swells due to the sand under the paint. The white and black areas, on the contrary, are smoothed: the surfaces bear no trace of the brush; the stroke is concealed. As for the guitar, its surface is covered with sinuous parallel lines, possibly pulled across the surface with a metal comb, a technique the artist borrowed from French Cubism. As a result of all these experiments on the canvas, contrasts are set up as different color patches and different textural zones are juxtaposed. This interest in textural combinations may have been awakened not only through the influence of French painting but also in response to the various textural experiments of Tatlin,

Kliun, Puni, and others of the Russian avant-garde.

The emphasis on the planar character in this version of *Guitar* also represents one extreme point on the artist's rather broad front of investigations. The opposite point is the pictorial reliefs done in 1915 that arose out of her still-life experiments. We will touch on these compositions later. For now let us turn to the other still lifes Popova did in her Cubo-Futurist period.

"OBJECTS"

Popova often called her still lifes "objects," referring to the realistic motif she depicted on the canvas. True, the actual word "object" was then transferred to the picture, in accord with the idea of the "thingism" of painting. Meanwhile, as Popova was evolving from Cubo-Futurism to nonobjective art, the objects themselves were becoming less and less recognizable. Or else another tendency emerged: the object remained, but its surroundings lost their objective character and took on an abstract interpretation. The early, more "recognizable" still lifes include *Objects from a Dyeworks* (1914; page 80).[32] All sorts of things—gloves, ribbons, feathers, tasseled drapery,[33] and finally, a newspaper with a headline—seem to be placed on the plane, sometimes overlapping or intersecting one another. By weaving themselves into one common *represented* plane, they leave a neutral zone along the sides and in the corners of the canvas.

In *Objects from a Dyeworks* we can establish many other characteristics of Popova's manner of the mid-1910s: she varied the texture in different places on the canvas; she broke up objects and at the breaks shifted them or broke them off; she looked for harmony in her color relationships, as if she were tearing the active dark blue, green, red, and yellow dots out of the colorful composition's gray background. But there is still another important feature that involves more than the actual means of formal expression and pictorial language: the selection of objects shown to the viewer attests to a real-life situation. The motif of the still life refers to a real combination of objects in concrete space and time. There are no traces of the usual still-life setting. The artist does not "place" the objects, does not organize their interrelations in any real place and then record them in the picture. The canvas transforms the impression of a real-life situation, moving significantly away from it.

Several versions of *Clock* (1914; page 73) belong to the group of fully recognizable objects. They are also more traditional in their pictorial and compositional resolution, although they have virtually no iconographic analogies in European Cubist painting.[34]

The *Clocks* also possess something of a concrete situation. They have not only the cogs of the mechanism, the gears and the swinging pendulum, but also the wall, hung with wallpaper. In one version (page 73, top right) the arrows on the clock face are displaced but accurately tell the time. The "Russian situation" is expressed in this composition not only in its love for the bared mechanism, which we spoke of in connection with the problem of the iconography of Russian Cubism, but in the object itself: the clock Popova chose is the grandfather clock that was popular in Russia then and can still be found today all over the Russian provinces and countryside.

The "situationness" that we have established in the *Clocks* facilitates the formation of the Cubist interior and not simply the still life, although compositions like this can be called interiors only in the broadest sense, since they ignore real space. But the feeling of an interior released through a whole series of abstract barriers lives on. We can note this feature in the works of Udaltsova as well, for example, in *Kitchen* (1915), in several works by Rozanova (*Hairdresser's, Sewing Box,* both 1915), and in earlier works of Goncharova (*Laundry,* 1913; *Mirror,* 1912). We can assume that this characteristic dates back to the classics of French Cubism. But in Russian Cubo-Futurism it takes on a specific coloring in its choice of objects, its unique attraction to a naïve, folk beginning, and its interest in the inner life of things not put out for view but hidden in the corners of the room, in the parts of people's homes guests never see.

In Popova's graphics archive (private collection, Moscow) there is an entire series of sketches that characterize her intentions. Here we find the Dutch tile oven with the iron door (page 76, top left), tables set with dishes, little tables with small table lamps (page 74, left), and carafes (page 76, top right), compotes (pages 84 and 86), and bottles drawn on a large scale. One of these horizontal oval drawings has a composition with a carafe, as well as other objects very reminiscent of Gris's, and on the lower right in a pattern of slanting lines we read the name "Juan"—unnecessary proof of the artist's interest in the Spaniard's works.

As is usually the case with Popova, all the drawings described above were sketches for future paintings, some of them merely planned and never executed. But in this specific instance we are interested not only in the actual work process, which for Popova scarcely differed in any serious way from that of other Cubists in the 1910s, but in that special "situationness" we noted above.

In this respect two *Still Lifes with Tray* (1915)—one of which was in her posthumous exhibition and is now in a private collection in Moscow (page 75), and the other of which we know only from a contemporary photograph (page 74)—are characteristic. Both of them include the inscription "chai" ("tea"), as if thereby drawing the viewer into whatever action is unfolding around the table. The newspaper pasted onto the canvas in one of the versions is not simply a formal device; it is a newspaper at a tea table, as ordinary a phenomenon as the tray, the vase, the carafe, the goblet, and the other objects.

In both *Still Lifes with Tray* there is almost no dismantling of the object; it would be more appropriate to speak of a "dismantling of space," of its thoroughgoing transformation. If in the lower part of the canvas we can imagine a real section of a table with a goblet or other objects on it, then by stepping back a little from these objects we can begin to sense a nonreal space in which the goblet "floats," the planes start overlapping one another—"burdened," moreover, with volume—and only the flat objects—the newspaper, and especially the semicircular tray that peeks out from under the other things—confirm the actual painting surface.

It is interesting that in Popova's still lifes not only does the cult of favorite objects establish itself, but the visual formulas for referring to them evolve, one of them being the depiction of the compote that is repeated in several instances: in one of the versions of *Still Life with Tray,* in *Still Life* of 1915 (page 86, top right),[35] in the painting *Objects* (1915) in the Russian Museum, in the painting-relief *Compote with Fruit (Plastic Painting)* (page 85), shown in 1915 at the "0.10" exhibit and known today from an old archive photograph. The Vesnin-Aksionov list mentions a still life with compote and bottles, as well as a sketch for it (1916). The compote motif so fascinated Popova that she returned to it anew in 1920, when she did three replicas of *Still Life with Compote* in gouache,[36] where the beloved object of depiction stands alone and therefore is placed in the center. In the version that has survived (page 84) it is set off by gaps, surrounded not so much by other objects as by abstract shapes, precisely defined and already seeming to come from "painterly architectonics"—a visual approach that she would soon evolve.

Popova's compote functions in much the same way as Braque's violin or pipe, Picasso's bottle, or Gris's carafe—it is another "formula of Cubism." Of course, the white compote was part of the still life in Cézanne and many Cubist works as well, but only in Popova did it take on such an original and expressive form.[37] On one hand the compote's base is vertical, strictly perpendicular; on the other, curved. This curve seems to set off the circular motion so desired among the Cubists, and the motion brings us to the semicircular foundation of the base, at first marked by a distinct line, then broken off, but quickly regaining its contour. The upper portion of the compote, where the fruit lies, is shown not only from different points of view but in what seem like different sections. Looking at similar experiments with Cubist form, one is inevitably reminded of the words of the then popular Russian philosopher Piotr Uspensky, a follower of the renowned philosopher of the fourth dimension Charles Howard Hinton—words the painter and theoretician Mikhail Matiushin quoted in his article on Gleizes and Metzinger's book *On Cubism:* "For us, every thing exists in time; only a *section of the thing* exists in space. By transferring our consciousness from the section of the thing to the part of it that exists in time, we achieve the illusion of motion in 'the thing itself.'"[38] Indeed, Popova's compote does seem to go into motion: it unfolds, reveals its inner structure, manifests all its

plastic potential in a highly meaningful form.

Let us turn our attention to how, within the confines of the still life, nonobjective painting developed, how things gradually lost their real appearance, and how the painting retained only an abstract reminder of them. A few of Popova's works of the years 1915–16 demonstrate this evolution quite specifically, beginning with works in which a more or less concrete object is depicted on an abstract ground, as in the *Still Life with Mask* (page 81).[39] The white mask, which looks as though it has been placed on a plane and therefore appears somewhat in perspective, is the sole object here to retain any traits of a concrete thing, although even that is very difficult to recognize. Some of its parts seem to have been lopped off, truncated. The perspective effect becomes somewhat suspect, for the abstract forms, the incrustations on the canvas, the newspaper clippings covered with paint, bring us back to the surface. Here the depiction of space ceases to be a goal for the artist, and the task of identification is shifted to the viewer.

In their book on Cubism, Gleizes and Metzinger wrote: "From the fact that the object is truly transubstantiated, so that the most practiced eye has some difficulty in discovering it, a great charm results. The picture which only surrenders itself slowly seems always to wait until we interrogate it, as though it reserved an infinity of replies to an infinity of questions."[40]

In some of the paintings that lie at the very boundary between the objective and nonobjective, Popova certainly relied on this curiosity in the viewer, on his wish to supplement objectlessness with concrete associations. Cases in point are *Still Life* (page 86, top right) and *Grocery* (page 87). Both these canvases were painted when Popova had already begun to work on nonobjective compositions. These paintings could be considered nonobjective because of their ambiguous, encoded nature. However, they differ from the nonobjective works, not only in their titles, and not even in the fact that the forms engender reminders of specific objects. The *Painterly Architectonics* also have reminders of the objective world. That is not the point. The forms themselves in these two compositions continue to refer to the still life: they intertwine, break up, block each other out. Inscriptions have a place here: letters and numbers, labels, sprinkles of sand. From time to time the contours of geometric forms break off and later are picked up again; lines and planes that had been lost find themselves once more. This device compels the viewer himself to follow the motion, to "catch" the lines, to fill in the lost contours, to guess the origins of the forms. These origins can easily be just as far from the depictions as in works of nonobjective painting. However, the very forms in this *Still Life* "behave" like concrete things, whereas in nonobjective painting they acquire an ideal completeness and perfection.

Compared with the *Still Life, Grocery* goes further to confirm Popova's already architectonic language of painting. In her explication for the painting, the artist wrote: "The object is almost totally deprived of its concept; all that remains are the forms necessary for the linear building of the color construction" (see Appendix X). The forms are more geometric in *Grocery*; they tend toward rectangles, triangles, and half cylinders. The placement of these forms over the spatial planes is right. Done the year the artist was possessed by the ideas of nonobjectivism and Suprematism, *Grocery* is a phenomenon of the avant-garde in the rearguard. For among the *Still Life Interiors* this composition stands at the furthest remove from the traditional interpretation of this genre. However, it has not yet broken off from its old roots, testimony to the gradualness of the break that was occurring in Popova's art.

There is yet another point that is illuminating for the place *Grocery* occupies in the evolution of Popova's art. In this painting the formal problems are resolved on the whole through purely painterly means. The artist depicts draperies rather than pasting them on; she depicts half cylinders rather than constructing a relief as she did in many works of 1915 that marked her fling with sculpto-painting. By 1916 that fling was already well behind her.

RELIEFS

Popova's interest in sculpto-painting was not accidental. She was by no means the only artist to experiment with this important and interesting tendency in the development of the European and, especially, Russian avant-garde movement. Popova's inner impulses constantly provoked her to go beyond the limits of the pictorial surface. We have seen how actively she utilized any opportunity to transform the surface of the canvas into a kind of relief, employing sprinkles and collages, and truly achieving a real spatial texture. Another inner impulse is her desire, evidenced in 1913, to achieve objective illusion. As we have already said, this desire was best manifested in *Tin Dish* (page 56), where the things seem to want to take on three-dimensionality; they are ready to "poke out" of the surface of the canvas, although the paint layer does not create a relief and the impression of the illusion is made purely through graphic means.

These inner impulses coincided with the general movement of European painting, beginning with the synthetic stage of Cubism.[41] As in many other situations, at the source of the new tendency we find Picasso, and his "picto-sculptural" experiments. As for Russian artists, in the years 1913–15 Baranov-Rossiné, Puni, Tatlin, and Kliun all shifted over from pure painting toward three-dimensional work. For some of them— Tatlin, for example—this shift meant a long break with painting. For others—Kliun, for instance—the sculpture acquired total independence, and the artist continued his painterly work at the same time. Puni's sculptural experiments taught him to use

set three-dimensional forms, which he often combined with the pictorial plane. "Sculpto-painting" ran a different course in Popova's art.

In the first place, her interest in this form of art was short-lived, lasting only one year: 1915. Neither before nor after, as far as we know, did she work on pictorial reliefs. Further, she never emerged into total three-dimensionality but always maintained the initial surface—the plane; her works remained "sculptural pictures" in which color, and not the combination of materials, played the most important role. In other words, Popova remained first and foremost a painter, whereas Tatlin, with his combinations of materials, presaged Constructivist design.

From lists and catalogs we know only a few works by Popova of a sculpto-pictorial nature. At the "0.10" exhibition, Popova showed three: *Portrait of a Lady (Plastic Drawing)* (page 83), *The Jug on the Table* (page 82),[42] and *Compote with Fruit* (page 84). The last two works are labeled "plastic painting" in the "0.10" catalog. To these we should add *Card Game (Painterly-Plastic Balance)* (location unknown), which was shown in "The Store" exhibition and dated 1915 in that catalog, and *Volumetric-Spatial Relief* (page 86)—the title under which it was listed in the catalog to the posthumous exhibition of 1924.[43]

Unfortunately, we have no picture of *Card Game*, a lack that terribly impoverishes our understanding of Popova's "sculpto-painting," for this work departs from the still life. If we were to imagine how Popova's other "reliefs" fit into her evolution, we could easily draw a line to represent the artist's general development, a line passing from the rather objective and "real" *Jug on the Table* and *Compote with Fruit* to the conventional *Portrait of a Lady* and, finally, to the "nonobjective" *Volumetric-Spatial Relief*. Nevertheless, all of them remain fundamentally two-dimensional.

The most simply, but at the same time highly effectively, resolved is *The Jug on the Table*. Here Popova used wood and cardboard worked, as in a traditional painterly composition, with oil paint. She did not try to reveal texture and use it as a medium for artistic expressiveness. As before, she was interested in the relationship between volume and plane. She doubled the volume: the convex surfaces of the jug bring the depicted object into the third dimension, but through her painting Popova revealed parts that jut out (milky white) and parts that recede (gray). In this way, the light and dark modeling of the volume appears as the consequence of the real distribution of surfaces in space and as a result of the painterly modeling of an already real volume. The artist herself (see Appendix X) explained the device this way: "The desire to structure the distorted sculptural . . . abstract volume more powerfully necessitates that the painted volumetric form be replaced by real volume and also that its sculptural expressiveness be strengthened through the use of subdued color."

But there is another important point, which brings Popova back to the painter's initial position: the plane as a reference point in the spatial elaboration of the composition. On this plane we find certain traces of visual illusion — letters, numbers, the sand-sprinkled textured surface typical for Popova, the chessboard with colored squares. This is not the plane of departure for a sculptural relief.

If in *The Jug on the Table* the painterly-illusory and real three-dimensional treatments are fairly well defined and clear, in *Portrait of a Lady* they are more complicated: some parts of the head and half figure begin life in real three-dimensionality but conclude with the illusion of a two-dimensional depiction on a plane of that three-dimensionality. These shifts are elusive; they engender a sensation of unique interdependence between the real relief and its painted depiction. The viewer is presented with a kind of rebus that is reinforced by the absolute conventionality of the depiction of the human face, individual parts of which are likened to details of a three-dimensional construction: the eyesockets to apertures and funnels; the ear holes to semicircular embrasures.

The combination of painting and relief in *Portrait* is striking above all for its wit, its inventiveness, its discoveries of similarities and transformations. But simultaneously another effect comes into play: the organization of forms, the harmonic relationships between volumes and the plane. This latter quality becomes primary in *Volumetric-Spatial Relief*. We cannot evaluate the resolution of this relief today. From the surviving photograph, we can only confirm that here again real volume coexists with illusory volume, and the basis is the plane on which the composition unfolds.

FACES, FIGURES

More significant in the artist's Cubo-Futurist period than the relief were her portraits and figure compositions. Most famous and perfect of the compositions of this series are the two versions of *Traveling Woman* (pages 96 and 97) and *Portrait of a Philosopher* (page 92), which represent the two lines she followed in treatments of people: portraits and figure compositions (with rare exception, single figures). Let us first consider the portraits.

One might suppose that *Portrait of a Philosopher* was preceded by the series of very similar compositions that were called *Study for a Portrait* (1915) in the posthumous exhibition and on the Vesnin-Aksionov list (pages 91, left, and 102, left and right).[44] We have no grounds for linking these studies directly to *Portrait of a Philosopher*. In the latter and in the preparatory drawings for it there are two major differences from the *Studies for a Portrait*: in the direction in which the head is turned and in the "facial features" (we can speak of these at least to some degree despite the very relative portrait nature of

the work). The model for the *Studies for a Portrait* is not known; it may have been imaginary. Nevertheless, the *Studies for a Portrait* clearly lead to *Portrait of a Philosopher*, for the problems posed in both are similar.

Each *Study for a Portrait* was worked out on the plane. The half figure and head are depicted strictly frontally; there is no perspective; they are presented as projections of volumes on the painting surface. The device of stratifying painted planes typical for Popova is here realized very sparingly. It does not create the sensation of spatial depth. The parts of the face are split up. The nose has almost the same shape in all the versions; it is turned to one side so that it looks more like the silhouette of a key or a musical instrument. Given the frontal position of the head, figure, and eye, the profile view of the nose completely destroys the real space that the object depicted seemed to occupy. In *Portrait of a Philosopher*, there is an element of space, however; there is a suggestion of perspective, although it is balanced out by the abstract rhythm and the abstract "figures" spread out over the surface. Consequently, in *Study for a Portrait* we encounter a somewhat deliberate planar resolution of the composition, which could have arisen as a kind of contrast to the artist's escape into real space in her reliefs.

Various versions of *Study for a Portrait* include inscriptions; in the majority of cases this is a combination of letters that, taken together, form the word "Cubo-Futurismo." On one of the preliminary pencil sketches for the *Studies* (private collection, Moscow), Popova wrote, along with the word "Cubo," the unfinished name of the Italian Futurist Ardengo Soffici (Popova's enthusiasm for his work is evident in her *oeuvre* of those years).[45] We cannot, of course, link the conception of this portrait only to Italian influence; the composition derives basically, as ever, from ideas in Picasso. We have only to recall Picasso's 1910 *Portrait of Daniel-Henry Kahnweiler (The Aficionado* or *Toreador)* of 1912. In these works we find certain devices adopted by Popova: the twisting configurations of the hair, the straight line of the nose, the darkness of the eyesockets. But in Picasso's compositions we sense an ambivalence of the planes in space, and taken together, these planes seem to be feeling out the volume, determining its place in its surroundings. Popova, as we have already remarked, held to the plane. Green, yellow (or orange), dark blue, or black strata overlap one another, recede only barely into the depth from the front plane. Even her use of letters does not conduce to spatial development: unlike those in many other paintings by Popova, the letters in *Study for a Portrait* have no "thickness" but lie on the surface in incorporeal silhouette. This device confirms yet again the existence of an experimental principle in *Study for a Portrait*; Popova never used this "squeezed" space anywhere else.

Comparing the various versions of *Study for a Portrait* it is hard to imagine where the artist's inquiries were heading.

Although similar in linear composition, the two are treated quite differently by the painter. In the gouache version (page 102, right) the color is used more decoratively; the green, black, and light yellow that predominate seek serene interaction. In the oil version from the Costakis collection (page 91, left) the same colors have warmer shadings, and the color relationships are more intense. In the version from the Moscow private collection (page 102, left) there is more contrast and genuine drama among the colors. This drama is enhanced by the white patches of the face and clothes, which seem to bare the construction of the forms—their skeleton. The white patches dispersed over the canvas attest to the application of the device of contrast. But the white details do not penetrate the surface; they contrast with the green and orange in the same spatial layer.

In *Study for a Portrait* Popova did not take any traditional portrait forms as models for imitation or polemic. *Portrait of a Philosopher* was constructed differently. Its very title implies something traditional. We know numerous "standard portraits" in the history of painting, after all: philosophers, artists, astronomers, doctors. Usually the type in these instances is born out of the image of the actual person who served the artist as model. This is the case with *Portrait of a Philosopher* as well. It is a portrait of the artist's brother Pavel Sergeevich, who was a philosopher both by education and by profession. The yellow cover of the journal with the inscription *Revue Philos . . . .* placed not far from the center of the composition confirms the painting's title.

The traditional quality goes beyond this, however. Because of the pronounced spatial development of the model, its location (a figure seated by a table), the well-tailored suit, traces of which can be pieced together from the jumbled and transformed shapes, the work acquires a formal tone. Popova wanted to give the image importance; the composition has stability. All this "formality" has a double meaning: on the one hand, positive; on the other (although scarcely noticeably), ironic. Popova's old comrades from the Jack of Diamonds group had been using the formal portrait in an ironic way since the early 1910s. Recall Yakulov's portrait by Konchalovsky, the self-portraits of Mashkov and Lentulov. The artists were either dressing up in a luxurious fur coat or a hunter's outfit or posing as "the great artist," as if a halo encircled their head with sunshine. We find elements of irony in the portrait images of French painters as well, but in Russian painting of the 1910s it was stronger, a direct reflection of the influential role of Neo-primitivism, which considered irony an important part of its program.

Still other sources than the Jack of Diamonds contributed to the *Portrait of a Philosopher*. As in many other instances, we cannot neglect Popova's favorite Paris painters—especially Metzinger with his portrait of Gleizes (1912) and Gris, whose

The Man in the Café (also 1912) may have been a prototype for *Portrait of a Philosopher*. This definite dependence on Gris is felt especially clearly in a preliminary drawing for the portrait, in gouache (1915, page 93, left). Here, as in *The Man in the Café*, the model's head stands out against the lighter background, not blending into it but sharply baring its own construction. In the portrait itself this separation of the head and figure from the background is lost: despite the fact that Popova overcame rigorous planarity, she never opened up any depth. The model, surrounding objects (table, goblet), and background are all of a piece. Background ceases to be background. First using planes to create the shape of the body and head and then using original formations that seem to feel out the space, the artist realized the objective essence of that space by not making a fundamental distinction between the body, the thing, and the air. It is this quality that distinguishes *Portrait of a Philosopher* from Gris's *The Man in the Café*. For Popova this was an essential difference because it laid the groundwork for her move into nonobjective painting, where the difference between form and "antiform" was first reduced to the bare minimum and later made to disappear altogether.

Popova resolved the interactions among the various color planes in an original way. Only a few of them possess opaque solidity—for example, the yellow-green corner of the wall with the figured draperies in the upper right corner of the canvas or the yellow plane of the newspaper cover. In other cases—even when Popova uses dark blue, almost black, or a deep brown—she relieves the color planes each time in certain places, breaks them up, forcing them to glow, to shine, either along the edges or within relatively large sections; these planes then become transparent.

The artist frequently resorts to white, which plays a completely different role here than in *Study for a Portrait*. If there it provided a dramatic contrast to the dark colors, then here it helps to create the special illusion of a stained-glass window, which, however, does not become the chief characteristic of the color structure. It does, however, help to place the color planes inside a rather narrow spatial stratum. Letters receive interesting treatment in this respect. Some are silhouetted on the plane and therefore flattened; others have a white "countershadow," which metaphorically implies their volume; still others glow, as if light were shining through them. All these three interpretations of form coexist in the painting, creating a harmonious unity through their interaction.

Portrait of a Philosopher must be considered one of the high points of Popova's Cubo-Futurist period. Another work also from 1915, appearing on the Vesnin-Aksionov list and in the catalog as *Portrait*, is in fact a self-portrait (page 101).[46] The self-portrait introduced a definite corrective into the artist's method, since it required at least some minimal reference to reality for recognition of the model's identity. Popova loved to draw self-portraits; several have been preserved in various private collections (see page 342). They are all similar, although they may have been executed at different times.[47] Almost all the self-portrait drawings possess an element of caricature. The nose becomes sharper, the eyesockets deeper; the curls of the hair, the creases of the lips and nose take on an almost ornamental quality. This honing renders Popova's face almost unrecognizable for those who know her pleasant appearance from photographs. The image in the self-portrait drawings is equally distant from the image in the self-portrait paintings of 1915. If the drawings involve a sharpening, then the paintings involve a distancing from the concrete manifestations of the original model. And although inevitably this distancing is not realized completely, the portrait image is interpreted more as an idea, a thesis.

The actual placement of the half figure and head on the painting plane is quite traditional for Cubist painting. An analogy can be seen with the series of *Studies for a Portrait*: the depiction is strictly *en face*; the basic compositional lines radiate from the center to the corners; some parts of the face seem to have been stripped bare and stand out in isolation. We encounter these kinds of *en face* "portrait diagrams" in the artist's drawings of those years as well, and they were widespread in Cubist painting in general. In particular, Popova had the example of Malevich, who did portraits of Kliun and Matiushin—intricate works, like a special kind of rebus requiring imaginative answers on the part of the viewer, and permeated with the idea of alogism. Malevich's portraits characteristically displayed a trait present in other Cubists as well: the conjunction of the mechanical and the living. The constructive idea sometimes transformed the human organism into a unique mechanism soullessly performing the life function. Juxtaposing the living and the mechanical intensified the effect of alogism.

Popova profited from her predecessors' experience, of course. But the *Self-Portraits* differ in essential features both from the works of her predecessors and from her own painting and portrait drawings. The composition in the *Self-Portraits* is significantly simpler; it is cleansed of complicated linear and spatial movement so as to seem almost somewhat elementary. The details of the face—eyebrows, eyes, nostrils, corners of the mouth—are outlined in black and tend toward the simplest shapes: oval, circle, straight line. The elements of similarity with the artist's face, which possessed a unique purity of form, are rooted in those shapes. But the essence of the portrayal is manifested not only in the direct resemblance. Popova was striving for its metaphorical embodiment: by scrambling the parts of the face she configured them in such a way that the central axis lies on a smooth plane, thereby informing the face with a unique openness.

The *Self-Portraits* differ from other works from the mid-1910s because the very problem of the subject prevents them from participating in the artist's generally consistent development. As in the other portrait genre, so in the figure compositions, this development went directly from overcoming representation to comprehending Malevich's experiment in total abstraction, which he called Suprematism. At the ultimate point in their evolution, Popova's figure compositions were in direct proximity to Suprematism. The paintings by Popova that interest us in this context are, in chronological order, *Smoker* (1914, location unknown; only a contemporary photograph survives, page 88),[48] *Lady with a Guitar* (1915; page 95, bottom right), *Pianist* (1915, location unknown),[49] and the two versions of *Traveling Woman* (pages 96 and 97). To this list we might add a painting-relief that has not survived, *Card Game* (1915).

Smoker, Lady with a Guitar, and *Pianist* fall within French Cubism's sphere of influence, and their models can be found in French painting of around 1910–15. We recall Picasso's *Girl with a Mandolin* (1910), Villon's *Girl at the Piano* (1912), Gris's *Smoker* (1913), and Gleizes's *Woman at the Piano* (1914). These examples could be multiplied. In Popova's *Smoker,* which depicts the figure of a man, evidently seated at a table in a café, we go back to the café scenes beloved of the French Cubists. But even from the old photograph of the work we can pick out distinctive features in the Russian version. It is more decorative; Popova used labels; her composition tends much more toward the plane, which corresponds to the characteristics we have already seen in the portraits of 1915.

Lady with a Guitar recalls Popova's portrait works in another aspect as well: the very principle of construction for the head and figure refers us back to *Portrait of a Philosopher*,[50] although it does not aspire to the perfection of the latter, nor does it achieve the same unity of figure and milieu. In *Lady with a Guitar* perspective is not neutralized; it seems to provide spatial reference points, allowing us to distinguish the primary and secondary spatial planes within the picture. One need only compare the treatment of the head in the two compositions to sense that Popova was taking a fundamental step that marked her departure from Cubo-Futurism. In *Lady with a Guitar* the head is in a three-quarter pose; the lips and nose stand out in relief from the cheek and jut out into the viewer's real space. *Portrait of a Philosopher* has the same pose, the same treatment of the face. All its parts, however, despite the fact that they are marked by light-dark contrasts, seem to be woven into a single plane. Perspective is not perceived; the integrity of the painting surface triumphs.

Popova reaches the culmination of this process in the two versions of *Traveling Woman* (pages 96 and 97). We can assume that the first version of the painting is the one that belongs to the Norton Simon collection, and the second is the one in the Costakis collection. Both of them are of impressive size (52 × 41½" for the former; 62⅜ × 48¾" for the latter); they are majestic, imposing. But the second, larger version is more generalized in its rhythm and composition. At its base lie one definitely expressed and two implied triangles, which take up almost the entire painting field. Meanwhile, in the first version, the generalizing principle is weakened—the rhythms prove to be finer and the composition more splintered. Moreover, in the first version the viewer can make out many more concrete details—including the beads on the traveling woman's neck and the chair's curving armrest. The details in the second version are much more "removed" from the figure itself and create only an associative link with the subject. We can make out some stairs, arches that lead us far beyond the limits of discrete space and concrete fact. We find approximately the same relationship between the inscriptions on the canvases. In the first version almost all of them can be deciphered, whereas in the second they are quite fragmentary and enigmatic.

Meanwhile, one important feature brings the two versions together, making the overall idea of *Traveling Woman* a unique synthesis of Popova's previous investigations. She has gathered together here details and devices encountered in other works. The rounded cylinders and cones take us back to the *Female Models*, the undulating parallel lines and imitations of wood grain to earlier still lifes, the hair on one of the heads to *Self-Portrait*. But the greater the number of different details and devices from previous compositions in these paintings, the stronger the pull toward a generalized artistic image. In many ways this image is now built upon expressive color. Popova's main goal is harmony and integrity. In the first version she juxtaposes two color motifs: in the lower left portion of the canvas she concentrates dark blue, green, and red; in the upper right, black, red, and yellow. These same color patches—but smaller—are dispersed over the other areas of the canvas as well, but there they look more like an accompaniment to the main color accents. The artist is concerned with balancing the color patches and distributing the amount of one color or another uniformly over the painting surface.

The second version employs a somewhat different principle of color harmony. Here two colors dominate—deep red (sometimes taking on a crimson tinge) and gray-black. Much as the fundamental lines forming the triangles subjugate the other linear and rhythmic motifs to themselves in this composition, so too these two colors drown out the others. We perceive the relationship between red and black as an intense, dramatic chord, depriving the travel theme as such of its primary significance.

It is interesting that in both versions Popova was concerned with harmony and beauty, with the significance and unique grandeur of the painting image. There is a Renaissance spirit in the *Traveling Woman*. By performing a Cubist dismantling of the object and the world, the artist returned to a total image that "wants to become" the image of the world, albeit allegorically expressed—and allegorically is the only way it can be

at a time when figurative art is on the wane. A universally meaningful image requires abstract shapes. *Traveling Woman*, especially the second version of it, takes us to the limits of the new artistic thinking. Popova was only half a step away from being freed from complicated internal rhythms, from concentrating expressive color on juxtaposed color planes, from overcoming distracting elements meant to denote concrete phenomena or events.

THE LAST LANDSCAPES

In the catalog to the posthumous exhibition, the only *Painterly Architectonics* listed is dated 1915. The year 1916 belongs wholly to a new stage in Popova's development. And only a few—fairly representational—landscape compositions manage to slip into this realm of nonobjectiveness. This fact is hard to explain. Possibly the reason is to be found in personal or outside circumstances. Possibly the architectural landscape (and the landscape works of the years 1915–16 routinely include architectural elements to a greater or lesser extent) was linked in Popova's consciousness with the version of abstract painting she herself called painterly architectonics. But the fact remains: the last representational compositions to cross into "enemy territory" were landscapes. The artist had returned to them after a long interval. The last cityscapes before this had been done in 1912, abroad, evidently. In the three intervening years Popova had quickly traversed the whole of Cubo-Futurism and circled all the way back to the genre with which she had begun. It is interesting that also in 1916, at the "Jack of Diamonds" exhibition, she showed her first nonobjective works, but they bore the name of Samarkand's famous medieval architectural landmark, Shah-i-Zinda (six versions), and as a consequence they too were linked by association with an architectural-landscape image.

The short list of works of the last representational genre in Popova's painting begins with *The Kremlin: Tsar-Cannon* (1915; page 98, bottom left).[51] There are numerous analogs for this work in French Cubism, Italian Futurism, and Russian Cubo-Futurism of the 1910s. Suffice it to recall Aleksandra Exter's paintings dedicated to Italian cities—Venice, Florence—or Lentulov's large panels—*Ringing: The Kremlin Bell Tower, Saint Basil's Cathedral, Strastnoi Monastery*—for specific and immediate analogies. As for Italian Futurism, the closest prototype here is Ardengo Soffici's *Painterly Synthesis of the City of Prato*. *The Kremlin* differs from its Russian *confrères* in several essential aspects. If Exter retained at least some elements of a visual image and Lentulov composed his paintings out of arbitrarily selected and juxtaposed architectural structures or created his image by adopting various points of view on the object, then Popova proceeded differently: she created a whole out of fragments. The viewer sees by turns a chunk of a portal, or one or two Kremlin embrasures, or a fragment of the wall of the Guard Corps barracks. Naturally, given this type of approach there can be no question of creating a unitary space, even one transformed and idiosyncratic. In addition, each fragment is allotted its own discrete spatial plane. These planes have almost no connection with one another. Popova offers a unique version of the Futurist conception: if by conveying various views of a motion, "pure" Italian Futurism created the sensation of time, composed of a series of discrete entities but nonetheless remaining somehow nonrepresentational, then in Popova the chunks of juxtaposed space made it possible to comprehend but not depict an overall space. As for the category of time, as in Cubism it again was left to the viewer.

In the later landscapes—from 1916 on—there is a return to the overall image; the shift from Cubism to nonobjectiveness is realized. We know two pictures, *Birsk* (page 104) and *Box Factory* (page 98, top),[52] as well as a series of preliminary drawings for them. Judging from the motifs themselves, all this work was done in the summer of 1916 in the town of Birsk, located in Bashkiria, where Popova often went to visit her former governess, Adda Dege.[53] In both the paintings and the graphics, Popova expressed her interest in the unique architecture and landscape of this small district seat. Her attention was drawn to the unique "cubic" buildings, with their strict parallelepiped volumes and annexes, the high picket fences. Many of the drawings convey the distinctive topography of the city—its numerous landslides, ravines, and precipices. As we shall see, the artist re-created all these characteristics of the town in *Birsk,* although she took it quite a distance from nature.

The existence of drawings done evidently from nature and later used for a painting image allows us to follow how Popova proceeded to "overcome nature." Of the two landscapes *Box Factory* resembles its prototype more closely. The preliminary drawing, in which the grounds of the factory are depicted from a high vantage point and in complete detail, including the factory gates, walkways, stairs, and a couple of boxes by the building, is the basis for this work in gouache. In this composition everything seems to have remained in its place. Overall, however, the factory has changed beyond recognition. The composition has been subordinated to the abstract rhythm of the geometric figures. Space has become absolutely arbitrary, having retained something of the dismemberment into discrete fragments that made itself felt so strongly in the landscape *The Kremlin.*

Birsk is also exceptional for its even greater remove from nature. It is difficult to say immediately what it depicts.[54] You have to look closely to make out details we already know from the drawings—the yellow-brown landslides, over which sprawl green, grass-covered planes of earth, concertina fences, building cubes. The main stress shifts to the relationship between the rhythms and the color patches. True, the viewer can easily guess that something real lurks behind these shapes, for there is a stronger feeling for the whim of nature that created this fantastic phenomenon than there is for its organization. Popova constructs a color composition in her favorite colors—green, yellow-brown, dark blue, reddish-pink—all softened with neutral grays. The harmony of the color relations eases somewhat the intense staccato rhythm of the lines and planes, a rhythm that is the fruit of Popova's skill, of her experience at organizing the canvas. Nonetheless, her inspiration remains this unique phenomenon of nature itself. In *Birsk* the language of abstract forms, plasticity, and color triumphs over reality. In the first *Painterly Architectonics,* done also in 1916, abstract forms will seem to "recall" reality.

Still Life. ca. 1914. Oil on canvas, dimensions unknown. K. Rubinger Collection, Cologne

Guitar. 1914–15. Location unknown. Contemporary photograph

Still Life. ca. 1914. Oil on canvas, dimensions unknown. Private collection

Musical Instruments. ca. 1914. Oil on canvas, 38⅝ × 23″ (98 × 58.5 cm.). Private collection, West Germany

Above: *Clock.* 1914. Oil and pasted wallpaper on canvas, 27⅝ × 18½″
(70.5 × 47 cm.). Private collection, Moscow

Above right: *Clock.* 1914. Oil and pasted wallpaper on canvas,
34⅝ × 27½″ (88 × 70 cm.). Private collection, Moscow

Clock. ca. 1914. Location unknown. Contemporary photograph

Still Life with Lamp. 1914–15. Pencil on paper, 9 × 6¼" (23 × 18 cm.) (along the penciled frame). Private collection, Moscow

Still Life with Tray. 1915. Location unknown. Contemporary photograph

Still Life with Tray. 1915. Oil and pasted paper on canvas, 15¾ × 22⅞″ (40 × 58 cm.). Private collection, Moscow

Above left: Still Life with Stove. Study. 1914–15. Pencil on paper, 6¼ × 5⅛"
(16 × 13 cm.) (inside the penciled frame). Private collection, Moscow

Above: Still Life with Carafe. Study. 1914–15. Pencil on paper, 12⅝ × 8¼"
(32 × 21 cm.). Private collection, Moscow

Still Life with Kitchen Utensils. 1914–15. Location unknown.
Contemporary photograph

Guitar. 1914. Oil and plaster on canvas, 28 × 32⅞″ (71 × 83.5 cm.).
Private collection, Moscow

Violin. 1915. Oil on canvas, 34⅞ × 27¾″ (88.5 × 70.5 cm.). Tretiakov Gallery

Italian Still Life. 1914. Oil on canvas, plaster, and pasted paper, 24½ × 19⅛″ (62.2 × 48.6 cm.). Tretiakov Gallery

Guitar. 1914. Oil on canvas, 34⅝ × 27⅝″ (88 × 70 cm.). Private collection, Moscow

Objects from a Dyeworks (Early Morning). 1914. Oil on canvas, 27¾ × 35″ (71 × 89 cm.). Collection, The Museum of Modern Art, New York. The Riklis Collection of McCrory Corporation (fractional gift)

Still Life with Mask. 1915. Oil and plaster on canvas, 13 × 19⅝″ (33 × 50 cm.). Private collection, Moscow

Portrait of a Lady (Plastic Drawing). 1915. Oil and cardboard relief, 26⅛ × 19⅛″ (66.3 × 48.5 cm.). Ludwig Museum, Cologne

The Jug on the Table. 1915. Wood, cardboard, and oil relief, 23 × 19″ (58.5 × 48.5 cm.). Tretiakov Gallery. Gift of George Costakis

Still Life with Compote. 1920. Gouache on paper, 13 × 10⅜″ (33 × 26.5 cm.).
Private collection, Moscow

Compote with Fruit (Plastic Painting). 1915. Location unknown. Contemporary photograph

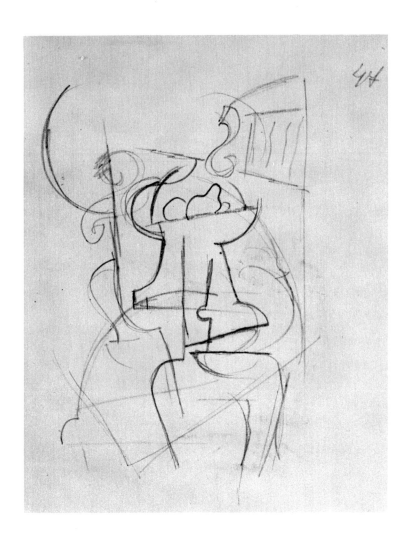

Still Life with Compote. Study. 1914–15. Pencil on paper, 11¾ × 8¼" (30 × 21 cm.).
Private collection, Moscow

Still Life. 1915. Oil on canvas, 21¼ × 14⅛" (54 × 36 cm.). Gorky Museum of Art.
Picture taken from an old photograph

Volumetric-Spatial Relief. 1915. Location unknown. Contemporary photograph

Grocery. 1916. Oil on canvas, 28⅛ × 21″ (71.5 × 53.5 cm.). Russian Museum

Smoker. 1914. Location unknown. Contemporary photograph

Study for a Two-Figure Composition. ca. 1915. Charcoal on paper,
17½ × 14" (44.5 × 35.5 cm.). Private collection, Moscow

89

Preliminary drawing for *Study for a Portrait*. 1915. Pencil on paper, 14⅛ × 8¼"
(36 × 21 cm.). Private collection, Moscow

Study for a Portrait. 1915. Oil on cardboard, 23⅜ × 16⅜" (59.5 × 41.6 cm.). Costakis Collection, Athens

Preliminary drawing for *Study for a Portrait.* 1915. Pencil on paper, 14 × 8¼" (35.5 × 21 cm.). Private collection, Moscow

Drawing for *Portrait of a Philosopher*. 1915. Gouache on cardboard,
20½ × 15″ (52 × 38 cm.). Tretiakov Gallery. Contemporary photograph

Preliminary drawing for *Portrait of a Philosopher*. 1915. Pencil on paper,
14 × 8¼″ (35.5 × 21 cm.). Private collection, Moscow

Portrait of a Philosopher. 1915. Oil on canvas, 35 × 24¾″ (89 × 63 cm.). Russian Museum

Preliminary drawing for *Portrait of a Philosopher*. 1915. Pencil on paper, 14 × 8¼″ (35.5 × 21 cm.). Private collection, Moscow

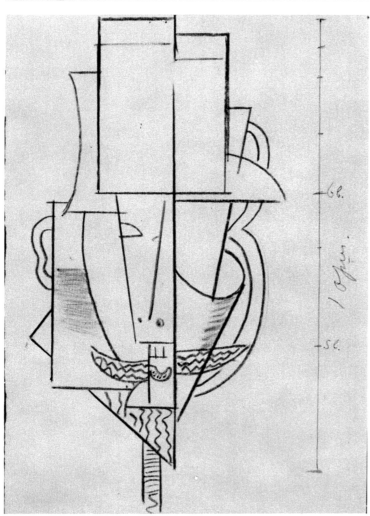

Study for a Portrait. ca. 1916. Colored pencil on paper, 10⅞ × 8⅛″ (27.5 × 20.5 cm.). Private collection, Moscow

Preliminary drawing for *Portrait of a Philosopher*. 1915. Pencil on paper, 14 × 8¼″ (35.5 × 21 cm.). Private collection, Moscow

Study for *Lady with a Guitar*. 1915. Pencil on paper, 10½ × 8¼″ (26.7 × 20.9 cm.). Costakis Collection, Athens

Study for *Lady with a Guitar*. 1915. Pencil on paper, 8⅛ × 6⅞″ (20.8 × 17.4 cm.). Costakis Collection, Athens

Lady with a Guitar. 1915. Oil on canvas, 42⅛ × 28⅛″ (107 × 71.5 cm.). Smolensk Regional Museum of Art

Traveling Woman. 1915. Oil on canvas, 52 × 41½" (132.2 × 105.5 cm.).
Norton Simon Museum, Pasadena, California

Traveling Woman. 1915. Oil on canvas, 62⅜ × 48¾" (158.5 × 123 cm.).
Costakis Collection, Athens

Box Factory. 1916. Pasted paper and gouache on wooden board, 16½ × 12¼"
(42 × 31.1 cm.). Private collection, United States

The Kremlin: Tsar-Cannon. 1915. Oil on canvas, 42⅛ × 36"
(107.1 × 91.4 cm.). Private collection

Study for *Box Factory*. ca. 1916. Pencil on paper, dimensions unknown. Tretiakov Gallery

Study for *Birsk*. 1916. Pencil on paper, dimensions unknown. Costakis Collection, Athens

Study for *Birsk*. 1916. Gouache on paper, dimensions unknown. Private collection

Self-Portrait. 1915. Oil, wallpaper, and pasted paper on canvas, dimensions unknown. Private collection, United States

Study for a Portrait. 1915. Gouache on paper, 14 × 10½″ (35.5 × 26.7 cm.).
Private collection, Moscow

Study for a Portrait. 1915. Oil and plaster on canvas, 27¾ × 18¾″ (70.5 × 47.5 cm.).
Private collection, Moscow

Study for a Portrait. ca. 1916. Pencil and colored pencil on paper, 7⅛ × 5½"
(18 × 14 cm.). Private collection, Moscow

104   *Birsk.* 1916. Oil on canvas, 41⅜ × 27⅜″ (105.2 × 69.6 cm.). Solomon R. Guggenheim Museum, New York. Gift of George Costakis

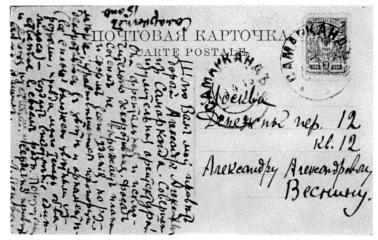

Postcard Popova sent in 1915 from Samarkand to Aleksandr Vesnin.
Private collection, Moscow

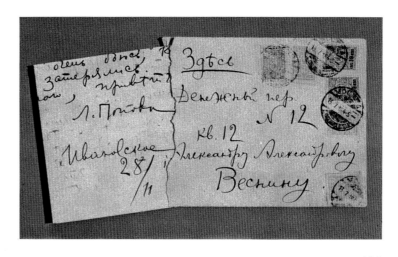

Letter Popova sent in 1918 from the village of Ivanovskoe to Aleksandr Vesnin.
Private collection, Moscow

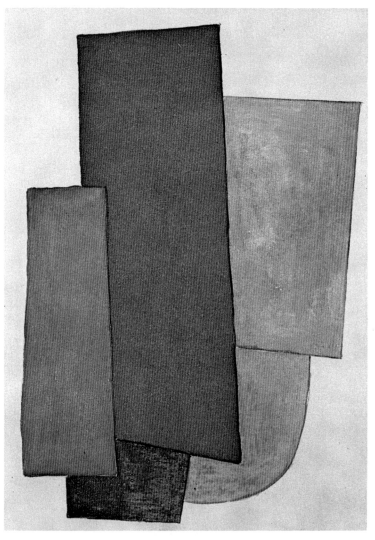

Above left: Painterly Architectonics. 1916. Gouache on paper, 7⅛ × 4⅞″ (18 × 12.5 cm.). Private collection, Moscow

Above: Painterly Architectonics. 1916. Gouache on paper, 7⅛ × 4¾″ (18 × 12 cm.). Private collection, Moscow

Painterly Architectonics. 1916–17. Oil on canvas, 17⅛ × 17¼″ (43.5 × 43.9 cm.). Costakis Collection, Athens

Untitled. ca. 1917. Colored paper pasted on paper, 13 × 9½″ (33 × 24.3 cm.).
Costakis Collection, Athens

Logo of the *Supremus* society. 1916–17. India ink on paper, 3½ × 4⅜″
(9 × 11 cm.). K. Rubinger Collection, Cologne

Logo of the *Supremus* society. 1916–17. India ink on paper, 3½ × 4⅜″
(9 × 11 cm.). K. Rubinger Collection, Cologne

Three plates from 6 Prints. 1917. Color linocut, top left: 13¾ × 10" (35 × 25.5 cm.);
top right and bottom: 13⅜ × 10¼" (34.1 × 26.1 cm.)

POPOVA AND SUPREMATISM

This is how Popova herself conceived of her path to nonobjective art: "The Cubist period (the problem of form) is followed by the Futurist period (the problem of motion and color); the principle of the abstraction of the parts of an object is followed with logical inevitability by the abstraction of the object itself. This is the road to nonobjectiveness. The representational problem is followed by the problem of the construction of color and line (Post-Cubism) and of color (Suprematism)."[55]

These words do not necessarily imply that Popova considered herself a member of the Suprematist movement. When you compare the formulation above with her other pronouncements, you are likely to conclude that her own experience was connected with "the construction of color and line"—with what she called Post-Cubism. Of course, today all these definitions seem less than precise and concrete. But at this point what concerns us is whether or not Popova identified with the Suprematist tendency that Kazimir Malevich propounded.

As we know, Malevich was the first to exhibit his Suprematist compositions widely, at the "0.10" exhibition in December 1915 in Petrograd. The new shepherd of the Russian avant-garde had not displayed his nonobjective paintings prior to this. Popova's first opportunity to view these works was at this exhibition, where she herself showed a series of Cubo-Futurist paintings. She and Malevich were not on friendly terms; she was much more in the orbit of Tatlin, who, as we know, feuded with Malevich.

Only in rare instances during the period of Popova's development within Cubo-Futurism do we find certain parallels and analogies with Malevich. Very probably the first of her paintings to keep exclusively to nonobjective forms was made before she became acquainted with Suprematism. We have reason to believe that one of the *Painterly Architectonics* was done in 1915.[56]

Let us recall several of the compositions with guitar done in 1915 and from those compositions draw a straight line to the first *Painterly Architectonics*. The correlation of rounded forms and triangles, the concentration of basic figures in the center of the canvas, the "supplementary figures" designated only by an outline on the background and not painted in—all this links these compositions of the same year. We can point to the black triangle in the *Guitars*, presaging the device in *Painterly Architectonics*. This black triangle, abstracted from a real thing, takes us straight from the figurative to the nonfigurative, the nonobjective.

Popova proceeded logically toward nonobjective forms. The very logic of her creative development drew her toward them. It was a straight path; it could not have culminated in anything but nonobjective art. Malevich's Suprematism became merely a companion impulse, a supplement to the movement taking place

inside the artist's work. The example of her senior comrade-in-art probably enabled Popova to overcome her last doubts, especially since his "geometric abstractionism" proved to be closer to Popova than any other forms of nonobjective art engendered theretofore by Russian art—Kandinsky's Abstract Expressionism or Larionov's Rayism. There was no question of her relying on the experience of those two artists, given her alliance with the traditions of Cubism and her study with Metzinger and Le Fauconnier.

Popova's independent approach to nonobjective art does not contradict the fact that after the appearance of Malevich's Suprematism she found herself among a group of artists that began to be attracted to this latest innovator and prophet, especially since Malevich reinforced his painting experiments with theoretical formulations: in 1915 he had put out the first edition of his book *Ot kubizma k suprematizmu* (From Cubism to Suprematism), which could not fail to affect each and every Russian artist of the avant-garde movement. In the years 1916–17 a society of artists—among them Popova—was formed under the name "Supremus." In addition to Malevich himself, the group included Rozanova, Udaltsova, Kliun, Menkov, Pestel, Natalia Davydova, the poet Kruchenykh, and Aliagrov (the pseudonym used by Roman Jakobson).[57] The artists' gatherings were held in Udaltsova's studio. The first issue of a magazine went into production, but never saw the light of day.

Several sketches of the Supremus logo created by Popova have been preserved (Costakis collection). Judging from the Vesnin-Aksionov list, they date from 1917. These sketches combine several forms borrowed from Malevich's Suprematist canvases in the "0.10" exhibition and some of Popova's own "plastic symbols," which would undergo further development in her paintings. This mixture is quite understandable; Popova was creating a logo not for her own artistic signature but for the entire movement, at the base of which lay the painting of Malevich.

Particularly telling is the quadrangle that is drawn into a square and has three of its corners touching the frame (page 107, bottom). This composition is extremely close to one of Malevich's Suprematist paintings exhibited in "0.10" and well known from a photograph of Malevich's section of the exposition (hanging to the right of *Black Square*, which is up in the corner under the ceiling). This quadrangle can be regarded either as aspiring to the square or as an achieved square now distorted. One way or the other, this form, which is in a state of disharmonic tension, is strong and expressive.

In other sketches for the Supremus logo Popova used compositional schema from her own paintings of that period. One of them can be numbered among the artist's better early nonobjective compositions. Moreover, it is marked by a certain influence from Malevich. The work in question is the *Painterly Architectonics* (page 120, top left), with a black quadrangle and two parallelograms (red and gray). We can date this work with some accuracy as 1916.[58]

Not very large (35 × 30″), this economical painting makes a strong impression. Its composition is one of the simplest in Popova's legacy. Malevich's example undoubtedly played a role in her choice of a few very simple forms to serve as a base for the compositional resolution. Naturally, Popova could not simply repeat Malevich's device and fill the canvas with a single figure. That would have been a repetition, tantamount to plagiarism—even if the form were other than the square, circle, and cross Malevich used. Popova selected three "figures," but she united them in an indivisible whole, "tied them with a knot." This was the first time she was to use the principle of overlapping planar forms (what she called an "interleaved" construction) so consistently in an abstract painting. Malevich used this device, but for him this overlapping of figures was something of a visual necessity, dictated by the real interactions of primordial elements that seemed to float in infinite space. For Popova the device served to concentrate the painting planes, to solidify the forms, to distribute them harmoniously over the painting surface, to create the impression of the indissolubility of its parts.

Other compositional elements as well were subordinated to these goals. We should point out that the basic three-part "figure" is placed dead center; not a single part escapes the limits of the canvas; the edge of each part clears the frame by a good margin. All this intensifies the centeredness. This compositional conception not only does not repeat but even contradicts Malevich's "Dynamic Suprematism." Popova is preventing the forms from "floating away." They stay where they are; you might even say they stand fast, resting on the corners of the black quadrangle and gray parallelogram and forming something along the lines of a pyramid. In the painting the bottom is sharply delineated: earthly gravity is in force; the quadrangle does not become the burst into infinity it did in Malevich's *Black Square*. On the contrary, by imposing itself on the red and gray forms, it secures their position on the plane.

In certain other early nonobjective compositions we discover similar principles. In a sketch for *Painterly Architectonics* (1916; page 106, top left),[59] done in gouache on paper, we again find the combination of three planes (this being the minimum number of "figures" for Popova), placed on top of one another and seemingly affixed to the surface of the sheet. Compositional stability is achieved by balancing the parts and also by having all three planes intersect in the center of the field—an intersection that ensures the security of their being. Another study (page 121) uses the same compositional device, the same forms (with the addition of just two new ones), and a yellow background unusual for Popova. Due to the background's intensity, the overwhelming black and gray alter neither the purpose nor the nature of the image's forcefulness.

In all such compositions by Popova, the forms seem to be searching for a point of support; the corners rest on the edges of the frame but do not pierce it. Even in the more fluid compositions created under the influence of Malevich's Dynamic Suprematism, Popova looked for an opportunity to neutralize the dynamic principle and lead the composition into her usual "earthly" confines. An example of this kind of approach is the *Painterly Architectonics* (page 106, bottom).[60] Unlike some works of Malevich, in this painting the forms do not let themselves get very far away from one another; they cling. The diagonal that directs the movement from the lower left corner to the upper right is interrupted by a massive gray "figure," which halts this movement, and presses its corners into the painting frame as if especially to acquire stability. Even here the artist was modifying Malevich's conception in order to assert her own principles.

Approximately the same interaction with Malevich makes itself known in the series of linocuts done in 1917[61] and in the series of collage designs for Davydova's Verbovka enterprise (see page 273), dated 1917 on the list.[62]

Of seven linocuts only the cover (page 122) invites associations with Malevich's works. The old cohesive force is no longer active in the cover composition. The black parallelogram has ceased to act as a bracing form, and the interactions between the two quadrangles have destroyed the balance. The dark blue triangle has already broken away from the central "figure," which is destroyed right before our eyes. Neither geometric forms nor the letters of the title fill even half the whole page; the space created permits free movement. All this is much more typical of Malevich's Suprematism than of Popova's nonobjective compositions.

One essential difference in principle separates Malevich and Popova even in these instances: their understanding of the connotations of color. The euphony of colors—both in their interrelationships and in their optimal interaction with specific forms—was never an important matter for Malevich, for whom the treatment of color was just one of the vast philosophical concepts that had become the content of his artistic images: black opened up the abyss of infinity; white signified the limit of the light possibilities of the cosmos, the universe. Frequently it was more important to destroy than to affirm color harmony, for doing so facilitated direct expression of an idea. Malevich never gave a thought to the elements of decorativeness.

The cover for 6 *Prints by L. Popova*, like all her subsequent linocuts, immediately reveals a different principle. The green and bright blue, softly pulling together, neutralize the black. Their combination gives birth to the color of the letters; it fixes the forms even more, creating chromatic unity. In another (page 124)—constructed on the principle of the logical overlapping of rectangles, triangles, and trapezoids—azure and yellow are added, intermediate shades between black and green,

green and yellow, appear; the color scale acquires an elegance that the severe Malevich never would have allowed. Occasionally Popova built a gray-blue scale, setting it off with softly contrasting brown, black, and even white. But the whites are shot with azure, and the black with dark blue. One of these compositions (page 126) uses only three colors—red, black, and white. However, Popova did not intensify their relationship; on the contrary, she found it necessary to weaken the red and black with white.

All these examples are sufficient to show that in the most "Suprematist" cycle of her easel works—and in her linocuts— Popova is following a course in many ways different from that of Malevich. The same might be said of the two large collages (close in size to the linocuts),[63] one of which is found in the Costakis collection (page 107, top left) and the other in a private collection in Moscow (page 297, left), and of the previously mentioned cycle of collage designs.

The collage designs were of an applied rather than an easel nature; therefore they will be examined in Part Two of this book. Here we shall touch briefly once again only on the problems of the relationship between Popova's principles and Suprematism. Obviously, Popova felt it was possible and even, probably, necessary to employ the by then accepted Suprematist vocabulary used not only by Malevich but also by Puni, Udaltsova, Rozanova—everyone doing sketches of one kind or another intended for execution later by sewers for Verbovka. Naturally, the decorative problem itself necessarily would alter the austere language of Suprematism. But it was in Popova that this alteration came about most easily and organically (mostly at the expense of color). Not because her art sought decorativeness but because it tended toward harmony. Popova often used complementary colors, green and red, yellow and bright blue; sometimes various shades of the same color are present, which ensured their peaceful interaction. The artist was concerned with the qualitative equilibrium of color patches and did not permit one color to win out over another when any opposition arose.

As we see, Suprematism did act as a kind of stimulus, a catalyst in Popova's art, but it never became her "native language."

REMINISCENCES OF REALITY

Popova's art, as we have already shown, basically followed a line from depicting reality to abstracting it. Traces of the reality that only recently had been an object turn up frequently in Popova's nonobjective paintings, especially during 1916–17. It is interesting that the concrete impressions that stimulated the images could be landscapes, architectural landmarks, or things. Let us recall that among her first nonobjective works were paintings grouped together by the name of a well-known

architectural landmark in Samarkand, Shah-i-Zinda,[64] and done after her trip to Central Asia. This was not the only time the artist gave a nonobjective composition a concrete name. In the Irkutsk and Perm museums two similar paintings by Popova bear the same title, *Portrait* (pages 115 and 116), whereas they seem like rather typical *Painterly Architectonics* for 1916. One more example: in the Ryazan Museum one of the linocuts discussed above bears the author's title *Spring*. We are no longer talking about the numerous landmarks (real objects) to be found right up to and concurrent with the *Painterly Architectonics* designations on the Vesnin-Aksionov list. In the latter instance it is difficult to be sure that this was how Popova herself titled these paintings—the compilers may have drawn on concrete distinguishing features, traces of reality, that made it easier to recognize the painting. But it is important that these features are present. A *Painterly Architectonics* may have a black board, or a yellow or gray one, it may have a saw, or perhaps a thermometer.

Later—precisely by force of these concrete associations— several of these mistakenly acquired other titles. Such is the case with the 1916 painting from the collection of Baron Thyssen-Bornemisza often called *Musical Instruments* or *Instruments* (page 119).[65] This large composition has a grand, formal quality, like quite a few others in Popova's oeuvre. Some of her forms remind us of the outlines of violins or guitars, the sounding board of a stringed instrument—that is, those objects or parts of objects that a year or two before she had been working on with such interest in her still lifes with musical instruments. But Popova's memory held not only those objects but also the forms of recent reliefs executed in 1915. One of the planes in the composition curves, turning into part of a cylinder. We remember how the cylinders and cones in the *Female Models* (page 55) of 1913 seemed to be trying to leave representation behind in order to enter reality—which did happen in the 1915 reliefs. Now once again these forms returned to the confines of representation. It is interesting that the *Painterly Architectonics* do not show the technical contrivances typical of Popova's Cubo-Futurist works—collages, marble or metal sprinklings, underlayers beneath the paint layer, artificial protuberances on the surface of the canvas.

The *Painterly Architectonics* from the Thyssen collection is rather different from the other paintings of the years 1916–17. It stretches out upward (some of the studies for it [page 113] have an even more elongated format). The forms, which cover almost the entire surface of the canvas, have a slight tendency toward motion, but instead they seem to tower over one another. The great complexity of relationships among the individual forms is emphasized by the fact that some are placed on the plane and are themselves flat and like sheets of paper or metal stuck onto the painting surface, whereas others turn. These two principles clash. In the end, the flat forms win out.

Simultaneously there is a concentration of the individual parts in the center of the canvas. The irregular white quadrangle against the black oval forms the center, which is not only the compositional but the color center as well, for in a multicolored painting constructed with a rather harsh treatment of red, dark blue, green, orange, yellow, and crimson—there white on black has the virtue of simplicity.

Among other works revealing reminiscences of reality is *Painterly Architectonics with Yellow Board* (1916; page 118), which, due to an erroneous inscription on the back of the canvas, was incorrectly titled *Italian Still Life*.[66] In the center of the composition is the chief object of attention—an orange board with two cutouts along the right edge. Were it not for these cutouts we would not associate it with a concrete object; it would be Popova's usual painting of a long, colored quadrangle. Now we have what is certainly a board, but from this main association others seem to radiate out: the white side of a guitar comes up again, and below, under the orange board—a stripe, which could have been a saw if its uneven edge were jagged instead of wavy. But transformations like that do happen in Popova, and we have brought up the saw for a reason: among the paintings of 1916 is *Painterly Architectonics with a Saw* (page 114, right), and at one of the exhibitions at the Galerie Gmurzynska in Cologne a collage was shown that may have been a study for the vanished painting.[67] The saw in this collage, although severely distorted and simplified in its shapes, can be read quite distinctly.

Immediately following *Painterly Architectonics with Yellow Board* on the Vesnin-Aksionov list is another with a black board (1916). This painting is not known, but there is a study done in gouache, dated 1916 (page 118, bottom left), that we may assume bears some relation to the vanished work. Here again the main attention is on the board, somewhat different in form from the so-called yellow board, it is true, but with a similar cutout. Were that cutout a hole, the board would remind you of a guitar.

Both versions of *Portrait* (pages 115 and 116), mentioned earlier, contain a complete set of the forms that are so traditional for Popova's paintings of that period—boards, quadrangles, half cylinders. But one detail in both paintings lets them become "portraits": in the upper part of the composition the cylinder starts to look like a hat with a brim, whose form seems to be doubled by its shadow.

It should be noted that all these returns to reality concern the first years of Popova's work in nonobjective painting. As she developed, she moved even further away from her sources. The second reality, that of the painting construction itself, was more important for her than objective reality. It was to this second reality that the *Painterly Architectonics* were essentially devoted.

Study for *Painterly Architectonics* in the Thyssen-Bornemisza Collection. 1916. Watercolor, gouache, pencil, and lacquer on paper, 7⅜ × 4¾″ (18.7 × 12 cm.). Private collection, Moscow

Left: Study for *Painterly Architectonics* from the Thyssen-Bornemisza Collection. 1916. Watercolor, gouache, and pencil on paper, 13⅜ × 8½″ (34 × 21.5 cm.). Private collection, Moscow

Far left: Study for *Painterly Architectonics* from the Thyssen-Bornemisza Collection. 1916. Watercolor, gouache, and lacquer on paper, 13 × 9½″ (33 × 24 cm.). Private collection, Moscow

Painterly Architectonics. Study. 1916. Pencil on paper, 7½ × 5⅜" (19 × 13.7 cm.).
Private collection, Moscow

Painterly Architectonics with a Saw. ca. 1916. Colored paper, pasted on paper,
dimensions unknown. Private collection

Portrait. 1916. Oil on canvas, 21⅛ × 14″ (53.5 × 35.5 cm.).
Irkutsk Regional Museum of Art

Portrait. 1916. Oil on canvas, 21⅛ × 17½″ (53.5 × 44.5 cm.). Perm State Art Gallery

Painterly Architectonics with Three Stripes. 1916. Oil on canvas, 42⅛ × 35″ (107 × 89 cm.). Private collection, Moscow

Painterly Architectonics with Yellow Board. 1916. Oil on canvas, 34½ × 30¾"
(87.5 × 78 cm.). Tretiakov Gallery. Gift of George Costakis

Painterly Architectonics. Study. 1916.
Watercolor, gouache, and pencil on
paper, 7⅝ × 5¾" (19.5 × 14.5 cm.).
Private collection, Moscow

Painterly Architectonics with Black Board. Study. 1916. Watercolor, gouache, and
pencil on paper, 8⅛ × 5⅞" (20.5 × 15 cm.). Private collection, Moscow

Painterly Architectonics (Still Life: Instruments). 1916. Oil on canvas, 41½ × 27¼″ (105.5 × 69.2 cm.). Thyssen-Bornemisza Collection, Lugano

Painterly Architectonics with Black Rectangle. 1916. Oil on canvas, 35×28"
(89×71 cm.). Tretiakov Gallery. Gift of George Costakis

Painterly Architectonics. ca. 1916. Gouache on paper, 9⅛×7⅝" (23.2×19.5 cm.).
K. Rubinger Collection, Cologne

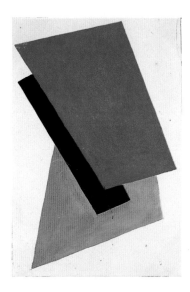

Painterly Architectonics. Study. 1916.
Gouache on paper, 6⅞×4¾"
(17.5×12 cm.). Private collection,
Moscow

Painterly Architectonics. Study for a
painting in the Tretiakov Gallery. 1916.
Gouache on paper, 7⅛×4¾"
(18×12 cm.). Private collection, Moscow

Painterly Architectonics. Study. 1916. Gouache and watercolor on paper, 12⅝ × 9⅝"
(32 × 24.5 cm.). I. Dychenko Collection, Kiev

Cover design for *6 Prints*. 1917. Color linocut, 13 × 8⅞″ (33 × 22.5 cm.)

Plate from 6 *Prints*. 1917. Color linocut, 13¾ × 10¼″ (34.5 × 26 cm.)

Plate from *6 Prints*. 1917. Color linocut, 13¾ × 10¼″ (34.5 × 26 cm.)

Plate from *6 Prints*. 1917. Color linocut, 13¾ × 10¼″ (34.5 × 26 cm.)

126   Plate from *6 Prints*. 1917. Color linocut, 13 × 9½″ (32.9 × 24 cm.)

Painterly Architectonics. 1916–17. Oil on canvas, 62⅝ × 49¼" (159 × 125 cm.). Tretiakov Gallery. Gift of George Costakis
(on reverse: *Painterly Construction.* 1920; page 179)

128   *Painterly Architectonics.* Study. 1916–17. Gouache and pasted paper on paper, 16¾ × 11¼″ (42.5 × 28.5 cm.). Private collection, Moscow

Painterly Architectonics with a Pink Semicircle. 1918. Oil on canvas, 23 × 18¾″ (58.5 × 47.5 cm.). Tretiakov Gallery. Gift of George Costakis

Painterly Architectonics with a Black Quadrangle. 1916. Oil on canvas, 42⅛ × 35″ (107 × 89 cm.). Private collection, Moscow
(on reverse: *Painterly Architectonics with Turquoise Rear Plane.* 1917; page 131)

Painterly Architectonics with Turquoise Rear Plane. 1917. Oil on canvas, 42⅛ × 35″ (107 × 89 cm.). Private collection, Moscow

PAINTERLY ARCHITECTONICS: MEANING, PRINCIPLE, EVOLUTION

The most widely used title for Popova's works is "Painterly Architectonics." At the 1924 posthumous exhibition alone at least thirty works so titled were shown, and on the Vesnin-Aksionov list there are forty-four. To these we should add those not included in the list because the artist had sold them during her lifetime. All of these were done in the period 1916–18, with the exception, of course, of the one executed in 1915. After 1918 the artist no longer did *Painterly Architectonics*. Her paintings had other titles.

There is a reason for the word "architectonics" in these titles: it conveys the complete agenda for Popova's mature art. The concept of architectonics is tied up with — but not confined to — architecture. The process of putting together forms on the canvas was, indeed, akin to construction; her understanding of this kinship is testimony to the creative principles of this artist, who was by no means alone in asserting the tendency of painting and architecture to converge. Let us recall a few very obvious facts that do not require lengthy digression. Malevich began working on his architectonics in the 1910s. He was a painter who applied his experience and plastic ideas to architecture. Coming from the other direction, in the late 1910s the architect Le Corbusier, having broken off his own architectural practice briefly, turned to painting, which opened up new perspectives on his architecture. It is generally recognized that early twentieth-century painting was a unique laboratory for architecture (although it certainly did not limit its endeavors to architecture). Given this context, Popova's architectural strivings are wholly understandable.

Nevertheless, we do need to keep in mind that architectonics is not simply architecture, even if it is realized most completely in architecture. More than that, it is "painterly." Architectonics, after all, is not necessarily the direct expression of a construction; in some instances it expresses constructive relationships. Painting, too, therefore, can convey architectonics as the logical interrelations of parts, their harmonious interaction. Often even in architecture architectonics can be more decorative than real/constructive. Of course, decorative, as opposed to real, architectonics does contain an element of idealism, a utopianism — and it is this idealism that Popova's *Painterly Architectonics* possess. They overcome the chaos of reality for the sake of the utopia, resurrect the harmony lost in the dismantled world of Cubo-Futurism.

The utopianism of Popova's *Painterly Architectonics* has a dual meaning. It can be compared to the general utopian conception of the Russian avant-garde, to which Popova's art belongs. Avant-garde artists were creating a new world that bore no direct relation to the real-existing — and even less to the real-past — world. Their images are a secondary reality, an ideal reality, in which the interrelations among the parts of the universe and the smaller phenomena and things in man's orbit are constructed in a different manner. Here other means of knowing prevail, here intuition holds sway, invisibly instituting its own laws. We have only our approximate earthly knowledge with which to appreciate this world; our opportunities to enter into it are limited. Nonetheless, artists assume the roles of both creator and investigator of this world. In creating it, they honor it as a reality; in exploring it, they comprehend just how complex this task is and how relative all its possibilities are.

Russian avant-gardists had good reason to try to value the idea of the fourth dimension, which intrigued Hinton and Uspensky, striving in every way possible to apply the teaching of those men to their own artistic endeavors. The idea of a fourth dimension offers the enticing prospect of moving into that new ideal world of which they dreamed.

The utopia of the avant-garde was akin to the many utopias in the general history of art. The foremost of these — the utopia of the Renaissance — so impressed mankind that it held fast in minds and memories for many centuries, passed on from generation to generation like an inheritance, a formula for perfection and true beauty. There are problems, of course, with comparing the Renaissance and the avant-garde; too great a distance intervenes, and their artistic principles are far too disparate. Nevertheless, utopianism draws them together. Although it was dominated for many centuries by the symbolic and the speculative creative method, the Renaissance, while seeming to take a step toward reality, at the same time was retreating from it. It created its utopia right when the world was opening its reality up to art. The avant-garde, too, was working toward its own utopia, gradually leaving behind the imitation of reality, which did not provide adequate means for them to express their ideas, and then even more decisively building a new world subjugated to the nonreal world, to metaphysical necessities. The avant-garde seemed to be going right back to what the Renaissance had rejected. In their enthusiasm, however, both moved away from the life structure and, in overcoming it, advanced their own ideal conception of the world order.

Russian avant-gardists felt no sympathy for the Renaissance utopia. They rejected it along with all dominant European culture from the beginning of the sixteenth century right up to the nineteenth. Popova was one of a very few who respected Renaissance culture and to some extent fed off it. Recall the many copies, sketches, and drawings done from frescoes and paintings in Italy and at the Hermitage in Petersburg. Remember as well the interest Italian art sparked in Popova during her travels through Italy. We can surmise her interest in Renaissance architecture: the portals of Italian palaces seem to loom over the *Painterly Architectonics*.

She was interested in architecture of all kinds — Renaissance, ancient Russian, Central Asian. The last initially attracted her

Painterly Architectonics. 1917. Oil on canvas, 17⅜ × 13¾" (44 × 35 cm.). Tobolsk Museum of Art

during her trip to Samarkand in 1915. She was impressed by the unique utopianism of Central Asian architecture, in which ornamental and decorative expressiveness achieves total independence from the construction.

Comparing the works of Popova and Malevich, we have already concluded that her works tend toward harmony and balance; she did not try to make her images express the idea of the fourth dimension or an escape into unknown worlds accessible only to the intuition. The best *Painterly Architectonics* demonstrate this harmonic principle.

Viewing generally the discrete stages in the artist's development within the *Painterly Architectonics* theme, we can establish a distinction between the works of the years 1916–17 and those of 1918. The most obvious, most immediately striking fact about them—in many instances the clue to dating them—is that in the earlier paintings the basic compositional forms stand out on a white or, much less frequently, colored background. In the paintings of 1918 there is no room left for a background; the forms fill the surface, and there is no longer any reference point for determining the spatial depth of one or another form. This could be considered a superficial feature, but more than likely it expresses inner creative shifts that represent the first tentative steps on the artist's path to her later nonobjective work.

The best early works are notable either for their unabashed monumentalism or for the economy of their compositional resolution; occasionally both qualities coexist. Some of the best *Painterly Architectonics* have already been discussed. Among the high points Popova attained in her first years of work in nonobjective painting is the *Painterly Architectonics* in the Tretiakov Gallery (1916–17; page 127), which has a later composition on the verso (to which we will turn later) and which gained renown and "success" at the "Paris-Moscow" and "Moscow-Paris" exhibitions in France and the Soviet Union in 1979. Of unprecedentedly large dimensions (62⅝ × 49¼"), it creates an impression of being even more grandiose. The many forms relating the painting to several linocuts of 1917 do not interfere with the composition's compactness, cohesion, or stability, at the base of which lies the red rectangle. Its strict form is flawed in only one place by a triangular cutout created out of a white stripe. This white stripe and, on the other side, a black stripe, edge the central "figure," flanking it like columns flanking a portal. As the remaining forms get farther from the center, they gradually grow smaller, thereby creating their own compositional structures, shaping their own motifs. Equally multifaceted is the color scale, which is constructed in approximately the following manner: the main theme—red, edged in white and black—stands firm, while all the other colors merely support the basic color melody. Due to the small size of the shapes, these color patches escape gaudiness and leave the main color chord in the center of our attention.

Frequently this grandness of Popova's is found in some of the smaller-scale paintings, for example, the *Painterly Architectonics* at the Dallas Museum of Fine Arts (ca. 1916). Unlike the previous composition, in this one the basic forms are placed at acute angles but fixed there so as to form a strong and stable figure. The right-hand cut of the two basic rectangles is so accurate and precise that it is almost not perceived as a cut—it is as if new forms had been devised to fit the edge of the painting. The main black rectangle rests its sharp lower corner on the edge; it is fixed in place. With their right angles the accompanying forms seem to set the rectangular format of the board. At first glance all these devices might seem elementary, but on closer examination we see how subtly and carefully the axes shift, how the equilibrium ceases to be arithmetic and becomes algebraic.

The classic example of an early *Painterly Architectonics* is the one in The Museum of Modern Art in New York (ca. 1917; page 153, top right), with the red triangle in the foreground. Here another principle of composition prevails: all the forms do not coincide with the format of the canvas; they are drawn into the rectangle freely. But the countervailing movements cancel one another out.

In the majority of the large-scale canvases the levels and planes are "sorted," they follow logically one after another, and together the figures form an integral "construction." The large painting in a private collection in Moscow that we can identify as the *Painterly Architectonics with Three Stripes* (1916; page 117) on the Vesnin-Aksionov list was the result of prolonged investigations. A private collection in Moscow and the Rostov Museum-Archive both hold graphic works that we can assume to be studies for *Painterly Architectonics with Three Stripes*. The artist was moving away from using a large number of forms and colors and toward "consolidating" the canvas. She harmonizes colors around the grays, giving the yellows, greens, and browns a restrained tone and avoiding sharp color contrasts. The organization of space around more than a dozen overlapping plane forms was a difficult task. This is not a matter of spatial neutralization as in the painting in The Museum of Modern Art in New York. On the contrary, some forms (for example, half of the gray cylinder) have volume in space; others are lit up from the sides or at the corners and therefore start to sway in space. This swaying pushes adjacent planes back. The presence of depth requires that forms be constructed not only on the plane but also in space—a space, however, seen as illusory, not real as in the 1915 reliefs.

Another large-scale canvas (42⅛ × 35"), *Painterly Architectonics with a Black Quadrangle* (1916; page 130), is resolved more flatly. Here there are no rounded forms jutting out from the plane of the canvas; there are no illuminated edges, with the exception of an oval inside which yellow modulates to white. Rather than enhance the effect of light moving, it merely indicates a color change. The color figures are virtually welded to each other. The black quadrangle fixes all the other forms. The smooth texture, the paint layers that seem to have melded together, accentuate how thoroughly worked each element is. Nonetheless, the paint does not lie mechanically on the canvas. Although the brushstroke is nearly invisible, the work put into the canvas is obvious: we can feel the color surface breathe.

On the reverse of the canvas there is another composition, evidently the one cited on the Vesnin-Aksionov list as *Painterly Architectonics with Turquoise Rear Plane* (1917; page 131). This is a combination of three planes, two of which overlap; the third is displaced to the side to flank the composition. The front plane is painted black, the rear plane has a complicated color pattern: a lively dark blue, concentrated in the corner, lightens as it nears the center, becoming almost white. Where it makes the transition from dark blue to white it becomes turquoise. This treatment of dark blue achieves the spatial resolution of the composition. The rear plane recedes. The "heavenly" association wrenches the turquoise figure even farther away from the black and makes it "float." Here we note new plastic qualities characteristic of Popova's later nonobjective painting.

In examining the *Painterly Architectonics* of the years 1916–17 one must mention three other important compositions—from the Russian Museum (1916), from the Costakis collection, 38 × 31⅛", and from the Krasnoiarsk Museum (both 1916–17). Even more attention, perhaps, though, should go to the 1917 composition (page 294) that harks back to the studies for the *Supremus* logo, which we know from a few graphic versions executed in gouache or collage (private collections in Moscow and West Germany). This composition consists of two planes, yellow and bright blue, at the top of which, where they connect, lie two black segments of a circle touching at the edges.[68] This is one of her most economical compositions. Evidently, while Popova was in the process of searching for the *Supremus* logo, the design she devised took on a life of its own and demanded material embodiment and may have been painted on canvas. She did a masterful job of arranging the three forms on a rectangular sheet. Their corners almost rest on the frame. Likewise, the centrifugal force created in the fan-shaped motion of forms becomes centripetal, yielding to the reverse motion from the edges of the sheet. The opposition of two pairs of colors, dark blue and yellow, black and white, is used to maximum effect.

Earlier we defined in the most general terms the difference between the *Painterly Architectonics* of the years 1916–17 and those of 1918 and spoke of the new principle of compositions without a background. In a later version the interrelationships of forms become more dynamic; the forms interpenetrate, sometimes change color where they intersect, often break off, as in Cubism, frequently disappear, only to resurface later. They lead an energetic, secretive, sporadic, impulsive life.

Achievement of cohesion in her composition becomes more difficult. Often she has to struggle to unite seemingly disparate linear and color compositions. The artist describes one of her *Painterly Architectonics* like this:

[it] comprises three constructions: chromatic, volumetric, and linear. The volumetric is built on the intersection of planes and their extension in space. Space does not have perspective; therefore the color composition and gradation of tone may not coincide with it but build their own relationships on the weight of color. Drawn form, like volumetric form, is independent of color and sometimes coincides with the volumetric, since it is created from the lines of intersection of the planes and their extension in space, but it can also be constructed independently of it. All three compositions are united in a single effort expressed in the overall dynamic composition [see Appendix X].

It might be said that a shift toward dynamism is taking place in Popova's art—similar to that which occurred in Malevich's work. But unlike Malevich, Popova tried to incorporate her recent experience with Cubo-Futurism. This forward motion, which contains elements of "reverse," is quite typical for Popova. She would promote forward motion as an important creative goal, even, as Aksionov recalls, boasting about how quickly her manner was changing, how little she lingered in any one place. At the same time, though, her art, much more than that of other avant-gardists, retained the memory of her overall artistic development and her own past work.

The *Painterly Architectonics* of 1918 can be divided into several groups, each of which is connected with works of the two previous years. One group, consisting of a few paintings and several watercolor studies (*Painterly Architectonics*, 28 × 28", Hack collection, Cologne; watercolor and gouache studies from the Costakis collection and a private collection in Moscow), has the following distinctive qualities: many different forms, the mandatory presence of an acute triangle or several acute angles, a few echoes of Suprematist motifs, a combination of straight and curved lines, and a number of colors. Popova practically hurls what for her were usually the elements of logical and integral structures into dynamic chaos. By entering into complex, confused relationships, the various forms find themselves in a process of transition, transformation, a process that is incomplete: stability is absent.

To a certain extent the architectonic element returns in the gouache studies (Hack collection) that use circles and semicircles. The combination of curved and straight lines here takes on a different character—simpler, more severe, more regimented. Popova used this combination freely. To judge from the Vesnin-Aksionov list, she did several *Painterly Architectonics* with semicircles of different colors. Only one of them, for which the semicircle's color is indicated as pink with black, can be identified as a painting in the Tretiakov Gallery (page 129). The color density of this canvas is reminiscent of much earlier *Painterly Architectonics*. Only to a very small extent are the planes whitened up toward the edges. Here and there the color from one plane shifts to another. But the overall balance is retained—at a subtle, calculated cost. While moving the main red quadrangle to the right of the central axis, the artist saturates the left portion with smaller forms. The balance becomes dynamic. The concentration and centeredness of the composition are preserved, although at much greater expenditure of effort now due to the slanting lines and intersections.

One of the 1918 compositions, a yellow-orange plane on dark blue (page 153, bottom), recalls in its relative simplicity the works of a previous era and in its modulations from dark blue to white the *Painterly Architectonics with Turquoise Rear Plane* (page 131) discussed earlier. It is easy to observe how in the later compositions the tendencies born in an earlier period are strengthened. The lighted planes along the edges become more important. The dark blue form undercuts the yellow-orange in the foreground, where it would seem to be protected from any external activity; in several places the texture thickens, the paint surface becomes rough. The lighting helps the color planes subdue their material substance. Harmony is created no longer on earth but in space; however, it continues to ensure the architectonics their full value.

One of the new devices characteristic of the *Painterly Architectonics* of 1918, and not used before, was the unique slicing of one plane by another. In a painting from the Costakis collection (page 176),[69] a green quadrangle is sliced by a dark blue triangle. Popova did not try to achieve the full illusion of that slice: the upper portion of the blue triangle lies on the plane; here it is firmly welded to the red-brown triangle, even sharing its colors, thereby strengthening even more their plane, which is parallel to the painting surface. Strictly speaking, it cannot cut the green quadrangle, which also lies on the plane. But here Popova returned to the devices characteristic of her Cubo-Futurist period: her shapes do not behave according to the laws of perspective; frequently they arbitrarily hide behind one another, merge, break off, and intersect. Seeking out the logic of this trespass becomes the artist's chief task, as she persists in trying to reassert harmony precisely where it has been destroyed.

Among the *Painterly Architectonics* of 1918 there are several paintings in which this idea of reestablishing the harmony of a virtually demolished world is realized thoroughly and exquisitely. These works include paintings in the Tretiakov Gallery, the Costakis collection, the Gorky Museum of Art (page 154, top left), and the Yaroslavl Museum of Art (page 177). All of these demonstrate the same programmatic purposes characteristic of Popova in 1918, purposes set out in the catalog of the "Tenth State Exhibition," which opened in Moscow in 1919 and at which Popova showed eleven 1918 paintings and the 1917 linocuts. From the artist's introduction to her section of the

catalog, we realize that she was making a decisive break with referential reality in her works. We also learn that she was excited by the problem of "energetics," which she understood as something akin to the idea of dynamism dominant at that time in the minds of artists and critics, for whom it was very nearly the leading idea of the period (see Appendix I).

In the painting from the Tretiakov Gallery (page 174, left) the idea of architectonics is realized in the harmonized contrast, which comes out in various aspects. First, the main movement in the composition, created by the elongated white rectangle, has a "negative," difficult direction—along the right-left diagonal. In its very essence this movement is disharmonious, conflicting. It is immediately neutralized by the red triangle, which sends its shapes in the other direction and serves as a background for the conflict of movements. Other shapes also hold fast, amortize the original impulse, and as a result, the composition calms down. The second aspect of the contrast is the incorporeality of the white rectangle as opposed to the substance of the red triangle. But the white is "undercut" by the red, while the red is diluted by the white. In another spot this red changes to dark blue, highlighting yet another conflict—between warm and cold, between arousing and restraining. These interchanging shapes of the conflict interpenetrate, creating a complex system that brings a "difficult" harmony.

As in all the paintings of 1918, the *Painterly Architectonics* in the Tretiakov Gallery resolves the problem of light perfectly. Here we observe the familiar situation of the artist's looking back—in this case, to the light conception of the years 1913–15. In many paintings of that period light does not fall on the figure or objects from outside but illuminates them from within. In *Painterly Architectonics* light loses its former staccato; it no longer makes shapes smaller. In the Tretiakov Gallery painting the main form consists, for all intents and purposes, of light. From the pure form of the rectangle in which this light is embodied it spreads to other forms, but there it behaves differently: in places it flares up and spills over; in places it shades the dark edges of neighboring forms. Light eases the entire picture; it transports the idea of architectonics out of its earthbound sphere and into the sublime, and as a result the harmony of the painting takes on an ideal and simultaneously somewhat unsteady quality.

In a painting from the Yaroslavl Museum (page 177) and in a rather large canvas from the State Museum of Art of the Uzbek S.S.R., Tashkent (page 154, bottom), Popova complicated the color structure somewhat by applying a greater number of colors and the composition by structuring it in what seems like several levels. This experiment engenders a more complicated harmony—but not chaos, as before. She achieved the same complicated harmony in the *Painterly Architectonics* in the Dallas Museum of Fine Arts, in the gouache in a private collection in Moscow, and finally in a watercolor in the

Yaroslavl Museum.[70] This last, which is rather complex in composition, is remarkable for the special translucency, lightness, and purity of its colors.

Very different from this painting is the *Painterly Architectonics* with dark blue and black acute angles on white, which exists in two nearly identical versions, one from the Costakis collection (page 155) and one from the Rostov-Yaroslavl Museum-Archive of Architecture and Art (28¾ × 19¼"). The artistic image created in these paintings is tense and dramatic. Although emotion had no part in her program, Popova nevertheless imbued her painting with definite emotions. The acute angles that dominate in the composition arouse Gothic associations. They pierce the white space like arrows. The strong feeling of a struggle between light and dark is created. The austerity of the chromatic structure intensifies the drama of this inescapable struggle. There is a sense of irresolution in the painting. The white triangle that stands at a sharp angle in the lower edge of the canvas is doomed to this eternal instability. At the same time the painting does have its own harmony—the harmony of a conflict that leads it to a definite, complete form of existence, to an image of the world.

In analyzing *Painterly Architectonics* we have often relied on traditional categories, including the category of harmony. But the majority of European avant-gardists rejected such categories. Nevertheless, in an analysis of Popova's work—not only in her nonobjective period but in her Cubo-Futurist period as well—one cannot avoid the category of harmony. The artist herself may not have used the term in her comments on these concepts, but it arises naturally out of her art.

In concluding our survey of Popova's nonobjective painting of 1916–18, we must pose one question important for understanding the uniqueness of the artist's work: her attitude toward the traditions of ancient Russian painting. Articles about Popova often discuss this attitude, comparing her paintings with the Russian icon and finding in them the same planarity and decorativeness. On the whole, of course, this is correct. One might even expand the formal analogy—for example, find a similarity between the wavelike mountains called "*leschatki*" in ancient Russian icons and the painting *Birsk,* a likeness between the "gaps" typical of ancient Russian painting and the white patches and brushstrokes in *Study for a Portrait* (page 102, left); one might note the artist's frequent use of the typical colors of the Russian icon: red, green, yellow, dark blue. But this does not exhaust the issue.

What about the question of the understanding and interpretation of space, especially in *Painterly Architectonics,* on the one hand, and in the Russian icon, on the other? Popova did not use linear perspective. Superimposing plane on plane, she narrowed the spatial layer in which all the forms are located. Her space does not serve to create the illusion of reality. The image the painting creates therefore is of a philosophical

nature. In this respect Popova's paintings—especially the nonobjective ones—do find an analogy in the icon.

Another important trait, linked with the first, is that Popova was creating an ideal world, lofty and abstract; in it concrete, real things were either totally lacking or reduced to a minimum. The best examples of *Painterly Architectonics* are models of restraint, of economy of artistic means, of integrity. It is these qualities that give her paintings the air of icons.

Finally, an important factor is the artist's desire to create a harmonious image whose content is founded on objective categories. Popova's images are *ontological.* She does not allow subjectivity to determine the construction of her compositions but tries to make her artistic composition correspond to the eternal foundations of the world order.

Most likely it is these general positions that allowed Popova to look on icon painting as a native phenomenon, although, of course, she remained an artist of the twentieth century. She was incapable of transforming herself into an ancient Russian master and had no desire simply to imitate or borrow features directly from this richest of sources of ancient Russian art.

THE PAINTINGS OF 1920

As has already been stated, in 1919 Popova did not work. In March of 1918 she married Boris von Eding, an art historian and expert on Russian antiquities. After intensive work, in November there was a lull: Popova had given birth to a son, who absorbed all her strength and attention. In the summer of 1919 Liubov Sergeevna, her husband, and her son went to Rostov-on-the-Don. There von Eding contracted typhus and died. Later Popova too got typhus—and then typhoid fever. Her old governess, Adda Dege, barely managed to get her back on her feet. Not until November did Popova return to Moscow, but with serious heart disease. For a long time she was unable to pull herself together and really work; reluctantly she sold off her paintings because she needed the money. In 1921 she finally got her strength back, whereupon there was a new surge in her art.

In the catalog to Popova's posthumous exhibition there is not a single work dated 1919. It is the same on the Vesnin-Aksionov list. Only a few works are listed under 1920—four *Painterly Architectonics,* eight graphic studies, a few graphic rejoinders to her old compote motif, a few monochrome prints. Not very much for a whole year! We must bear in mind, of course, that in 1920 easel painting was beginning to be viewed unsympathetically in the Soviet Union—and soon ground to a dead halt. In its place came other types of activity.

The main issue in connection with Popova's works in 1920 is that of the *Painterly Constructions.* At present we have too little foundation to label unequivocally any of the paintings we know with that title. On the other hand, we do know that only four

Painterly Constructions have been established from the lists. Consequently, we can consider any painting of 1920, with some exceptions, a *Painterly Construction*. Then it is simply a matter of dating a particular work 1920.

One of the paintings we can presumably so date is on the reverse of a large *Painterly Architectonics* (page 127). Our reasons for dating the other side (page 179) 1920 are that the painting's motif is a mirror image of the motif of a 1920 linocut (page 158) and that a preliminary study in India ink dated 1920 is on the back (page 159, left).

This date is confirmed by the fact that the painting under examination—let us call it *Painterly Construction*—possesses features that distinguish it sharply from *Painterly Architectonics* as well as from any later *Spatial Force Construction*. In it once again we encounter multiple objects, an abundance of different motifs, complex rhythms, countervailing movements, a large number of "figures" of various sizes. To these qualities we can add one more—a highly significant one in fact: more and more the "figures" in Popova's painting lose their stability, they head off into space and seem to move on different intersecting planes. The old interleaving principle is finally overcome here. The chief instrument of its destruction turns out to be the spiral movement of the lines and bands that form the conical funnels and the cylinders. This movement clears a path for itself, intersecting the color planes, changing their coloration along the way, and shoving the spiky acute angles, the crescent moons, the numerous small shapes, to the edges. The energy of this spiral's movement depends a great deal on the resistance of other shapes; they demand conquest.

Comparison of the painting with the print confirms just how essential a means of expressiveness color was for Popova. In the print space gets shorter, the shapes are brought out to the surface. In the painting we can pick out several interacting spatial layers, an interaction expressed in the color changes. Sometimes the color of the "victorious" plane is retained, although it acquires a slight admixture of white or of the adjacent colors; sometimes a new color will appear as a result of the mixture; sometimes the form (the black crescent) is placed on top of the others and its color remains utterly untouched. In this last case we have before us echoes of the 1916–17 *Painterly Architectonics*, but here stability is forfeited, since similar fragments wind up in a different sphere—they tend to turn into "floating" forms rather than forms permanently occupying a specific place.

Despite the fact that the painting of 1920 creates a strong impression both through its monumentalism and through the energy the artist invested in it, it is impossible not to feel how transitional it is. There is a breaking away from earthly gravity, although as before the law of equilibrium remains in effect. Finally, in making an attempt to penetrate to the "fourth dimension," Popova nevertheless retained many of the laws arrived at

over mankind's centuries of experience. If behind all these shapes there is the idea of an infinite space incalculable by ordinary earthly means, then these shapes themselves in their interrelationships comprise an independent whole, albeit one fraught with internal conflict. It seems as though with one more step that unity will be shattered. In the *Spatial Force Constructions* of 1921 Popova frequently presented shapes as a fragment, a part of a world that knows no bounds. But as long as the painting still has this self-sufficiency, it remains an image of a world, not a fragment.

Let us turn to other works from 1920. One of them (gouache, India ink, watercolor, brush, with a date on the reverse, exhibited at Sotheby's in 1970, cat. no. 72, current location unknown to the author) harks back much more to the *Painterly Architectonics* of 1918. The motif of the crescent moon, repeated several times, contrasts in its softness with the motif of acute angles and stripes that intersect in the center of the page. The crescent moon shape comes up fairly often in Popova's later works. It has something in common with the spiral motif, which is either its precursor or its echo.

Two more compositions, done in gouache, can be assigned to 1920. Let us call one of them *Composition with White Crescent Moons* (page 156, left)[71] and the other *Composition with a White Half-Moon* (page 180).[72] In *The George Costakis Collection* these two compositions are reproduced as a pair (figs. 81 and 82), although the one with the half-moon is called *Spatial Construction* and the other *Composition*. They are included along with other "pairs" done by the masters of Inkhuk during the period of their construction-composition debate. In the drawings of Aleksei Babichev, Karel Ioganson, Nikolai Ladovsky, and others, the construction-composition opposition is indeed felt. Popova's graphic works do not demonstrate this theoretical distinction. It is probably incorrect to treat these works as a pair.

But let us return to the paintings themselves. In *Composition with White Crescent Moons* we can identify a new device: if before the edges of shapes were lightly washed out or whitened, now they take on a feathery quality.[73] This device further underscores the figures' shakiness, unsteadiness. In addition, their homogeneity brings back Popova's familiar principle: the circle segments and acute angles are a few elements that in close conjunction create the effect of cohesion. The composition's decorative richness is traditional: the orange and dark blue, black and white, are mutually reinforcing. As we see, *Composition with White Crescent Moons* looks both forward and back, which is typical for the works of 1920.

In *Composition with a White Half-Moon* the difference between the versions is more basic. It is not only that the color versions are very close to the black and white ones. The different versions are saturated with compositional elements to different degrees. The main motif of overlapping irregular rhombi is brought out, or it appears alongside others, which take on real compositional importance. It is this difference that determines the composition's degree of stability. In the "green" version the rhombus, set at an acute angle, is not stable; the yellow-brown color of the cardboard creates an abstract space—the atmosphere for the "flight." Evidently, Popova herself sensed a problem here. Like the preceding work, *Composition with a White Half-Moon* proved transitional.

Meanwhile the new device of shape entering shape through the "feathery" treatment of the edges of those shapes was mastered. Popova used it in other works as well, for example, in the gouache in the Tretiakov Gallery, acquired from George Costakis (fig. 849 in *The George Costakis Collection*), done most likely in 1920. Even more characteristic is a sheet from a private collection in Moscow with two compositions (1921; page 182, bottom).[74] They are notable for their decorativeness, for the vigor of the fringing motion of the brush, which provokes the reverse movement of the background or, more likely, of the adjacent shapes, since usually the background turns into a silhouette and thus a shape as well.

The "feathery" manner found its embodiment in graphics as well, but there it was modified in accordance with the properties of graphics. We believe it is possible to date as 1920 an entire series of Popova's graphic works, mostly in gouache and India ink. Some of them were shown at recent exhibitions, as sketches for the *Supremus* magazine or drawings for the linocuts, and dated 1917. Here we have the same motifs as in the paintings of 1920—crescent moons, spirals, acute triangles. The "feathery" edges have been transformed into parallel lines set closer, more thickly. Sometimes these lines point not away from but into the shapes. In some places parallel hatchstrokes are crossed by perpendiculars, forming a net. There are more shapes here than in the paintings; a tendency toward the ornamental manifests itself.

A definite overall look develops for 1920. But the main issue—whether we can positively identify certain works as those Popova herself entitled *Painterly Constructions*—remains open. None of the works enumerated above demonstrates much that is specific to construction. No more so than *Painterly Architectonics*. Possibly this title came about under the influence of Kandinsky, who used the term "construction" in a broader sense than the Constructivists did. One way or another, Popova eventually rejected it. Nevertheless, her paintings of 1921, which have much more constructive meaning, she entitled *Spatial Force Constructions*.

SPATIAL FORCE CONSTRUCTIONS

Popova's last easel works are dated 1921–22. They sum up her work in the fields of painting and graphics and do it great credit. Her easel work seemed to come to an end at the very moment when it could be put to most logical use in design, theater, and applied graphics, so that one would hardly expect any notable achievements at the easel. This assumption is not borne out, however. Obviously painting and graphics had not exhausted all their possibilities in Popova's art; they were forcibly restrained—for the benefit of a program that was false, albeit consistent to the logic of the Constructivist thesis about the end of easel painting. All in all, the final stage in Popova's painting investigations was one of the high points of her career.

At the time the artist herself was already embarrassed by her easel work. In the catalog for the "5 × 5 = 25" exhibition, she treated her works "merely as a series of preliminary experiments leading to concrete material constructions." This refers to five paintings exhibited, one of which is reproduced in the catalog and which in its composition was very close to many paintings entitled *Spatial Force Construction*. So that, one way or another, the statement refers to these as well.

By no means do Popova's last paintings seem like mere "preliminary experiments" to us, however. They are self-sufficient; they require no translation into another language. Popova may well have extracted not only this experience but also the artistic principle from her easel works in her sketches for fabrics and covers; this does not detract from the paintings' significance. On the contrary; it adds.

Popova's last easel works share several general characteristics. In the catalog to the posthumous exhibition these paintings are represented by nine *Spatial Force Constructions*, all dated 1921. On the Vesnin-Aksionov list there are four *Spatial Force Constructions* dated 1921, but there are an additional four paintings entitled *Work in Oil*. As for the graphic works (water paints), in 1921 the list included approximately forty (including a large number of *Construction Sketches* on cardboard). In the catalog the *Constructive Drawings* are dated only 1918 (a mistake, obviously). This "quantitative description" approximates what we have today in museums and private collections (with significant losses only among the graphics).

In terms of the technical changes in Popova's art of the last years, there is a marked preference for wood (plywood) over canvas. Quite often a significant portion of the plane is not covered with oil paint. Therefore the texture of the wood, which in these works is not primed, plays a large role. Frequently the paint layer "swells," since the artist freely uses an "underlayer" of sand or metal or marble dust. The unprimed plywood promotes the impression of the wood plane being "painted over"—an emphasis on the material used in keeping with so-called Tatlinism, which is utterly natural for the years when Constructivism was taking shape as a movement. Let us recall what Nikolai Punin said about Tatlin's painting, likening it to "housepainting," or to the traditional icon painting that had survived to the twentieth century.[75] True, for Popova (as, for that matter, for Tatlin), paint was not just paint but color as well.

But what is important for us at present is to underscore the materiality of Popova's late painting, her "thing-ness,"[76] the idea of which was extremely popular at the time in all of European art. These qualities had all been present in Popova's painting in earlier years, too, but in the last years they intensified and acquired a programmatic quality.

The most widespread motifs in Popova's late painting were the circle (or the spiral) and a "net" of stripes that formed a unique grating pressed onto the painting surface. Sometimes likenesses of machines or mechanisms appeared in the paintings or graphics. Some graphic works can be viewed as (and many indeed were) drafts for theatrical productions. In all these instances Popova came especially close to embodying the ideas of Constructivism. But those ideas were also realized in works that were far removed from any practical tasks. For the Constructivists themselves, the most important criterion was expediency, if not practical then artistic—serving the image, we would say. "On the whole, Constructivism is motivated art," wrote Constructivist poets and critics Ilia Selvinsky, Kornelii Zelinsky, Vera Inber, and others in their "Constructivists' Declaration."[77]

Popova was looking for just this inner motivation in each stroke, each dot of color, in the logic of the composition, while bringing all her previous experience to bear. Much had been preserved unchanged in her art, and she made use of a good deal of it (especially the devices of her Cubo-Futurist period). In this respect we cannot forget Aksionov's appraisal of Popova in writing about her 1924 posthumous exhibition:

The attentive visitor to the exhibit will see clearly that from the time of the pencil drawings of 1912 the principle of constructing compositions remained invariable. It can be formulated mathematically (during the period of her last works L. S. loved to talk about the mathematical rigor of her constructions and relied less and less on the eye, eagerly turning to mechanical means of dividing lines and planes). At points of intersection the lines of a graphic construction are reciprocally divided into segments at a 1:2 ratio; the angles formed by the two lines with a third and pointed in the same direction retain the same relationship. It is curious that this system remained unchanged throughout the course of the artist's work, even though she enthusiastically altered the outward appearance of her compositions in accordance with the current novelty of the Paris masters.[78]

Taking Aksionov's overstatement into account, we still cannot help but agree with his basic idea. And it is not just a matter of the internal unity of Popova's various stages but also of the use of similar devices. The stripes of the last *Spatial Force Constructions* are pushed to the forefront to "hang," recalling the depiction of letters in her Cubo-Futurist pictures. The underlayer beneath the painting layer also takes us back to Cubo-Futurism. Some of the *Spatial Force Constructions* remind us in their

outlining of shapes of the *Painterly Architectonics* of 1918; only the triangles and rectangles of this period have been preserved, but in outline form, thereby revealing the figures' "ribs." This device demonstrates the link between the *Spatial Force Constructions* and the painting of the years 1916–18. In turn, the unique rib forms in the late Popova refer us back to her early "Gothicism," about which Aksionov spoke so willingly in characterizing the artist's early independence. Thus we see an indisputable connection among the various stages; the late stage encompasses many of those features we have observed before.

The artist's last painting and graphic compositions were born in this unique combination of old and new. Obviously new were the "technical"—one might even say "industrial"—motifs in Popova's paintings. The pictures of powerful beams poured from molten metal or planed from wood, with openings for bolts and rivets, fragments of constructions, stretched cables, wheels strung from cables—all this is in the paintings and drawings of 1921. At this point, however, we should make two qualifications. In the first place, we have no way of certifying that these are really beams, cables, wheels. At best we can say that the details depicted look like these industrial objects. They evoke associations with the world of technology. Second, these motifs are not the beginning and end of the iconography of Popova's late easel art. The majority of her works remain "pure" geometry—triangles, curves, parallelograms. Nevertheless, the advent of "industrial" motifs was highly indicative of Constructivist tendencies in this art of the early 1920s. This line probably ought to have led Popova directly to Production Art.

Among such compositions is the *Spatial Force Construction* (1921, Tretiakov Gallery; *The George Costakis Collection*, fig. 854) with a cross-shaped construction. We have several preliminary drawings for this composition. Comparison with the final painting version shows that in the course of work Popova tried to leave behind superfluous concreteness in treating her chosen motif. The drawings precisely fix the cross's angle of incline, and the shaded beam ends are hatched. The picture seems like a design for a construction; it looks like the numerous sketches for set details for *The Magnanimous Cuckold,* which Popova did in 1922. Naturally, the drawings are not strictly a matter of construction either; they have plastic strength, dynamics, color equilibrium (red and black). But in the painting Popova took a much bigger step away from construction toward the image. For this she had not only to affirm the delicate balance of red, black, and white, but above all to destroy the illusion of a real object. Spatial definition vanished: the volumes and planes entered into a complex interweaving, "entangled," turned inside out in places, and destroyed the straight perspective by tipping the beam ends out at us. The basic structural lines are lost in the interpenetration of shapes, and only in a few places do they emerge, having secured the basic directions of the "force currents."

In another *Spatial Force Construction* (1921; page 160, left), one of Popova's largest paintings (48⅞ × 32¼"), the volumetric forms are again replaced by planes, true, of other proportions and shapes. They bear the traces of constructions and mechanisms—openings, spikes. The natural texture of the wood's surface is left unpainted in several spots and so retains all the marks of its machining and seems ready to be machined again. But if we ignore these signs of the "Production period" in Popova's art, we can easily discern behind the new details elements of the old *Painterly Architectonics* structure. Red and dark brown stripes overlap and form an acute angle. The small white trapezoid can be characterized as a special "minus form." Unlike the earlier white planes, its angles have acquired a "notch," hooking into the adjacent planes and thereby confusing the spatial levels. A new system of line rays is added to the basic elements of *Painterly Architectonics*.

Combining diverse compositional structures is quite typical for the "Production" *Spatial Force Constructions*. In an entire series of sketches, done in gouache, watercolor, or India ink, we find a conjunction of "ray cables," planes, and Production details. As we already wrote, all these motifs do not reproduce the real objects precisely; instead they merely provide hints, spark associations. Popova seems to be maintaining the nonobjective principle. However, there is an essential difference between the late *Painterly Architectonics* and the works described here. In the paintings of 1918 the very proportions of the planes, the shapes of the triangles, had a nonobjective character. Real objects did not stand behind them: the everyday world of things that echoed in the first abstract compositions had already gone its way, and the new—Production—world had yet to be born. When you look at paintings or graphic sketches with Production motifs, you get the feeling that another world already prevails in the artist's consciousness. Its reality destroys nonobjectiveness. The proportions of shapes change. The "figures" become longer and narrower. Sometimes Popova adopts a deliberately straight-on perspective, frankly confronting the horizontal and the vertical. In many instances the dominant acute angle disappears and the right angle prevails. However, we are talking here about the extreme manifestations of Production tendencies. Most often Popova's compositions were as before dominated by aesthetic problems, even when that new real world of which we just spoke lives in the painting.

Illustrative in this regard is the *Spatial Force Construction* (1921) from the Primorsk Art Gallery in Vladivostok, where it is incorrectly titled *Construction*. This is one of Popova's last paintings[79] whose genesis we know: in a private collection in Moscow there is an India ink study for the composition (page 163, top left).[80] The technical elements are softened in the painting. What seemed a rigid diagram in the study becomes vague; the former spatial precision is destroyed, spatial planes are confused, the line-rays that stretch across the whole painting field give the space a certain abstractness.

Popova's "rayist" paintings form the majority among her late paintings and graphic compositions. The word "rayist," bringing to mind the works of Larionov and Goncharova, is not mere coincidence here. In fact, some of Popova's works do come close to examples of Larionov's Rayism. Nevertheless it is hard to say whether this analogy was a conscious creative act or a consequence of Popova's inexorable advance toward her predecessors. Moreover, the similarity turns out to a large extent to be superficial. Larionov conceived of his Rayism as a method of achieving reality, by capturing the rays emitted by the objects. Popova, like all the Constructivists, did not see the goal of art as achieving reality. Constructive reality was chief for her. Life-building—not life-knowing: that was the slogan of the Constructivists.[81]

Most likely Popova's "rayic" system (we will call it rayic rather than rayist) was conceived as a result of an evolution whose beginning must be sought in the *Painterly Architectonics* of 1918, where acute-angled triangles prevailed. Later the artist seemed to free herself of the triangle plane, preserving merely their contours—"ribs." These contours acquired an independence and were transformed into stripes, "arrows," "rays." All feeling of the triangle was lost behind these contours. The lines, set at an angle to one another, stretched out into long zigzag stripes. The acute angles retained their "Gothic nuances." A powerful dynamic was realized in the movement of these line-arrows; they hold an inner force, a charge of some sort. The stripes float out to the foreground, and behind them a free, almost limitless space takes shape. Truly, the idea of a "spatial force construction" seemed to arise in and of itself.

A whole series of graphic and painting compositions (for example, page 165, left), two sheets from the Costakis collection (page 156, left), a few graphic works from a private collection in Moscow (pages 156, right, and 157) demonstrate this evolution. But this line reached its apex in the famous *Spatial Force Construction (Composition)* in the collection of Mr. and Mrs. Roald Dahl (1921; page 166, left), which at one time was published as a postcard along with a few other paintings by Popova.

It is easy to imagine how Popova logically went from compositions of this sort to the *Spatial Force Constructions* with straight lines intersecting along the vertical or horizontal or diagonally across the whole painting field. There are quite a few graphic sketches for compositions of this kind in Popova's legacy: *Vern 34* (fig. 875 in *The George Costakis Collection*), a few sheets with India ink studies in a private collection in Moscow (page 163, top right and bottom, and page 164). To one degree or another all of them are drawn toward two constructions found in the Tretiakov Gallery (acquired from the Costakis collection).[82]

Both paintings, on plywood, are similar in their basic scheme: approximately the same lines, tending toward the diagonal and crisscrossing in the center, with some difference in the format (the first of them stretches upward) and color structure. The small, almost square *Construction* (on page 186) has only white stripes; the large one (page 167, top right), white, black, bright blue, and yellow. The white stripes appear like some material light. The light ray is objectified; it is placed in an abstract space made up of two color bases—the red-brown of the impastoed triangles and the yellow of the plywood surface, which has been left unpainted. Only the small black triangle introduces another principle into this "tricolor," but right at that point something is lost in the overall harmony of light tones. However, it does fulfill its role: it reminds us of the unrealized possibility of contrast. The interweaving of rays, their flight in space, although it assumes some sort of infinity opening up beyond the limits of the painting field, nevertheless possesses a certain independence—not to say, exclusivity. This is a knot of energy lines that do not so much escape the painting as penetrate it from without. Therefore the composition itself comprises a concentration of energy—it is a *force* construction, although by no means is force identified with mechanical energy or mass; rather, it acquires a supraearthly, "rayic" nature.

The larger picture is more dramatic, not only because of its multicolored rays but because of the color contrasts in the intervals between the lines. Added to the scale of red-yellow triangles, which signified space in the previous work, are the relationships between the blacks and whites that stand next to, penetrate, separate each other. The triangles filled in with black and white seem like spatial abysses, chasms, unique "aerial holes." The former ideal structure is exploded by spatial contradictions. For the most part, in her other "rayic" works Popova rejected contrasts like these, although she did retain black.

Here we have in mind those works in which the stripes tend toward the horizontal and vertical. These lines help form a unique net. One of these painting combinations is among the best of the *Spatial Force Constructions* (1921; page 167, top left).[83] There is a whole series of preliminary works that show that the construction had been under development both in the artist's consciousness and practically, on paper, for quite some time, leading through extensive investigations and consistent movement toward the final version. In one of the closest studies (oil and gouache on cardboard, private collection; page 167, bottom) the stripes and background are colored in the direct opposite of the final resolution. In the study the stripes are black (in the painting, white), and the intervals between them are filled in with orange and white (in the painting, orange and black). The basic composition is exactly the same in the study

and the painting. However, the color relations fundamentally change the object-spatial structure. The black stripe-rays in the study are somehow separated from the space that opens into the depth. In the painting this distance between the foreground and middle ground is eliminated. The levels are not discrete. The black angles jut out rather than delve deep. The opaque orange-brown "background" also comes quite close to the painting surface. But this principle of bringing the planes closer is not like the earlier interleaving principle. Now Popova wreaks havoc on the simple logic of an orderly juxtaposition of planes on the same level. The distribution of color acts as a counterweight to the linear perspective. This destruction of simple logic corresponds to the new understanding of the idea of space as well. Its infinity cannot be directly expressed by visual pictorial means. In order for the viewer to feel its limitlessness, the feeling of the presented object's fragmentariness must be intensified. The stripe-rays seem to come here from infinity. The viewer is presented with only a piece of it, its smallest part. The fragment of the limitless world makes it possible to feel the infinity precisely because visible phenomena are made maximally abstract; they are the elements that make up the universe. The fragmentariness Popova now employed implies resistance. Consistency is attained at the price of composition. Popova was concerned with defining the fundamental axis: the two verticals, running parallel, close to one another. How much this problem of the vertical axis concerned the artist is evident from the numerous studies done in 1921 that are like the examined painting in composition. Particularly interesting are five small drawings done in gouache and ink and published by George Peck and Lilly Wei[84] (private collection, New York). Two of them have a pair of stripes at their center; three have only one. In all five compositions these stripes dominate, unquestionably subordinating all the other elements—triangles, lines. They "hold up" the composition, create balance, balance not on earth now, but in space.

There is yet another characteristic of the works Popova executed in her "rayic" manner. In her earlier works we noted the concept of the form that "floats" in space. But this concept did not provide a basis for displaying energy. The *Spatial Force Constructions* demanded a different solution: a ray that possessed its own force and penetrated space, thereby developing energy. Here a fundamentally new thought was expressed, differing at base from what we were able to observe in the *Painterly Architectonics*. New horizons were opening up for Popova; she was reaching the cosmic infinity that Malevich had touched on boldly several years before. He had been trying to reach the universe. Popova was propounding the idea of a kind of cosmic building. She was building a fantastic structure by relying on a particular material—rays—a material that appeared to lead beyond the limits of ordinary earthly parameters. Popova's experiment seems to link up with the lessons of

Tatlin and the last trends of Constructivism. In this combination of largely contradictory positions we can discern Popova's uniqueness, her constant desire to go her own way, on the basis of the experience of modern art, but proposing her own solutions.

Popova's "rayic" system was not simply a phase in her artistic career, although not very many works were executed within the bounds of this system. Nevertheless, the "rayic" paintings were not the last of Popova's easel works. Evidently the compositions whose main motif was circular movement (the circle, the spiral) were created not only then, in 1921, but later as well; many graphic works with this motif are dated 1921–22 by the artist herself.

Popova had used the motif of circular and spiral movement before, too, but in later years this motif became the basis for the creation of what may have been the artist's greatest achievements in easel painting and graphics. Moreover, it received a fresh interpretation and became the main—and, in her best works, the sole—motif.

The "circular" compositions entitled *Spatial Force Construction* at the posthumous exhibition can be put into several groups. Two of them consist of paintings that, despite their high artistic quality, need not necessarily be considered her culmination. The paintings are dated 1921 both in the posthumous exhibition catalog and on the Vesnin-Aksionov list, although several graphic works the artist herself dated either December 1921, or winter 1921–22, or simply 1922. Consequently, not all the graphics can be considered studies; it is possible that some of them are further elaborations of a motif created after the paintings.

One group of "circular" compositions exists in graphic form (or else we have never found the paintings). The most important of these versions are in the Costakis collection, the Tretiakov Gallery, and the Perm Picture Gallery (all page 172). The last is signed and dated by Popova 1921.[85] It is possible that this version is the basic one. In composition they are all extraordinarily similar, and quite sketchy in nature. From the center, as if (and possibly in fact) with a compass, several circumferences are drawn. But not one of them is complete. Sometimes the compass draws only a third of a circle. Sometimes the curve breaks off and picks up again on the opposite side of the sheet. The closer to the center, the more energetic and concentrated the movement of the lines seems. Toward the edges of the composition, on the periphery, it is the dotted line rather than the line or the stripe that prevails. Not far from the center a few more circles appear with their own centers. The consistent planarity of the composition is striking. There are no overlapping planes, no abstract space sliced by stripe-rays. The entire motion of the composition is not into the depth but on the plane. The movement is equally restricted in two other important dimensions—only supplementary lines and forms are aimed

beyond the limits of the sheet. All the rest are concentrated in or cluster toward the center.

The same could be said about other compositions based on the circle motif. *Spatial Force Construction* from the Tretiakov Gallery (page 183), which has a signature and a date (1921), combines painterly perfection and draftsmanly calculation. The basis of the composition is three intersecting circles (red, bright blue, and black) and two diagonal stripes. In the colored pencil drawing that anticipates the painting (page 171, bottom), the draftsmanly tendency makes itself felt with special clarity. The line becomes abstract; it acquires a sterile purity, as if it were distancing itself from the hand of the concrete artist who drew it.

Among the works of Popova's last years we encounter drawings like this—two intersecting circles or a circle and square, zigzags drawn in variously colored pencils, not unlike those devised for the cover of the "5 × 5 = 25" exhibition catalog (page 187), a cross drawn into a circle. These drawings are very much like the works of Rodchenko. We see something different in the painting, however. Here Popova did not abandon her previous path. She was not abstracting from the material, from the plane. The painting surface once again takes on life: the paint swells (with metal dust as an underlayer), the edges of the color areas take on their former "featheriness," the texture of the plywood contributes its own rhythm with the movement of its lines. The spatial concept takes a back seat (although in the "circular" compositions there are traces of the "rayic" system). Popova was trying to unite the experience of her early nonobjective works with her attempts to escape into infinity and with the Constructivist innovations of the early 1920s. This combination of hers is especially successful in the large *Spatial Construction* (page 172, bottom) in the Costakis collection.

As in other instances, this painting is accompanied by a large number of graphic compositions elaborating the same motif (page 182, top), some of which are dated 1922 and consequently were done after the picture was painted. Despite the compositional similarity in the painting there is one essential difference: the drawings are long up and down, the painting is square. The square format is unusual in Popova's easel works. It is a difficult format for a nonobjective construction, necessitating a rectilinear compositional solution. Popova successfully avoided this rectilinearity. She sent a spiral movement down a diagonal from corner to corner. She squeezed the red circles with bladelike black stripes and triangles, having concentrated the basic force more in the very heart of the painting. The force construction includes stripes that enter the painting field from beyond its limits. But this "rayic principle" does not become dominant. Both those stripes and the Constructivist dotted line are subjugated once again to the relationships of the main shapes. This time these forms would best be called energetic rather than architectonic. Forms change, but the goals remain as before. Harmony must now be built not through the relations of masses, volumes, or patches, but through the relations of energetic principles.

It is the small circles and spirals that possess the most strength in the painting. They convey a sense of heightened tension. The large curves yield to the central ones, as if discovering some possibility of movement but simultaneously holding back the pressure. The balance between centrifugal and centripetal forces guarantees the harmony of the energetic principles. Unlike *Painterly Architectonics*, this painting does not have any large color planes, or "figures." A large portion of the painting field is unprimed plywood. The circular red ribbon lines and black straight lines assume almost all the energy. White, black, yellow, and crimson patches seem to create a dramatic environment for the force struggle, accompany it, and facilitate resolution of the conflict.

As we see, the harmonic principle, which had been so important for Popova during the Cubo-Futurist stage of her development, remained primary for her in the last stage of her easel work as well. The paths to an artist's utopia turned out to be complicated. Before crossing over along with all the Constructivists to direct life-building through useful, practical activity, Popova, at the most critical point in her development, when purely artistic categories already seemed to be losing their meaning, continued to maintain intact the *artistic* kernel of the image while at the same time employing the new language of Constructivism, the whole Constructivist arsenal. The intrinsic worth of the artist's last works is obvious. All the traditional criteria of harmony, perfection, integrity, and completion apply.[86] As before, we have before us an ideal construction, and the utopian, harmonious world realized in this painting rises up over reality.

As we have seen, some of Popova's easel works were done in 1922—after Popova herself rejected easel art. Evidently that rejection did not come easily. Her new spheres of endeavor would be rewarded by successes, the source of no small gratification in the last years of her life.

NOTES TO PART ONE

1. Biographical information about Popova has been taken primarily from the questionnaire compiled after Popova's death by Tatiana M. Pakhomova of the Institute of Artistic Culture (now in a private archive in Moscow). These facts have been clarified and augmented by information from relatives, descendants, friends of the artist, and others who remembered her. The authors also used the reminiscences of the sculptor Vera Mukhina and the diaries and memoirs of Nadezhda Udaltsova, as well as other materials. The authors would like to thank Maria V. Zubova, N. I. Tolstoy, and Elena A. Drevina for their assistance.

The authors wish to express special gratitude to the late George Costakis, who was responsible for resurrecting the name of Liubov Popova, who collected her works, and who always graciously allowed study of the works in his collection.
2. Several books mistakenly name an imagined sister Vera in photo captions instead of Liubov Sergeevna's brother Pavel.
3. The authors have in their possession a typewritten list of Popova's works taken from the archive of Aleksandr Vesnin that enumerates the works of the artist found in her studio and apartment after her death. To judge from the compilers' comments, dates were set either from Popova's own list (not found in her archives), on the basis of earlier explanations by the artist, or from memory. Taking part in the compilation were members of the Commission of the Institute of Artistic Culture: Vesnin, Ivan Aksionov (for biographical sketch, see Notes to Part Two, n. 80), Varvara Shamshina, and Popova's brother Pavel. Since Vesnin and Aksionov were close friends of Popova, whose artistic work went on in their full view, the facts in the list can be considered completely reliable. Hereafter in the notes and the text we will refer to the "Vesnin-Aksionov list."
4. In the Vesnin-Aksionov list in the table "? list of L.S.P." under no. 1 is *Composition with Figures* (1913), which the artist did after her return from Paris.
5. In *The George Costakis Collection: Russian Avant-Garde Art* (New York, 1981; hereafter, *The George Costakis Collection*), p. 345, there is a picture entitled *Still Life*. Our title and date are taken from the Vesnin-Aksionov list. Henceforth, as a rule, we shall not point out discrepancies with *The George Costakis Collection* in dates and titles.
6. Of the works from the years 1910–12 only one still life, dated 1909–11 and as of the present time not located by us, was shown at her posthumous exhibition. We can, however, get some idea of it from one of the photographs taken at that exhibition. As regards the Vesnin-Aksionov list, it includes approximately thirty paintings from that period, of which only six or seven are available for viewing.
7. I. A. Aksionov, "Posmertnaia vystavka L. S. Popovoi" (Posthumous Exhibition of L. S. Popova), *Zhizn iskusstva* (Life of Art), no. 5 (February 3, 1925): 5.
8. Ibid., p. 4.
9. The greater part of the Russian avant-garde regarded Vrubel, as they did the other Symbolists, negatively. In those instances when artists or art theoreticians were prepared to recognize his role in the development of Russian and European art, they either linked him to Cézanne or treated the Russian artist as a forerunner of Cubism. See S. Yu. Sudeikin, "Dve vstrechi s Vrubelem" (Two Encounters with Vrubel), in *Vrubel. Perepiska. Vospominaniia o khudozhnike* (Vrubel. Correspondence. Reminiscences About the Artist) (Leningrad, 1979), pp. 291–95; N. Kulbin, "Kubizm" (Cubism), in *Strelets. Sbornik pervyi* (Archer: The First Collection) (Petrograd, 1915), pp. 197–216.
10. Liubov Popova most certainly knew the work of the artists of this group. We know, for example, that on her advice Vera Mukhina in 1911 spent some time at the studio of Ilya Mashkov—one of the group—where she drew diligently. See O. I. Voronova, *Vera Ignatievna Mukhina* (Moscow, 1976), p. 18. (Popova's advice suggests that she herself had some contact with Mashkov's studio.) Ivan Aksionov, in his aforementioned essay, stated that the artist did join the Jack of Diamonds group. See Aksionov, "Posmertnaia vystavka," p. 5.
11. Ibid., pp. 4–5.
12. See Andrei B. Nakov, *Alexandra Exter* (Paris, 1972), p. 10.
13. Diary of Nadezhda Udaltsova (private collection, Moscow). Elsewhere in her diary Udaltsova explains similar deficiencies by the fact that until then Popova and Prudkovskaia had used a stroke that was much too staccato. She also voices concern that her friend's Cubism was taking on an ornamental-decorative quality, and continually refers to the critical comments and praises of Le Fauconnier and Metzinger. Gradually the praises come to predominate.

14. This series comprises 281 drawings, of which the author knows only a limited number. Among the known sketches and cityscapes mentioned in the list, however, are nos. 245, 246, 247, 270–74.
15. Published in *Künstlerinnen der russischen Avantgarde 1910–1930/Women-Artists of the Russian Avantgarde 1910–1930* (Cologne: Galerie Gmurzynska, 1979), p. 178 (bottom).
16. Quoted in the Pakhomova questionnaire, cited by Pavel Popov in his article in *Katalog posmertnoi vystavki khudozhnika-konstruktora L. S. Popovoi* (Catalog of the Posthumous Exhibition of Artist-Constructor L. S. Popova) (Moscow, 1924), p. 6.
17. Beginning with 1913, we base our dating of Popova's works on two main sources, the Vesnin-Aksionov list and the 1924 posthumous exhibition catalog. Both make it possible for us to include among the works for 1913 the *Still Life with Tin Dish*, *Composition with Figures* from the Tretiakov Gallery (in various catalogs it is called *Two Figures*), and all the compositions with a single female figure. As for the still life, we know it only from an old photograph. The compositions with a female figure are designated in the catalog and the list as either *Female Model* or *Study for Female Model*. At the 1924 exhibition there were ten paintings by that name; the list gives fourteen. At the present time we know four single-figure compositions. One—with a standing figure—was acquired from the Costakis collection by the Tretiakov Gallery. Three—with a seated figure—are from the Rubinger Collection, the Ludwig Museum in Cologne, and the Russian Museum, where the painting is entitled *Person + Air + Space*. This basic version may have been in the "Tramway V" exhibit in Petersburg in 1915 under the title *Figure + House + Space*.

One more argument for dating the single-figure compositions 1913 is the mention on the Vesnin-Aksionov list of a "Copy of the Cranach Madonna" on the reverse of one of the *Female Models*. As we know, in 1913 Tatlin did several "rephrasings" of the Cranach Madonna. Since Popova was working in Tatlin's studio at that time, we can be fully confident of the simultaneity of these experiments. As a sidelight we should mention that in one of the private collections in Moscow, in an album of Popova's drawings, there is one of a woman and child in the traditional Madonna pose right beside studies for the single-figure composition with a seated woman.
18. Popova must have known Gleizes and Metzinger's *Du Cubisme* (On Cubism) in France. Let us note as well that in 1913 there were two editions of that book, and in March of the same year the third issue of the Union of Youth anthology appeared; in it Matiushin summarized and commented on the book. There the Cubist tenet that the expressive quality of a painting must be based on the conjunction of straight lines and curves is particularly emphasized. See Mikhail Matiushin, "O knige Gleza i Metsenzhe 'Du Cubisme'" (On *Du Cubisme* by Gleizes and Metzinger), *Soiuz molodezhi* (Union of Youth), no. 3 (March 1913) (Petersburg): 32.
19. One of the paintings on the Vesnin-Aksionov list is called *Female Model with Still Life*.
20. Popova calls him Guido da Verona, but evidently she means Guido da Siena, an artist of the Italian duecento. In one of Popova's autobiographical notes, where she has listed the Italian cities on the travelers' itinerary and several names, after the name of Guido da Verona, in parentheses, is "Siena."
21. P. K. Suzdalev, *Vera Ignatievna Mukhina* (Moscow, 1981), p. 7.
22. Ibid., p. 85.
23. A. M. Rodchenko, *Stati. Vospominaniia. Avtobiograficheskie zapiski. Pisma* (Essays. Reminiscences. Autobiographical Notes. Letters) (Moscow, 1982), p. 85.
24. N. A. Udaltsova, *Moi vospominaniia* (My Reminiscences) (Private collection, Moscow).
25. See Giovanni Lista, "Futurisme et Cubo-futurisme," *Cahiers du Musée Nationale d'Art Moderne*, no. 5 (1980): 458–59.
26. About this, see Charlotte Douglas, "Russian Art and Italian Futurism," *Art Journal*, vol. 34, no. 3 (1975): 229–39; Charlotte Douglas, "Cubisme français/ Cubo-futurisme russe," *Cahiers du Musée Nationale d'Art Moderne*, no. 2 (1979): 184–93.
27. About this, see N. Khardzhiev, "Maiakovsky i zhivopis" (Maiakovsky and Painting), in *Poeticheskaia kultura Maiakovskogo* (The Poetic Culture of Mayakovsky) (Moscow, 1970); D. V. Sarabianov, "Noveishie techeniia v russkoi zhivopisi predrevoliutsionnogo desiatiletiia" (The Newest Trends in Russian Painting of the Pre-Revolutionary Decade), *Sovetskoe iskusstvoznanie* (Soviet Art Studies), vol. 80, no. 1 (Moscow) (1981).
28. The very title—*Italian Still Life*—and the dedication to the Italian Futurists

inscribed on the stretcher confirm our assumption that the composition appeared after the Italian trip. On the back of the canvas is a label with a second title—*Violins and Cannons* (although the musical instrument pictured looks more like a guitar than a violin). It may well be that the very idea of uniting these disparate objects may have had something to do with the onset of World War I.

29. Two of them were in the Galerie Gmurzynska in Cologne and a third in a private collection in Moscow. We do not know what titles Popova gave these works. On the listing for 1913 in the posthumous exhibition catalog and on the Vesnin-Aksionov list for 1914 there is only one title that we can identify as belonging to the group called *Musical Instruments*.

30. The painting was shown at the posthumous exhibition with this date. Popova wrote 1915 on the back of a photograph in the author's possession as well. Only at "The Store" exhibition of 1916 was *Violin* exhibited with the date 1914.

31. The final (?) version of the painting was shown at the posthumous exhibition with the date 1915 and was reproduced in the catalog. This date is confirmed by a signature in Popova's own handwriting on the back of a photograph in the author's possession. The location of the painting remains unknown. On the Vesnin-Aksionov list for 1914 there are three *Guitars*—one of which has the still life *Clock* on the back. This version, close to the basic one, and another, which has only half a guitar on a white and black abstract background, are in a private collection in Moscow. Both of them are obviously from 1914.

32. This painting acquired the incorrect title *Early Morning* from the name of the newspaper pictured in the still life, but this title does not appear in any list or catalog, whereas *Objects from a Dyeworks* figures both on the Vesnin-Aksionov list and in the posthumous exhibition catalog. In one of the photographs of the posthumous exhibition, where the artist's works are set out in the same order as in the catalog, the still life is fully discernible and corresponds to the order of the titles.

33. Rarely do we encounter this type of detail in Western European Cubism. The only thing that comes to mind is Juan Gris's *The Watch* (*The Sherry Bottle*; 1912). Reference to Gris is rather frequent in Popova's creative work of the mid-1910s.

34. We know three versions of *Clock* (see page 73). One, the basic one, is established in an old photograph from Popova's archive (fig. 67). The other two are on the backs of *Study for a Portrait* (figs. 65 and 83) and an incomplete version of *Guitar* (fig. 66 and 62). The latter two *Clocks* are in a private collection in Moscow.

35. This figures in the posthumous exhibition catalog under the title *Still Life* (1915) and is distinguishable in one of the photographs of the exposition.

36. On the Vesnin-Aksionov list ("List No. 2: Works in Water Paints, Drawings, Prints") under numbers 34–36 is *Study for a Rejoinder to a 1915 Work*. On the list these works are dated 1920. One of these three versions, listed as on the reverse of no. 35 and dated 1920, is in a private collection in Moscow. The later date is also confirmed by the presence in the picture of the letters "RSF" ("Russian Soviet Federated," a portion of the initials "R.S.F.S.R," for "Russian Soviet Federated Socialist Republic"), which could have appeared only in the post-Revolutionary period. In its composition this graphic work does not coincide with a single still life of 1915 that we know of. It is possible that the object of the rejoinder has not survived (on the Vesnin-Aksionov list under 1915 there is a *Still Life with Compote*).

37. Of the Paris works of the mid-1910s only one—Juan Gris's *Still Life in Front of an Open Window* (*Place Ravignan*)—offers an analogy to Popova in the depiction of that object so beloved in still-life art. But this time Gris's work appears not before but simultaneously with Popova's compositions.

38. "O knige Gleza i Metsenzhe 'Du Cubisme,'" p. 30.

39. We have assigned this title arbitrarily. The still life—although there is no question of Popova's authorship, since it comes from Aleksandr Vesnin's collection—does not correspond precisely to anything in the lists or catalogs. More than likely, to judge by the manner of its painting, it was done in 1915. Some of its shapes are reminiscent of the 1915–16 landscapes.

40. "O knige Gleza i Metsenzhe 'Du Cubisme,'" p. 34.

41. See Margit Rowell, *The Planar Dimension: Europe 1912–1932* (New York, 1979).

42. Exhibited and reproduced in the posthumous exhibition catalog under the title *Relief*.

43. Often this work is dated 1916. This is arbitrary: to refute it, in the first place, is the posthumous exhibition catalog and, second, the artist's dated inscription on the back of a postcard reproduction of the relief (in the author's collection).

44. There are three painting versions of *Study for a Portrait* (there are three in the Vesnin-Aksionov inventory also): one belongs to the Tula Picture Gallery, another to the Costakis collection (page 91, left), and the third—the largest—to a private collection in Moscow (page 102, left; on the reverse is a *Clock*, page 73). This collection also has a version in gouache (page 102, right; dated 1915 on the back), as well as several pencil sketches.

45. Popova could have met Soffici in the spring of 1914 in Paris, where he was working in a studio with Aleksandra Exter. See Nakov, *Alexandra Exter*, p. 11.

46. In one of the lists of works designated for exhibition at the "0.10" show Popova included a self-portrait. This list, handwritten on the back of a drawing held in a private collection in Moscow, matches almost perfectly the list of Popova's works in the exhibition catalog. It lacks only two still lifes, which evidently were added later. The order of placement of the pictures matches almost perfectly, too. This list includes several portrait works. First is *Portrait*, then *Drawing for a Portrait*. It is not hard to guess that these refer to *Portrait of a Philosopher* and the study for it in the Tretiakov Gallery (page 93, left). One other portrait is mentioned in the exhibition catalog and in Popova's own handwritten list as *Portrait of a Lady* (or *Lady*) with *Plastic Drawing* in parentheses tacked on. This is the relief examined earlier (reproduced on page 83). There is one more portrait, which the list calls *Self-Portrait* and which we identify as the work under discussion. To that add a certain likeness in the structure of the eyes, the nostrils, the eyebrows, and the waves in the hair, which can be established by comparing the portrait with photographs from the 1910s, as well as in the shape of the brooch and the style of the collar, for which we once again find analogies in the photographs.

47. There are problems with assigning specific dates to the self-portrait drawings. Dating one of them 1912 (see *The George Costakis Collection*, fig. 739) seems questionable, due to both the nature of the drawing and the age of the model herself.

48. In the possession of the author.

49. A very rough idea of this painting can be obtained from the photograph of Popova's posthumous exhibition.

50. It is no accident that the compiler of *The George Costakis Collection* mistook a preliminary drawing for *Lady with a Guitar* (fig. 804) for a study for *Portrait of a Philosopher*.

51. This is the title given on the Vesnin-Aksionov list. The posthumous exhibition catalog gives a shortened version of the title—*The Kremlin*. This work was in an exhibition in 1980 in Los Angeles, *The Avant-Garde in Russia 1910–1930: New Perspectives* (no. 238), with the incorrect date 1914 and the title *Cubist Cityscape*, and after that was reproduced in print several times with these same mistakes. It is not hard to make out this work in an old photograph of the posthumous exhibition. Meanwhile, among the paintings mentioned in the exhibition catalog, the only one the painting can be identified with is *The Kremlin*. The details of the landscape—the embrasures, the parts of the portal and arches, the barrels of the Tsar-Cannon, piled in a pyramid as they are today, the striped walls of the Guard Corps barracks—testify to the fact that before you is the Moscow Kremlin.

52. The gouache version of *Box Factory* (page 98, top) was shown at the 1980 Los Angeles exhibition under the title *The Factory* and with the incorrect date c. 1914–15. *Birsk*—also incorrectly dated (1914–15) and named—is in *The George Costakis Collection* (fig. 820). We submit our names and dates on the following grounds. The Vesnin-Aksionov list and, what is particularly important, the posthumous exhibition catalog cite oil and watercolor (in fact, gouache) versions of *Box Factory* as well as *Birsk*. All three works are dated 1916. There were no other landscapes from the Cubo-Futurist period (with the exception of *The Kremlin*) at the exhibition. Meanwhile, we can distinguish both landscapes on a photograph of the posthumous exhibition.

53. The Costakis collection and a private collection in Moscow have a series of letters from Popova to Adda Dege that mention frequent visits to that city. One of the drawings that served as a preliminary study for the large landscape *Birsk* (judging from the Vesnin-Aksionov list, there were eight such preliminary works altogether) has written on the back "Summer 1916." The actual landscape pictured in *Box Factory* recalls *Birsk*. It is, thus, not difficult to conclude that the former, which we now know in its gouache version, was also done in Birsk or else immediately upon her return to Moscow.

54. It is no wonder the landscape was exhibited turned on its side and with the title *Head of a Woman* at several Moscow shows.

55. *Katalog posmertnoi vystavki,* p. 6.

56. As the reader is already aware, one of the photographs of Popova's posthumous exhibition demonstrates the sequence of paintings exactly as it occurs in the catalog. In it under no. 3 we have *Painterly Architectonics* and a date—1915. We may assume that the catalog's compilers learned this date from the artist herself, who must have discussed the question of her first experiments in the field of nonobjective painting with her friends. From the same photograph we can not only re-create the painting's composition but also identify it as the *Painterly Architectonics* in the Tretiakov Gallery (inv. no. 11938) and, before that, in the Museum of Artistic Culture. Other versions of this composition, one of which is in the Rubinger collection in Cologne (a collage) and another in a private collection in Moscow (gouache, 1916), retain the same colors of its component parts—black, gray, green, yellow, and terra cotta (brown).

57. See Larissa A. Shadova, *Malevich: Suprematism and Revolution in Russian Art 1910–1930* (London and New York, 1982). Originally published as *Suche und Experiment* (Dresden, 1978), p. 122.

58. We can establish the dates of several works from the Vesnin-Aksionov list. In the painting section, the compilers have attributed various identifying marks and signs to the *Architectonics* (in some cases we use these titles, although they are not the author's). On "List No. 2: Works in Water Paints, Drawings, Prints" numbers 1 through 26 cover "preliminary works for paintings of 1916." In compiling this list, its authors simultaneously put the corresponding number and, sometimes, date on the back of the work. A private collection in Moscow has two nearly identical studies that wholly coincide with the painting under discussion and are numbered on the back 7 and 22.

59. On the back of the sheet is the number 11. Consequently, it belongs with the preliminary works for the paintings of 1916. Either the actual painting from this study was never executed or it has not survived.

60. This work is dated 1917. Presumably it can be identified as the painting *Painterly Architectonics: Orange, Black, Gray* mentioned on the Vesnin-Aksionov list.

61. Usually this series of color linocuts, consisting of six sheets and a cover executed in the same technique, is dated 1917–19. The reason for this broad dating, we may assume, is the information in the posthumous exhibition catalog, in which all linocuts (there are ten of them) are dated 1917–20. Those from the later period were black and white, which is the reason for this broad dating. On the Vesnin-Aksionov list the series of color prints is dated 1917. It also enumerates the preliminary drawings for the prints (at the present time, partially in the Costakis collection). Impressions of the prints are held in various museums and private collections.

62. According to the list there were fifty-six watercolor studies and collages for Verbovka. A private collection in Moscow has over a dozen collages—small, as a rule—with corresponding numbers on the back.

63. It is possible that there were originally more such collages and that, because they were almost identical in size to the linocuts, they served as studies for the latter.

64. Unfortunately, we have been unable to identify any of Popova's known paintings with works of this group, although they were in exhibitions.

65. A private collection in Moscow has a series of studies for the composition dated 1916 on the back and numbered correspondingly with that year. The studies' dates and numbers enable us to fix the picture itself as 1916, which is wholly substantiated by its artistic characteristics.

66. Among the inscriptions on the back, only one is the author's (on the stretcher)— with the author's name and the number 29. This is the number from Popova's own vanished list. In the Vesnin-Aksionov inventory a series of works from 1916 opens with *Painterly Architectonics with Yellow Board,* next to which, in the column "Nos. of L.S.P.'s list," is the number 29. We can, therefore, identify the work with this title and date with utter confidence.

67. *Künstlerinnen der russischen Avantgarde,* p. 203. In the exhibit this collage belonging to a private collection was dated 1920. This date seems too late. If the collage was indeed a study, then it must have been done in 1916. If it was an echo of an earlier work, it should be dated no later than 1917, when Popova was doing collages as studies for embroidery and was in general enthusiastic about collage.

68. The question of the correct approach to this composition is complicated and not completely resolved. In one of the photographs of Popova's posthumous exhibition the composition is hung so that the circle segment is on the left near the bottom. In the studies for the Supremus logo we find the exact opposite positioning. We hold with the latter version, believing that when the 1924 show was hung a mistake was made.

69. In *The George Costakis Collection* (fig. 832) this work is dated 1918–19. In our view the year 1919 was added arbitrarily. From the biographical information compiled by Pakhomova we know that in 1919, due to her husband's serious illness and death (from typhus), Popova for all practical purposes did not work. In those instances when the artist herself put this date on the back of a canvas or sheet of paper, the dating, evidently, was done at the time of sale.

70. On the back is a watercolor dated 1919 by Popova herself. But more than likely it was done in 1918. This may have been another of those instances when the artist dated a work at the time of sale.

71. Executed by the artist in several versions, which differ from one another to a very slight degree. One of them (shown at Sotheby's in 1973, cat. no. 47), entitled *Architectonic Composition with Orange, Dark Blue, White, and Black,* has a date on the back—1920—and a number—40, which, according to the Vesnin-Aksionov list, does belong to 1920. Another is in the Costakis collection, and a third in the Tretiakov Gallery (on the back is the date 1921).

72. There are several very similar versions. One, in color (green, black, and white), is in the Costakis collection. Another was shown in 1922 at the "First Russian Art Exhibition" in Berlin under the title *Composition* (reproduced in the catalog *Erste russische Kunstausstellung* [Berlin: Galerie van Diemen, 1922]). Its current location is unknown. A third version was exhibited at Sotheby's in 1972 (cat. no. 86); a fourth— black and white—is in a private collection in Moscow. It is signed by Popova in the lower left corner. The signature attests to the fact that this composition is usually reproduced rotated on its side. On the back of the sheet is an inscription in an unknown hand: "Composition. 1920." This is just the date we would like to assign this work, considering its stylistic similarity to other works of 1920.

73. In the 1910s Aleksandra Exter used a similar device.

74. On the back is a number, 53, which on the Vesnin-Aksionov list corresponds to the year 1921.

75. N. Punin, *Tatlin. Protiv kubizma* (Tatlin: Against Cubism) (Moscow, 1921), p. 12.

76. About this, see N. L. Adaskina, "Liubov Popova. Put stanovleniia khudozhnika-konstruktora" (Liubov Popova: An Artist-Constructor's Formation), *Tekhnicheskaia estetika* (Technical Aesthetics), no. 11 (1978): 18.

77. *LEF. Zhurnal levogo fronta iskusstva* (Lef: Journal of the Left Front of Art), editor-in-chief V. V. Maiakovsky, no. 3(7) (Moscow-Leningrad) (1925): 142.

78. Aksionov, "Posmertnaia vystavka," p. 5.

79. On the back of the painting is a number—86—a number from Popova's own vanished list. Judging from the Vesnin-Aksionov inventory, the artist's last painting was numbered 90.

80. In a private collection in Moscow there is a notebook of drawings and studies by Popova. The notebook is dated 1921 and contains thirty-seven drawings, in ink and India ink. Sheet no. 17 is a study for a composition in the Primorsk Museum.

81. See N. F. Chuzhak, "Pod znakom zhiznestroeniia (opyt ocoznaniia iskusstva dnia)" (Under the Banner of Life-Building [An Experiment in Realizing the Art of the Day]), *LEF,* no. 1 (March 1923).

82. At the posthumous exhibition all the late works were called *Spatial Force Construction.* At the "5 × 5 = 25" exhibition, in addition to this title, "constructions" were described as "spatial-volumetric," "of color planes," or "enclosed in spatial constructions." Obviously this expansion of titles was excised in the course of organizing the posthumous exhibition. In the Vesnin-Aksionov inventory, besides the *Spatial Force Constructions,* there are four numbers with the general title "Works in Oil Paint." We assume that the last compositions with circles belong to these. One of them has Popova's own number on the back—89, which corresponds on the Vesnin-Aksionov list to precisely this title. However, this title did not figure in the posthumous exhibition, although compositions with circles were shown.

83. A postcard was also done from this painting.

84. George Peck and Lilly Wei, "Interpretations of Space," *Art in America* (New York) (October 1982): 101.

85. One version of this composition (in colored pencil) was published in 1978 in the catalog of an exhibit at the Bargera Gallery (no. 69) and dated 1922, without reference to the source for this date.

86. It is telling that in the last years of her life, when the artist was starting to write a different sort of commentary—sketches for articles—she expressed in them great interest in the problem of style, which, as a rule, did not interest practitioners and theoreticians of the European avant-garde.

Liubov Popova in her studio. 1920

Painterly Architectonics. Study. 1916. Pencil on paper, 8¾ × 7⅜" (22.3 × 18.7 cm.). Private collection, Moscow

Painterly Architectonics. 1916–17. Oil on canvas, 37 × 30" (94.1 × 76.3 cm.). Costakis Collection, Athens

Painterly Architectonics. 1916. Oil on canvas, 20⅛ × 13" (51 × 33 cm.). Russian Museum

151

Painterly Architectonics. Study. 1918. Gouache on paper, 15¾ × 11¾″ (45 × 30 cm.). Private collection

Painterly Architectonics. 1918. Gouache and lacquer on paper,
13⅛ × 11⅜" (33.5 × 29 cm.). Private collection, Moscow

Painterly Architectonics. ca. 1917. Oil on canvas, 31½ × 38⅝"
(80 × 98 cm.). Collection, The Museum of Modern Art, New York.
Philip Johnson Fund

Painterly Architectonics. 1918. Oil on canvas, 22⅝ × 17⅜" (57.5 × 44 cm.).
Ludwig Museum, Cologne

Painterly Architectonics. 1918. Oil on canvas, 22⅞ × 20⅞" (58 × 53 cm.).
Gorky Museum of Art

Painterly Architectonics. 1919. Watercolor on paper, 13½ × 10" (34.2 × 25.5 cm.).
Rostov-Yaroslavl Museum-Archive of Architecture and Art, Yaroslavl

Painterly Architectonics. 1918. Oil on canvas, 41½ × 35" (105.5 × 89 cm.).
Museum of Art of the Uzbek S.S.R., Tashkent

Painterly Architectonics. 1918. Oil on canvas, 28¾ × 19″ (73.1 × 48.1 cm.). Costakis Collection, Athens

Composition with White Crescent Moons. 1920. Gouache on paper, 13½ × 10⅞" (34.3 × 27.5 cm.). Costakis Collection, Athens

Composition. 1920–21. Gouache on paper, 13⅝ × 10⅝" (34.5 × 27 cm.). Private collection

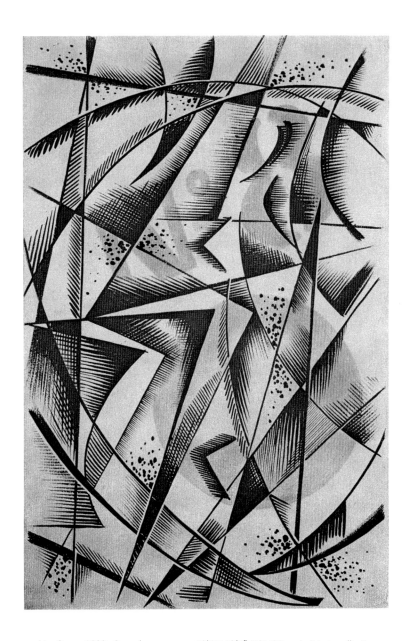

No. 8. ca. 1920. Gouache on paper, 19¼ × 12⅝″ (49 × 32 cm.). Private collection

Study for the *Painterly Construction* in the Tretiakov Gallery. 1920. India ink and pencil on paper, 9⅞ × 7⅛" (25 × 18.2 cm.) (inside the penciled frame). Private collection, Moscow

Untitled. ca. 1920. Color linocut, 9⅝ × 8" (24.2 × 20.2 cm.). Location unknown

Painterly Construction. 1920. Linocut, 9⅝ × 7¼" (24.5 × 18.4 cm.). Private collection, Moscow

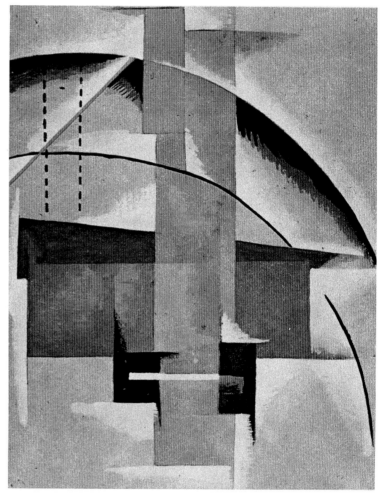

Spatial Force Construction. 1921. Oil on plywood, 48⅞ × 32¼" (124 × 82 cm.).
Tretiakov Gallery. Gift of George Costakis

Spatial Force Construction. 1921. Gouache on cardboard, 13¼ × 10⅝"
(33.5 × 27 cm.). Tretiakov Gallery. Gift of George Costakis

Spatial Force Construction. Study. 1921. Pencil and India ink on paper, 13⅜ × 9⅞"
(34 × 25 cm.). Costakis Collection, Athens

Composition. 1921. Pencil and charcoal on paper, 15⅛ × 10¾" (38.5 × 27.3 cm.). Private collection, Moscow

Above left: Spatial Force Construction. Study for a painting in the Primorsk Picture Gallery. 1921. India ink on paper, 10⅜ × 8⅛" (26.5 × 20.5 cm.). Private collection, Moscow

Above: Spatial Force Construction. Study. 1921. India ink on paper, 10⅜ × 8⅛" (26.5 × 20.5 cm.). Private collection, Moscow

Spatial Force Construction. Study. 1921. India ink on paper, 10⅜ × 8⅛" (26.5 × 20.5 cm.). Private collection, Moscow

Above left: Spatial Force Construction. Study. 1921. India ink on paper, 10⅜ × 8⅛"
(26.5 × 20.5 cm.). Private collection, Moscow

Above: Spatial Force Construction. Study. 1921. India ink on paper, 10⅜ × 8⅛"
(26.5 × 20.5 cm.). Private collection, Moscow

Spatial Force Construction. Study. 1921. India ink on paper, 10⅜ × 8⅛"
(26.5 × 20.5 cm.). Private collection, Moscow

Composition. 1920–21. Oil on plywood, 19⅝ × 16⅛″ (50 × 41 cm.). Albright-Knox Art Gallery, Buffalo, New York

Composition. 1921. Gouache and India ink on paper, 20⅛ × 13¾″ (51 × 35 cm.). Private collection

Spatial Force Construction (Composition). 1921. Oil on plywood,
36⅝ × 24¼″ (93 × 61.5 cm.). Collection of Mr. and Mrs. Roald Dahl.
Contemporary photograph

Composition. 1921. Watercolor and gouache on paper, 13⅞ × 10⅜″
(35.1 × 26.5 cm.). Costakis Collection, Athens

Above left: Spatial Force Construction. 1921. Oil and marble dust on plywood, 28 × 25⅛″ (71 × 63.9 cm.). Costakis Collection, Athens

Above: Spatial Force Construction. 1921. Oil on plywood, 32⅞ × 25⅜″ (83.5 × 64.5 cm.). Tretiakov Gallery. Gift of George Costakis

Spatial Force Construction. 1921. Oil and gouache on cardboard, 13⅝ × 10¾″ (34.5 × 27.2 cm.). Private collection

Above left: Spatial Force Construction. Study. 1921. Gouache and ink on paper, 4¼ × 3¼" (10.8 × 8.2 cm.). Private collection, New York

Above: Spatial Force Construction. Study. 1921. Gouache and ink on paper, 5½ × 3¼" (14 × 8.2 cm.). Private collection, New York

Spatial Force Construction. Study. 1921. Gouache and ink on paper, 4⅛ × 3" (10.4 × 7.5 cm.). Private collection, New York

Spatial Force Construction. Study. 1921(?). Gouache and ink on paper, 4¼×3⅛″ (10.8×7.9 cm.). Private collection, New York   169

Above left: Spatial Force Construction. Study. 1921. Materials unknown, 10⅜ × 8⅛"
(26.5 × 20.5 cm.). Private collection, Moscow

Above: Spatial Force Construction. Study. 1921. India ink on paper, 10⅜ × 8¼"
(26.5 × 20.8 cm.). Private collection, Moscow

Spatial Force Construction. Study. 1921. India ink on paper, 10⅜ × 8⅛"
(26.5 × 20.5 cm.). Private collection, Moscow

*Above: Spatial Force Construction. Study. 1921. India ink on paper, 10⅜ × 8⅛"
(26.5 × 20.5 cm.). Private collection, Moscow*

*Above right: Spatial Force Construction. Study. 1921. India ink on paper, 10⅜ × 8⅛"
(26.5 × 20.5 cm.). Private collection, Moscow*

*Spatial Force Construction. Study. 1921. Colored pencil on paper, 14 × 8½"
(35.5 × 21.5 cm.). Costakis Collection, Athens*

Spatial Force Construction. 1921. Watercolor on paper, 18⅛ × 15¾" (46 × 40 cm.).
Tretiakov Gallery. Gift of George Costakis

Spatial Force Construction. 1921. Gouache and watercolor on paper,
17⅜ × 14⅛" (44 × 36 cm.). Perm State Picture Gallery

Spatial Force Construction. 1921. Oil and marble dust on wood, 44⅜ × 44⅜"
(112.6 × 112.6 cm.). Costakis Collection, Athens

Painterly Architectonics. Study. 1918. Watercolor, gouache, and pencil on paper, 13¾ × 10⅝″ (35 × 27 cm.). Private collection, Moscow

Painterly Architectonics. 1918. Oil on canvas, 24¼ × 17½″ (62.2 × 44.5 cm.). Tretiakov Gallery

Painterly Architectonics. 1918. Gouache on paper, 18⅛ × 9″ (33.5 × 23 cm.). Private collection, Moscow

Painterly Architectonics. 1918. Oil on canvas, dimensions unknown. Private collection

Painterly Architectonics. 1918. Oil on canvas, 27⅞ × 22⅛″ (70.8 × 58.1 cm.). Costakis Collection, Athens

Orange Painterly Architectonics. 1918. Oil on cardboard, 23¼ × 15½″ (59 × 39.3 cm.). Rostov-Yaroslavl Museum-Archive of Architecture and Art, Yaroslavl

Study for *Painterly Construction* (?). 1920. Gouache on cardboard, 7⅜ × 4⅝″
(18.7 × 11.8 cm.). Private collection, Moscow

Painterly Construction. 1920. Oil on canvas, 62⅝ × 49¼″ (159 × 125 cm.). Tretiakov Gallery. Gift of George Costakis (on reverse: *Painterly Architectonics.* 1916–17; page 127)

Composition with a White Half-Moon. 1920. Gouache on cardboard, 13⅛ × 10⅝″ (33.5 × 27 cm.). Tretiakov Gallery. Gift of George Costakis

Composition with a Half-Moon. 1920. Gouache and lacquer on cardboard, 14 × 10¼" (35.5 × 26 cm.). Private collection, Moscow

Spatial Force Construction. Study. 1921. Colored pencil on paper, 10⅞ × 8⅛″ (27.6 × 20.6 cm.). Costakis Collection, Athens

Part of a page with two compositions. 1921. Gouache on paper, 10½ × 9⅞″ (26.8 × 25 cm.). Private collection, Moscow

Spatial Force Construction. 1921. Oil and metal dust on plywood, 27½ × 20¼″ (70 × 51.6 cm.). Tretiakov Gallery

Spatial Force Construction. 1921. Oil on plywood, 28⅜ × 24¾" (72 × 63 cm.).
Tretiakov Gallery

Spatial Force Construction. 1921. Gouache and lacquer on paper, 13⅝ × 10¾"
(34.6 × 27.2 cm.). Private collection, Moscow

Spatial Force Construction. 1921. India ink on paper, 17 × 10⅞″ (43.2 × 27.5 cm.). Costakis Collection, Athens

Spatial Force Construction. 1921. Oil on plywood, 25¼ × 23⅝" (64 × 60 cm.). Tretiakov Gallery. Gift of George Costakis

Cover sketch for the "5 × 5 = 25" exhibition catalogue. 1921. Colored pencil and collage of two-color lithographed paper on cardboard, 8⅛ × 13⅝" (20.6 × 34.5 cm.). Tretiakov Gallery, Manuscript Division

PART TWO: THEORY, TEACHING, THEATER, AND DESIGN

A TIME OF CHANGES

The Revolution brought radical change to the entire spectrum of artistic life. Liubov Sergeevna Popova's artistic fate—despite its unquestionable integrity and clearly visualized core—also underwent radical change, taking on new, heretofore uncharacteristic forms.

Before this, Popova had seen herself as the classic easel painter immersed in problems of craft and artistry, living the concerns and problems of her artistic circle, her milieu. The pressing need to discuss theory and solve creative problems logically had been a constant in Popova's life, as it had been for her colleagues. This was an essential aspect of artistic life, a direct consequence of avant-garde art itself, of its specifics. However, during the pre-Revolutionary years Popova's theorizing about professional problems usually had been limited to spirited discussion and debate, a kind of sociability, and the same had been true for many other artists. Even then, however, Popova had been intrigued by the idea of organizing leftist artists and elaborating a theoretical basis that might become a solid foundation for such an association.

Under the new conditions, the status of private life, of living-room debates, and of informal communication took a sharp plunge. In their place new social forms for artistic life arose, forms unlike anything Popova had ever known before. The private market for artistic production vanished. The Maecenases and collectors scattered. And a new type of artist—the artist as a civil servant[1]—was born. Artists were assigned to staging political and social events; a network of art schools and educational institutions grew up despite the harsh economic circumstances; and finally, research institutes, something hitherto unheard-of, were created to study living artistic practice. All this radically altered the nature of the artist's creative work, his social status, and his consciousness.

Previously accustomed to solitary labor, to a narrow professional circle, the artist was transformed into a participant in collectives large and small, a citizen working within an institution to solve pressing governmental problems. To some degree this was an extension of the old discussions and debates, a discussion of the same issues of craft and the future of creativity, but clearly the new reality put its own stamp on everything, lent everything its unique character.

It was during the post-Revolutionary period that Popova discovered the need to think with pen in hand, to raise and attempt to solve the fundamental problems of creativity—her own and that of the artists of her circle. All her theoretical texts date from this period.

The humanistic education the artist had received and the poetic experiments of her youth, of which her archive gives us some idea, facilitated the task of composing theoretical deliberations in literary form.

Thus, both the artist's altered social position and the very nature of her work—her teaching and research jobs, which were utterly new for her—required new forms of artistic activity: research and theoretical formulations. All this led to the development, or, possibly, the revelation, of qualities of her personality, her nature, and her mind previously not evident.

Apart from external circumstances, personal circumstances also played a role in this process. The years 1918–19 were a vivid, happy, and tragic period in her life: marriage, the birth of a son, and the swift death of her husband, serious illness that nearly took her to her grave as well—all this could not help but take its toll on her character and art. There is a striking dissimilarity between the marvelous, intelligent, confident, and somewhat arrogant young lady Popova appeared to those around her in 1916 (as she appears, for example, in Aleksandr Rodchenko's reminiscences of "The Store" exhibition),[2] and the image we can piece together from contemporaries' stories about the last years of her life. These reminiscences testify to her being a tireless worker, a loyal comrade, a disciplined and competent organizer, an impassioned fighter for the ideas of the new culture, honest and unbending.

Although she was neither an undisputed innovator in her art, as Kazimir Malevich and Vladimir Tatlin were, nor a wholly independent theoretician, Popova was remarkable for the amazing purpose and discipline of her practical and theoretical work. To a great degree these qualities determined her activity at Inkhuk (Institute of Artistic Culture, established in May 1920 in Moscow), and, especially, at Vkhutemas (Higher State Art-Technical Studios, which held its first classes in September of that year).

Setting aside for a time the factual side of Popova's pedagogical, production, and theatrical work, we shall attempt to illuminate the fundamental issues of her theoretical legacy, with one proviso, however: it is not only natural but essential that we examine purely theoretical, pedagogical, and other materials in their entirety, since they were born in a single stream of creative work. The very same artists, carried away by their ideas, united to work on common problems at Inkhuk and to realize their new creative aims in teaching at Vkhutemas, in theatrical presentations, and in production work in factories.

The connection between Inkhuk and Vkhutemas was particularly strong. At moments, art pedagogy and the organization of art education became the focus for research at Inkhuk, whereas the creative life of Vkhutemas, the difficulties and contradictions of the new pedagogy, necessitated framing the theoretical problems of studying contemporary art and its prospects in a new way. Vkhutemas was a true experimental base for Inkhuk's theoretical elaborations.

POPOVA'S CREATIVE EVOLUTION
IN THE EARLY 1920s

Swift development, quick shifts from one stylistic stage to another, from one mood to another, were characteristic of the creative evolution of Russian avant-garde artists in general. Time after time one is amazed by the swiftness of the evolution of these artists' theoretical and creative conceptions during the early 1920s.

Such was the flow of Popova's artistic ideas and creative aims in the years 1920–22. In late 1920 and early 1921 she was fully immersed in the abstract analysis of the mediums, devices, and methods of artistic creation, but late 1921 was marked by the "5 × 5 = 25" exhibition (page 187), where the easel works shown turned out to be meant as future "concrete materialized constructions," and during 1922 she categorically rejected both the system of "formal-analytic" disciplines she had created during that time (1921–22) for Vkhutemas's introductory course as well as the aesthetic criterion in artistic creation, replacing it instead with the principle of expediency, the degree to which a form attains its goal (through the appropriate use of material).

That is, as soon as theoretical positions and creative goals took shape, while they were still in the process of becoming, Popova subjected them to revision and cancellation. After one was rejected, recognition of other positions followed immediately. This feature of her creative activity in the area of theory and artistic concepts was determined, on the one hand, by the highly intensive development of the artistic process, the constant influx of new artistic ideas, of impressions from executions of new plastic conceptions by other artists, and by other creative tendencies that were developing at the same time. On the other hand, the need the artists of Popova's circle felt to reshape their personal goals was stimulated by the participation in the artistic movement of such theoreticians—more sociologically than critically or artistically oriented—as Boris Arvatov and Boris Kushner, whose ideas, although connected at a profound level with the course of artistic evolution, did not evolve out of the inner tendencies of the development of the artistic process at all; rather, they expressed the needs of the general cultural movement. As a result, the logic of sociocultural deliberations was applied in the artists' consciousnesses to the needs of immanent artistic development, outstripping them, changing their scale and goals.

As a corollary to the burning intensity of the intellectual work of the theorizing artists of the avant-garde, artistic ideas and concepts were rejected before they ever had a chance to be worked through or fully digested. But they survived, nevertheless, not only in creative practice but in the deliberations themselves. In any event, that is what we observe in Popova's art. Naturally, this feature injects an internal contradiction into the artist's outwardly logical discussions; however, it also enriches them with nuance and obviates oversimplification.

The speed of these changes greatly complicates dating individual texts by the artist, complicates tying them to a specific point in her swift evolution from the analytic stage of nonobjectiveness to the Constructivist synthesis of "abstract objects" and then on to Production. In sorting Popova's disorderly archive into individual documents, trying to comprehend and date them, and then link them to her artistic practice, one naturally must compare the fragments from the archive with the facts of the artist's creative biography, with the landmarks of her teaching at Vkhutemas and GVYTM (State Higher Theater Workshops), and last but not least, with the work of Inkhuk, the events of its history, and the ideas discussed within its walls.

A FIRST APPEAL TO THE FORMAL METHOD

Popova's first, very laconic, but also highly principled statement was her credo in the catalog for the "Tenth State Exhibition," which was held at the Svomas Free State Art Studios on Rozhdestvenko in January 1919, where she showed her *Painterly Architectonics* of 1918 and her linocuts of 1917. In her text for the catalog (see Appendix I) a declaration of biases for and against (for Cubism, Suprematism, and Futurism, against the representation that had replaced painting)[3] is accompanied by an attempt to enumerate the component parts of the art of painting and to point out how they have been utilized in the latest tendencies in painting. It is, in other words, an attempt to apply the formal method to the analysis of modern painting.

Of course, Popova was not the first to define and differentiate the basic elements of the painting form. In the pre-Revolutionary quasi-scholarly journalism of the artistic avant-garde such concepts as color, line, texture, and pictorial space had already been heard. These writings were clearly analogous to the first works of Viktor Shklovsky and other linguists who applied this method to the analysis of contemporary literature. In addition, one must point out the immaturity and relative randomness of the order constructed. What is important, though, is the artist's desire not only to name the basic elements of the painting form but also to explain their content and role in the building of the whole. For example: "Line, as the contour and trace of the passing plane, participates in and directs the force of the construction."

It is important to emphasize as well that unlike the other participants in the "Tenth State Exhibition" (Varvara Stepanova, Aleksandr Vesnin, Ivan Kliun, Kazimir Malevich, Aleksandr Rodchenko), Popova, despite the extraordinary emotional saturation and vivid imagery of her paintings of 1918 shown at the exhibit, wholly rejected any poetic-romantic interpretational style in conversations about painting, and was quite precise that the craft and creative problems of the artist were the only important and essential ones.

Popova participated actively in the work at Inkhuk from the very beginning. Her name was on the first list of the Council of Masters—an Inkhuk prototype—in December 1919. Popova participated regularly in the sessions of the Section on Monumental Art led by Wassily Kandinsky, within whose framework Inkhuk's work was conducted from May to December of 1920.

For her this was not simply a matter of being in direct creative contact with Kandinsky. For Popova this whole period was profoundly influenced by Kandinsky, as was reflected later in theoretical works of hers seemingly free of his influence. In the initial period, Inkhuk's work followed Kandinsky's program for the complex study of artistic creativity. In the Section on Monumental Art they discussed his paper "Osnovnye elementy zhivopisi. Ikh sushchnost i tsennost (kratkoe izlozhenie teorii zhivopisnoi formy)" (The Fundamental Elements of Painting: Their Nature and Value [a brief exposition of the theory of pictorial form]) and devised responses to Kandinsky's artists' questionnaire, which through a system of questions was supposed to reveal the (semi- and unconscious) psychological foundations of visual activity.[4]

Popova's responses to Kandinsky's questionnaire (see Appendix II; the questionnaire itself has also been preserved in her archive) are very valuable both insofar as they reveal the logic of her own creativity, her internal logic in constructing her painting images, and also from a more general standpoint: as a clarification of characteristic color-shape-image schemes for determining the proportions and degrees of both the individual and the general in her thinking on colors and shapes (pages 210 and 211). In composing his questionnaire on painting, Kandinsky, addressing intuition and experience in analyzing visual impressions among a wide circle of painters, was trying to reveal through nonpictorial artistic means—rather than through symbolic forms that are rooted in the fundamental culture—which impressions are directly connected with the objective laws of perception. He was searching for the "basis of a general law," as he put it in the questionnaire.

In her responses to the questionnaire, as in the catalog to the "Tenth State Exhibition," Popova resisted the temptations of literary-associative expression, resisted delving into any psychology not directly and immediately connected with the painting craft. She consistently set aside the problem of making the abstract visual image concrete, which was such a burning issue for Kandinsky. Her response was terse and concise.

Popova actually responded to only two points on the questionnaire (no. 8 and 9), that is, to the second group of questions on color form: "8. Which color do you feel is most appropriate for the triangle, square, circle? Make drawings and color them. 9. If you feel that any basic color is not appropriate to any geometric shape, try to find a free form rather than geometric

shape that does suit it. Make a drawing and color it. If possible, explain why it is better that way."[5]

Popova's responses most certainly reflected her experience as a painter-analyst. This is especially obvious from the gouache drawing-diagrams she did to support what she felt were logical combinations of color and form, combinations that demonstrated the seemingly mutual attraction between a color and a shape (pages 210 and 211). These diagrams look like typical starting points for many of the artist's compositions, unique compositional blanks for her canvases.

Unfortunately, the Inkhuk archive does not have the responses of other artists to the questionnaire. Possibly they have yet to be discovered in private archives.

Nevertheless, by comparing Popova's opinions with the known opinions of other painters, we can, following Kandinsky's ideas, at least try to reveal just how much she shared with them and how much was unique in her positions. First of all, we have to compare Popova's conclusions with those of Kandinsky himself, which he set forth in his paper on the fundamental elements of painting mentioned above. On the question of the correspondence of colors and shapes, the text, which was found among the Inkhuk papers, says: "The color yellow manifests two tendencies: one toward the viewer and one centrifugal. Both display great impetuosity, bordering on importunity (especially the former) and insanity (especially the latter). This is a color that expresses great wit. Thus its link with the triangle is obvious. . . ."[6]

At this point agreement between Kandinsky and Popova on the correspondence of colors and forms ends. Crucial divergences emerge. Kandinsky felt that "the properties of dark blue and the circle have such a kindred description that their inner connection cannot be subject to question," whereas Popova insisted on the enmity of dark blue toward curved, circular shapes, and so on.

Popova found two allies among her fellow artists in her judgment of the geometric attractions of cold colors. Mikhail Matiushin, who made his comments at another time and in another connection, came to the conclusion that "the cold colors have an attraction for straightness of edges and the formation of angles, if even acute shapes in warm colors lose the acuity of their angles."[7] Less categorically but with the same attention to the essence of the phenomenon, Kuzma Petrov-Vodkin, one of the originators of new art movements in Russia, wrote in one of his remarks that "dark blue in a circle is not the same as dark blue in a triangle."[8]

Malevich maintained the opposite opinion. Proceeding from the experience of his Suprematist compositions, he emphasized the importance of the whole—the scale of the elements, which was chiefly determined by the nature of the color. In his opinion, color never existed yoked to any specific shape, and vice versa.[9]

Comparison of several artistic discussions tells us that the research on the means of artistic expression planned out and begun by Kandinsky at Inkhuk and embraced at the time by many, including Popova, was anything but fruitless. Reliable results, however, can be obtained only by working up a large body of statistical material. Moreover, all positions on visual language are probably not equally universal. And if some of them (for example, the tendency of cold colors to retreat and warm to approach) are perceived identically by all normally seeing people, then others bear a more specific, particular nature.

Popova's attempt to analyze form in modern painting (apparently she was talking about nonobjective painting) in terms of the "concretization of color" is obviously linked with the early stage of study at Inkhuk, which fell within the compass of Kandinsky's ideas. In building a "new form of color," the painter must take into account such new (in Popova's opinion) qualities as the color's "force effect," which reveals in all their basic relations such things as duration, intensity, weight, materiality, and rhythm.[10] The artist also felt a need to reveal and formulate the fundamental problems of form in painting, and to do analytical work on it, during that period in her teaching practice at Vkhutemas as well. This was the beginning of the development of her scholarly-analytical work in the color discipline in the second half of 1921 and early 1922.

INKHUK: THE IDEAS OF OBJECTIVE ANALYSIS

We know that Kandinsky did not succeed in uniting Inkhuk solidly behind his program. The essence of the contradiction between Kandinsky and his opponents came down to two fundamentals. First was the artists' reluctance to devote all the institute's research work to solving the problem of whether or not painting is a "temporal art." The creative practice of these artists, along with their stage of development in the artistic process at the time, was tending to bring nonobjective painting and sculpture together with architecture, which was understood at this time of research and experimentation as abstract construction in space.

The second reason was the method Kandinsky proposed for analyzing creativity, which ranked in first place the problem of association in artistic thinking and the problems of making the themes and imagery of nonobjective compositions concrete, as the questionnaire on painting and his paper on painting's fundamental elements revealed. To the artists this seemed much too subjective and "psychological."[11] One has to think it a conscious decision on Popova's part not to answer those questions.

Kandinsky's rivals on the best methods for studying the laws of artistic form were striving for greater definition and "objectivity" in their conclusions. Popova was, along with Aleksei Babichev, an active figure in the "parallel" Inkhuk.[12] If one keeps in mind Popova's later, by then independent, work on the analysis of painting form in the Primary Division of Vkhutemas in the years 1921–22, her collaboration with Babichev on the curriculum for the Objective Analysis Group[13] can be looked on as a starting point, a broad theoretical platform for further research. At Vkhutemas Popova was already concentrating on the elements themselves of painting form, delving into their individual problems and constructing a system for studying them.

It is no accident that one of Popova's earliest curricula for the color discipline (the program for Discipline No. 1, "Color," coauthored with Vesnin; see Appendix XII) is strikingly similar in its initial positions and the logic of its exposition to the program of the Objective Analysis Group.

Color becomes an independent element in the Vkhutemas program, which examines its qualities: the most spectral colors, the law of complementary colors, tone, weight as a qualitative characteristic in the comparison and relationships of colors; color's intensity or "inner energy"; texture. Color is also examined in connection with such formal elements of painting as the line and the plane. Significant attention is paid to the principles of building pictorial space, the chief one of which was called Construction.

This single word—Construction—serves as a vivid illustration of the extraordinary dynamism of the phenomena we are studying (the theory and practice of the Russian avant-garde) and the artistic views of Popova in particular. It comes up first as an element in the formal analysis of art in her reflections on concepts close to Kandinsky's directives. Gradually the word becomes saturated with the new, more effective meaning not only of painterly but also of vitally practical organization, turning into a term filled with Productivist life-building determination and utterly devoid of any aesthetic intent or ring.

The concept of Construction was key for the wing of Cubo-Futurist painting to which Popova belonged. It was already popular among nonobjective artists in 1920, when Popova and Vesnin's studio produced the Vkhutemas program. Characteristically, Kandinsky was making wide use of the concept at the time. In an article published in early 1920 setting forth his organizational principles for the planned Museum of Artistic Culture, Kandinsky proposed gathering in the museum "experiments in formal construction according to the principle of comparison: color and the drawing plane . . . the relationship between the plane and volume," and so forth.[14]

Constructiveness was beguiling, intriguing; it seemed like the essential, determining quality of the new art. Participants in the artistic process, however, were dismayed by the ease with which the concept of constructiveness spread from architectural and objective forms to the area of painting.

A famous discussion—"Analiz poniatii konstruktsii i kompozitsii i moment ikh razgranicheniia" (An Analysis of the Concepts of Construction and Composition: Aspects of Their Boundaries)—proved the most important event in Inkhuk's work of 1921. Gradually the discussion clarified artists' ideas about the contemporary status of art as absolutely new and specific to its era, an era when art was acquiring not only new forms but also new goals and functions. Late that year this idea found a formula: "from representation to construction." Preparations were underway at Inkhuk for a collection of essays and other materials elaborating on this slogan.

Popova took active part in the debate. Like other artists, she also presented, apart from actual speeches, graphic works from several done previously that provided a schematic-visual demonstration of her ideas about the essence of construction and composition.

In the artist's archive there are drafts of her paper "O konstruktsii novoi formy predmetnoi i bespredmetnoi" (On the Construction of New Objective and Nonobjective Forms; Appendix III), clearly a response to the topic under discussion. Absolutizing and idealizing the principle of Construction as the essence and specific nature of modern art was characteristic at that moment for all participants in the Inkhuk discussion, Popova included.[15]

I will not dwell right now on the details of Popova's understanding of the principle of constructiveness as expressed in the paper, which takes the artist's activity beyond the boundaries of art and into life itself; that is, it manifests a life-creating nature. I will only underscore the tight interlacing, the merging of strictly artistic, professional-formal issues with issues of outlook and attitude. Removal and destruction for the sake of future building in art represented a direct parallel to the destruction and building going on in real life. The pathos of an organization wrested from social reality itself, gripped by the fever of organization, reorganization, and self-organization, became a principle and an ideal uniting art and life.

Popova's notes are vivid testimony to the attitude of the person and artist. She wrote: "We are breaking with the past because we do not believe it anymore, because its hypotheses are unacceptable. We ourselves are creating them anew, our own hypotheses . . . and on the basis of them alone, on our own invention, can we build our new life and new worldview"[16] (see page 205 and Appendix III).

Popova's notes reflect the complicated process of elaborating this new worldview, or rather its application to creativity and the understanding of creativity. Life and its problems, tasks, and nature were touching and entering the artist's professional consciousness and self-appraisal. For Popova this process was intense and vivid.

OBJECTIVE AND NONOBJECTIVE: THE MODERN STYLE?

A large part of the surviving Popova archive consists of comments, drafts, and relatively complete summaries that cluster around one theme—modern painting, the modern style in art (Appendixes IV–VII).

The occasion for these deliberations and notes on this theme was more than likely Popova's speech on painting, which had been under discussion at Inkhuk as far back as August 18, 1920, as part of the agenda for a meeting of the Section on Monumental Art.[17] Due to conflicts within Inkhuk the speech was not given. Beginning in late November, Popova was working in the newly formed Section of Individual Arts, or the Objective Analysis Group, in which, as has already been mentioned, the artist took active part in organizing and determining goals and methods. Thinking about the direction of the group's scholarly work forced Popova to write down her analysis of the problems of modern art. Moreover, she may have resorted to writing her thoughts on this theme during the discussion of the actual problems of art ("an analysis of the elements and laws of their organization according to works of art") at the meetings of the group at the Museum of Modern Western Painting. It is known that during December 1920 six sessions of the group "were devoted to discovering art's fundamental and dominant elements and the nature of their organization in three modern art movements: Impressionism (with the example of Claude Monet); Pointillism (the works of Paul Signac), and the works of Henri Matisse."

Yet another occasion for bringing into the system her ideas about the specifics of modern art, its place in historical evolution, and its connections with reality was her work in organizing the Museum of Artistic Culture and developing a scholarly rationale for the Department of Contemporary Russian Painting (Appendix IV)—work that was going on inside Inkhuk during 1921.[18] For Popova the question of the specific nature of modern painting grew into the problem of the new style of modern art, its sources and its formation. The criterion by which Popova defined whether or not artistic phenomena pertained to the new style was not a work's formal, outward marks but its method of creation. The true basis, in her view, for a style's appearance were the specifics of the era's worldview and perception.

The essence of the new style, according to Popova, was the "abstraction of the artistic form from the form visible in reality." She saw the development of style in the growth of this abstraction of the artistic form, the liberation of the artistic task from any motivations. "The degree of abstraction," she wrote, "indicates the stage in the process of the style's formation, although the basic characteristic 'forms' began to become clarified at the very first step of distortion—historically, we can recognize the new style in Cézanne!"[19] (see Appendix V).

Thus, in Popova's deliberations, the methodological pivot for composing the new style of modern art becomes a strictly *formal* creative principle, in other words, a formal method. She discovers its beginning all the way back in Impressionism.

In her conception, all the stages modern art passed through were merely steps leading to a logical culmination, the complete triumph of the new principle, which she linked with the concept of objectivism as a creative movement wholly realizing the formal-analytic approach to art. The term is undoubtedly connected with the name of the Inkhuk Objective Analysis Group. Objectivism had no development as a creative movement, having merged quickly with the tendencies of the then-embryonic Constructivism. Popova wrote:

In the latest movement [meaning objectivism] a new demolition is taking place, on an entirely new plane: the goal is not achievement in one of the areas of elements; rather, once again the whole building consciousness in its entirety has shifted. From the representation of the object to its concrete, material organization. What is happening with the whole object is also happening with all its separate parts or elements. . . . They have broken away from their centuries-old applied meaning right through to significant formal painterly relations and made themselves as such a part of the construction of the painting organism.[20]

Let us note briefly some characteristic points in Popova's discourse on style. First of all, as is already clear from before, she was seeing the new style not only in the form of nonobjective art but also in the form of objective painting (witness her glimpsing its beginning in Impressionism). However, she was distinctly aware as well of just how unique the newest nonobjective art was, arising, as it had, naturally out of the history of art, from a series of styles that had sprung up with abstraction (here Popova refers to and cites Wilhelm Worringer, the early twentieth-century aesthetic theorist), a logical step in the development of this principle.

She wrote: "Nonetheless, never before have we encountered any such law necessitating construction of such an entirely new approach, such a new attitude toward the visible world, especially one so compatible with the new historical norm and consciously geometric construction."[21] Two theses are important here: the theme of the historical norm and the motif of the conscious geometrism of the new style.

Popova directly compared the abruptness of the demolition in the development of the artistic process with the radicalness and irrevocability of the revolutionary break that had come about in the life of society and that the artists of the Russian avant-garde had experienced so sharply. "Just as a break occurred in all areas of practical and theoretical life, catastrophes have come about after which the forms and images of lives past were no longer possible," she wrote, "so a break or overthrow occurred in the sphere of artistic style."[22]

Popova's theoretical remarks convey the author's emotional state and trials just as immediately as her mature paintings do. Reading into these texts, we realize how tightly art and reality were interwoven in the artist's perception, how indissoluble the problems of craft and the attitude toward the life of society were in her consciousness. We have not found in Popova's archive any evidence of a specific, conscious attitude toward concrete political slogans or a clear appraisal of the events that had come about, but the emotional shadings of her perception are perfectly clear. She was rocked by the immensity of the changes that had gone on in front of her, their elemental sweep and momentum. For her it was clear: the life of every person had changed radically and irrevocably. In all spheres of social life, science, and technology, she saw a precise boundary between "before" and "after." That is why the break in art was so abrupt. And why it expressed itself in strong, expressive forms. Probably the chief mark of the new style that had coalesced in art, according to Popova, was this power, which expressed the intense upheaval of the day.

For Popova, several practical issues of modern art were bound up with the problem of style, and she was quite conscious of these connections, making them the theses of her discourse: objective and nonobjective, analysis and synthesis, "the problem of the characteristics of the form in which the modern style is expressed."

Relying on her creative practice, and, moreover, on the incomparable intensity of the development of the artistic process, Popova took the solution of each of these questions outside the discussion of the painting form she had sketched out in late 1920 and early 1921. The course of her thought, which reflected the movement of art, gradually and relentlessly led her to the principles of life-building.

For Popova it was clear that nonobjective form was a logical culmination of the process of freeing artistic (form-building) principles from representation. She recognized and agonized over the moment of liberation of the creative principle that had created the painting form independently and offered mankind an ideal plan for constructing the world. Contemplating the problems of artistic-investigative work and the state of art, she wrote in her notebooks: "The goal . . . is the theoretical foundation and practical laboratory elaboration of artists' activity, which at the present moment is focused on creating new objects for the world."[23] "In nonobjectiveness, which is the natural conclusion of free reliance on the painterly elements of the object," she continued, "we see all the means placed in the hands of the subject, and he is free."[24]

By force of the above-noted speed of movement of artistic ideas characteristic for Popova and her colleagues, however, the victory and rapture of this *conscious* freedom of creation without canons or prototypes were quickly replaced by doubts, questions about the direction of further development, and a conviction that this stage of art was transient, temporal in nature.

It is important to emphasize that all of these vacillations and this feeling of having exhausted this path emerged before the ideas of Productivism had been planted and had begun to develop actively among the Inkhuk avant-gardists. These ideas had come to rest on the ready soil of "intrinsically artistic," abstract Constructivism. Thus it was with highly abstract slogans — "Struggle Against the Artistic Culture of the Past" and "Agitate for a New Worldview" — that the most inherently radical group of Constructivists, with whose members Popova became increasingly close in her views in the years 1921–24, took its first steps at Inkhuk in early 1921.

In articles of recent years the following words of Popova have been cited several times: "I don't think that nonobjective form is the final form: it is the revolutionary condition of form. We must reject objectiveness and the old conditions of representation connected with it altogether, we must feel absolutely free from all that was created before in order to listen closely to burgeoning necessity and then start to look differently on the objective form, which will emerge from this work not only transformed but totally different in general."[25]

This statement seems to demonstrate not only and not so much Popova's critical look at the nonobjective phase in the development of her art before her entry into the Productivist period, as it does the *very nature* of the consciousness and experience of the artistic movement — a feverish glance into the future, a desire to forestall reality with an idea.[26] Thus, one of Popova's statements is entitled: "And Now? What Next?" (Appendix VII).

Popova linked the solution of artistic problems indissolubly with the period's revolutionary suffering, which permeated and determined all aspects of life. Her responses at first were rather vague and indeterminate, but their emotional base was unmistakable: " 'Revolution' is always 'revolution' . . . always onward, more, even if it is sad and hard to part with the immense labor of one's achievements — but, after all, once they are achieved, what more can you do with them? Of course onward, to new struggle, new labor, but always with the revolutionary banner in the front rows of the human assault"[27] (see Appendix VII).

Gradually the direction of the path became clear to Popova and those of like mind: *through the organization* of artistic form, through the *construction* of works of art — to the organization of life itself, to the construction of its concrete environment. But this realization was achieved only very slowly and gradually, through repeated deliberations on the *nature* of the artistic experience acquired, on the *specifics* of modern art.

The modern style, the modern form, in Popova's opinion, was still far from perfect or complete. Style would reach its culmination through the synthesis of the disparate elements of

artistic form discovered by Cézanne and the Cubists, Futurists, Simultaneists, Orphists. "Of course, these are all still elements of the new understanding of form," wrote Popova; "the synthesis lies ahead, the whole joyous work lies ahead, the hardest part has been done."[28] She felt that the basis for the desired synthesis, the most important step of principle on the path to it, was the shift to nonobjectivity accomplished by Russian artists: "another element has been introduced into the construction of the new form — the element of abstraction or nonobjectiveness. This may in fact be the most important."[29]

In these deliberations of Popova, style does not seem to possess any precise visible characteristics; it emerges more as a creative method. However, by concentrating on works that most fully embody her conception, her version of the modern style, the artist attempted to designate as well its marks, its characteristic features. Thus her notes bring up the principle of rationality, the theme of the mathematical regulation of modern artistic form, the problem of geometrism as a specific form of the modern worldview and picture.

Comparing the art of the past and the present, Popova wrote: "There the arbitrary organization of form is everywhere; here there is an inner law and necessity."[30] And further: "One might say, continuing Lipps's thought about the geometric line (that it is not found in nature), that abstract line and form are forces of consciousness, whereas natural forms are a mechanical force."

In this regard Popova enthusiastically recalled that the newest theoreticians of art, such as Alois Riegl, Theodor Lipps, and Worringer, considered mathematics one of the highest art forms and even quoted the Romantic Novalis on how "pure mathematics is religion" and "the life of the gods is mathematics."[31] There is no need to repeat here how widely and vividly the theme of rationalism and the idealization of geometric form was represented among the masters of the Russian avant-garde, especially in the creative and theoretical conceptions of Malevich, El Lissitzky, and their followers.

Thus we see that, right on the heels of the special expressiveness, the vividly felt "tension" of modern artistic form, Popova turned to the rationality of that form, its logical structuring and thorough structural development in the work. For Popova, the "nature of the arrangement of intensity" in modern art was determined by its rational regulation.

"FROM REPRESENTATION TO CONSTRUCTION"

Here we shall move into the sphere of constructing and relevant debates: first to constructing the pictorial plane, then the abstract object — the ideal model for imagined things and structures — and beyond, to real constructing for life. In Popova's view, the most important stage on the theoretical level was the first: "The leading factor in our creative consciousness in this era of great organizations is the replacement of the art of painting, of representation, by the principle of organization or *construction*."[32] Popova saw the meaning and result of the artistic evolution of the recent decades in the development of construction, in its liberation from any attendant representation.

This series of discussions on constructiveness echoes the same logic we saw in the examination of painting elements and their liberation from representation. Only now constructiveness was harnessed to the theme of "distortion," "transformation," abstraction. That is, the same phenomena were being described but in different terms. Popova pointed out that, in the history of art, devices of distortion (Russian and Byzantine painting, the art of primitive peoples, and so on) have always been used, but only the newest art used distortion and transformation "for the sake of painterly or sculptural construction—that is the revelation of our artistic revolution," she concluded[33] (see Appendix VII).

The construction of a new form was gradually liberated in Popova's theoretical deliberations from the traditional forms of illustration in pictures and from the very principle of easel painting, with its characteristic system of criteria and associations, echoing the logic of an analogous emancipatión in art itself.

The art Popova was contemplating, completely cut off from representation, directly addressed the problem of an ideal "organization" for the world. Such was the general sense of the artist's discourses in late 1921—the period of the "5 × 5 = 25" exhibition, when she began her work at the State Higher Theater Workshops (GVYTM) and was starting to consolidate the innovative pedagogy of the Basic Department. This transitional moment in Popova's creative development, in the evolution of her theoretical views, was extremely interesting and productive on many fronts and, like so much else, was never fully digested, either by the artist herself or by those around her.

In dealing with the materials from this stage we must carefully delineate one clear-cut theme: art and life. On the one hand, these two principles are distinct and autonomous. Art appeals to and shapes consciousness. Popova still was not ready to interfere in the real planning of her objective environment—life had to grasp the new form by becoming aware of the new form. She wrote in a notebook: "The past is for history. The present and future are for the organization of life, the organization of consciousness, which is will and the building imperative"[34] (see pages 204–5). On the other hand, Popova was becoming increasingly convinced that by rejecting representation the plastic arts were coming perilously close to life, to reality, to practice; art was losing its ideal character and taking on the qualities of a thing. Her notes reflect this as follows: "Through a transformed and abstracted reality the artist has freed himself

from all the conditions of the worldview that has existed up until this moment. The principle of constructiveness renders a work not a means but an end in itself; it objectifies it, thereby making it really existing, necessary, and therefore *utilitarian*"[35] (see Appendix III).

Both the works themselves—the "objects"—and their idea equivalent in the artist's consciousness were tottering on the brink: art on the brink of reality, representation on the brink of the thing, the aesthetic on the brink of the utilitarian. Such were the works exhibited in "5 × 5 = 25." Their impetus was still purely investigative. They were still mere "representations" of constructions.

A year later, in December 1922, in an explanation for the Museum of Artistic Culture of her works of the preceding years (Appendix VIII), Popova saw clearly the direction and purport of her artistic evolution: "From an analysis of the volume and space of objects (Cubism) to the *organization of the elements*, not as means of representation but as integral constructions (whether color-planar, volumetric-spatial, or other material constructions)."[37]

By late 1922 Popova had already switched over completely to life-building. She felt drawn not so much to the idea of the organization of consciousness through art but to that of the creation of the life environment through the building of utilitarian things. She also appraised her works of former years from these new positions: "The significance of each of these elements (line, plane, volume, color, material) of the means of representation is made the concrete work of the given material, determining the function of the thing itself (be it utilitarian or abstract)"[38] (Appendix VIII; illustrated on page 358).

It is important to note that for Popova the creation of constructive and wholly utilitarian objects amounted to neither prosaic pragmatism nor technicistic construction. For her, objective creation was replete with lofty ideological (or, perhaps, figurative) significance. Besides "hands-on mechanically visible work, construction involves ideological work," Popova wrote, "inasmuch as, in its forms, it is the reflection of its time, and by baring the principle of organization, it replaces this principle with criteria of an aesthetic order"[39] (Appendix VIII).

The next step was the fundamental rejection of easel art ("abstract constructions") for work "within the context of concrete production."[40]

Here let us emphasize once again two points that are essential for understanding the evolution of Popova's art and artistic views and that may also have been characteristic of an entire circle of artists.

First, individual aesthetic adjustments were never fully digested, fully exhausted, so they continued to live on in the artist's consciousness. Herein lies the potential significance of stages of artistic evolution "completed" so quickly, so hastily.

Thus, having firmly rejected by late 1921 the creation of

(purely artistic) abstract constructions, Popova a year later clearly recognized the figurative significance and profound artistic meaning of these things, of this incomplete stage of artistic development.

Second, her verbal rejection, her idealized, mental resolution of problems was at times at extreme variance with her creative practice, forestalling it in any case and often proving a source of creative contradiction and inner conflict. Thus, Popova overcame her doubts as to the moral possibility of a Constructivist working for the theater and did her first production at Vsevolod Meierkhold's theater. Her creative work as a whole was encountering these kinds of problems at the very time when she was just starting to embrace the positions of Productivism.

In December 1921, fresh from the famous Inkhuk meeting of November 24, at which easel painting was anathematized, Popova wrote: "It is perfectly obvious that the revolution that has occurred in the sphere of artistic goals, issues, means, and forms . . . has clearly posed for us the question of the superfluousness of representational art as such, of its absolute irrelevance today, given the new social conditions, even as an object of production and not just as a product of psychometaphysical necessity"[41] (see Appendix XIV).

This understanding of the meaning and issues of art and the demands of the times could mean just one thing for someone with Popova's steady and decisive nature: the rejection of easel art. And indeed, after the "5 × 5 = 25" exhibition she no longer exhibited easel works, and in the posthumous exhibition there were no such works dated after 1921. We know that Popova did not cease her easel painting altogether, but both for the artist herself and for her milieu it was no longer a fact of the social function of art. It lingered on solely as the artist's absolutely personal affair, as a private creative laboratory. In the beginning, there were few forms for the social existence of art that satisfied the principles of Productivism. During that period Popova's art, like that of many of her colleagues, was gripped in the strange vise of a voluntary taboo, in a state of profound contradiction between the incompleteness of certain creative ideas, the extraordinary incandescence of certain creative potentials, and the artificially imposed limits of ideo-aesthetic dogmas. These were the circumstances surrounding Liubov Popova's teaching and theater work during the years 1922–23. It is entirely possible that the very complexity of the situation described determined the energy and brilliance with which she realized these aspects of her art.

VKHUTEMAS: "THE ESSENCE OF THE DISCIPLINES"

It was very lucky for Vkhutemas that the best artists of the time worked within its walls. Not that there could be any question of unanimous agreement among them all on the new school's goals and tasks, or of a peaceful, undisputed process for devising new methods of art pedagogy. On the contrary, the history of Vkhutemas, of its formation and development, is one of clashes, conflicts, disputes, and contradictions. Nevertheless, nearly every major artist made a contribution to its history, made his or her artistic and pedagogical achievements the property of others.

Since we cannot examine the history of Vkhutemas and the development of its pedagogical system in their entirety here, we will select those aspects with which Popova's work was directly connected, stressing right off that these aspects, these stages in the school's history, were in fact crucial.

Liubov Popova was one of the most active organizers of the school-wide introductory course, which was called the Basic Department and was wholly structured around the methods of formal-analytic pedagogy. This pedagogy, according to its creators, was intended to serve as a unitary, universal method of art education for all the various spatial arts practiced inside the institute's four walls: from architects to draftsmen, from designers to easel painters. It was supposed to ensure the creative ties of artists and the unity of artistic culture. As the Basic Department's organizers, including Popova, evolved creatively from formal experiment in easel art to Production Art, the goals and scale of the pedagogical methods they had created changed as well.

Popova's name is usually linked with the establishment of design education for Vkhutemas, which replaced the traditional applied art of the Stroganov Art School. This artistic-pedagogical trend, part and parcel of the ideas of production art, was vividly colored by stylistic Constructivism; more precisely, it was itself an active creative principle in the formation of the artistic methods and devices of Constructivism.

Both these problems of Vkhutemas's pedagogical theory and practice were closely linked with the investigations going on at Inkhuk, the evolution of its ideas, its history.

In February 1922, when Rodchenko became director of the Basic Department,[42] intensive work began on shaping the many studios, which shared little in the way of aims or methods, into a well-organized course of study. This process may already have been started as early as late 1921. Judging from Popova's archive, the bulk of the work fell to her. After analyzing her colleague's programs,[43] Popova tried to devise a system of academic disciplines based on the formal-analytic method and covering as much as possible the professional problems of painting.

It is characteristic that her pedagogical conception wholly excluded representation as an issue. Nature was immediately (programmatically) conceived of as a combination of nonobjective elements. We know that both Rodchenko and Popova—and other artists as well—went the traditional route for art education: they assigned academic still lifes. But for these nonobjectivist pedagogues the very nature of these still lifes—which combined along with more or less ordinary things (glass vials, porcelain electric insulators, a rolled-up piece of paper, and so forth) nontraditional objects (painted pieces of plywood, metal, or paper) perceived not as things but as abstract color and texture planes—was steadily moving away from natural, objective perception to the abstract construction of the painting surface.

In creating her formal pedagogy, Popova did not reject altogether the necessity for artists to study the skills and methods of representation. She simply obviated the problem for herself with a reference to how students should learn "correct drawing" at an earlier stage; at the Painting Faculty they would be studying painting as a "special art." The artist wrote her rationale: "Apprentices from the Probationary-Preparatory Department will enter the Basic Department having already mastered elementary accomplishments in painting, such as: the ability to use paints and other painting materials, the ability to see nature and draw it correctly or in the pictorial forms in which the eye perceives it."[44]

The fact that Popova accorded the cardinal problem of representational art only negligible attention speaks to her total preoccupation with the new analytical tasks and new possibilities opening up for her in nonobjective art. It was this new knowledge, the experience of modern painting, that Popova was eager to transmit to the students: "Participants in the Basic Department must train their chief attention on the study of the fundamental elements of painting in their pure and differentiated form."[45]

Popova mapped out a plan for "study of the elements of painting" for the entire First Department that consisted of four cycles (disciplines). Her archive demonstrates how doggedly she worked to transform the very personal and loose methodological aims of a few pedagogues into a streamlined, logical program of study for the profession of painter, albeit painter of a particular background. In a text written in the fall of 1921 and entitled "Sushchnost distsiplin" (The Essence of the Disciplines; Appendix XIII), Popova unfolded the content of each of the program's four cycles. We can easily recognize her logic in the discussion of the evolution of her own painting and the entire movement from passively conveying nature to Cubism and post-Cubist analysis. The problems of color as such play a secondary role in this discussion.

First of all she postulated the very principle of the purely formal resolution of the painting task: "Discipline no. 1 establishes the painterly conception of the object. . . . The emotions emanating from the object are purely formal."[46] It is important to emphasize that although the object was present in these discussions, as it was in the still-life arrangements at the academic studio, the attitude worked out toward it was not direct and sensual but logical and conceptual. "What is depicted is not the impression of the object but its essence, the essence of its color, volume, characteristic construction, materialness; everything incidental to, or uncharacteristic of, the given painterly image of the object is omitted."[47]

The rationality we see in the analysis of objective (from nature) impressions naturally merges in Popova's discussions of pedagogical requirements with the rationality of painting construction itself. The premeditated coincidence in Impressionist compositions is categorically rejected. At the base of her work on the pedagogical system, for which "The Essence of the Disciplines" served as a study, Popova put the logic of Post-Impressionist development, from the experience of Cézanne to the modern nonobjectivists, making it the logical crux of the system. In doing so she relied on her own conception of the "modern" style discussed earlier.

It is characteristic that although she did have a theoretical understanding of Impressionism's historical significance for the development of the "new style," in her teaching practice Popova went to great lengths to remove from Impressionist representativeness the formal (color) problem inherent to that method.

In composing a program for the study of painting at his studio at the Second Free State Studios in 1919, Malevich had proposed the same logical path: from Cézanne, through Cubism and Futurism, to Suprematism as his own version of modern nonobjective art.[48] These artists, like many other masters of other persuasions, Petrov-Vodkin, for example, categorically excluded their own beginnings—Impressionism—from their educational programs.

It is clear, therefore, that the system of disciplines for the Basic Department of the Painting Faculty, composed in the course of Popova's methodological work of late 1921 and early 1922, combined her own pedagogical conception, based on the logic of development of the modern style, with the pedagogical issues posed by other artists involved in the department. This system was founded on the formal-analytic method, which by that time had already been very thoroughly worked out at Inkhuk.

Several sporadic attempts had been made to apply this method to art education in the practice of the preceding years, and there was lively interest at Inkhuk in Vkhutemas affairs. The inculcation in the Basic Department of the formal-analytic method, on which Inkhuk's research was founded, attracted especial attention. In this connection, Popova was asked to report on the new method of study for Inkhuk's Pedagogical Section (see Appendixes XV and XVI). In her draft, Popova examined the history of art education since the time of the Renaissance masters. She allotted special attention to the Paris académies, where the masters' individual methods (Henri Matisse, Maurice Denis, Antoine Bourdelle, Fernand Léger, Jean Metzinger) flourished. She had a good notion of the Paris schools both from her own study experience and from the work of her friends. It was in Cubists' *académies* that she had discovered the principle of the new method of teaching, which she extracted directly from the new method of artistic creation, in which "understanding representation takes the place of presenting it."[49]

However, Popova and her colleagues at Vkhutemas in the 1920s were not at all pleased with the individualistic tendencies of study they had found in the pedagogical directives of the Paris artists. They were not at all pleased that these masters had led their students, as Popova noted, "down their own little road, their own branch, rather than down the channel of history."[50] Popova saw the task of Vkhutemas and Inkhuk in the scientific elaboration of unified programs for teaching formal problems. These artists saw the formal tasks and principles themselves as utterly objective and of absolutely universal significance.

In late 1921 they began putting together a unified course for the Basic Department of the Painting Faculty, converting the separate studios into its stages, its subdivisions. That is, they started to build art education from scratch (as had once been done in the academic system), on unitary bases shared by the entire teaching collective, on the basis of the "objective" method about which so much had been said during the organization of Vkhutemas in the summer of 1920 and which had proved rather difficult to put into practice after Svomas's essentially opposite establishment on individual methods.

What is important, though, is that the Basic Department of Vkhutemas did not by any means rest with the creation of a system for the painting disciplines. The system for studying painting that Popova sketched out in late 1921 had not yet been put into practice when the problem arose of creating a unitary system of preparatory disciplines for teaching all the visual arts.

Bringing the idea of a unitary preparatory course for all disciplines to life was helped somewhat by the fact that the architectural studios of Nikolai Ladovsky, Vladimir Krinsky, and Nikolai Dokuchaev (the so-called OBMAS, or Joint Studios of the Left), which worked at Vkhutemas, had been given their own department in the fall of 1921 and had acquired a certain independence from the Architecture Faculty, so that there was an opportunity to spread Ladovsky's architectural preparatory course to the other faculties.[51] Since then the architect-teachers had rightly been a constant presence at the meetings of the Basic Department at which this work was actually carried out. Creative ties and shared artistic-educational goals also attracted the sculptor Anton Lavinsky to this work.[52] As before, Popova was among the most enterprising and active; she fulfilled the duties of secretary for the department, and her archive has preserved for us this page in Vkhutemas history.

A group of Constructivists at Aleksandr Rodchenko's studio. 1924. *Left to right:* Zakhar Bykov, Anton Lavinsky, Varvara Stepanova (in the foreground), Aleksandr Vesnin, Rodchenko's mother (against the curtain), Liubov Popova, N. Sobolyev. Photograph by Rodchenko

Popova (wearing a white pompon on her hat), Aleksandr Vesnin at her right, with their Vkhutemas students. 1922

Study for a Composition. 1921. Colored pencil on paper, 67⅜ × 57⅛″ (171 × 145 cm.).
Tretiakov Gallery, Manuscript Division

Fragment of a manuscript by L. Popova. Private collection, Moscow (see Appendix III)

О новой Организации

Мы должны сознательно гордиться тем, что живем в эту новую Великую Эпоху Великих Организаций.

Ни один исторический момент не повторим.

Прошлое для истории. Настоящее и Будущее для организации Жизни, для организации сознания, которое и есть воля и необходимость созидающая.

Мы порываем с прошлым потому-что не верим ему больше, потому-что не привлекаем его гипотезы. Мы создаем их сами вновь, роим собственные гипотезы, и только на них, как на новом изобретении, и можем ли строить нашу новую Жизнь и новое миропонимание.

Study for a Composition. 1921. Colored pencil on paper, 10⅜ × 8⅛″ (26.5 × 20.5 cm.). Private collection, Moscow

Study for a Composition. 1921. Pencil and colored pencil on paper, 10⅜ × 8⅛″ (26.5 × 20.5 cm.). Private collection, Moscow

Study for the cover of the "5×5 = 25" exhibition catalogue. 1921. Pencil on paper,
5⅛ × 3⅛" (13 × 8 cm.). Private collection, Moscow

32

Study for a Composition. 1921. Colored pencil on paper, 10⅜ × 8⅛″ (26.5 × 20.5 cm.). Private collection, Moscow

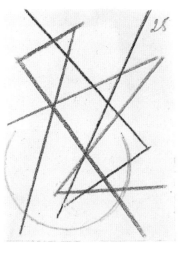

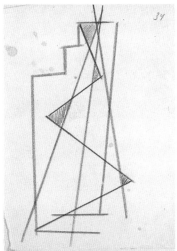

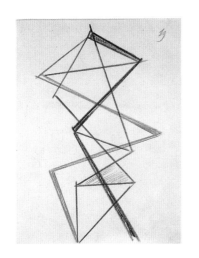

Four Studies for a Composition. 1921. Colored pencil on paper, 10⅜ × 8⅛" (26.5 × 20.5 cm.). Private collection, Moscow

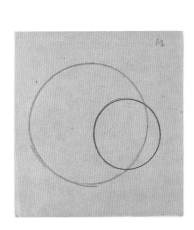

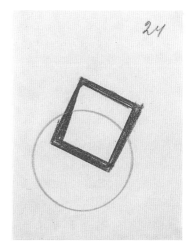

Above: Study for a Composition. 1921. Colored pencil on paper, 7⅜ × 7" (18.7 × 17.7 cm.). Private collection, Moscow

Drawing accompanying Popova's response to Kandinsky's questionnaire on color. 1920. Gouache on paper, 6⅞ × 16¾" (17.5 × 42.5 cm.). Tretiakov Gallery, Manuscript Division (see Appendix II)

Drawing accompanying Popova's response to Kandinsky's questionnaire on color. 1920. Gouache on gray cardboard, 7½ × 10⅝" (19 × 27 cm.). Tretiakov Gallery, Manuscript Division

Drawing accompanying Popova's response to Kandinsky's questionnaire on color. 1920. Gouache on paper, 6⅞ × 16¾" (17.5 × 42.5 cm.). Tretiakov Gallery, Manuscript Division

Drawing accompanying Popova's response to Kandinsky's questionnaire on color. 1920. India ink on paper, 8½ × 10⅝" (21.5 × 27 cm.). Tretiakov Gallery, Manuscript Division

VKHUTEMAS: "DISCIPLINE NO. 1—COLOR"

By the spring of 1922 a fundamental break had taken place in the work of the Basic Department: having functioned first as the preparatory course for the Painting Faculty, it now became the general preparatory course for the entire complex system of easel and production arts taught at Vkhutemas. With this purpose in mind, the program for the color discipline, which Popova had written together with Aleksandr Vesnin, was reworked.

Teaching practice as such had changed. Now less attention was paid to work from nature, even in the special "nonobjective" still lifes of which we spoke earlier. Abstract construction on a specific compositional "theme" ("on the cross," "on the diagonal," "on the circle," and so forth) was now most important. However, organization from nature was not eliminated altogether, although it was no longer conceived exclusively within the confines of the painting surface (the plane of the canvas, plywood, cardboard). Apart from these planar variations, the "still life" was resolved volumetrically as well. Color as a universal element of artistic creativity had become the point of these painterly-textural, planar-volumetric exercises in Popova and Vesnin's course. Popova formulated this new attitude toward the teaching issue in her "Programma distsipliny tsveta Osnovnogo otdeleniia" (Program for the Color Discipline in the Basic Department): "Color is a constructive element in the structure of every consciously created thing regardless of which sphere of material culture the given thing belongs to, be it painting, architecture, sculpture, graphics, ceramics, textiles, woodworking, or metalworking. The meaning of color and its properties are special in each type of production."[53]

For the course's directors (as before, Vesnin headed up a studio together with Popova), what was important now was not only the material qualities of the coloring medium that colored the canvas or other support but the chromatic qualities of the materials, and not as an object for painterly interpretation but as a constructive material for creation. This is how, with the development of both fundamental hypostases, the problems of color discipline were formulated. The problem of "color volume and color space on the plane" was approached as a painting problem. Next came "the comparison of color materials on the plane and in space," that is, "the selection of materials" on the plane was supplemented by work associated more with nonobjective sculpture than with painting. In posing these problems Popova and Vesnin did not merely dissect analytically the work of the new type of artist experimenting with coloring medium and real coloring material or work out separately the methods for constructing on the plane and in space. The themes of volume and space permeated all the tasks as individual problems: "volume on the plane," "space on the plane," "volume in real space." They indicated the initial compositional "mate-

rials" of such a construction as well: "volumetric elements: prisms, cones, cylinders." Similar tasks were proposed for spatial objects out of diverse materials: wood, glass, black lacquer, porcelain, bronze, and so on.

What, then, did Popova and Vesnin's preparatory art course actually involve that was fundamentally new? Their "color discipline"? First of all, they consistently brought in the experience of contemporary art, its method, the lessons of its evolution. Painting ceased to be conceived of as the traditional work in paints on canvas. Textural innovations invaded painting, which Popova taught: different materials, their combination on a colorful painting surface. In teaching, painting was now breaking away from nature. In many cases the teacher himself was already completely free from the formal-analytic problems related to representation.

Moreover, in this art pedagogy we observe something characteristic of this era, when painting was expanding from the plane into space, having passed through an intermediate stage of compositions like Tatlin's three-dimensional "counterreliefs."

A painting innovator who herself had traversed all the basic paths of contemporary painting, Popova boldly brought material from the artistic experiment into her teaching. That is, she tried to devise an art education that would respond to the demands and trends of artistic development. It is another matter that the Soviet Union's artistic process was not destined to continue for long in this direction. By 1922 a turn toward realism could be noted in the artistic life of the country. The problem of artistic traditions had been revived once again; pedagogy once again faced the problem of nature.

All these circumstances impeded a thorough appraisal of Popova's innovative pedagogy in the area of easel art in her own time. She was accepted and judged above all as a design- and architecture-oriented educator. Such is the pedagogical legacy of Popova and her colleagues we have received.

This was related to another fundamental feature of "color discipline," the extension of the artistic problem of color beyond the confines of painting. In turn, this reflected the tendency of the contemporary artistic process to erase the boundaries of genre and form in art, basing its search for a new synthetic universality in the arts on a unity of laws for artistic training. In laying the foundations for the new profession of artist-constructor (designer), the Vkhutemas pedagogues placed these general laws of education at the base of design education.

Despite the energy and passion displayed in Popova's pedagogical work at Vkhutemas, she was not one of those fortunate teachers who leave an indelible mark on their students' souls. We have no evidence to that effect. This may have been due to the brevity of her time at Vkhutemas (from the fall of 1920 to the fall of 1923)—three academic years in all. It would be more accurate to speak of Popova as a scholarly-theoretical pedagogue rather than as an organizer of the academic process or a methodologist.

Popova's teaching on theater design, under Vsevolod Meierkhold, however, did leave a distinct mark on the art of her students, artists, and directors.

THE SEARCH FOR A NEW CREATIVE OBJECT

Popova's work with Meierkhold was preceded by a chain of events in late 1921 related to various aspects of her activity: her practice as an easel painter; her activities at Inkhuk; and her pedagogical work at Vkhutemas. At the point where these phenomena intersected, a new quality arose that determined and colored her further creative development: she was becoming an artist-constructor.

In September 1921, a painting exhibition entitled "5 × 5 = 25" opened at the All-Russian Union of Poets Club (VSP) on Tverskoi Boulevard, where Popova's friend Ivan Aksionov was permanent chairman. It continued for approximately two months. Popova's fundamental creative issue, which had developed in the course of preparing and hanging the exhibition — an issue she had hoped to illuminate in her short "credo" to the catalog — was the evaluation of her own works on a scale ranging "from representational art to objective creation." She found a unique compromise, proposing that the works shown be examined as "preliminary experiments for concrete, materialized constructions."[54]

This formulation demonstrates the artist's dissatisfaction with the traditional forms of easel painting, her desire to give quite complete and self-sufficient works a new meaning. Popova was continually arguing for a nontraditional and unaccustomed meaning for her latest nonobjective works during the autumn months of 1921. She tried to explain the essence of the break that had come about in the creativity of the artists of her circle by proceeding from the logic of the formal-analytical experiment. A painter's analytic problems, for example, the building of an integral color construction, require a certain form — an "object." "That is why," explained Popova, "we are devising an imaginary but ideological [conceivable] object that possesses an ideological similarity to the real object."[55]

But it was this abstractness, the nonreality of the artistic object that had ceased to satisfy the artist. "What is needed is concrete production," she wrote in her notebook, "in order to materialize material concretely, to the requirements of the object's construction,"[56] or its "expediency," as she put it in another note. Now, in the fall of 1921, she absolutely required "experiment in the functional study of the element [that is, the formal elements of artistic creativity] with utilitarian examples."[57]

In the process of forming the artist-constructor's consciousness, artistic-theoretical assumptions (the formal analysis of artistic activity) became enmeshed with socioideological assumptions (the influence of the conception of Production Art on creativity). In the Productivist journalism that was gathering steam about then, the decision of artists to reject easel painting in favor of production was connected with Inkhuk's session of November 24, 1921. All the questions and misunderstandings that had accumulated up till then seemed to find a simple and unambiguous solution: easel art must be replaced by concrete production of utilitarian things.

In turn, decisive changes had to be made in pedagogical work as well. The desire to find a utilitarian object for artistic creativity so intrigued Popova that abstract formal experiments and exercises now seemed out of place even in the academic context. The totally new pedagogy that had just come into being and had not yet taken final form no longer suited her because of its genetic link with the rejected representational art. In an essay on the "disciplines" of the Moscow Vkhutemas, Popova wrote: "in the very best case, even the new objective method of analysis of the formal elements of each given 'art' . . . ultimately is still a matter of the same representational formal elements"[58] (Appendix XIV).

Consequently, late in 1921 Popova was faced with the problem of finding a new object for her theory, creativity, and pedagogy.

GVYTM: "THEATER AS PRODUCTION"

It was in response to this situation that she welcomed the challenge of working at GVYTM (State Higher Theater Workshops).[59] At this stage she understood theater as a type of production with its own specific technology, a unique potential for the creation of life. Moreover, in her understanding the emphasis fell not so much on the ideospiritual or sociopsychological as on the material-concrete aspect.

In Popova's art, theater thus functioned as both paths and means, leading from the "dead ends of representation," through the knowledge of production technology, "to the method of creating those production objects, the products of organized material design" that the artist wrote about and whose birth she and her colleagues so passionately awaited in the imminent future.

This will help to explain why her teaching at GVYTM, which went on parallel to her Vkhutemas work, immediately took on the aspect of life-building art, was immediately colored by the urgency of "concrete production." However, all this was dependent upon corresponding progress within the theater and its experimental pedagogy toward life-building and the utilitarian aspirations of the production-oriented artist. Such movement did exist. Without in any way trying to cast Vsevolod Meierkhold's theatrical activity wholly within the framework of "production art," we can point out several notions among the participants in "theatrical October" (Meierkhold's use of spectacle theater at the service of the Revolution) that brought them closer to the position of the Productivist artists.

First was the principle of expediency, which in and of itself, of course, had no production connotation and which, although used to confirm the new "production" aesthetics, was not itself regarded as an aesthetic.

At the center of Meierkhold's conception of the theater (and consequently of his pedagogical theory and academic exercises) stood the principle of theatrical action—the work of the actor in action. "The standard was expediency," wrote the contemporary theater scholar David Zolotnitsky. "If the result gave the impression of beauty, then this was the beauty of the well-thought-out treatment. Meierkhold considered this alone worthy of the era; only it, in his view, could express the dynamics, the rhythm, the style of the times."[60]

The idea of expediency in movement, costume, sets, and script permeated the work of the theater and became the foundation for theatrical pedagogy. Biomechanics was the theory and academic discipline of the actor's expedient functioning.

It was from the start of her work at GVYTM that the word "expediency" became Popova's favorite term and principal creative criterion. She saw the artist's sole path in the maximal subordination of art to the precise and well-defined laws for working with materials.

Theatrical action, understood as the dynamic "work of the actor," broke down into several elements: individual stunts and music-hall numbers, and so on. The GVYTM artist had to work directly on equipping the stage and therefore on instructing the audience. This allowed—and, perhaps, compelled—Popova to move away from abstract construction on the plane and in space and toward mastering technical contrivances and actually constructing objects conceived from a practical standpoint. Naturally, there can be no question of any special virtue or inventive priority regarding these constructions. What is important, rather, is that ideoartistic aspirations led the artist-painter, a person of humanistic education, to want to study and master technical mechanisms: fastening angles, various types of joints, and so forth. On the basis of these studies Popova herself had already invented a device (a "formovariator") made of laths that enabled her to preview a three-dimensional design. When she planned her "installations" for the plays, she was already fully conversant with the technical side of the project.

Individual sheets and entire notebooks of drawings by Popova (Tretiakov Gallery and private collection, Moscow) distinctly demonstrate the highly unusual process that went on in her creative laboratory in 1921 as she backtracked from creating nonobjective form to depicting a real construction. Complex planar compositions with arc-shaped and rectangular elements in a series were transformed into studies of intersect-

ing, constructively linked beam shapes—all done almost with the precision of a skilled engineer (see pages 222 and 223). In their final form they recall the spatial constructions of Rodchenko or Karel Ioganson. There are clear inklings of the cross-shaped constructions of the future stage settings of Popova herself and of her followers.

Here we must emphasize that both in practice and in theory this new stage of Popova's work as a creator of forms in space was a direct result of and closely linked to all the preceding stages of her creative evolution. This was the extension of Constructivism as an artistic movement from constructing on canvas to constructing in space, from abstract work in materials to work satisfying practical demands. In the academic buildings of GVYTM, abstract exercises in constructing on the plane and in space acquired the concrete character of technical solutions.

GVYTM: "THE CONSTRUCTION OF FORM AND SPACE"

From its history, we know the enthusiasm of Popova's students for every possible technological innovation in the theater, for adapting mechanisms to the problems of dynamic and gestural action.

It is the simple, comprehensible exercises that Popova worked out and that with time became the ABCs for all basic design training that interest us here, first of all, because of their novelty (in the winter of 1921—22 no one at Vkhutemas was training students so purposefully toward real constructing) and, second, because of the theoretical and methodological emphasis on continuity between representation and creating an object according to the laws for developing form. Moreover, due to certain socioideological factors, objects were acquiring an "industrial," technical appearance.

Naturally, the focus on, and preservation of, this connection forced artists like Popova in that period, as they evolved from widely varied artistic backgrounds, to distinguish and develop those aspects of it that were close to the logic of technical development, and to cut out and discard everything else. The Constructivists' artistic style was channeled into rationality, asceticism, into acquiring quasi-industrial forms. The orientation toward industrial production was conscious. "Our age is the age of industry"—the realization of that fact determined a great deal. The logic of technical construction based on satisfying functional requirements through intellectual effort was transformed into a true logic of artistic formation in general and a law for designing things in particular. For Soviet artists of the 1920s, working out a functionalist approach to artistic constructing proceeded in precisely this way, from general creative principles, from style.

The abstract principle of industry and the ideal image of industrial production played a bigger role here than the actual real demands of production when the artists came into contact with them. The conscious insistence on the object's "industrial" traits, as if they had been engendered by the production process itself, was the consequence of artistic will, of the play of the creative consciousness, forestalling the real demands of life in the name of an ideal, however understood. This was the case with Constructivist books and textiles. It was even more so with Constructivist theater—a fantastic model of industrial society.

But it was this artistic, playful (for all the creators' seriousness) nature of this absolutization and this aestheticization (in conjunction with the total rejection of the propriety thereof) that compels us to feel and appreciate the artistic value and beauty of the Constructivists' often naïve and programmatically ascetic creations.

This is our reaction, for example, when we look at Popova's famous *prozodezhda*, her work uniform for an actor. First of all, we would like to do away once and for all with what has become an accepted, even inevitable connection between the design of this work uniform and the 1922 production of *The Magnanimous Cuckold,* which was the first stage endorsement of both the costumes themselves and the idea of an actor's work uniform[61] (pages 224 and 225, 246 and 247).

The work uniform had been conceived, as the artist's archive makes clear, within the context of her academic work, totally independent of the play. That is where it acquired its ideoartistic rationale. In late 1921 Popova worked out a syllabus for her course on "Costume as an Element of Material Formation." In the "ideological" section, the artist formulated three basic approaches to the problem: "1. Costume as a material element of the performance in conjunction with other material elements. 2. Costume in conjunction with the laws of biomechanics and speech. 3. Costume as a production object of material formation . . . based on the utilitarian principle."[62]

With respect to the first approach, which we might call formal-compositional, Popova proposed a multifaceted examination of costume "as a plastic object" (construction, color, texture, rhythm). The form was studied from many aspects: the spatial arts—linear, volumetric—and movement in space. The text of the syllabus also reflects the craftsmanly side of the matter: materials, the technology of work. Moreover, costume is compared here with such "material" elements of the performance as speech and movement.

Popova's work uniform was born in the context of Meierkhold's system of actor training—his biomechanics. In its most primitive interpretation, the actor's work uniform was supposed to serve the same purpose as a leotard for a circus artist—the special garb of the acrobat and the contortionist. The image of the circus artist—the contortionist and the gymnast—was Popova's point of departure in this work as well. The Meierkhold archive in the Bakhrushin Central Theatrical Museum has a study for a gymnast's costume labeled by Popova "Work Uniform for Actor No. 1." The gymnast is pictured in a leotard with a diagonal ornament, as if it had been draped with colored ribbon rays, a trademark of Popova's painting style of those years. The head is draped in a band of ribbons rather like a turban. As we know, however, Meierkhold's biomechanics had an ideoartistic significance as well—to magnify the actual scale of the acting, its visual forms, and its graphic idea. While abandoning the "psychological personality," that is, character, for magnified images, Meierkhold's theater was resurrecting the ancient devices of the theatrical mask, trying to create new "social masks."

It is hard to tell from the photographs of the productions we now have how much the features of Futurist dynamism were characteristic of the actual costumes; what you see in them seems more like extreme and typical simplicity and a conscious departure from the individual. However, in the press of those years we come across comments on the work uniform's capricious forms ("the blue-bloused Popova costume with its varied lengths").[63]

In a speech at Inkhuk on April 27, 1922, during the discussion of the production of *The Magnanimous Cuckold* (Appendix XVII), Popova provided a glimpse into another significance for the work uniform—the utilitarian, practical side. In her draft for the speech she wrote: "the costume was intended for the actor's daily, ordinary life and work and therefore had to be utilitarian both for this purpose and to replace all other clothing, so that it was necessary to add, for example, an overcoat, and so forth. In all, the costume is intended for seven or eight sorts or types of work."[64]

In clothing design, theatrical work crossed directly into artistic construction for real-life needs and served as a first step for the later fashioning of the clothing the artist designed in the winter of 1923–24. Popova's theatrical work did not merge with the resolution of the practical problems of equipping the everyday environment as it did in Rodchenko's theatrical works. However, the necessary premises were in place: a design treatment for the play's sets and costumes had been worked out in keeping with a unified milieu for facilitating specific functional processes.

GVYTM: "THE MATERIAL ELEMENT OF THE PLAY"

In order to clarify this subject we must address one more issue: the correlation between formal-analytic methods and the new principles of artistic construction employed by Popova in her teaching at GVYTM. It was here that she achieved that convergence of the formal-analytic method and the artistic construction of concrete equipment and entire complexes that had been sought without success at Vkhutemas.

It is characteristic that in this work, abstract formal "disciplines" no longer concerned her. Popova perceived that the formal-analytic approach to art, which lay at the base of the era's overall artistic movement, was the foundation of the "modern" style, and essential both to her and to design education.

In Popova's painstakingly elaborated syllabus for "The Material Element of the Performance," what strikes us apart from her rationale for the functional approach to designing is her extraordinary concern that the audience's attention be turned away from the "academic study of the design's elements" and toward the "real utilitarian purpose." That is, the principle of expedience—keeping the goal in mind—must be part of the final stage in the academic (formal-analytic) study of the design's elements.

According to Popova's program, though, the actual study of the artistic craft is built on the formal-analytic principle. She proposed separate assignments in color-plane construction, in volumetric-spatial construction, in the organization of the material elements of a stage production, and in the organization of the material elements of a photographic and film production. Each of these cycles began with a purely abstract exercise and ended with fully concrete works that built on all the preliminary exercises.

As we have already stated, Popova's pedagogical work at GVYTM was more successful and fruitful than her teaching at Vkhutemas. Aksionov even felt it possible to speak of the "school of Liubov Popova." After the artist's death he wrote of her pupils: "They are many: in speaking of the late master's theatrical activity one is obliged to remark upon the enormous pedagogical work L. S. conducted among theater students, although the details would take up too much space. Suffice it to point out that Sergei Eisenstein, German Fedorov (*The Forest*), Vladimir Liutse, Yuri Ekk, and many other young masters of the stage were, as far as the material design of the performance went, her disciples, and they continue . . . the untiring and uncompromising artist's activity."[65]

On the whole, Popova's intensive work at GVYTM, generally quite effective, if not totally free of complications, and her participation in Meierkhold's productions brought her greater satisfaction than did her teaching at Vkhutemas, which seemed to her excessively academic. In contemplating a reorganization and the development of a preliminary course for Vkhutemas aimed at concrete production of a new "utilitarian" object, Popova tried above all to extend the experience she had had at GVYTM.

VKHUTEMAS: THE PLAN FOR A "PRODUCTION STUDIO IN THE BASIC DEPARTMENT"

There was a plan at Vkhutemas to create an Experimental Studio.[66] The formal justification for organizing the studio was a petition to the Vkhutemas administration from fifteen students in the Basic Department requesting that "a separate studio be organized for equipment, theatrical models, utilitarian spatial constructions."[67] At the very outset their statements proposed "creating ties with the production faculties of Vkhutemas, GITIS (State Institute of Theatrical Art), the Free Theater Studios, and the theaters in general." The statement was read at a meeting of the Basic Department on October 25, 1922, and two weeks later Popova was preparing a "Memorandum to the Vkhutemas Administration on an Organization Plan for the Studio of Vkhutemas Professors Vesnin, Lavinsky, Popova, Rodchenko," which, as the students' petition had already mentioned, she was willing to direct. In this memo the set studio was quickly transformed into an "experimental production laboratory," which, according to the author's idea, was supposed to ensure the "practical synthesis or concretization of the abstract studies of the disciplines in the Basic Department"—supposedly by executing various orders. The memo clarifies their nature: "Thus, for example, the studio's jobs might be: to work out designs and partially execute the interior design of structures—commercial, public, cinemas, theaters, circuses, stores, cafés, and so on; official and residential quarters; all types of industries, household objects and clothing; all types of advertisements (posters, signs, shop windows, exhibits, magazines, book publishers, and so on); to organize festivals and performances of various types, and so on and so forth."[68]

As we can see, she contemplated the studio's future largely as design work; moreover, most of its attention was to go to entire complexes, to the functional-graphic resolution of spatial environments with various uses. That is, Popova discarded the idea of a theatrical-set studio (even one initially oriented toward the new type of theatrical work, toward GVYTM) and began decisively to broaden its perspectives, consciously planning for a real design center—a broad-profile design institute.

As for her plans for organizing the new studio, Popova formulated the basic principles of the new profession of artist-constructor (designer), which she had derived in the course of her work at GVYTM in the years 1921–22: "The method of study throughout the entire course will be that approach to the object, to its material design, which in our age of industry comes about through the precise calculation of an object's material functions, designed in accordance with its utilitarian necessity. This ideological premise determines this artistic-technical profession's approach to work on the material object."[69]

It should be emphasized that the details of the artist's creative life were affected by her personal vision of this fundamentally new profession as being firmly linked with the theater. It was her theatrical work and that of her pupils that she felt and understood as the "new profession." When she undertook to organize design education at Vkhutemas, Popova naturally broadened the boundaries and scope of the new profession's application, designating it as "artistic-technical."

Since the spring of 1923, after the performance of *Earth on End*, Popova had switched over completely to "production" work (the printing trades, textiles, clothing design). All her creative efforts during this final, very brief stage of her life were informed by the conviction that "the artist's contemporary social position charges him above all with creating works that respond to the demands of the day. In this way, the modern artist's activity," she wrote, "inevitably stays within the limits of concrete production rather than making abstract constructions."[70]

The chief pedagogical problem now was to find the necessary transitions from the formal-analytical method of training to the real work of the artist-constructor. This aspect of her activities can be seen not only in her work at GVYTM and in the Basic Department of Vkhutemas but also in her work in graphic design at the Graphics Faculty of Vkhutemas[71] and in her preparation of a seminar on "Material Design" for Moscow Proletkult (Proletarian Culture Movement) in 1924, where her GVYTM student Sergei Eisenstein was active. In her syllabus for the Proletkult course (Appendix XXI), Popova once again affirmed the functionalist foundation of her design concept: "This principle is the construction of the object, or the search for its form proceeding from the function of the object itself. In our age of industry the thesis of 'functional form' is the principle that lies at the base of every material design."[72]

THE PARADOXES OF POPOVA'S THEATRICAL WORK

Liubov Popova's theatrical work is the best-known and most widely recognized area of her art. Popova's productions in Meierkhold's theater are a benchmark in the history of theatrical Constructivism: all that went before them is its prehistory; all that went after, its development and continuation.

Numerous rejoinders, pronouncements, comments, articles, and books from the 1920s to the present have been devoted to this theme. Strange though it may seem, however, the fame and commensurate academic interest have concerned only one part of the artist's theatrical legacy—her work with Meierkhold, and even that not in its entirety. All the rest drowns in a fog of unconfirmed facts and unresolved issues. The list compiled after Liubov Popova's death by people close to her often serves as virtually the sole source of factual information on the numerous surviving studies.

But the dearth of complete information on the artist's work in the theater is only one element in the atmosphere of mystery and obfuscation that clouds this aspect of her work; the other has to do with the actual understanding of her creative evolution. The classic performances mounted by Popova and Meierkhold are a brilliant demonstration of harmony in staging and directing, of mutual understanding and goodwill between the director and the artist, their joint efforts on common creative problems and

stylistic inquiries. This could not be said of Popova's other work for the theater. Moreover, in the majority of her theatrical studies not intended for Meierkhold productions, Popova the theatrical artist found herself in an awkward position with respect to her own easel art. Her studies for theatrical productions seem to refer back to another time, to much earlier stages in her own evolution as an avant-garde painter. This was due to a series of objective and subjective causes, some of which have to do with the specifics of the Russian theater's development in the 1910s, with its transitional stage from decorativism à la Sergei Diaghilev and the World of Art to mastering the newest achievements in avant-garde painting. The chief formal problem of this period, as we know, was the transition from the two-dimensional sets at the turn of the century (which comprised painted space as well) to the real space of Cubo-Futurist solutions. The path had been anything but smooth.

Meierkhold had attempted to set up these types of experiments in his work on Aleksandr Blok's *Neznakomka* (The Unknown Woman) in 1914 and in his classes at the Directors' Training Course in 1918 in Petrograd. But only Aleksandr Tairov had managed to pose this problem properly for himself and for the theater. The 1913 production of *Victory over the Sun*, with nonobjective sets by Malevich, and similar Futurist experiments that were far ahead of their time, signaled an expansion in painting and literature rather than any real contact between theater and modern painting. They fell more within the literary-painting movement, setting aside the theatrical essence of the performance.

Tairov was working from his own inner inclinations and the problems of theatrical art. To solve them he needed to be in contact with modern art. In his swift development of avant-garde tendencies he demonstrated an inkling of Cubo-Futurist thinking.

THE FIRST EXPERIMENT:
THE CHAMBER THEATER—*ROMEO AND JULIET*

Popova's theatrical work began with her studies for an unstaged production of *Romeo and Juliet* for the Chamber (Kamernyi) Theater (it was produced a year later by Tairov with sets by Aleksandra Exter). Popova had been acquainted with this theater since 1916, when Exter had designed the lobby, staircase, foyer, stage portals, and theatrical interior for a production of *The Merry Wives of Windsor* with sets by Aristarkh Lentulov and she had needed a sculptor to do a frieze, a head of Apollo, and other jobs. Popova had served as intermediary between the theater and Vera Mukhina, who carried out Exter's proposal.[73]

In subsequent years both friends of Popova—Mukhina and Exter—continued to work here, and in 1920 Popova and Vesnin were brought in as well. Vesnin staged Paul Claudel's *Annunciation*, and Popova began work on *Romeo and Juliet*. Because this was her first theatrical work, and thus required vast amounts of labor, and also because the Chamber Theater never did use Popova's designs, great numbers of studies for *Romeo and Juliet* were stored in the artist's studio, allowing us to penetrate the development of her thought, her work method, her difficulties, and her successes.[74]

It becomes clear that Popova wanted, perhaps unconsciously, to reproduce on stage the classic Italy of the Renaissance that she had seen and loved so well in her youth. In the studies we see accurately reproduced terraces of palaces, a marble-encrusted church facade, a panorama of an Italian town with towers, gates, and stairs. All these vivid, vital, but disparate image-impressions had to be gathered into a sound, unified theatrical form. Naturally, Popova used her customary devices, especially the collage. She isolated the most expressive details in order to combine them with others in a complex intersecting space. As in her easel compositions with collages, she built the proposed stage's spatial depth while achieving a compact and integrated whole.

In addition, she had to depart from actual impressions, just as she had so many times in her still lifes, landscapes, and portraits—she had to abandon the concrete while maintaining the expressiveness and characteristic definition of the artistic motif. As in her painting of 1914–15, once again the artist was traversing the logical path of abstraction and concentration of images—a path from detailed scenes to the architectonic building of volumetric forms and color planes, which only recalled Italian architecture in her treatment. This feeling "returned" at the expense of the plastic interpretation of the whole, either more detailed ("Gothic" or "Baroque"), in the spirit of the painting of 1914–16, or else more terse, as in her paintings of later years (1918–20).

So the study for the garden in front of the Capulets' home (page 240, top), thanks to the twisting shapes of the tree, which is more like an architectural-decorative motif than a depiction of an object of nature, brings up associations with Baroque shapes. The crypt is built on the direct example of Gothic constructions (page 241, top). The studies for the production recall earlier paintings by the artist, not only in these "stylistic" markers but also in their almost exact plastic coincidences. For example, the stair motif in the final version extends diagonally up and to the right, as in the landscape *Box Factory* (page 98, top). It is even more interesting to trace the kinship between the costume designs for *Romeo* and abstract landscape canvases of previous years. The folds of the dress and the coloration of one study for a female figure (Juliet's mother?; page 232) bear a striking resemblance to the fan-shaped motif that signified the steep slopes of the ravine in the *Birsk* landscape (page 104), and so on.

Examining all the numerous pencil drawings and watercolor and gouache studies, which are only sketches but quite on a level with her easel compositions, one is convinced that the artist's goal was gradually becoming the creation of a unified spatial-compositional structure capable of being transformed into the various zones of stage action. Her foundation became a system of volumes with platforms and stairs. Added details (an abstract-sculptural tree, a complicated tiered architecture of lamps, sarcophagi, and so on) transformed the compositional structure into the garden at the Capulet house, the hall, the crypt, and so forth, in turn (pages 226–29 and 234).

By this time a unified stage structure of an architectural nature had already been created for several productions at the Chamber Theater (for example, Aleksandra Exter's *Tamira of the Cittern*), and Vesnin had worked on this type of set for *The Annunciation*. There is every possibility that Popova began to develop her later, more monumental version under the influence of the architecturally oriented Vesnin.

As a whole Popova's work process on the set studies for *Romeo and Juliet* echoed the progress of her own painting style from the works of the years 1913–14 (an example of which might be *Objects from a Dyeworks*, page 80) to her architectonic painting of the years 1918–20.

This progression does not make itself felt as strongly in the costume designs (pages 230–33, 240, bottom, and 241, bottom). They do not have the emphatic monumentality present in Popova's architectonic painting of the late 1910s and early 1920s. The ringing staccato of the folds, the Cubist acuity of the faceted shapes, is closer to her mid-1910s style, and the manner of the drawing studies is close to that of the early Cubist nudes of 1913, which seem to be encased in an armor of geometric shapes (pages 54 and 55). At the same time, the costume designs are characterized by both literalism and realism in their fixation on details and attributes, their fear of breaking from reality, which reveals a certain timidity on the part of the artist.

The fate of the *Romeo and Juliet* production at the Chamber Theater deserves comment. Three artists worked on it in succession: Popova, Vesnin, and Exter. Popova was rejected. No documentation on this has survived. We can assume that Popova's relative lack of confidence as a beginning theatrical designer, and her lack of a vividly expressed plastic conception that could bring the whole visual performance together as a unified whole, did not go over well with Tairov. Vesnin was brought in, having already successfully completed *The Annunciation*.

Close comparison of Popova's work and Vesnin's studies supports John Bowlt's assertion that Vesnin simply elaborated what Popova had already discovered.[75] Indeed, Vesnin kept among his studies the system of volumes with platforms and stairs proposed by Popova, endowing it with more concise architectural definition and spatial clarity. He even maintained an insignificant feature in the foreground stage right: the tongue of a ramp descending from the wings. Vesnin's costumes were also constructed on the theme of stiff, armor-like shapes and folds, less jerky than in Popova's studies, but much more whimsical and subtle than in his *Annunciation*. For all their outward dynamism, these sketches look rationally balanced and less emotional than Popova's images. In this respect they are decidedly inferior to Exter's famous designs, which Tairov preferred; clearly what he had been looking for was elemental, unbridled passion. Exter took a bold step away from the rational geometrism characteristic of Vesnin and Popova's Cubism to a "baroquely Baroque" accessible to the post-Cubist painting of those years.[76]

Nevertheless, without a doubt, Popova's unstaged work on *Romeo and Juliet* gave her added confidence and freedom.

THE SECOND EXPERIMENT:
THE CHILDREN'S THEATER—*THE TALE OF THE PRIEST AND BALDA, HIS HELPER*

On the Vesnin-Aksionov list, the year 1920 is marked by Popova's work on a puppet show for the Children's Theater.[77] From the history of the Children's Theater we know that in the winter of 1918–19 Natalia Satz organized a puppet theater under the aegis of the Moscow Soviet (Mossovet) on Mamonovsky Street, where she staged various types of performances: Punch-and-Judy shows, marionettes, Chinese shadow shows. The sculptor Ivan Efimov and his wife, Nina Simonovich-Efimova, a puppeteer, established their theater here.

The organizers of the Children's Theater were trying to switch from puppet shows to an acting troupe. In 1920 the Mossovet Children's Theater became the First State Theater for Children of the People's Commissariat for Enlightenment (Narkompros) and began putting on true acting performances: in 1920, *Mowgli* (after Rudyard Kipling); in July 1921, *Adalmina's Pearl*, staged by Vesnin. However, the need for a traveling show to take to the schools, along with a desire to be accessible to the youngest audiences, compelled the theater to experiment once again with puppet shows.

In all likelihood Popova was brought in to stage the Pushkin tale of Balda because of this new enthusiasm for puppet theater. The chronicles of the theater have not preserved any information on this performance. Evidently *The Tale of the Priest and His Helper, Balda* was part of a literary-musical evening devoted to Pushkin. Satz has written about this 1920 series of evenings organized around a theme.[78]

In Popova's studio after her death there were seventeen studies for this show depicting puppet characters and horses. In these studies (pages 236–39) the artist put the folk background of the Pushkin tale to good use to create crude, "blocky" forms. At this new stage we encounter a primitivist and folklorist motivation emphasized by the idiosyncratic shape characteris-

tic of avant-garde art. Popova's devices are quite complex and varied. Along with the volumetric Cubist form of the puppets, which look as if they were chopped with a carpenter's tool in the spirit of Bogorodsk toys, we see figures of horses stylized in the shallow relief of the traditional peasant carving and broadly applied in wooden architecture, in utensils, and in the relief of gingerbread trim. Here a harsh but confident line outlines not the sculptural volumetric form but a quasi-graphic, quasi-sculptural flat relief intended to be viewed from only one side. Along with this there are painterly studies of puppets: devils and horses. These may have come first, before her intentions had coalesced. It is characteristic that in all these studies the artist used color arbitrarily and purely decoratively, in the spirit of folk art. The smooth lines and outlined dots of individual studies recall dark blue and white Gzhel porcelain more than carvings.

The artist achieved particularly lively color and festivity in her study for the booth for the traveling puppet show (page 238). The combination of her favorite lush green with ocher-gold is grand and magnificent. The tent is crowned with a tiny red flag, a detail the artist tried to repeat later in her design for Meierkhold's *The Magnanimous Cuckold*.

It is safe to assume that *The Tale of Balda* was not the only puppet show Popova worked on. Among her studies there are pictures of a cock and a cat, a wolf and a fox—characters from Russian fairy tales—but we have no precise information on whether these projects were ever realized.

THE THIRD EXPERIMENT:
THE COMEDY THEATER—*THE LOCKSMITH AND THE CHANCELLOR*

In 1920 Liubov Popova also worked on a production of Anatoly Lunacharsky's *The Locksmith and the Chancellor* at the Comedy (formerly the Korsh) Theater, presented in the 1920–21 season. The surviving materials raise another entire sequence of questions and misunderstandings. We know of fewer than ten studies.[79] Two of the set studies are complete, confidently and beautifully executed easel compositions in the Cubist manner (page 244). The actual sets (which we can judge from an album of excellent photographs in the Bakhrushin Central Theatrical Museum) retain the studies' compositional scheme, but in place of the Cubo-Futurist romanticism of sharp edges and scattered, splintering shapes, there are comfortable interiors with real furnishings. In the offices, halls, boudoirs, and other rooms shown on the stage, the frankly modern style is replaced by the neo-Gothic, and so on. Only one of the closing scenes, when the rebels have broken into the palace with their flags, is filled with the spirit of dynamism and expressiveness characteristic of Popova's studies for the production and her painting style in general. We do not know how this translation from painting studies to stage furnishings was brought about or by whom. It is quite possible that Popova herself was powerless to oppose the conservatism of the theater and was forced to relinquish her Cubist forms and to cooperate with the theater's property man in bringing the stage space "to life" with "stylish" furniture, lamps, vases. Several details speak in favor of this scenario. In the setting created on stage we see natural objects that seem to be trying to relate to the artist's intention, although on the whole, the lack of correspondence between the studies and the sets is striking. In her work for the Chamber Theater, Popova finally accomplished what she had been struggling toward, but the Comedy Theater proved unequal to her innovative intentions.

The reviews for the production were lukewarm. Neither the Comedy Theater nor Lunacharsky's play attracted any particular notice—although Lunacharsky was the head of Narkompros. The production was treated as a "Philistine melodrama." However, within the theater itself it was considered a complete success.

Not until a year later, toward the end of 1921, did Popova, now teaching in the Higher Directors' Workshops, return to the theater. This year changed a great deal in her artistic signature and, most important, in her aesthetic views. However, one thing links the studies for The Locksmith and the Chancellor and her future work at GVYTM: her costume designs. Comparing her costume designs for The Locksmith and the Chancellor (page 242) with her slightly earlier designs for Romeo and Juliet

(although both were done in 1920), we can see the artist moving away from simple striking graphicness in the direction of a more clear-cut constructiveness and prosaicness of treatment not only in the images of characters, which is natural, but in the forms themselves: the volumes, the folds, the details. The costume material for Romeo brings to mind stiff paper or tin and recalls Popova's still lifes and architectonic compositions. In her studies for The Locksmith the forms tend to be wooden, carved (her puppet show experience), but at the same time amazingly precise in depicting faces (for example, Man with a Pipe; page 235), in the details of the cut and finish of the clothing: it is an easy form for a theatrical costumier—utilitarian and seemingly without any pretensions to asceticism, even if they do lack the deep, resonant colors of the earlier studies.

Unlike the set designs, the costumes for The Locksmith clearly lead toward a precise and realistic depiction of nature, in striking contrast to the general movement of Popova's easel art toward increasingly abstract constructions, toward the unique artistic "schematism" of her rayic compositions of 1921.

This internal contradiction, of course, may have been connected with the Comedy Theater and that theater's demands on the artist. However, it does seem closely linked to Popova's artistic evolution. The realistic tendency in her later theatrical, printing, poster, and other studies may have been a natural counterbalance to the spiritualization going on in the basic easel compositions, a linchpin in restoring the harmony of spirit and flesh, the spiritual and the earthly, in the artist's art.

At Popova's studio. Left: Pavel Popov, Liubov's brother and the model for Portrait of a Philosopher (pages 92–94), with Aleksandr Vesnin. On the wall, center: Spatial Force Construction, 1921; lower right: Sketch for a Portrait, ca. 1915 (page 94, bottom left). Photograph by Aleksandr Rodchenko

Picture of building constructions and diagrams. 1921–22. Pencil and India ink on tracing paper, 6⅜ × 9¼" (16.3 × 23.5 cm.). Tretiakov Gallery, Manuscript Division

Study for a construction in space. 1921–22. Pencil on paper, 10⅜ × 8⅛"
(26.5 × 20.5 cm.). Private collection, Moscow

Studies for constructions in space. 1921–22. Pencil and colored pencil on paper,
10⅜ × 8⅛" (26.5 × 20.5 cm.). Private collection, Moscow

Work uniform design for Actors No. 2 and 4. The Free Studio of Vsevolod Meierkhold at the State Higher Theater Workshop (GVYTM). 1921

Work uniform design for Actor No. 6.
1921. India ink, gouache, and collage on
paper, 12⅞ × 9⅜" (32.7 × 23.8 cm.).
Costakis Collection, Athens, cat. no. 881

Work uniform design for Actor No. 3. The Free Studio of Vsevolod Meierkhold at GVYTM. 1921. Pasted paper, India ink, gouache, and collage on cardboard, 13 × 10⅛" (33 × 25.7 cm.). Tretiakov Gallery. Gift of George Costakis

225

Study for a set for *Romeo and Juliet*, Moscow Chamber Theater. *The Square*. 1920. Pencil on paper, 7⅞ × 10⅝" (20 × 27 cm.). Private collection, Moscow

Study for a set for *Romeo and Juliet*, Moscow Chamber Theater. *The Square*. 1920. Pencil on paper, 7⅞ × 10⅝" (20 × 27 cm.). Private collection, Moscow

Study for a set for *Romeo and Juliet*, Moscow Chamber Theater. *The Square.* 1920. Pencil on paper, 8 × 10⅝″ (20.3 × 27 cm.). Private collection, Moscow

Study for a set for *Romeo and Juliet*, Moscow Chamber Theater. 1920. Whitewash and gouache on cardboard, 9½ × 14⅛″ (24 × 36 cm.). Private collection, Moscow

Study for a set for *Romeo and Juliet*, Moscow Chamber Theater. 1920. Dimensions unknown. Gmurzynska Collection, Cologne

Costume design for *Romeo and Juliet*, Moscow Chamber Theater. *Youth*. 1920. India ink and gouache on paper, 14¼ × 11¼″ (36.2 × 28.5 cm.). Private collection, Moscow

Costume design for *Romeo and Juliet*, Moscow Chamber Theater. *Romeo in a Mask*. 1920. Pencil on paper, 13⅞ × 10½″ (35.2 × 26.7 cm.). Private collection, Moscow

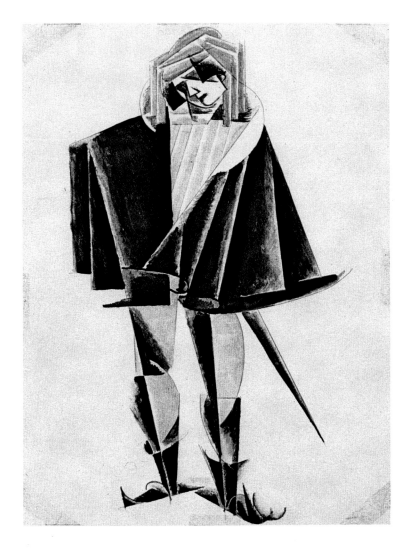

Costume design for *Romeo and Juliet*, Moscow Chamber Theater. *Youth in a Cape*.
1920. India ink and gouache on paper, 14 × 10⅝″ (35.5 × 27 cm.). Private collection,
Moscow

Costume design for *Romeo and Juliet*, Moscow Chamber Theater. *Servant with Tray*.
1920. India ink and gouache on paper, 14 × 10⅝″ (35.5 × 27 cm.). Private collection,
Moscow

Costume design for *Romeo and Juliet*, Moscow Chamber Theater. *Woman*. 1920. Pencil on paper, 13⅞ × 10½" (35.1 × 26.7 cm.). Museum of Decorative and Applied Art, Moscow

Costume design for *Romeo and Juliet*, Moscow Chamber Theater. *Woman*. 1920. India ink and watercolor on paper, 14 × 10⅝" (35.5 × 27 cm.). Private collection, Moscow

Costume design for *Romeo and Juliet*, Moscow Chamber Theater. *Friar Laurence.* 1920.
Pencil on paper, 13⅞ × 10⅝″ (35.2 × 27 cm.). Private collection, Moscow

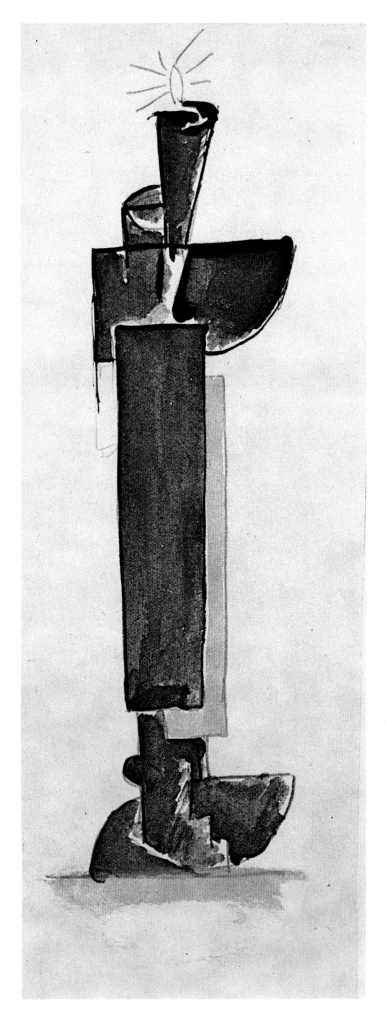

Design for *Romeo and Juliet*, Moscow Chamber Theater. *Tree*. 1920. Pencil, India ink, and watercolor on paper, 6⅞ × 5¾″ (17.4 × 14.7 cm.). Private collection, Moscow

Design for *Romeo and Juliet*, Moscow Chamber Theater. *Lamp*. 1920. India ink on paper, 9¼ × 3¼″ (23.4 × 8.2 cm.). Private collection, Moscow

Costume design for *The Locksmith and the Chancellor*, by Anatoly Lunacharsky, Comedy
(formerly the Korsh) Theater. *Man with a Pipe (The Locksmith?)*. 1920. Gouache on
paper, 15¼ × 10¼" (38.8 × 26 cm.). Private collection, Moscow

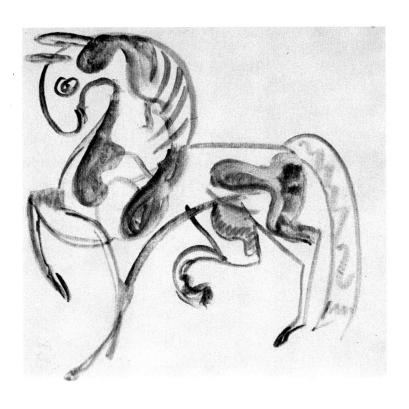

Three designs for a puppet show. *The Tale of the Priest and Balda, His Helper*, by Aleksandr Pushkin, Moscow Children's Theater. *Horse*. 1920. Gouache on paper, above: 8⅝ × 8″ (21.9 × 20.4 cm.); above right: 16½ × 21½″ (42 × 54.5 cm.); left: 14⅝ × 21¼″ (37 × 54 cm.). Private collection, Moscow

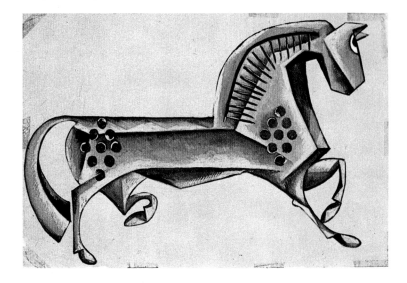

Designs for a puppet show. *The Tale of the Priest and Balda, His Helper*, by Aleksandr Pushkin, Moscow Children's Theater. 1920. Gouache on paper. *Left: Balda*. 16½ × 12¼″ (42 × 31.2 cm.); *right: The Old Devil*. 17⅛ × 12″ (43.5 × 30.5 cm.). Private collection, Moscow

Design for a puppet show. *The Tale of the Priest and Balda, His Helper*, by
Aleksandr Pushkin, Moscow Children's Theater. *The Young Devil*. 1920. Gouache on
paper, 19⅝ × 14⅛" (50 × 36 cm.). Private collection, Moscow

Curtain design for a puppet show. *The Tale of the Priest and Balda, His Helper,* by Aleksandr Pushkin, Moscow Children's Theater. *The Puppet Show Booth.* 1920. Collage of paper and gouache on cardboard, 23¾ × 28⅛" (60.3 × 71.3 cm.). Private collection, Moscow

Design for a puppet show. *The Tale of the Priest and Balda, His Helper,* by Aleksandr Pushkin, Moscow Children's Theater. *The Priest's Daughter.* 1920. Gouache on paper, 20½ × 13⅛" (52 × 33.5 cm.). Private collection, Moscow

Study for a set for *Romeo and Juliet*, Moscow Chamber Theater. *The Garden in Front of the House*. 1920. Gouache on paper, 9⅛ × 13¾" (23.2 × 35 cm.). Private collection, Moscow

Costume design for *Romeo and Juliet*, Moscow Chamber Theater. *Romeo in a Mask*. 1920. Gouache on paper, 15⅛ × 12⅜" (38.5 × 31.5 cm.). Private collection, Moscow

Study for a set for *Romeo and Juliet*, Moscow Chamber Theater. *Friar Laurence's Cell.*
1920. Gouache on paper, 9¼ × 13⅜″ (23.6 × 34 cm.). Private collection, Moscow

Costume design for *Romeo and Juliet*, Moscow Chamber Theater. *Soldier.* 1920. India
ink and gouache on paper, 14 × 10⅝″ (35.5 × 27 cm.). Private collection, Moscow

Costume design for *The Locksmith and the Chancellor,* by Anatoly Lunacharsky, Comedy (formerly the Korsh) Theater. *Woman with a Briefcase.* 1920. Gouache on paper, 17½ × 9⅛″ (44.5 × 23.2 cm.). Private collection, Moscow

Costume design for the unstaged *Priest of Tarquinia*, by S. Polivanov, at GITIS. *Soldier*. 1922. Gouache on paper, 23 × 16⅛" (58.5 × 41 cm.). Private collection, Moscow

244   Set design for *The Locksmith and the Chancellor*, by Anatoly Lunacharsky, Comedy (formerly the Korsh) Theater. *The Study*. 1920. Gouache on paper,
18⅛ × 14⅝" (46 × 37.2 cm.). Private collection, Moscow

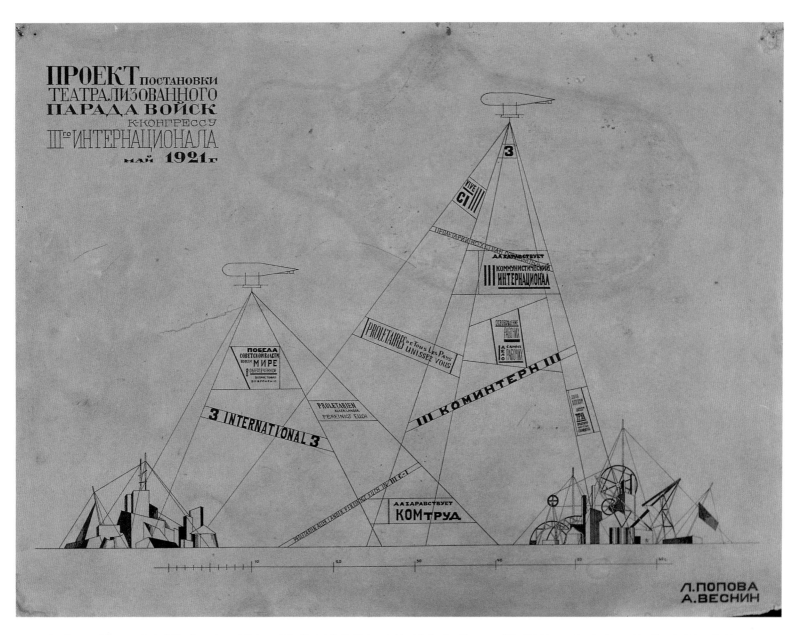

Design for the set of the mass festival *The Struggle and Victory of the Soviets* (with Aleksandr Vesnin), for the Congress of the Third International, directed by Vsevolod Meierkhold. 1921.
India ink on paper, 18⅛ × 34⅜″ (46 × 62 cm.). Tretiakov Gallery. Gift of George Costakis

Work uniform design for Actor No. 7. The Free Studio of Vsevolod Meierkhold at GVYTM. 1921. Pasted paper, India ink, gouache, and collage on cardboard, 13⅛ × 10⅜" (33.5 × 26.2 cm.). Private collection, Moscow

246

ПРОЗ ОДЕЖ ДА АКТ ЕРА № 5

ЛПОПОВА 1921.

Work uniform design for Actor No. 5. The Free Studio of Vsevolod Meierkhold at GVYTM. 1921. Pasted paper, India ink, gouache, and collage on cardboard, 13½ × 9⅝″ (34.2 × 24.6 cm.). Private collection, Moscow

Set design for *The Magnanimous Cuckold*, by Fernand Crommelynck, Actor's Theater. 1922. Watercolor, gouache, and collage on paper, 19⅝ × 27⅛″ (50 × 69 cm.). Tretiakov Gallery

Prop design for *The Magnanimous Cuckold*, by Fernand Crommelynck, Actor's Theater. *Geranium in a Pot.* 1922. Black and red pencil on paper, 14⅜ × 8⅞″ (36.4 × 22.5 cm.). Tretiakov Gallery. Gift of George Costakis

COLLABORATION WITH MEIERKHOLD:
FIRST EPISODE—A MASS FESTIVAL
ON KHODINSKOE FIELD

In the spring of 1921 Moscow was getting ready for the Third Congress of the Communist International (Comintern). Meierkhold was preparing a grand mass festival on Khodinskoe Field. The idea of this newly revived revolutionary type of popular theatrical parade-spectacle—theatrical October— excited him greatly. Even before the Revolution he had experimented with ancient popular theater forms and had tried to synthesize traditional forms with the innovations of the latest artistic ideas and images.

The spectacle was conceived on a grand scale. Called *The Struggle and Victory of the Soviets*, and using both symbolic and very concrete military action, it was supposed to evoke the era of worldwide proletarian revolution and its victory over the bulwark of capital. Ivan Aksionov wrote the scenario, and more than likely it was he, Aksionov, Popova's old friend, who acted as liaison between her and Meierkhold. Evidently it was Aksionov's doing that Popova and Vesnin were invited to help stage the festival.

Aksionov was a man of unusual destiny, unusual even for that period of complicated and changeable lives.[80] A historian and expert on the theater and a direct participant in military operations and revolutionary events, he was assigned to write the scenario for the presentation. All the action was broken down into episodes and was supposed to take place on a large field around two basic monumental structures: "The Fortress of Capital" and "The City of the Future" (pages 245 and 258).

Samuel Margolin explained how the presentation was supposed to unfold:

According to Ivan Aksionov's scenario and Vsevolod Meierkhold's plan, in the first five episodes of the festival various national groups of troops for the Revolution are supposed to come from different directions to lead a united attack on the bastion of capital, forming a tight ring around it, engulfing it in smoke, and exploding ten-pound land mines. In the smoke of an artificial fire the armored cars let the tanks by to pass through artificial barricades and obstacles. The smoke screen disperses. The emblems of capitalism disappear from the bastion and all the national flags fall. A high, fiery *cone of flamethrowers* rises over the bastion. The bastion's silhouette takes on the features of a factory with this slogan on the wall: "Put what workers' hands make into workers' hands!" *Sixth episode of the action:* The troops—infantry, artillery, cavalry—file past the tribunal, where all the members of the Congress of the Third International are to be present. The parade is joined by teams of trick riders dressed up as Worker, Peasant, and Red Soldier. *Seventh episode:* Searchlights create a *light curtain*. Trucks decorated with emblems of labor and carrying athletes from Vseobuch [General Education—an umbrella group in charge of educating workers] playing the people of

labor drive out onto the field and arrange themselves in front of the City of the Future. *Eighth episode:* "And having conquered, they do not abandon their arms!" They hurl the discus! They hurl the javelin! *Ninth episode:* Hammer and sickle. To the beat of the orchestras, the former warriors re-create the movements of a blacksmith and a reaper. The sickle bearers move in between them and stop next to the tribunal, crossing their sickle with their neighbor's hammer. *Tenth episode:* "Joy and strength—the victory of the workers." Free movement by the Vseobuch student participants in the Mass Festival. They approach and pass the tribunal, then stop at the City of the Future, where they form into groups, which are joined by military units. *Eleventh episode:* Airplanes with Zeiss spotlights fly over the illuminated portion of the field at an altitude of no more than 2,000 yards. Searchlights beam slogans against the forest and the City of the Future. *Twelfth episode:* The orchestras and all those participating perform the *Internationale*. Fireworks. A shot signals the end of the festival.[81]

The spectacle contemplated was never staged. During the preparations in the bleak, famine-struck year of 1921, the government issued a decree prohibiting mass festivals and celebrations that consumed colossal means. The performance of *Struggle and Victory* "proposed the participation of 200 riders from the cavalry school, 2,300 infantry cadets, 16 artillery weapons, 5 airplanes with Zeiss spotlights, 10 automatic searchlights, 5 armored cars, tanks, motorcycles, ambulances, Vseobuch, the physical-education department of Guvuz [Main Administration of Higher and Secondary Pedagogical Institutions], military orchestras, and choruses."[82]

The idea alone of Meierkhold's unstaged event played an important role in the evolution of theatrical performance from the chamber theater to the mass audience, from complex psychological subtleties to the frank agitational slogan. This evolution, which responded to the demands of revolutionary propaganda, came about both in Meierkhold's own performances and in a wide circle of attendant phenomena— professional, semiprofessional, and amateur.

Meierkhold's conception played a crucial role in the development of theatrical performances in the broad sense and, more narrowly, in the evolution of Popova's own theatrical art. According to Aksionov, "Work had reached the point of submitting a maquette and laying it out in place. L. S. supervised this laying out personally."[83] As in other instances of coauthorship between Popova and Vesnin, it is not easy to separate out the role of each artist. A final production design signed by both authors was found in Popova's studio, along with a sketch done at an earlier stage and maquettes of the "cities."[84]

The designs for the mass festival fell well within the boundaries of contemporary architectural thought—well within the formulations of architectural Constructivism. They represent a logical step on the path from Tatlin's *Monument to the Third International* to the Vesnins' architectural plans of the early

1920s (the Moscow office of *Leningrad Pravda*, the Palace of Labor, and so on). At the same time, these sketches are a natural link in Popova's own creative evolution—from architectonic compositions based on the dynamic articulation of two-dimensional color shapes to the openwork spatial constructions of her last stage. Here we also see—and this is wholly understandable—the principles she was to develop in subsequent Meierkhold productions. The scaffolding motif is found in simplified form in the set for *The Magnanimous Cuckold*. The crane from the study for "The City of the Future" is transferred almost exactly in the studies for *Earth on End* (Bakhrushin Central Theatrical Museum).

The importance of this project in Popova's creative evolution becomes clearer and greater when we recall the importance the production's scenario assigned to color architecture: a great many beams from searchlights and projectors lighting fragments of the action and specially prepared panels with slogans. Popova's late painting is largely built on the motif of the ray-cable, a form that is incorporeal and spiritual, almost immaterial, but at the same time strictly constructive and architectonic. Popova's canvases and drawings of 1921 are ideal models of the delicate, pure-energy architecture of force lines and fields. In the theater she supplemented the material reality of her architectural structures with the dynamics of brilliant spotlights and projectors.

When we try to imagine how the mass festival on Khodinskoe Field would have looked, we mentally picture a whimsical but strictly Constructive and logical web of pull-cables that are fastened to the earth, holding down the vertical turrets of fantastic cities and balloon-like kites straining upward. An enormous net, raised up high on cones, covers a broad expanse of Khodinskoe Field like a tent. The clusters of matter sprinkled on this sharp-angled web are slogans. The entire system is permeated with a network of searchlight beams that pluck the posters out of the darkened sky. The poetics of Popova's late painting are clearly felt throughout all this. Especially significant here is the motif of the great openwork circles and semicircles that define the image of the City of the Future. The circle, the whirlwind motion—these are also characteristic of the artist's painterly poetics in the late 1910s and early 1920s. It was obviously no mere coincidence that she worked out this motif so spiritedly in *The Magnanimous Cuckold* and later in her textile designs.

COLLABORATION WITH MEIERKHOLD: SECOND EPISODE—*THE MAGNANIMOUS CUCKOLD*

When Popova began work on Fernand Crommelynck's *The Magnanimous Cuckold* she was a full member of GVYTM. She was already familiar with the theatrical experiments at the Chamber Theater and the Comedy Theater, and most important, she was fully conversant with Meierkhold's theatrical quests, his "Productivist" ideas, his bold and unexpected mix of cultural traditions and contemporary slogans.

In his essays written soon after Liubov Popova's death, Aksionov stressed her reluctance and resistance to agree to design this production: "It proved very difficult to secure Popova's participation in the given work; she agreed to undertake it only after long hesitation and under the pressure of very complicated methods of persuasion and entrapment—but once she did, she followed through quickly and easily. The design for the maquette took all of two weeks, and the work uniform a few days."[85]

In Aksionov's interpretation Popova's prolonged hesitation was related purely to the moods in the Constructivists' camp: Popova did not want "to discredit Constructivism with overly hasty realization."[86] We can recall her similar dissatisfaction with the excessively abstract nature of her work, with the creation of purely "artistic objects," and with her desire to participate in "concrete production," of which we spoke earlier. What was the proper attitude toward the theater? Should it be regarded as a production or as yet another version of the artistic laboratory? So long as it was a matter of purely academic work, the artist looked on it as preparation for the new profession of life organizer and planner of which the Productivists dreamed. Could a real, concrete performance serve these goals? One may also assume that she was put off by the lack of resolution and clarity in those new forms in which the artist's work "in planning the material element of the performance" might be expressed. After all, her own theatrical experience had been on a totally different plane.

Popova's work at GVYTM, in that atmosphere of constant collective discussion and collective creativity, both helped and hindered her. It helped her to work out precise principles for the new design, to conceptualize her goal, but it kept her from seeking an immediate, vital solution, first, because it set extremely high standards for innovation and for the theoretical purity of accepted solutions, and second, because once again it detracted from the performance's integrity for the sake of a purely experimental elaboration of partial problems.

We shall try to reconstruct briefly how the sets for *The Magnanimous Cuckold*, which have become so popular throughout the world, evolved. While Popova and Rodchenko (Aksionov names him as well) were still weighing the theater's proposal, it was accepted by the young Stenberg brothers, Georgii and Vladimir, and their friend Konstantin Medunetsky, all of whom were young, pragmatic, self-confident, and not inclined to excessive reflection or intellectualizing about their work. In recent literature the role of these artists in conceiving the sets for *The Magnanimous Cuckold* has been mentioned and discussed several times.[87] We shall make one more attempt to evaluate the influence of these young artists' original idea on Popova's final resolution.

Judging from Vladimir Stenberg's recollections, both those published and those he related to the author directly, what they proposed that captivated Meierkhold and that, as the painter Georgii Yakulov later asserted, "would never have occurred to a Soviet mademoiselle like Popova," was the rather scabrous idea (but one absolutely in keeping with Crommelynck's farce) of playing up the mill chute—down which grain or sacks of grain are supposed to slide—for Stella's "processed" lovers to descend from her bedroom. This idea naturally implied bringing the image of the chute rather than the traditional interiors to the foreground. Moreover, the whole architecture of the mill was transformed into a scheme of "acting" elements: the platform, the stairs, the chute, the vanes of the mill. By all accounts, the idea of the mill turning during the course of the action also came from the Stenbergs and Medunetsky. There is no indication of any notion of the overall stage setting in this initial idea. There is no question that Popova's entire plastic conception for the final staging was worked out quite outside the original plan.[88] Vladimir Stenberg recalled that when they talked with Meierkhold, they had no sketches with them and drew their idea on a piece of paper right there. More than likely Meierkhold transmitted this idea to Popova orally. That this was a verbal image rather than a sketch is supported in part by the mill's lack of definition as a basic component in the set's construction. Stenberg speaks clearly of the vane, that is to say, the mill. At first, in the spirit of the plastic system developed in her painting, Popova began to elaborate a scheme of wheel circles. Only later did she combine all the usual mill attributes into one, creating a sort of synthetic, ideal, abstract image of "a mill in general."

To add to all this, the Stenbergs and Medunetsky's idea also reached Popova through the intermediate sketches of her pupil Liutse, to whom The Magnanimous Cuckold had been proposed as an academic assignment. "By inspiring the pupil and leading him away from illusionistic representation, Vs. Meierkhold suggested the basic elements of the future set, proposing they be taken from the construction of a wooden windmill (a montage of real givens). V. Liutse submitted a design that L. S. Popova took as a basis for further elaboration."[89]

The idea of constructing a freestanding set evidently took shape gradually during classes at GVYTM and in heated debates over the theater's development. This was Meierkhold's secret dream; it defined his attitude toward Constructivist-oriented artists who moved from depicting the object to real construction in space.

One gets the impression that Popova's concept was originally tied to the proscenium stage. This compromise theatrical construction would be used more than once in the future in Meierkhold's theater as well as in others.[90]

The set designs for The Magnanimous Cuckold in the Tretiakov Gallery (page 261, top) demonstrate an initial stage in the development of Popova's concept. The composition completely fills the stage and resembles the future set only in individual motifs and details: the cross-shaped supporting structures, similar cruciform doors, the diagonals of the staircases, the as yet weakly delineated circles of the wheels. We have no absolute, total assurance that these studies relate to The Magnanimous Cuckold rather than to some other academic production at GVYTM. Our assumption is supported, however, by the sketches' similarity to what we may consider the next stage of work (page 260, bottom), depicting a set already familiar to us from the final version but having in addition in the upper portion a rather massive girder, a sort of rudiment of earlier fortifications, as well as wheels that are significantly larger than in the final version and equally large windmill blades now placed on the right. Sketch by sketch the vertically oriented set gradually takes on a horizontal silhouette, the upper girder, repeated one more time (Tretiakov inventory p. 47238), disappears once and for all, the wheels get smaller and acquire sharply contrasting dimensions, the large windmill on the right becomes a small, purely symbolic propeller on the left (page 248, top). In eliminating the large windmill the artist evidently considered replacing it with a flag such as the one that decorated the booth of the puppet theater (page 260, top).

Despite the wholly independent resolution of the problem by Popova and her students, a scandal arose at the premiere when Georgii Yakulov accused Popova of plagiarism. Popova was outraged. A few days later Inkhuk investigated the case, and the meeting established Popova's total innocence. For the history of art, however, it is not the clarification of the relations between Popova and the Stenbergs and Yakulov that is most important here but the discussion of the artistic question of theatrical Constructivism that flared up in Inkhuk in response to Popova's production and that vitally affected all its participants. Various memoirs refer to this meeting as "Popova's trial."[91]

The Inkhuk discussion of April 27, 1922, brought into focus many creative contradictions in the artist's concept of the performance—those terribly fruitful contradictions that ensured a vivid artistic result and artistic success where theory saw insurmountable complications and incompatible principles.

Popova spoke most candidly and passionately about her doubts, intentions, and goals in entering into the discussion (Appendix XVII). She evaluated her own work quite harshly, emphasizing that her resolution of the tasks she had set herself was far from complete. The artist insisted on the "production" treatment of theatrical work: "my desire is to translate the problem from the aesthetic to the production plane."[92] This is precisely how she treated the theater in her classes at GVYTM; it was here that she saw the meaning to herself of her work in the theater since that crucial moment in the fall of 1921. Popova was absolutely sincere and convinced in these declarations. She stressed that formal problems (of color, space, and so on) were for her merely the functional conditions of a given work, the concrete solution to the given theoretical problem: "equipping theatrical action with its material components." She persisted in shifting the stress from formal-compositional to utilitarian-functional problems; the figurative problem seemed not to exist for her at all. She insisted that her goal was to create the "equipment, a set or prop for the given action. In this, one criterion should be utilitarian adaptability and not the resolution of any formal-aesthetic problems such as the question of color or volume, or the organization of the theatrical space, and so on."[93] And then she notes: "In this case, of course, the pure resolution of the issue did not work out because (1) it was hard for me at the start to reject outmoded aesthetic customs and criteria, and (2) I was hindered by a condition of an aesthetic order, that the action bore a farcical, visual character and made it impossible for me to consider the action merely as an ongoing work process, and this to a significant degree lent everything the aesthetic character of the visual action."[94] That is, theater itself, which Meierkhold's experiments had to quite a strong degree abstracted and mechanized but which had by no means been deprived of its acting and visual essence, interfered with the renunciation of the theater for the sake of abstract action.

The artistic significance of Popova's work for the stage consists, as the art historian Elena Rakitina has magnificently demonstrated, in the counterpoint among the seriousness of the acting, the theory, and the immediacy of creative expression, of asceticism and luxury, of rehearsal and improvisation. While accusing herself of inconsistency in applying precisely formulated "production" principles and dogmas, Popova suddenly confessed: "I had a very hard time deciding to accept this job. I will not do easel painting, and this was an attempt to discharge some energy."[95]

This job, about which the artist spoke so many harsh words, gave her the vital joy of creation, a joy stemming from the direct funneling of creative energy, the manifest materialization of inner ideas and fantasies. Aksionov recalled: "As Popova herself admitted, the theater gave her the happiest moment in her life. That moment, she felt, was when the set for Cuckold was assembled for the first time, and she, the author, having taken refuge in the dress circle, saw for the first time what was her largest work so far—ready for action."[96]

When characterizing Popova's work in designing this production as a whole, it is essential to emphasize that, first of all, what was achieved here was a magnificent accord, a coming together of the aesthetic and creative aspirations of the artist and a director—Meierkhold. Their creative contradictions were shared, on a single plane, of a single order. The produc-

tion achieved an essential balance of theatrical action and design, which was not present, for example, in the Tairov-Vesnin work on an adaptation of G. K. Chesterton's The Man Who Was Thursday, where the painstakingly constructed theatrical architecture overshadowed the performance's theatrical significance.

In the second place, this work was an essential step in Popova's own creative evolution, her own personal version, her own edition of Constructivist stylistics. It is extremely important that Popova brought all her artistic temperament, as well as the refined sensibility and tact peculiar to her as an artist, to bear on these stylistics. The result was a composition that was harmonically consistent in its proportions and in the relations between the scale of the set and the figures of the actors—a light but stable structure whose wheels and windmill echoed the Romantic theme of wind and water, elementary and enigmatic in its singularity, gladdening the eye with its clear combination of light, unpainted wood, which looked as though it had just left the carpenter's hands. Its black and red details underlined the enigmatic, mysterious letters: CR ML NK. This set engendered pleasure, amazement, and amusement, but it also worked like a machine, an apparatus, subordinating itself to the action of the performance.

There are a number of analyses of both the production as a whole and the artist's role in it that reveal the rich and contradictory essence of this phenomenon. Let us turn to several aspects that illustrate its role in the artist's creative evolution. To a greater degree than other such works, the production of The Magnanimous Cuckold was pulled in two directions simultaneously: toward the abstract model of the theater in general, to theatricality in its pure form, and also toward the theater as an organizer of life, a school of optimism, courage, and harmony. Both were achieved by identical means: abstraction from everyday reality, historical concreteness, psychological complexity, alienation from the literary plot, and visual authenticity. In this abstractness lay the pledge of the production's purity and brightness in defiance of the play's farcical plot. This abstractness beyond the contours of "pure" theater clarified a model for the theater-workshop that shapes the "effective harmonious social personality."[97] The work of Popova-the-theater-designer comprised these principles: refinement of form, taking it to the purity of the sign, the overall scheme, and the effective organization principle. She was firmly convinced: "The theater's new production is not the depiction of life but the exemplary illustrative organization of life and people (whether positive or negative)."[98]

The incisive viewer consciously perceived or unconsciously sensed the bold, lively rhythm of the action, felt behind the strange peripeteia of the theme the true significance of the young, provocative, gay, and human production. He was not called upon to suffer through questionable actions and words born of a vaguely pathological psychology but was drawn into the very process of merry alienation, of acting *joie de vivre* in a psychological drama. Popova's set and the costumes (the work uniforms) in which the actors were dressed embodied very well the spirit of creativity-in-process, which as such demanded the viewer's inclusion and full participation. "The Constructive set," wrote Sergei Tretiakov, "is a forest of buildings under construction. It is our stairs and floors, our walkways and crossings, which our muscles must overcome. And the wheels—these are the decorations themselves laughing and joking during the course of the action."[99]

Both Meierkhold's production and Popova's work acquired world fame, a place in the history of the theater, in the history of the arts—and for good reason. In my opinion the sets for *The Magnanimous Cuckold* cannot be judged only by an external criterion related to their role in the development of architectural Constructivism, and so forth. They are important in and of themselves as an indicator of the aesthetic value and artistic possibilities of Constructivist stylistics.

It is absolutely clear that the set for *Cuckold* grew wholly out of Popova's later painting—from the poetics of linear constructions and those "visits" from the world of abstraction to the world of reality, where the speculative interlacing of painting and graphic elements gave birth to the reality of the articulation of wooden beams and laths. (We should note that although the windmill theme lay at the base of the set's image, it did not actually appear in the sketches right off. It was initially contemplated as an abstraction and a diagram, which the artist hoped to give the character of a real structure with a specific construction and appearance; pages 260, bottom, and 261, left).

What turns out to be altogether vital in Popova's work is the essential graphic quality, the draftsmanliness of the set and the relative lack of depth to its space. The artist did this consciously. To a question from Boris Kushner at the Inkhuk discussions as to whether she had planned the set in two dimensions she replied: "I had in mind resolving everything in two dimensions; the stairs, for example, I showed not *en face* but in profile. I was working from the idea of a planar resolution, I made sort of a sketch; the problem of space did not interest me."[100]

The reasons for this, in my opinion, are related to the fact that the structure's graphic quality accentuated its schematicness, the image's abstractness from the natural prototype, that is, something other than the usual make-believe. The structure into which the former windmill, being in essence a three-dimensional structure in space, was transformed doubly emphasized its abstractness: as an abstraction from nature and as a complement to the acting, without any pretensions to a leading role. A few months later a GVYTM student, A. Pozdneev, in an essay in the magazine *Zrelishcha* (Performances), argued for a parallel between the *Cuckold* set and abstract circus apparatuses, which have absolutely no pretensions to any direct psychological effect on the viewer but are wholly subordinated to the gymnast's work.[101]

The poetics of draftsmanly graphics was Popova's principal artistic means in this work. Despite the fact that the set design had been sketched out in painstaking fashion—which may have been unavoidable for the craftsmen constructing it—Popova carefully drew all the details of the action, from the pot of geraniums (page 248, bottom), which like the flower (page 260, right) was to be executed in wire, to the rattle, pen, and inkwell. Everything was supposed to acquire a conceptual, unreal character—this, evidently, is how she survived the transfer from the world of planar representation to the world of real three-dimensional things. Fear may have exacted its toll here—fear that in translating the sketch into the substance of the artistic image, into reality, the same thing would happen that had a year before with *The Locksmith and the Chancellor*. Now she was depriving the world of things of its flesh and naturalness in advance, wittingly. This is also how she saw the actors in their work uniforms: two-dimensional and abstract, people-signs, masks, types.

The director and the acting gave them life and flesh, overcoming the impersonal schematism imparted by the artist. But this schematism meshed perfectly with Meierkhold's theatrical-educational theories, his system of "biomechanics." The performance itself, the director and the acting, overcame the narrowness of the theoretical setting in precisely the same way as the artist did in designing the production. A fortunate distinction was achieved here between acting as a demonstration of the actor's training and as a vital improvisation executed with cheerful ardor and sincerity.

But Popova's compositions, after all (both the large final drawing and the preliminary sketches), were by no means simply drafts but draftsmanly graphic images both of the set itself and of the production as a whole. The image of the production was far from unambiguous and simple, rather it seemed to be concealed behind the ascetic simplicity of the work uniforms. The emphasis on the "production" treatment of the theatrical action and the actual eccentric, dynamic (nearly on the level of circus tricks) acting of the actors led Popova toward a technical treatment of both the sets and of the image as a stage-workplace. Although the set was quite uncomplicated in the technical sense, the construction for *The Magnanimous Cuckold* clearly bore the theme of a machine-workplace for the actors' work, a concept that was also part of Constructivism's aesthetic ideal.

But, we repeat, the meaning and success of the staging, as of the production as a whole, was in the destruction of unified theoretical postulates, in the vital pulsing of creative energy destroying and facilitating the schematism of the original goals. Popova's work, which was looked on highly critically inside Inkhuk, enjoyed instant and immense popularity among audiences and in innovation-oriented theoretical circles. Evidence of this were the widespread imitations, variations, and paraphrasings. There was a new fashion in sets; arguments flared over the priority of one or another construction, over attempts to cleanse "true Constructivism" in the theater of deviant imitations.

The production's popularity was extraordinary, in fact. Successful and beloved, it played in the theater constantly. On December 8, 1922, the hundredth performance of *The Magnanimous Cuckold* took place. The journal *Zrelishcha*, which was sympathetic to Meierkhold's thinking, published an editorial saying: "When it was performed for the first time in April 1922, this play enjoyed absolutely exceptional success. Without exaggerating, one could assert that modern leftist art marches forward under *Cuckold*'s banner....*Cuckold* is a production of historical significance; as a landmark for all modern theater it is undisputed."[102] It added that viewers honored L. S. Popova—the artist-constructor: "the mother of Constructivism on the stage."

The resonance and artistic influence of Popova's work on sets was not limited to the theater. It could be seen in the evolutionary movement of the Constructivist architecture-in-formation (for instance, several pavilions at the 1923 Agricultural Exhibition had the motif of cross-shaped diagonal constructions). No less important was Popova's effect on the development of Constructivist style in graphics. Even more important was her influence on Constructivist theater aesthetics, which came into being together with the unique image of the spectacle: the director, the performance, the entire design concept.

THE PRIEST OF TARQUINIA: "A PRODUCTION NOT IN KEEPING WITH ITS CONCEPT"

A series of studies of traditional Oriental types was found in Popova's studio after her death (pages 243 and 262–69). To judge from the studio list and remarks on the sheets themselves, they pertain to an unstaged production at the Actor's Theater (which is what Meierkhold's theater was called in 1922) of the play *Zhrets Tarkvinii (The Priest of Tarquinia)* by S. Polivanov, the pseudonym of Naum Sheinfeld. The chronicle of Meierkhold's theater and art contains no mention of this work. We know from Meierkhold's correspondence that Polivanov's play was under consideration at the Actor's Theater in May 1922.[103]

Clearly the studies on *The Priest of Tarquinia* theme could not have appeared before then, that is, Popova had to have worked on them after *The Magnanimous Cuckold* and, in all likelihood, no later than the fall of 1922, when she was already busy with the preparations for a new production of *Zemlia dybom (Earth on End)*. The folder of sketches is dated in her own

hand "1922." But the date of their creation and their place in the artist's creative evolution are what make this work so paradoxical, incomprehensible, enigmatic.

The clear, logical development of Popova's art, justified and explained by a whole series of circumstances—the general nature of the evolution of those artists close to her, the progress of Meierkhold's theater from *The Magnanimous Cuckold* to *Earth on End*, the precise line of theoretical rationales expressed in the artist's own speeches—all this negated, in an unforeseeable, arbitrary, mysterious way, the spirit and style of these studies, of which there are a few dozen.[104]

All the studies bear the stamp of stylization, a lively admiration for the refined expressiveness of curved lines, of details inferred. They do not bear so much as a trace of the Constructivist bent toward asceticism and directness. The simplest and most economical are the pencil drawings (pages 264-67), which, as a rule, depict full figures. If we were to compare them to the studies for *Romeo and Juliet* done two years before (pages 230-33) we would be struck by the simplification and "distillation" of style that comes through in the reduction of the number of lines, their complicated intertwining, rhythmic repetitions, and the simultaneous complication of the nature of the lines themselves: instead of harsh Cubist angularity, they now acquire a vital and diverse flexibility.

If almost all the preceding drawings of the "post-nonobjective" period—the studies for *Romeo and Juliet, The Locksmith and the Chancellor* (pages 235 and 242), the actors' work uniforms—were placed logically in a line from Cubism to Constructivism, repeating to some extent the same evolution as Popova's painting in previous years, then the sketches for *The Priest of Tarquinia* would be seen clearly to initiate a new phase. It is characteristic that this new turn capriciously resurrects elements of the stylistics of the Modern movement long since departed. In trying to define the place of these works among all the rest, we note that the beginnings of this new free, unfettered drawing can be seen both in some of the puppet show studies (not all of them were built upon the fragmented Cubistic form) and in the illustrations for a volume of Oriental tales published in 1920 by Diez (Gavriil Dobrzhinsky). This project revived the artist's impressions from her 1915 trip to Samarkand.

Thus we see that in Popova's creative evolution the final five years were marked and developed—with varying intensity, it is true—by two lines: one that led clearly toward Constructivist stylistics and another that presupposed a wholly realistic path but for its development utilized Oriental ornament, artistic-archaeological material, and the ornamental linearity of Modernism.

It is important to understand whether the artist herself recognized these divergent possibilities and what might have served as a concrete stimulus for the manifestation of this second line, in this instance, in the studies for *The Priest of Tarquinia*.

I see two possible reasons here. One, which to some extent has already been illuminated, has to do with the need for a livelier, more spontaneous, more immediate expression of creative energy than seemed possible within the narrow channel of Constructivism understood as the art of rationalism, as the manifestation of a "divine mathematics." Drafting compositions with a ruler, having rejected easel work as well, Popova may well have felt the need of a counterbalance in the form of free, unfettered drawing, the play of associations, the traditional romanticism of Orientalism.

Another reason, it seems to me, involved the success of Aleksandra Exter's dazzling productions for *Romeo and Juliet* at the Chamber Theater and Vesnin's *Pearl of Adalmina* at the Children's Theater, in 1921. By trying to resolve the new production in a decorative vein, to saturate it with vivid color images, to convey through it her impressions of the art, architecture, and daily life of the Orient, Popova, unconsciously perhaps, placed herself in competition with the successful works of her friends.

Polivanov's play, as was stated earlier, was never staged. Of course, at the time Popova's work was unacceptable to the Actor's Theater. It would scarcely have been possible to explain all that she had done by the necessity for "expediency" or to prove the absence of aestheticism. And it was, after all, precisely these principles that she had propounded so ardently and so sincerely in the speeches and essays she has left us from that period.

EXPEDIENCY!

In the summer of 1922 Popova wrote and that September published an essay with a lengthy title: "O tochnom kriterii, o baletnykh nomerakh, o palubnom oborudovanii, o poslednikh portretakh Pikasso i o nabliudatelnoi vyshke shkoly voennoi maskirovki v Kuntseve" (On a Precise Criterion, on Ballet Steps, on Deck Equipment for Warships, on Picasso's Latest Portraits, and on the Observation Tower at the Military Camouflage School at Kuntsevo; Appendix XVIII).[105] In this article, parts of which have already been cited, Popova once again decisively rejected the formal style criterion in discussing art and artistic creativity (and anything aesthetic per se) that only recently (in 1920 and early 1921) had seemed absolute. In its place she advanced and asserted expediency—functional appropriateness to attain a goal—and the related ideas of universality, objectivity, *infallibility*. She saw this expediency in the precise and regulated movements of the deck crew and in the outfitting of warships, in a chemical formula and in the calculation for boiler walls. The meaning and vector of movement of the actor's thought should be clear—toward precise, emotion-free calculation, toward prosaic, life-conditioned goals, toward the rejection of fantasy and play. But this is what is characteristic: higher expediency illuminated and vindicated the new neo-

classical works of Picasso—rumors of which had reached Russia during those years and had upset the art world—which Popova elevated in her deliberations to the rank of a positive example.

Of Picasso's latest abusers she wrote: "The days of their 'art for art's sake' have long been numbered, but they persist with their 'formal-aesthetic point of view' in DISCUSSING PICASSO: as if he had turned realist and betrayed the Dardanelles of his 'formal inquiries'! Whereas Picasso," Popova heatedly retorted, "in the name of what if not 'expediency,' has started making *portraits like photographs* (what does Ingres have to do with this?!). Honestly, photographically, *in the name of representation* as a goal that is anything but aesthetic: that is what the photographers are doing now."[106]

Reading this text more closely, with the sketches for *The Priest of Tarquinia* that were "not in keeping with its concept" before you, you cannot help beginning to suspect a certain ambivalence, an ambiguity in Popova's quick-tempered, seemingly very precise statements. Suddenly the new criterion is overly broad, equally applicable to *"formulas of work for the given materials"* and to "representation as a goal" in Picasso's portraits. One gets the impression that the problem of the new representation had taken on increasing urgency at that moment for this artist, who had passed not only through the experiments of nonobjectiveness but also through those of doctrinaire Constructivism.

One way out was photography, which Popova treats here as true representation in pure form, representation minus the author's will, aestheticization, or transformation, the presence of nature in and of itself.

She attempted to apply and experiment with these possibilities of photography in her typographical design works of the last two years of her life and in her last theatrical production, *Earth on End*.

COLLABORATION WITH MEIERKHOLD:
THIRD EPISODE—*EARTH ON END*

In this agit-play production the idea of the theater "as an exemplary demonstration organization of life and people" was no longer resolved metaphorically or abstractly but rather through direct impact on the consciousness and the psyche. It was a performance-poster: "By destroying stylized illusion and discarding the fetishism of theatrical form, this theater functions under the slogan of practical expediency and utilitarian life-building."[107]

According to Meierkhold's original idea, the production was to have marked the fifth anniversary of the October Revolution in 1922.[108] Meierkhold had to hurry. He was eager for a large-scale, splashy political spectacle. The director was preparing for an anniversary of his own, marking thirty years in the theater, and he dreamed of saying his piece about the Revolution at the top of his voice.

Stern sobriety and tragic pathos sharply distinguished the new production from the joyous, sarcastic *Cuckold* as well as from most other GVYTM works. Such moods, characteristic of that moment, were the artistic intelligentsia's unique reaction to the sociopsychological situation in the country as a result of the New Economic Policy (NEP), a form of limited capitalism by which Lenin hoped to relieve the Soviet Union of its postwar famine and shortages. The vulgarity of the numerous entertainments intended for high-rolling Nepmen, the atmosphere of prosperity, of smugness, stood in sharp although perhaps unacknowledged contrast to the stern, tragic, passionate productions, the realism of the brutally honest film documentaries, whose authors wrote "Kino-Pravda" (Cinema-Truth) on their banners, to the cutting, nearly Expressionist journalistic graphics. The members of the Meierkhold collective, who themselves had only recently rejoiced, carefree, in life during *The Magnanimous Cuckold*, now produced a show in a different, tragic key, wholly subordinate to direct and open propaganda for the Revolution and for Socialism.

Since they could find no appropriate material, they decided to adapt Marcel Martinet's play *La Nuit* (The Night), which had been translated from the French and already staged unsuccessfully in Moscow and Petrograd. Sergei Tretiakov did the adaptation. Meierkhold assigned Popova to break the play down into dynamically sequenced episodes (instead of the traditional acts and scenes). The treatment of text and plot development were pragmatic and arbitrary—they used the play frankly as material for their own purposes and constructions.

The theater had moved further down the path toward the metatheatrical propaganda play. In this instance the design actually made it possible to perform the play (actually a cut version), not only in the theater, but in open-air spaces such as parks and stadiums, which the troupe did several times. [109] The play premiered on March 4, 1923, and by May 1 there were already plans to perform it on Khodinskoe Field, where two years earlier Popova had laid out "The Fortress of Capital" and "The City of the Future" for *The Struggle and Victory* festival. The grandiose sweep of the performance was intended not only for "field conditions," but for inside a theater as well. In the theater, bicyclists and motorcyclists sped down the aisle. Soldiers formed columns and rows, marched, held mass meetings, shouted "hurrah." A model airplane flew over the hall (there wasn't room for a real one), a real truck drove on stage with the body of the murdered Ledru. The military technology, the agricultural implements, the typewriters at headquarters—all this was real. But all of it was "technology," not "daily life." They were afraid of daily life. The blue work uniforms the

peasants wore flashed past on stage alongside real military uniforms. This note brought the performance back from the digression on "nature" to the abstract realm of slogans.

Popova formulated the basic principles of the agit-performance precisely in her "Tezisy" (Theses), which she published in the journal *LEF* (Left Front of the Arts; Appendix XIX). [110]

Another manuscript shows that for the artist these general principles had been transformed into tactical rules: "(1) no decorativeness; (2) equip to suit the action; (3) plan the action along the horizontal (the plane of the hall) and along the vertical (the space of the hall); (4) lay out the principal areas according to the script...; (5) lay out the space: stairs, bridges, letters hung on ropes, lighted signs, searchlights, posters on walls and ropes. Technological points: (6) overall rhythm: extreme, totally bared dynamics; extraordinary swiftness; Americanism." [111]

The Magnanimous Cuckold was quintessential theatricality expressed in the careful tuning of all the acting elements (movement, gesture, voice), in the exaggerated artificiality of all the details of the action—recall Popova's sketches indicating how many inches of wire should be used to make the pot of geraniums (pages 248 and 261)—in the notoriously abstract nature of the *prozodezhda* (work uniforms). Here we have the opposite. The acting loses its theatrical refinement and acquires the sweep and strong, sharp accents of an agit-play. According to the reviewers, the intensity and intonations of the entire performance seemed to be heard through a megaphone, as in a mass meeting. [112]

For Popova, and to some extent for Meierkhold as well, *Earth on End* was simultaneously a continuation, a development of what they had begun and conceived—especially of their as yet unrealized idea for a mass spectacle—and to an even greater extent, the antithesis, the negation of what they had only recently discovered and mastered, above all, resolving the problems of art versus life, theater versus reality, illusion versus realism.

The rejection of artificial theatrical baggage, apart from the purely artistic calculation of the impression real things were supposed to make, had one more aspect to it: a move away from professional acting to broadly accessible acting. The notion of improvisational amateur acting had been latent during the staging of *Cuckold*, and paradoxically so, considering the basic tendency toward professionalism. Aksionov wrote about the idea of the development of the spectacle outside the theater: "in its further development, by freeing the stage, sets, costumes, the production ought to lead to freeing the actor and the play as well. The theatrical production ought to yield to the free acting of off-duty workers who spend part of their leisure on a presentation, improvised, perhaps, near where they have just left off work, following a script one of them has made up on the spot."[113] By rejecting purely theatrical trappings, in *Earth on End* the theater took a step toward the viewer-participant of the mass festival.

In contrast to the quick, joyous work on *The Magnanimous Cuckold*, the preparations for *Earth on End* proved a complicated matter for Popova, the source of many difficulties and doubts. Personal tragedy hovered in the background—the illness and death of Popova's mother, which clouded the artist's emotional state and her perception of her work.

Judging from Aksionov's fragmentary comments, Popova thought of the production in terms of Productivist doctrine, as a "demonstration of organized daily life," using purely propaganda effects, and was opposed to changes that brought it closer to the playful, entertaining Khodinskoe Field festival.[114]

What was the design scheme? Basically, it was a grandiose construction depicting a crane (pages 270 and 271, bottom). Actually, it would have been a real crane, but since that turned out to be too heavy for the theater building, a wooden model was substituted. For the open-air performances they did use a real crane, to which they attached plywood shields bearing slogan-posters (page 271, top left), and screens, on which they projected film clips, slogans, and the episode titles (page 271, top right).

The production's whole design was resolved like a poster, or perhaps more precisely, like a cinematic propaganda chronicle evolved from a poster. In one of the reviews we read: "In this production for the first time theater wins out over film."[115] These qualities determined the style and nature of the performance and gave its entire structure a visual concentration. These same qualities gave an essential terseness and emphatic expressiveness to all the sets and details. The viewer was fixed in a saturated propaganda field, not only following the development of the tragic theme of rebellion and defeat, a leader's betrayal and murder, but immediately tuning in to an active, up-to-the-minute, highly actualized perception of events. For this purpose an enormous shield with a quotation from a speech by Georgii Chicherin, commissar of foreign affairs, was introduced as a constant in the design: "Build, build, hold that plow, hold that hammer—take out everything the earth will give. Throw bridges across rivers, draw steel pathways across the broad fields, shatter their silence with the happy sound of trains.

Erect gigantic factory complexes, count, draw, administer, economize, count your pennies, save—that is our revolutionary front today." All the other slogans and representational film and film clips changed during the course of the action.

Aksionov stressed the special, totally symbolic treatment of slogan-texts—somewhat analogous to advertising—in this staging: "The slogans selected for projection were well known to everyone, so familiar that they had already lost their individual word articulation and were thought of as monolithic phrases, so familiar that they had already become *objects* of social custom."[116]

Popova's montage of real objects and slogan-texts was, as we have noted, analogous to the documentary film montages of those years, especially the works of Dziga Vertov, for example. It was on the basis of this cinematic principle that the part-episode titles were introduced. In the artist's studio after her death dozens of such texts were found (large quantities of them are in the Costakis collection).

There are numerous reproductions of Popova's montage design for the set. On the board we see a crane, slogans, documentary films, and parts of photographs—not concentrated inside a frame but freely distributed over the entire field. This composition is a highly expressive example of Constructivist monumental graphics, a graphic image of the "poster-performance." In the montage we can distinctly read the stylistics of Constructivism: the arrangement of the composition, the strict linearity of the basic shapes, the idealization and assertion of technical form, the extensive use of typefaces, textual fragments, and photographic images as graphic elements. All these points are characteristic for Popova's graphic design as well.

The montage the artist did for this play about war and revolution, *Earth on End*, demonstrates the amazing combination of concentration and economy in the image and, simultaneously, visual and informational wealth. It reconstructs vividly and precisely the image of the mass festival, enclosed within the walls of a theater only by chance. In this, as well as in her book design of those years, there is a special—I would call it "postnonobjective"—attitude toward representation and the figurative form that emphasizes its documentary authenticity, its nearly schematic clarity, its draftlike essentialness.

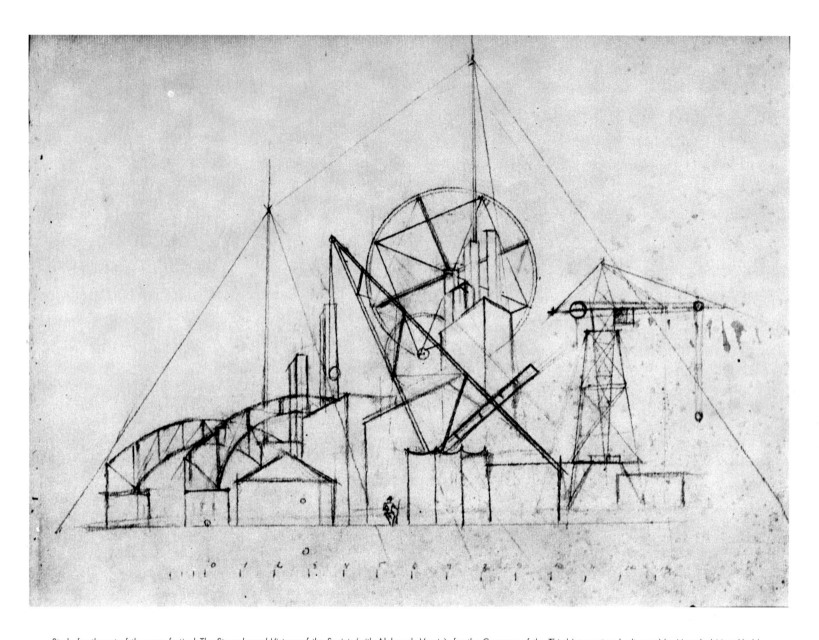

Study for the set of the mass festival *The Struggle and Victory of the Soviets* (with Aleksandr Vesnin), for the Congress of the Third International, directed by Vsevolod Meierkhold. *The City of the Future.* 1921. Pencil on paper, 9⅝ × 13⅛" (24.6 × 33.4 cm.). Private collection, Moscow

Scene from *The Magnanimous Cuckold*, by Fernand Crommelynck, Actor's Theater. 1922.

Set design for *The Magnanimous Cuckold*, by Fernand Crommelynck, Actor's Theater. 1922. Pencil, colored pencil, and India ink on paper, 9⅛ × 14⅞" (23.1 × 37.8 cm.). Costakis Collection, Athens, cat. no. 880

Set design for *The Magnanimous Cuckold*, by Fernand Crommelynck, Actor's Theater. 1922. Pencil on paper, 11 × 8½" (27.8 × 21.7 cm.). Tretiakov Gallery. Gift of George Costakis

Original set design for *The Magnanimous Cuckold*, by Fernand Crommelynck, Actor's Theater. 1922. Pencil on paper, 10½ × 8⅛" (26.6 × 20.6 cm.). Tretiakov Gallery. Gift of George Costakis

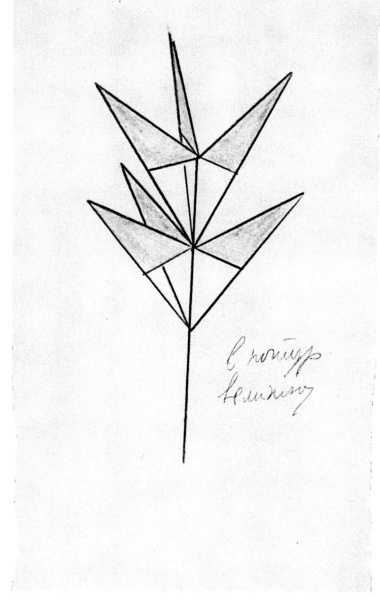

Prop design for *The Magnanimous Cuckold*, by Fernand Crommelynck, Actor's Theater. *Flower.* 1922. Black and red pencil on paper, 14⅝ × 9" (37 × 23 cm.). Tretiakov Gallery

Costume design for the unstaged *Priest of Tarquinia*, by S. Polivanov, at GITIS.
Astrologer (?). 1922. Dark blue India ink on gray paper, 10⅝ × 8¾"
(27.1 × 22.3 cm.). Private collection, Moscow

Costume design for the unstaged *Priest of Tarquinia*, by S. Polivanov, at GITIS.
Man in a Crown. 1922. Dark blue India ink on gray paper, 10⅝ × 8¾"
(27.1 × 22.3 cm.). Private collection, Moscow

Costume design for the unstaged *Priest of Tarquinia*, by S. Polivanov, at GITIS. *Man with a Fan*. 1922. Dark blue India ink on yellow paper, 15¼ × 8½" (38.6 × 21.6 cm.). Private collection, Moscow

Costume design for the unstaged *Priest of Tarquinia*, by S. Polivanov, at GITIS. *Man with a Fan*. 1922. Dark blue India ink on gray paper, 10⅝ × 8¾" (27.1 × 22.3 cm.). Private collection, Moscow

263

Costume design for the unstaged *Priest of Tarquinia*, by S. Polivanov, at GITIS.
Old Man. 1922. Pencil on yellow paper, 14 × 8⅝" (35.5 × 22 cm.).
Private collection, Moscow

Costume design for the unstaged *Priest of Tarquinia*, by S. Polivanov, at GITIS.
Priest. 1922. Pencil on gray paper, 10⅝ × 8" (27.1 × 20.2 cm.).
Private collection, Moscow

Costume design for the unstaged *Priest of Tarquinia*, by S. Polivanov, at GITIS.
Soldier. 1922. Pencil on gray paper, 10⅝ × 8" (27.1 × 20.2 cm.).
Private collection, Moscow

Costume design for the unstaged *Priest of Tarquinia*, by S. Polivanov, at GITIS
(Lunacharsky State Institute of Theatrical Art). *Priest*. 1922. Gouache on paper,
21¾ × 15⅜" (55.2 × 39 cm.). Private collection, Moscow

Costume design for the unstaged *Priest of Tarquinia*, by S. Polivanov, at GITIS.
Woman in a Yashmak. 1922. Pencil on yellow paper, 13⅞ × 8⅝″ (35.1 × 22 cm.).
Private collection, Moscow

Costume designs for the unstaged *Priest of Tarquinia*, by S. Polivanov, at GITIS.
Women. 1922. Pencil on yellow paper, 13¾ × 8⅞″ (34.8 × 22.5 cm.).
Private collection, Moscow

Costume design for the unstaged *Priest of Tarquinia*, by S. Polivanov, at GITIS. *Woman*.
1922. Pencil on yellow paper, 14⅛ × 9" (35.7 × 22.7 cm.).
Private collection, Moscow

Costume design for the unstaged *Priest of Tarquinia*, by S. Polivanov, at GITIS. *Women*.
1922. Pencil on yellow paper, 13⅞ × 8⅝" (35.1 × 22 cm.).
Private collection, Moscow

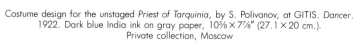

Costume design for the unstaged *Priest of Tarquinia*, by S. Polivanov, at GITIS. *Dancer*.
1922. Dark blue India ink on gray paper, 10⅝ × 7⅞" (27.1 × 20 cm.).
Private collection, Moscow

Costume design for the unstaged *Priest of Tarquinia*, by S. Polivanov, at GITIS. *Musician*.
1922. Dark blue India ink on gray paper, 10⅝ × 8¾" (27.1 × 22.3 cm.).
Private collection, Moscow

Costume design for the unstaged *Priest of Tarquinia*, by S. Polivanov, at GITIS. *Dancer.*
1922. Gouache on paper, 21½ × 16⅜" (54.5 × 41.7 cm.).
Private collection, Moscow

Costume design for the unstaged *Priest of Tarquinia*, by S. Polivanov, at GITIS. *Dancer.*
1922. Indigo India ink on gray paper, 10⅝ × 8¾" (27.1 × 22.3 cm.).
Private collection, Moscow

Stage design for *Earth on End*, adapted by Sergei Tretiakov from *La Nuit* by Marcel Martinet, Vsevolod Meierkhold Theater. 1923.
Collage on plywood, dimensions unknown. (From a photograph)

Fragment of a stage design for *Earth on End*, Vsevolod
Meierkhold Theater. 1923. Collage on plywood, dimensions
unknown. Photograph from the Costakis catalogue

Slogan-text for *Earth on End*, Vsevolod Meierkhold Theater. 1923. India ink and collage on paper, 6⅞ × 9″ (17.6 × 23 cm.). Costakis Collection, Athens

Poster with a part-episode title for *Earth on End*, Vsevolod Meierkhold Theater. 1923. India ink and collage on paper, 8¼ × 10⅛″ (20.9 × 25.8 cm.). Costakis Collection, Athens, cat. no. 904

Embroidery design for Verbovka. 1917. Collage on paper, 5⅜ × 3⅜″ (13.5 × 8.5 cm.). Private collection, Moscow

Embroidery design for Verbovka. 1917. Collage on cardboard, 6⅞ × 4¾″ (17.5 × 12 cm.). Museum of Decorative and Applied Art, Moscow

"PRODUCTION WORK": STUDIES FOR VERBOVKA

The emotional atmosphere and content of the final years of Popova's life provided a solid foundation for the conception of her art as an inevitable and unswerving progression from art to production, from the aesthetics of avant-gardism to the precise directives of Constructivism.

It is difficult to argue with this, impossible to refute it, but this one-dimensionality must be enriched with nuances, with real contradictions, with the idea that this progression included digression as well. It is important to understand that the evolution of Popova's art was more complex than the oft-repeated picture described above, and the artist's very personality, despite her real ideological intimacy and ties of friendship in her last years, cannot be wholly subsumed by a description of the Rodchenko-Stepanova circle and their students, her views and tastes by the ideas of Arvatov and Kushner, by the moods of the youthful nihilism characteristic of the Stenbergs, Ioganson, Gustav Klutsis, and others.

Liubov Popova was formed in a circle of the Russian avant-garde that had not yet lost its ties with turn-of-the-century art, in which the ideological directives of Symbolism, the stylistic traditions of Modernism, and the neo-Romantic ideals of times past were strong. People of the circle of Mikhail Matiushin, Kazimir Malevich, Olga Rozanova, Nadezhda Udaltsova, and Popova were intact threads tied to the era of the World of Art, of Viktor Borisov-Musatov, of Mikhail Vrubel, which had come to an end before their very eyes.

One of the connecting links between the two stages of Russian culture was the activity of the artist Natalia Davydova.[117] Davydova's goal had been to graft new artistic ideas, new images, onto the handicraft industry, which was now losing its vitality, and, in addition, to find a practical application for the innovations of professional artists. Both aspects of this problem had deep roots in the development of Russian culture of the preceding era.

This was a new elaboration of the ideas and activity of the late nineteenth-century Abramtsevo and Talashkino artists, with their romantic, Ruskinesque dreams of resurrecting the precious, synthetic creativity-craftsmanship of ages past. This was also a response to the Symbolist-oriented artists' ideas on the life-building functions of artistic creation, on the aesthetization of the objective environment expressed in the activity of the masters of the World of Art (Leon Bakst, Ivan Bilibin) and picked up later by such representatives of the avant-garde as Rozanova and Ksenia Boguslavskaia.

The site of Davydova's enterprise was the town of Verbovka in the Ukraine. Her undertaking stemmed from the fact that the sketches made for her craftspeople by professional artists hewed very closely to folk or traditional stylization. The most interesting contemporary artistic images—Cubist and Suprematist—could come to life in the hands of folk craftswomen and benefit by their influence and interpretation. Popova joined this work in 1917, at the time of her enthusiasm for Suprematist ideas, while working on the *Supremus* journal.

The surviving sketches for Verbovka (pages 272, 294, top, 295–96, and 297, right)[118] are miniature collages out of colored and white paper, glossy and matte, pasted either on a white (paper) or a gray (various shades of thin cardboard) background. The latter was evidently meant to approximate the unbleached canvas rural embroiderers used along with white canvas. All the compositions are resolved in a Suprematist vein. They demonstrate both a closeness to the artist's easel compositions in oil and gouache and a special "applied" principle—accentuated logic and transparency of thought. The coloration of these sheets differs somewhat from Popova's usual palette.

The compositions vary quite a lot, while keeping within the strict framework of their own internal logic. As a rule, the elements are arranged in compact groups: most often in one, usually with a complementary satellite element; less frequently there are two systems. The characteristic compact centripetalness here is inherent in Popova's Suprematist compositions.

The expressive effect of the collages is achieved chiefly through the use of colored forms and through the vigorous tonality of the gamut of colors. As a rule, the shapes of the elements are lapidary: rectangles, trapezoids, less often oblique triangles, segments, or the sharply cut silhouette of a guitar's sounding board.

On the whole, the compositions closely resemble her searches for a logo for *Supremus* (page 107), right down to precise coincidences. *The George Costakis Collection* catalog contains a silk-embroidered book cover and a study for it in colored ink.[119] The work is dated 1923-24. However, there has been a suggestion that this work may have been done for Verbovka in 1917. We do not know any other items of that period from Popova's sketches executed in fabric.[120]

The Verbovka collages straddle the fence between easel and applied art. Their components are exceptionally strong, as was true of the artist's easel works. These harmonious, balanced compositions are able to stand on their own. They do not look like fragments of something larger, but rather they seem to be models for them in reduced scale. Their decorative and applied intention is harder to see.

Nevertheless, this was a step from easel art to object art. The lessons of the Suprematist collages for Verbovka can be read clearly both in the method and in the visual descriptions of Popova's textile design, which she took up six years later. The lessons of these compositions were always present in the artist's numerous applied and Productivist graphics.

THE EXPERIMENT IN MONUMENTAL DESIGN: MOSSOVET—THE POETS CLUB

Popova's experiments in monumental design formed a unique prehistory to her Productivist work, her propaganda posters, and her design for the agit-play *Earth on End*, discussed above.

The fact that Popova helped design the Mossovet (Moscow Soviet) celebrations during the first years of the Revolution is mentioned several times in various sources: the Vesnin-Aksionov list, Pakhomova's biography for the State Academy of Artistic Sciences (GAKhN), the biographical note in the catalog of the posthumous exhibition, and articles published after the artist's death. All that varies is the date: May 1917 or May 1918. This discrepancy turns up in later publications as well. Clarity is introduced by Aksionov's article, where he speaks confidently about how Popova participated twice in preparations for Mossovet's May Day celebrations, in 1917 and 1918.[121] In 1918 she worked with Vesnin. Surviving sketches (Shusev Museum of Architecture) preserve no traces of Popova's participation.[122] In Popova's studio, as the inventory makes clear, there were two sketches for a "furniture design for the Moscow Soviet of Worker and Soldier Deputies" done for May Day 1917. To judge from her studio inventory, Popova executed this work independently. So far, the Mossovet design studies have not been uncovered.

In an article on Popova, Vasilii Rakitin mentions that Popova, S. Karetnikova, Vera Pestel, and Nadezhda Udaltsova painted the club of the Left Federation of the Union of Moscow Painters.[123] The federation was active in 1918, and that, evidently, was when the mural was done. At the same time, according to the oral testimony of Viktor Kieselev, Popova helped design the Café Pittoresque.

Yet another absolutely authentic and well-known experiment by Popova in monumental design was the banner studies for the All-Russian Union of Poets Club on Tverskoi Boulevard (page 290, top). The studies are dated 1921. Popova may have done them in connection with the "5 x 5 = 25" exhibition organized in the club's quarters.[124] In this work, which was intended for the elite viewer—the visitor to the club or its Bohemian café—Popova made no attempt to soften her style; on the contrary, she treated the letters of the banner like color forms in a nonobjective composition, preserving the bare minimum of readability, and plunged them into a space formed by the breaking up of color planes. Vivid colors merged into one another, not at all the norm for her painting of 1921, which was constructed, as a rule, on the principle of color asceticism. For the most part, in her painting of that period bright colors were kept within precise graphic limits.

The stylistics of these works, distinct from Popova's painting and graphics of 1921, as well as from her 1920 theatrical studies, hark back to an earlier stage in her art. We see that in works of an applied nature, the artist actively exploited the experience of her earlier painting experiments.

Among the diverse Popova materials from her studio that are now in a private collection in Moscow, we find two studies for compositions drawn in a semicircular frame obviously intended for some architectural object. Since these compositions are not described on the Vesnin-Aksionov list, there is a definite temptation to link them with the theme for the 1917 Mossovet design. However, the slogans included in the studies for the panels—"Cooperation is the bridge between the city and the country" and "The basis for cooperation is the real participation of the worker-peasant masses"—manifestly refer us to a later period, the 1920s. We know that Vera Mukhina, brought in by Yakov Tugendkhold, also worked on the cooperative's poster in 1922-23.[125]

POPOVA'S GRAPHIC DESIGN: THE TRADITIONS OF THE "FUTURIST" BOOK

Liubov Popova first became involved with books, industrial graphics, posters, and theatrical design in the post-revolutionary period. This distinguishes her from the broad circle of avant-garde artists who in the second half of the 1910s successfully developed a culture of the lithographed and typeset book based on the artistic principles of Primitivism and Cubo-Futurism. Popova undoubtedly knew these books, and her first book works did take that experience into account. Another source of Popova's book design were her own quasi-easel, quasi-applied Suprematist works (the logo for *Supremus*, the collages for Verbovka, and so forth).

The artist's works in the sphere of book design during the years 1920-21 indicate that she had mastered and combined two tendencies: the painterly construction of the page with complicated spatial relations and a head-spinning scattering of words torn to pieces; and the clear, perhaps even ascetic, simplicity of the compositions of words and graphic elements obviously leading to mature Constructivism.

Popova's work on the book cover for Sergei Bobrov's *Delta* is characteristic (page 292).[126] We can clearly see the artist's vacillation between a purely Suprematist version (*The George Costakis Collection*, fig. 824) and a "painterly" version (Tretiakov Gallery) reproducing the Cubo-Futurist relationship between letters and the dynamic color forms comprising their field and in general creating the "spatial-force construction" look of the artist's easel works. The *Delta* cover studies demonstrate the same tight immediacy between the easel work and its application as in the banners for the poets' club. We don't know which version the artist finally decided upon. In all likelihood the book was never published with her cover.[127]

The image of the handmade Futurist book—significantly more orderly and geometric, to be sure—shines through in

Popova's work in the cover and layout for Aksionov's 1922 book *Eiffeleia* (page 284, bottom). This is especially noticeable in the two-color (vermilion and black) collage layouts with the columns of text laid out in complicated ladders. On one of the pages black is combined with three shades of red. On the book cover we see a whimsical combination of a puzzling Futurist placement of texts and the characteristic splintering and ninety-degree turns, and details that invoked the new aesthetics: the incorporation of photography into the collage. Aksionov's book of poems was also never published with Popova's design.[128]

The same lot, evidently, was fated for the book cover for Nikolai Aseev's *Bomba* (Bomb) of 1922 (*The George Costakis Collection*, fig. 863, and page 277, bottom). The two versions are built entirely on the relationship between typeface and regular monocolor planes. The cover has only two short words on it: "Aseev" and "Bomba." In one instance, one red and one black word are combined on a common neutral field; in the other, the background is divided into two strips: red with white letters, and white with black letters. Here Popova had already found the style characteristic of her laconic posters for *Earth on End*, which to a great degree determined the production's entire structure.

It is symptomatic that the sketch for Aseev's book is marked on the studio list as the start of her "production period." This division, however, was evidently introduced for reasons not of style but of dating—after November 1921, after the Inkhuk "resolution" on production work.

THE "ORNAMENTAL" SIDE
OF POPOVA'S GRAPHIC DESIGN

At this point I should go back for a moment to 1920 and mention Popova's numerous studies for the illustrations to *Volshebnye skazki* (Tales of Wonder) (Tretiakov Gallery), by Diez. In her work on this children's book she was faced with a problem analogous to the design for the children's play. The resolution had to be representational and graphic. Popova made generous use here of her vivid impressions from her Oriental travels, which had never found any direct outlet in her art. The cover (page 293, right) is a capricious combination of complex color forms ordered in an ornamentally correct construction, with a picture of a hammer and sickle—or rather the customarily crossed state emblem of a hammer and a curved Oriental saber. The spaciousness of the composition is accentuated by the massiveness of the hammer. Bright colors create a festive and elegant impression.

The illustrations (page 283, top), which portray lively scenes and Oriental archetypes, are distinctive for the elasticity of their energetic curved lines, which accurately outline the silhouette of individual fragments of forms. They are witty and

sharp. The coloration of the sketches is particularly rich in nuance; color, as a rule, lies in thick dots that betray the experience of the Suprematist painter. The design of Diez's book stands alone in Popova's art. Only in individual episodes can a connection be felt with, for example, the costume designs for *The Priest of Tarquinia* (pages 243 and 262-69). These phenomena are important as branches in the artist's creative evolution. The basic channel for Popova's graphic design—the countless covers and magazine designs of the years 1921-24—led to the solution of entirely different problems by entirely other means. It is these works that were executed as full-fledged "production work."

THE BOOK COVER
AS A SPATIAL ORGANISM

The chief formal problem for the artist's principal group of print studies was constructing the composition as a spatial organism. In this respect the cover for *Rossiiskaia pochtovo-telegrafnaia statistika 1921* (Russian Postal-Telegraph Statistics 1921) (page 293, left) is characteristic. The basic ground of the page is a white space to which a depiction of a delicate radio tower lends a minor and (as in the paintings of 1920-21) not fully defined depth. A black line weaves through the drawing of the tower: *"statistika."* The orange inscription *"pochtovo-telegrafnaia,"* done in gouache in solid, very substantial red letters, calls up distinct associations with a telegraph tape running across the surface of the page. The black frame with the word *"Rossii-skaia"* holds the composition's front plane. The hammer and sickle emblem, while having no precise spatial reinforcement on the page, lends it a hint of abstraction that shatters the representational principle created by the radio tower.

Despite the simplicity of its elements—three colors, including the white of the background, one depiction, a few words—the composition is rich in relationships and rhythmic shadings. Each of the three colors, repeated in various shapes, comprises a specific spatial layer. The composition is structured of various typefaces, a distinctive feature of Popova's covers as opposed to those of other Constructivists.

In addition, features of mature Constructivist stylistics are also clearly visible: the draftsmanliness of some of the lettering, the spare refinement of the color scale, the idealization of the technological form. Her depiction of the radio tower was a unique symbol of the new technological era and the new aesthetics of Constructivism.

An extensive cycle of Popova's prints relates to music publishing: covers and layouts for music journals, sheet music covers. A series of covers for the compositions of the young Moscow composer Evgenii Pavlov (*The George Costakis Collection*, figs. 922-25) (page 281) demonstrates the artist's increasing confidence in creating visually rich, informative, and at the same time logically strict compositions by means of the simple variation of two colors on a white background and a sample of simple linear forms. Popova's covers were usually executed as lithographs. She produced expansive, subtle lettering, playing on the characteristics of Russian and Latin typefaces. The linear elements stylistically re-create in Popova's drawn or collage studies the random poetics of typographers' errors. But for the artist this is merely play, stylization, whose purpose is to enrich the page.

Popova's studies for typographical work in the period 1922-24 are an untiring variation on details and shapes within a relatively narrow stylistic framework. Color is limited, most often to white, black, one shade of red; occasionally black is replaced by dark blue. There are endless variations of white letters on a black background, black on white, red on white and black; straight inscriptions and slanted; capital letters linking the strata of the composition; the stripes and rectangles of pseudoaccidental details balancing out the whole—all these give the pages the precision of Constructivist designs. Characteristic is the inscription motif "packed" into a triangle or a trapezoid with growing or shrinking letters; the masthead and cover for the journal *K novym beregam muzykalnogo iskusstva* (Toward the New Shores of Musical Art) (pages 278–79); Aseev's *Bomba* (Bomb) (page 277, bottom); the masthead for *Muzyka i revoliutsiia* (Music and Revolution); and the cover for *Muzykalnaia Nov* (Musical Virgin Soil) (page 280).

Purely nonrepresentational typeface composition runs through many of the artist's works of the years 1922-24. Despite the brief span of time, it is possible to discern a definite evolution of this line in her graphic design. With time the compositions became more compact, retaining fewer and fewer fine details (tiny lines, gratings, and so on).

This is especially the case with her 1924 posters for the Society for the Struggle Against Illiteracy (pages 284, top right; 286, and 291). In a series of posters that play compositionally on the name of the organization and the text of the saying, "Learning is light; not learning is darkness," we see the artist's inexhaustible inventiveness weaving the text through bright decorative figures and endlessly changing the shape and scale of the typefaces and the overall configuration of the inscriptions. She had become freer—less fettered by the insistence on mandatory rectangularity that had so recently completely dominated similar works. Now, along with rectangular and diagonal inscriptions, she made wide use of complex but visually clear circular compositions. Such compositions began to appear on her covers as well as the literacy society posters.

THE POSTER:
REPRESENTATION IN POPOVA'S LATE WORK

In addition to her largely abstract typographical work, Popova's legacy also includes poster designs that make rich use of representation. It is altogether likely that these drawings were related to the artist's short-lived association in the fall of 1923 with the Engine (Dvigatel) society. Two small-format ink drawings for posters—"Brother worker, keep your sister from prostitution" (page 287, left) and another on the theme of physical fitness (page 287, right)—have survived. These studies exploit representation as actively as they do the text. The antiprostitution poster has survived in two sketches. Apart from the first there is a large two-color sheet done in gouache and India ink (page 289). In the original drawing the artist uses maximum expressiveness. The text of the appeal is called upon to overcome the gloomy chaos of the monstrous images of sin and doom. The character of the posters is similar to the Expressionist tendencies in graphics and painting of the mid-1920s, which were very widespread outside the Constructivist circle (the works of Antonina Sofronova, the students of Pavel Filonov, and others).

We see that in Popova's later sketches for typographical designs the energy of the composition increases, as does the variety of compositional devices, which as a whole fall within the strict framework of Constructivist stylistics. The use of typeface and composition becomes more complex, and there is more freedom and sweep to the designs. This development is unquestionably and beneficially related to her work in textiles.

The particular course of her development also took her through representation. We discussed one of the lines of Popova's postnonobjective representation in conjunction with the development of free drawing based on the curve and employing stylized motifs in the Modern spirit. The other, the expressive line, is related to the posters described above. Most essential—and central—is the line of intra-Constructivist representation, which in book design and the poster is closely linked with photorepresentation, with the montage of photo-images.

Characteristic of this representation is a definite schematism, an accentuated delineation of essential qualities, but not qualities of form, as was true on the path from realism to abstraction, but qualities of the thing along with a clear idea of its function.

In elaborating his theory of composition then, the well-known Inkhuk teacher and artist Vladimir Favorsky tied the principle of constructiveness in the spatial arts to the functional perception of the thing: "Constructive representation according to function will scarcely be representation at all but rather the creation of the thing as such, living in my space, participating in my practical life."[129]

We see how close the understanding of constructiveness Favorsky proposed is to the understanding of Constructivism as an artistic tendency that had made the function of form the meaning of its inquiries. This function reveals a tendency to pointed exaggeration, to a unique expressiveness in which the artist emphasized an individual function at the price of the integrity of the whole. Such, for example, was the extreme, exaggerated depiction of the worker's hand pulling a lever in one of Popova's magazine drawings. Here the form loses some of its visual attributes but remains completely recognizable, reaching a new symbolic level. Popova and Meierkhold achieved this kind of symbolic treatment of real things in the theater in their production of *Earth on End*. That is why they were criticized for combining real objects and theatrical pretense in one of the sets in an "outmoded symbolism."[130] This was not outmoded symbolism but the altogether new symbolism of "neo-thingism," the new documentariness, the new realism.

GRAPHIC DESIGN: THE "MONTAGE STYLE"

One of Popova's last works, a design done in 1924 for the third issue of *Voprosy stenografii* (Problems of Stenography) (page 284), serves as an example of the "montage" style—that is, the broad use of ready-made photo-images and their elements. Gradually she had moved away from the Futurist book and accentuated "handmadeness." Here Popova was pulling even with the ranks of Constructivist book graphics, paying less attention to the variety of typefaces (in this respect the design is more like works by Rodchenko). Typeface is consciously made to look like standard typography and typewriting; its mechanicalness is emphasized. This extraspatial textual mechanicalness fixes the plane of the page, whose spatial depth is not destroyed even by the introduction of complicated photomontage details: an architectural factory landscape enclosed within the massive frame of a dynamo's stator and an advertising image of a fountain pen with an aircraft pasted over it.

Fragments of photographs cut out of technical advertisements meticulously symbolize the technological age, but this function wholly exhausts the entire content of these depictions: from the standpoint of form they are incorporeal, weightless, empty even, next to the consciously mechanized but nonetheless "living" substance of typefaces.

After the stage of Cubo-Futurism and Suprematism (within the framework of nonobjective art) with its complexly harmonized, visually and sensually rich, spatially infinite compositions, Constructivist print design frequently produced a mechanistic, regular, single-plane resolution. This affected Popova less than others, but a definite tendency is visible in her work as well. The "montage" style did not always lead to a loss of spatial values, however, as exemplified by the abovementioned sketch for *Earth on End*—a brilliant example of how to use the montage method without anything sacrificed.

Top: Printed book cover for *Sol zemli* (Salt of the Earth), by N. Tserukavsky. Moscow: VSP, 1924

Bottom: Book cover design for *Bomba* (Bomb), by Nikolai Aseev. 1921. Pasted paper, India ink, and gouache on cardboard, 6⅝ × 4¾" (16.7 × 12 cm.). Tretiakov Gallery

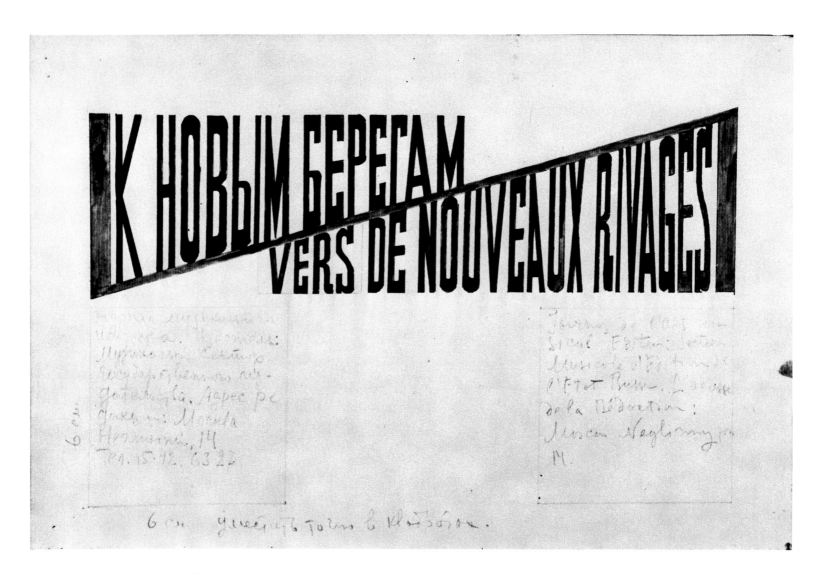

Masthead design for the magazine *K novym beregam muzykalnogo iskusstva (Toward the New Shores of Musical Art)*. 1923. India ink on paper, 6⅛ × 9¼″ (15.6 × 23.6 cm.). Private collection, Moscow

Cover design for the monthly magazine *Toward the New Shores of Musical Art*, no. 1, 1923. 1922. Collage on paper, 9⅝ × 7⅜″ (24.5 × 18.6 cm.). Private collection, Moscow

Cover design for the monthly magazine *Toward the New Shores of Musical Art*, no. 1, 1923. 1922. India ink and gouache on paper, 9⅝ × 7⅜″ (24.5 × 18.6 cm.). Private collection, Moscow

Cover design for the monthly magazine *Toward the New Shores of Musical Art*, no. 1, 1923. 1922. Collage on paper, 9½ × 7¼″ (24.3 × 18.5 cm.). Private collection, Moscow

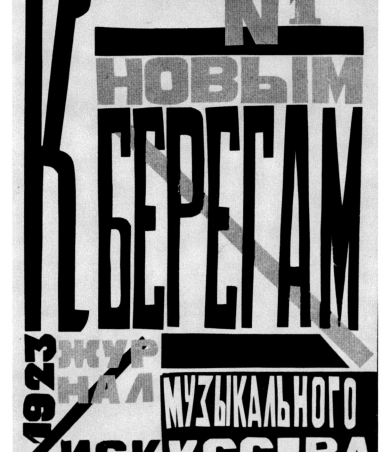

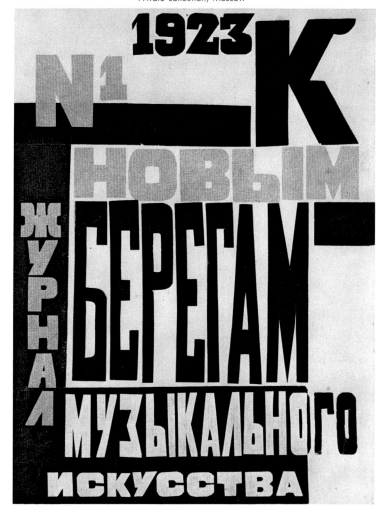

Magazine cover for *Musical Virgin Soil*, no. 1, 1923

Title page for *Musical Virgin Soil*. 1923–24

Layout detail for *Musical Virgin Soil*. 1923–24

Layout detail for *Musical Virgin Soil*. 1923–24

Proof of a page of *Musical Virgin Soil*, no. 1, 1923

Cover design for the musical score for *Vtoraia tetrad liriki. Dlia fortepiano*
(Second Notebook of Lyrics. For Piano), by E. Pavlov. 1922. 13¾ × 10⅛″ (34.8 × 25.8 cm.).
Private collection, Moscow

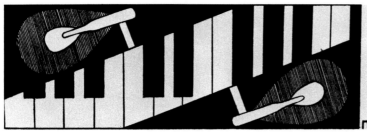

Layout details for *Musical Virgin Soil*. 1923—24

Advertisement page from *Musical Virgin Soil*. 1923

Sketch of an illustration for *Volshebnye Skazki (Tales of Wonder)*, by Diez (Gavriil Dobrzhinsky). *Man with a Small Bowl.* 1920. Watercolor on paper, 11 × 8⅝" (28 × 22 cm.). Tretiakov Gallery. Gift of George Costakis

Sketch of an illustration for *Tales of Wonder*, by Diez. *Man with a Sheep.* 1920. Watercolor on paper, 9¼ × 9⅛" (23.5 × 23.3 cm.). Tretiakov Gallery

Sketch for the cover of *Tales of Wonder*, by Diez. 1920. Pencil on paper, dimensions unknown. Tretiakov Gallery, Manuscript Division

Above: Magazine cover design for *Voprosy stenografii* (Problems of Stenography), no. 3, 1924. 1924. India ink and collage on cardboard, 11¾ × 6⅞" (30 × 17.5 cm.). Museum of Decorative and Applied Art, Moscow

Above right: Poster design for the Society for the Struggle Against Illiteracy. 1924. India ink and collage on cardboard, 17⅜ × 12⅞" (44.5 × 32.7 cm.). Private collection, Moscow

Book cover design for *Eiffeleia: 30 od.* (Eiffelia: 30 Odes), by Ivan Aksionov. 1922. Pasted paper, India ink, gouache, and collage on cardboard, 11 × 8⅝" (28 × 22 cm.). Tretiakov Gallery. Gift of George Costakis

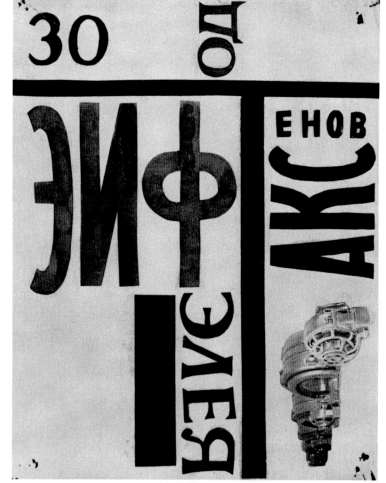

Printed cover for *Rebellion of Misanthropes*, by Sergei Bobrov. Moscow: Tsentrifuga, 1922

Poster design for the Society for the Struggle Against Illiteracy. 1924. India ink on cardboard, 10⅜ × 10¼″ (26.2 × 26 cm.). Museum of Decorative and Applied Art, Moscow

Poster design for the Society for the Struggle Against Illiteracy. 1924. India ink on cardboard, 17⅜ × 10⅛″ (44.2 × 25.7 cm.). Museum of Decorative and Applied Art, Moscow

Poster design for the Society for the Struggle Against Illiteracy. 1924. India ink on cardboard, 10¼ × 10½″ (26.1 × 26.5 cm.). Private collection, Moscow

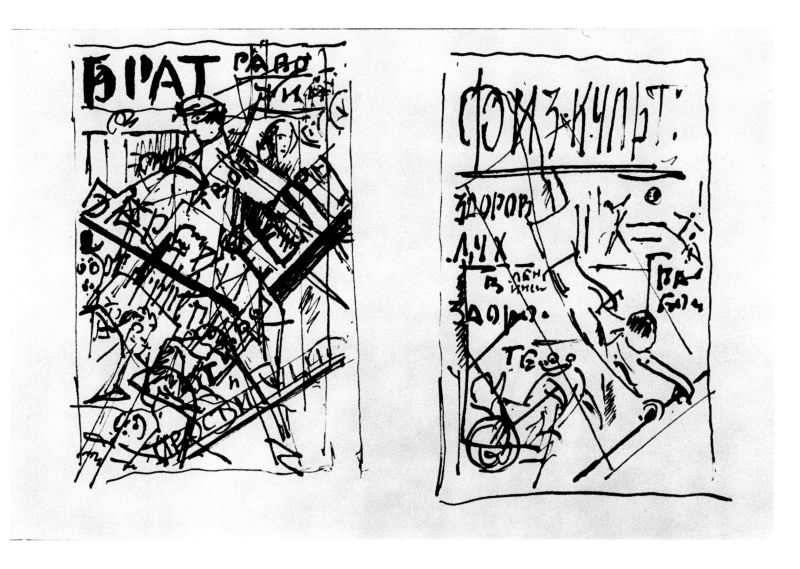

Two poster designs. 1922–23. India ink on paper, 3⅜ × 5¼″ (8.6 × 13.3 cm.). *Left:* "Against prostitution." *Right:* "For physical fitness." Private collection, Moscow

n. 47239

288   Poster sketch. 1922–23. Pencil on paper, 11 × 8½″ (27.8 × 21.7 cm.). Tretiakov Gallery. Gift of George Costakis

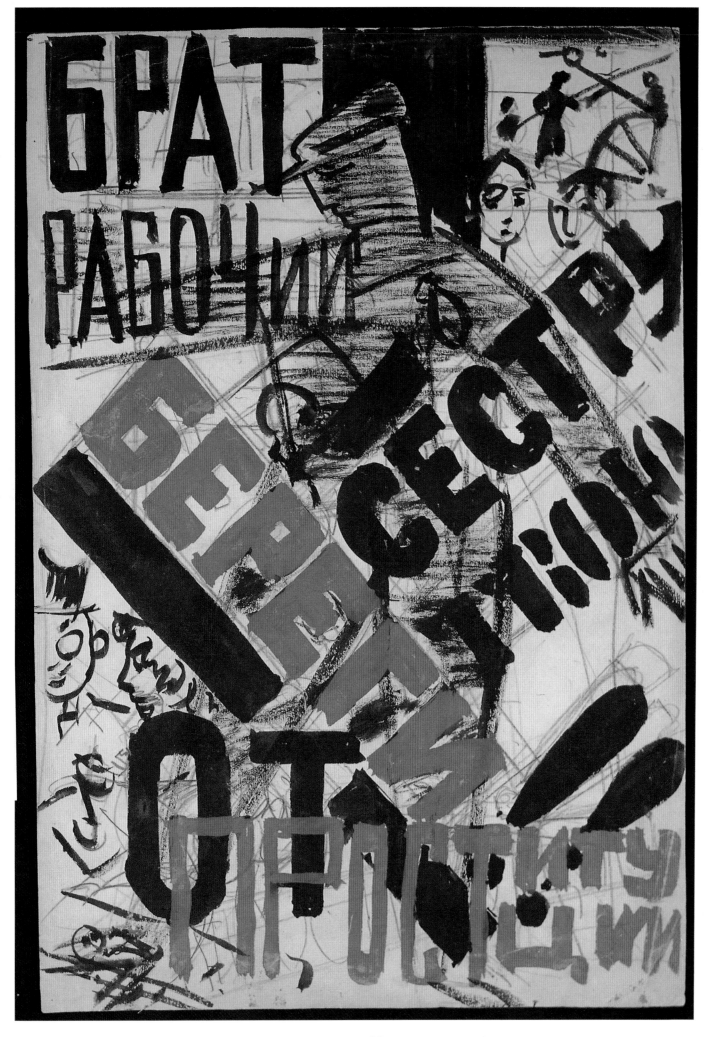

Poster design. 1922–23. India ink and gouache on paper, 15⅝ × 10¾" (39.7 × 27.2 cm.). "Brother worker, keep your sister from prostitution." Private collection, Moscow

Design for a banner for the All-Russian Union of Poets Club (VSP). 1921. Watercolor, pencil, and India ink on paper, 5⅝ × 30¼" (14.3 × 76.8 cm.). Tretiakov Gallery. Gift of George Costakis

Poster or mural design for the Tsentrifuga (Centrifuge) cooperative. 1922. India ink and watercolor on paper, 13 × 20½" (33 × 52 cm.). "Cooperation: a bridge between the city and the country. The basis of cooperation is the active participation of the workers." Private collection, Moscow

Poster design for the Society for the Struggle Against Illiteracy. 1924. India ink on cardboard, 14⅛ × 10⅜" (36 × 26.3 cm.). "Learning is light; not learning is darkness." Private collection, Moscow

Book cover design for *Delta*, by Sergei Bobrov. 1921. India ink and watercolor on paper, 7 × 7⅛"
(17.7 × 18 cm.). Tretiakov Gallery. Gift of George Costakis

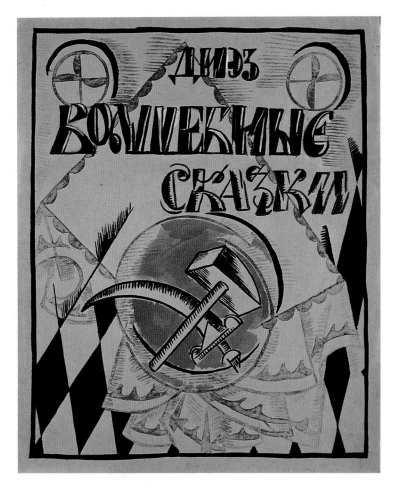

Cover design for *Rossiiskaia pochtovo-telegrafnaia statistika 1921* (Russian Postal-Telegraph Statistics 1921). 1922. India ink and gouache on paper, dimensions unknown. Museum of Decorative and Applied Art, Moscow

Book cover design for *Tales of Wonder*, by Diez. 1920. Watercolor on paper, 14 × 11½" (35.5 × 29.2 cm.). Tretiakov Gallery. Gift of George Costakis

Embroidery design for Verbovka. 1917. Collage on gray cardboard, 3 × 7⅞" (7.5 × 20 cm.). Private collection, Moscow

Painterly Architectonics. Study. ca. 1917. Gouache and lacquer on paper,
12¼ × 8¾" (31 × 22.2 cm.). Private collection, Moscow

Embroidery design for Verbovka. 1917. Collage on paper, 4¾ × 7⅜" (12.2 × 18.8 cm.). Museum of Decorative and Applied Art, Moscow

Embroidery design for Verbovka. 1917. Collage on gray cardboard, 3⅜ × 6½" (8.7 × 16.5 cm.). Private collection, Moscow

Embroidery design for Verbovka. 1917. Collage on paper, 7⅜ × 6⅛"
(18.6 × 15.7 cm.). Private collection, Moscow

Two embroidery designs for Verbovka. 1917. Collage on gray cardboard. *Top:*
2 × 2⅛" (5.1 × 5.5 cm.); *bottom:* 2⅛ × 2¼" (5.2 × 5.6 cm.).
Private collection, Moscow

Untitled. ca. 1917. Collage on paper, 12¾×9½″ (32.5×24 cm.).
Private collection, Moscow

Embroidery design for Verbovka. 1917. Collage on paper, 6×4⅜″
(15.4×11 cm.). Private collection, Moscow

Cup and saucer design. 1922 (?). Gouache on paper, 13½ × 10¼" (34.4 × 25.9 cm.). Private collection, Moscow

PRODUCTION ART

In recent years Liubov Popova's textile designs have become as popular as her productions for Meierkhold's theater. Textile design is one of the few production programs by Soviet Constructivists actually realized, one of the few clear demonstrations of the feasibility as well as the limits of life-building ideas. Popova's work in textiles is a remarkable illustration of the "overflowing," the "transference" of creative energy, of the creative temperament, of an artist's style with all its peculiarities and unique traits, from the confines of easel art to the objective environment.

Popova's design must be examined in two contexts: the Productivist ideology of Constructivism and the development of the inner qualities of her creative individuality. The former is more widely known. Popova's name is a landmark in any discussion of the evolution of Russian Constructivism from formal laboratory investigations in the late 1910s and start of the 1920s to their real flowering in the early 1920s. To understand the process properly it is important to remember that the ideas of Productivism, formulated in general and at the outset in highly abstract form, were advanced well before the artist-practitioners of the logic of their creative evolution were able to realize and master them.

In analyzing Popova's artistic and theoretical work we have seen that until the end of 1921 the idea of a Productivist application of artistic creativity was still completely superficial; art's chief zeal went to developing easel practices — a constant process of posing and solving formal problems. This zeal permeated her teaching at Vkhutemas as well at the very beginning. Popova's participation, described earlier, in Davydova's art-handicraft enterprise bore the romantic stamp of resurrecting traditional craft that had been characteristic of the previous era and was very distantly related to the Productivist ideas that had made industrial, machine production the center of attention and, as we have seen, was for Popova more a variation on easel painting than on designing things. Thus, her art developed idiosyncratically, gradually accumulating qualities that could be developed in future designs, and the atmosphere around her became increasingly saturated with the ideas and directives of the new "production" stage.

The problems of production, which the Revolution had brought into sharp relief, were being discussed more and more widely in artistic circles, were taking on more and more of a sociopolitical coloring.

The argument for social demand became entangled with the conviction that the development of industry had left its mark on art and had presented it with its demands. In 1920 David Arkin wrote: "Artistic consciousness and creation have already clashed sharply with both the machine and the mechanization of production (and, therefore, with life itself, which has produc-

tion as its base). If in the final analysis any artistic culture aspires to *transform life*, then this immense life event, the victory of the machine, cannot help but exert a powerful influence over the course of development of contemporary artistic culture."[131]

Before she began to work in textiles, Popova herself was already firmly convinced of the importance of the industrial, machine nature of production art. In 1921-22 she wrote: "The era modern humanity has entered upon is the era of the flowering of industry, thus the organization of the elements of artistic production, too, must address the design of the material elements of life, i.e., industry, and so-called production."[132]

THE TEACUP DESIGN

Before moving on to the story of how Popova and Varvara Stepanova were invited to join the First State Textile Print (formerly the Tsindel) Factory in 1923, a story that has been told many times before, a few words about the dish-designing episode. That Popova worked in a china factory[133] has become a conviction of the contemporary literature, but it was in fact never mentioned in the articles and biographies of the 1920s. The basis for this assertion is a single sketch of a teacup and saucer (page 298) found in the artist's studio (and not even listed in the famous inventory). In all likelihood it relates to the 1922 announcement by Glavsilikat (Main Silicate Administration) of a contest for china designs. An announcement about the contest and its rules was sent to various artistic organizations, Vkhutemas, for example, and possibly Inkhuk. The Productivists, who until then had had no connection with industry, exhibited lively interest in the proposal. In response, Rodchenko designed a "tractor service," and Popova did a sketch of a teacup. Despite the already well-known experiments of Malevich and his students in creating dishes, and her own Contructivist principles, Popova undertook a Cubo-Futurist style. Its sweeping decorativeness, evidently, derived from the artist's idea of the immutable features of the Russian teacup. She gave it an utterly traditional shape: broad, "for merchants."

We have virtually no information on the Constructivist artists' participation in the contest. All we know for certain is their interest and enthusiasm for practical activity of any kind. The way had been paved for the invitation to the textile print factory, which served as just such a stimulus.

AT THE TEXTILE PRINT FACTORY

The initiative had originated with Aleksandr Arkhangelsky, the director of the factory, and Vkhutemas professor Petr Viktorov, a textile expert and chemist, was actively involved in the negotiations. Around that time the Textile Faculty had been trying to get Popova to join their staff.[134]

At the time, D. M. Aranovich gave a thorough account of the reasons for inviting her to join the factory:

The First Textile Print Factory in Moscow (formerly the Tsindel) really started to resume activity at full capacity only in 1922. During the start-up period they worked off old reserves. The moment for completely independent activity came quickly, however, a moment that proved hardest of all for the factory's art department. Before the war the old Tsindel factory had received its textile designs straight from Paris. All its art had consisted of so-called secret work, in which they developed methods and formulas for coloring fabrics.[135]

We know that not only Emil Tsindel's factory but others as well, even the greatest Russian factories, lacked their own full-fledged design sections and used ready-made "Parisian" drawings. In the factories well-equipped technical laboratories, together with factory "designers," prepared the model drawings for production.

At the time Popova and Stepanova came to the factory, it was still in need of considerable restoration, and a great deal had been irretrievably lost. However, some of the experienced technicians, chemists, factory artisans, and draftsmen returned. More important, by that time all links with Paris as a supplier of textile "samples" had been wiped out, and fabric production had to be readjusted to work from native artistic ideas.

It is understandable that in the new "production" phase of her career Popova could not treat fabric design in the mechanical "applied" manner that had served her for the Verbovka designs. Neither she nor Stepanova lost any time in attempting to penetrate the specifics of production, to understand the requirements of technology.

This did not spare them complications in their work or conflicts with factory workers, though. Aranovich wrote: "Popova's designs, and especially Stepanova's, came out of Constructivist 'machinism' (flywheels, gratings, interlaced rails, and so on) in the planar and highly abstract textile drawings (both on the bolt and especially in clothing) and thus required thorough reworking by the factory's art-production team. . . . Moreover, this 'reworking' was so basic that the colors of the artist's sketches were changed completely, and only in relatively rare instances was the design itself retained in full."[136]

Despite its authoritative tone, Aranovich's testimony should not be taken at face value. Unquestionably it testifies to nothing more than real difficulties that were part and parcel of the work. The rare fabric samples by Popova that have survived (page 327) demonstrate a precise correspondence between the artist's drawing and the executed sample. True, the design that exists in two versions (turquoise and black) has survived as a fabric only in the black, and the other sample—dark blue—also turned out to be black and white in the sketch (page 326,

top right), but the drawing was retained in full. Most likely what we have here are clashes as well as compromises on both sides. Objective difficulties with the dyers and the technology, to which the artists had to respond with changes in their designs, may well have played a significant role.

In any case, we know that Popova was working at the very peak of her creative powers and inspiration. The Rodchenko-Stepanova family has a manuscript from a humor magazine in which there is a drawing of Popova and Stepanova carrying their designs to the factory (page 313, left). Stepanova is depicted carrying a small string bag with two or three designs in it; Popova is straining at an enormous wheelbarrow crammed with designs.

After Popova's death, less than six months after she started work at the factory (the time she worked may have been even briefer; no precise date for its start has been established), about a hundred textile designs and several dozen clothing designs were found in her studio. It must be remembered, moreover, that at the same time Popova was creating posters for Dvigatel (fall of 1923), was teaching a course in "The Material Design of the Performance" for Proletkult (1924; Appendix XXI), and was still designing magazines and books.

POPOVA AND CONSTRUCTIVISM
IN THE TEXTILE INDUSTRY

The reminiscences of contemporaries (Tugendkhold, Osip Brik, Aksionov) contain evidences of the profound satisfaction Popova derived from her work in textile design. Aksionov wrote in his review of Popova's posthumous exhibition:

For an evaluation of the rationale behind the solutions she had found to the textile drawing, L. S. now turned above and beyond the factory's official inspectors, to the mass purchaser, observing herself the class makeup of those who purchased the goods produced from her drawings, and it was her great happiness to ascertain some days before her death, amid the impending horror of the loss of the life that was much more precious to her than her own [her child's] that the fabrics printed with her drawings were enjoying widespread use both in the countryside and in the worker districts. L. S. told me this on the evening of May 12 (she lost consciousness on the 23rd).[137]

Tugendkhold wrote to the same effect in summing up the history of her art:

But most significant about Popova, I think, was her attempt to revitalize mass industry. The artist's straightforward nature was not content with the illusion of the theater; she was drawn on to the last logical step, to bringing art into production, into daily life itself. She was the first to breach the Bastille of our factory conservatism. Such were Popova's drawings at the Textile Print . . . Factory. Popova said that no single artistic success gave her such profound satisfaction as the sight of peasants and workers buying pieces of her material. And indeed, this past spring all Moscow was wearing fabric with designs by Popova without knowing it—vivid, strong drawings full of movement, like the artist's own nature.[138]

Art criticism established her success, and Popova's fabrics were shown at the Exposition Internationale des Arts Décoratifs in Paris in 1925. This success was especially notable against the backdrop of the textile industry crisis in the early 1920s. However, it did not last long. After Popova's death the Constructivist line in textiles quickly lost ground; her success was not followed up.

Aranovich explained this first and foremost by the general change in style in the mid-1920s:

Constructivism, which arrived at production much later than it did at exhibitions, here found itself *discarded significantly* sooner. The demand for abrupt and frequent changes in patterns proved too much for the Constructivists, and neither the viewer nor the purchaser wanted old colorings repeated over and over in one form or another. There was a rift between the art department of the First State Textile Print Factory and its "left" innovators that was hastened by the talented L. S. Popova's untimely death. In exhibitions, in graphics, in the theater, in literature, there was a decisive reverse move toward realism. Could textiles remain an exception? Of course not.[139]

Unquestionably, there is much that is correct in this judgment. But the speedy decline of the Constructivist trend in Soviet textiles has to be explained not only by a general change in style—Constructivist trends in literature, in easel art, in print, in the theater, and above all in architecture were developing and competing with other trends up until the early 1930s—but even more by the complexities of bringing Constructivism into daily life, its inability to transform the style of daily existence. The whole activity of the Constructivists in the 1920s in redesigning the equipment of daily life turned out to have been no more than a laboratory stage, the results of which were felt only in the 1930s, when Vkhutemas graduates made their mark in industry, preserving the traditions of Rodchenko and Tatlin. However, this concerns only industry per se; in textiles the experiment in inculcating Constructivism into life was limited to that one brief episode in the mid-1920s.

We shall try to understand the "textile chapter" in Popova's artistic career, the success of her designs and the complexity of her achievement, by examining first her personal creative tasks. This was more or less the same as what Davydova had undertaken—taking the style canons of modern art out of the studio and into the everyday world. This is more or less the same as what artists like Sonia Delaunay were doing in France—creating an acutely modern style for the everyday object. The conditions under which they accomplished these tasks, however, were entirely different.

In the first place, Popova lacked the specific elite clientele on which Davydova had relied and Delaunay in France could still rely to approve and adapt the latest trends. In Russia, the NEP provided a relatively prosperous public but this petit-bourgeois group, which had arisen chiefly through retail trade and speculation, on the whole displayed crass, vulgar tastes. Having no specific ideals in the field of art, they tried to surround themselves with what remained from the houses and clothing of those classes that had left the historical arena. This audience was incapable of becoming an elite consumer of artistic innovations in everyday objects.

Second—and this is more important—Popova had no desire to focus on a narrow elite. As we have already seen, she saw the meaning of her work in the broadest, most democratic possible inculcation of art into popular daily life.

This situation greatly complicated the problem of creating a new style for everyday objects. To judge from her sketches, Popova approached the problem with a broad range of solutions: from extremely simple, modest designs drawn from traditional folk weaving, to intricate ornamental designs with an irrational sense of space that created a magical effect.

At the same time, she tried to meet the consumer halfway, tried to anticipate the "personal taste of the peasant woman in Tula"[140] and to counter established tastes. Elena Murina wrote about the Constructivist artists' activities: "They did not pander to anyone's tastes (this may have been a weakness as well as a strength); they shaped those tastes."[141] Popova made use of her fabrics to agitate for a new style and for a transformation of daily life.

Popova's ornamental designs can easily be classified according to orientation: either toward "pungency" and perceptual surprise; or toward a calm and rather traditional feeling. There are a relatively large number of designs of the latter type, which the artist called "fine cotton prints in stripes and checks." These modest, "fine" prints were intended for shirts and blouses and were all structured around the straight line: the stripe, the regular, the rectilinear check, and wide variations thereof (pages 333 bottom, 322-23, and 329). Although these designs were intended for printing, they bear some resemblance to traditional textile patterns created by the interweaving of colored threads. You might say that Popova stylized her designs under the influence of handloomed fabric. There are, for example, studies where a solid line alternates with variations on a dotted line (page 330, bottom right). Fine-checked shirt-weight cottons also look quite traditional.

But gradually, from sketch to sketch, this typical traditional rhythm of lines and color resolutions gets more complicated, richer, bringing the drawings closer to those unique, incomparable fabrics that made Popova's name as a textile designer. Usually this happens through gratings, (checks) placed over the original drawing (page 326, right middle and bottom). Instantly the one-dimensional fabric takes on depth and spatiality.

As a rule, Popova's patterns are built on the principle of variation through combination. In some cases the artist unfurls a scale of variations from the "modest, ordinary" image to the intriguing visual illusion. In others she simply elaborates a maximum of variations on a single compositional basis (pages 334-35).

Examples: straight rows of squares resolved either as two-color or solid-color silhouettes, or as two-color silhouettes overlaid with squares in a third color set diagonally (page 313, bottom right), and so on. Entire "symphonies" are played out on the motif of circles, angles, gratings, and combinations thereof.

Although she used absolutely new motifs for her drawings (five-pointed stars, hammers and sickles, newly composed monogram-like miniatures; pages 328 and 329), Popova did not by any means always break with the usual rhythmic order of ornamental design, and she often introduced a rectilinear "constructive" element to the free field of the fabric dispersed exactly like the tiny sparsely sprinkled flowers of traditional cotton prints. In her hand, traditional circles took on an altogether new, unaccustomed feel.

Enthusiastically playing out the theme of circles and rings, Popova tested and combined all sorts of ways to place and color them. White circles with a painted segment on the right was one variation; another used the same pattern but with the narrow segment on the right remaining white and the rest painted instead; the same kind of circles with the side segments painted and the middle striped horizontally was a third variation; striped vertically was a fourth; with a star drawn inside the circles a fifth. Tiny circles and rings were either scattered freely across the field or gathered, "woven," into groups (pages 315, bottom, 317, bottom, and 334-35).

The effect of many of the studies, the purely decorative as well as—especially—the "fantastic," the spatial, is built on the qualities of color, on the great range of color combinations and means of applying colors. Here the artist brilliantly implements the experience of her painterly "color constructions."

The series of relatively simple fabrics that the artist called either "large cotton print," or "skirt-weight men's flannel," or "flannel cheviot for winter and autumn suits and coats" were usually built on the stripe motif—not necessarily infinite, solid stripes but often alternating in chessboard-fashion. The combination of dark blue and terracotta, of brown and gold and sky blue, of lilac tones with turquoise and crimson—all these are resonant, distinctive, beautiful. The overwhelming majority of her sketches make active use of black and white. Here, apart from any strict observance of correct geometry, the underlying trait of Constructivist stylistics comes through.

The renowned dynamism of Popova's textile designs may be rather overstated. Possibly they struck contemporaries with their unexpected, unusual color combinations and drawings, but to us in the late twentieth century, the overwhelming majority of Popova's fabrics look logical and programmatically harmonized in their colors, and as a rule the designs are well balanced also, and usually geometric. It is characteristic that the artist never resorted to free-style solutions in the manner of Suprematist compositions or *Painterly Architectonics*. Sonia Delaunay, for example, created textiles and decors with irregular patterns. Following the aesthetic principles of Constructivism, Popova totally rejected the notion of transferring irregular nonobjective compositions to textiles. Moreover, production itself presented its own conditions: the technology of the textile print factory was geared toward printing small repeats. In this sense Popova's sketches, constructed on the principle of overlaying several simple compositional layers, was well suited for printing, for example, and not for painting.

Among Popova's sketches there is only one that recalls free-style painting. The artist called it "large flower on a plain background." In it big interlocking rings of circles around a basic core, surrounded by sharp zigzags, coalesce in a strange way into the image of a large flower bordered with leaves. The final sketch, evidently, has not survived, but this design appears in a sketch for a chic dress (page 314, left), and we also find sketches for it on the back of one sheet.

The wide reputation of Popova's textile designs, their fame as dynamic, witty, brilliantly inventive, was based first and foremost on a group of frankly expressive sketches, all of them strictly regular and correctly geometric but also magical, spatially fantastic. As a rule, these works are based on various gratings, often placed on the diagonal.

The vague, minimal spatial depth inherent in these patterns recalls simultaneously both the space of the late "rayic," "crossing" compositions in painting and the flat space of *The Magnanimous Cuckold* set, as well as the delicate structure of metal girders she used in the studies for *Earth on End* and in various graphic works.

Popova began working out the stereoscopic effect of her future textiles in her sketches with simple compositions like the checked shirt cottons mentioned earlier and the big intersecting stripes that resemble the corner of a tablecloth or kerchief. Placing cold over warm, as she once had in her canvases—a solid blue cross over a cross made from a bundle of fine orange lines—and adding at the crossing of the blues a solid orange square (page 322, top right), the artist achieved a dynamic effect of pulsing visual energy. In other instances the sense of space and volume in the "checked" composition is accentuated by a supplementary color echo, somewhat like a shadow (page 323, top left). In other versions the sense of volume is born and extinguished before your eyes thanks to the introduction of solid and intact black crossings (page 324, right bottom), and so on.

Many of the diagonal gratings are structured on the special

device of syncopated rhythms. This is no accident. We know that Popova loved jazz and was acutely sensitive to its rhythms. Her hand produced compositions with "double" and "triple" rhythms harnessed together into a single sound; moreover, each "part" was carried by a distinctly expressed graphic structure. Sometimes two rhythmic themes coexisted on a single spatial level; in more complicated compositions they were distinctly divided into spatial strata.

Comparing Popova's late textile designs with her embroidery studies for Verbovka reveals both the similarities and the differences between these two stages, not only on the ideocultural level but in formal artistic thinking as well. At first glance we are struck by the resemblance of the devices; once again Popova resurrected her favorite method of collage: the literal application of elements, of spatial strata. But if in her Suprematist compositions the artist laid elements, details, one over the other, now she was working with whole, at times relatively complex, systems.

If in the Verbovka collages it was the form that was crucial, the configuration of elements (color-form), seemingly simple but in fact quite carefully refined, then now, in developed Constructivism, the element of composition was simplified to the basic primary, regular shape; it was rather the law by which she combined parts that became complicated.

Unlike the self-sufficient 1917 Suprematist collages, the 1923-24 studies are limitlessly spatial, just like the artist's later painting. On principle they have no distinct "central" compositional knots; balanced extension on all fronts prevails.

Moreover, their principal difference from those earlier studies — which were intended for concrete objects but never assumed that function — is precisely that attention to objects, that conscious orientation toward eventual manufacture (clothes, furniture, and so on). In many cases a textile design may well have begun with a dress design.

With rare exception, all the clothing designs Popova did — and about twenty of them have survived — had their "own" textile design. They show very clearly both her plans for the future fabric and the image she gave her textile designs. Apart from demonstrating the purely decorative qualities of the textile, which can be seen in the designs themselves, the clothing sketches bared their constructive qualities, their originality, individualized them, and thereby hinted at their human image.

FASHIONING CLOTHING

For a long time all the clothing designs Popova did were considered democratic, a version of the "proletarian style." This opinion persists to this day. Indeed, an entire series of her designs displays accentuated propriety, pragmatism, modesty, although they are infinitely removed from the stern prosaicness of the workers' outfits we know from the actor's work uniform.

Behind them looms the image of the woman laborer: perhaps not the "proletarian woman worker" but rather the Soviet office worker, the teacher, the salesclerk.

The majority of the models, however, were oriented toward a different human type, a different condition, and reveal other characterisitics of what are sometimes the very same fabrics. The woman Popova was thinking of when she designed could have been the Nepman's "lady from Kuznetskii Most [Bridge],"[142] but more likely it was a more artistic type, possibly slightly more unfettered, bearing both the traits of the "gay twenties" and that "purity of type" to which the twenties, with its strong sense of modernity and style, was so attuned — the artist, the film star.

Popova touched only lightly on the actual problems of dressmaking in her work, having made a few sketches for a magazine and a fashion studio window. However, these works of hers were important because they did not fall in with purely "Productivist" aesthetics but drew Popova closer to the work of her old friends Aleksandra Exter and Vera Mukhina. They showed not only concern for mass manufacturing but also a working out of the artistic principles of the modern suit, the discovery of the decorative possibilities of modern style.

Even more important for us is not the sociopsychological aspect of this activity of Popova's but her artistic conception of clothing as a spatial form and the qualities of the textiles that she consciously designed in the spirit of that conception. Here, too, Popova was closer to the works of Exter and Mukhina than to Nadezhda Lamanova or Evgeniia Pribylskaia, although they all worked in the same stylistic vein. This "spatial" conception of clothing may, as John Bowlt has found, have had its source in Leon Bakst's costumes for Sergei Diaghilev's ballets.[143]

The line of costume design Bakst began was developed further in Exter's theatrical designs (Romeo and Juliet). This did not make itself felt in Popova's initial theatrical works, but it suddenly broke through in her costume designs for The Priest of Tarquinia in 1922, which were constructed entirely on the motif of soft, draping, figure-enveloping fabrics — undoubtedly a Modernist "relapse."

In Popova's later designs all the various sources and trends in her work intermeshed. That is what distinguished her version of Constructivism. Her clothing was a spatial-architectural rather than a sculptural-architectonic phenomenon. The human figure was conceived merely as a constructive carcass bracing, supporting the clothing at precise, designated points. Otherwise the outfits had a life of their own — the construction of the human body and a spatial envelope of fabric. This spatial element, so "emancipated" from the figure, made possible the vivid decorativeness of the large geometric patterns, the color expression, the clearly articulated inner logic of ornament that does not quite fit the proportions of the body. This conception also facilitated the manifest "spatiality" of the fabric, as discussed above. It is characteristic that the majority of the experiments in inculcating avant-garde aesthetics into the sphere of textiles and clothing inevitably entailed this accentuated spatiality in the clothing.

Popova's patterns, apart from resolving problems in general, also demonstrated a more detailed probing of the object, a search for the highest correspondence between fabric and clothing. This once again naturally provokes comparison with Sonia Delaunay, who, like Popova, arrived at a suit uniform, a preregulated combination of smooth and patterned fabric. This combination was nearly mandatory for vividly colored, rhythmically intense textiles. [144]

When you take Popova's fashion experiments into account in a discussion of her fabrics, the problem of Constructivism in her art crops up even more urgently. If in our analysis of her fabrics we immediately felt the presence of the Constructivist aesthetic (regular geometrism, the use of black and white, the slight graphic tone), then all the phenomena as a whole—clothing and textile design both—clearly exceed the stylistic framework and aesthetic principles of Constructivism. Her unexhausted resources from her old "pre-Constructivist," "pre-Productivist" artistic experience were tapped to powerful effect.

The extremely brief but equally intensely bright textile design phase was a worthy culmination to Liubov Popova's tumultuous, abruptly changing creative life, which was irrepressible in its development of the internal logic of problems and accomplishments.

A PLACE IN THE RANKS—A PLACE IN HISTORY

Liubov Sergeevna Popova died May 25, 1924, at the age of thirty-five, her talent in full maturity, her mastery of the secrets of many types of artistic activity secure, able to execute whatever she conceived, bringing satisfaction and amazement to those around her.

She died tragically, after contracting a severe form of scarlet fever from her child, whom she survived by a few days.

With her death it was clear what a vivid artist and remarkable person Soviet art had lost. Numerous obituaries engraved her image as those around her understood it. This image, which remains in the literature, fixed the perception of a moment, a stage, the perception of a specific circle that insisted on its complete monopoly of the artist's spiritual legacy.

This circumstance was documented in an incident around an open letter to Mossovet in which a group of friends and supporters insisted on their right to handle the artist's civil funeral. They asserted Popova's place in the worker ranks of Constructivist-Productivists:

On the 25th of this May, artist-constructor Liubov Sergeevna Popova passed away. Her work, like her worldview, was linked in the closest possible fashion with the construction of a revolutionary culture. . . .

We, the undersigned, being well acquainted through collaboration with the worldview of Comrade Popova and the whole contribution of her personal life and the close personal friendship it involved for the entire period of the Revolution, affirm that she was a convinced follower and firm atheist and materialist. Her family, whose ideology she did not share, insists on a religious funeral, which, of course, is an act that directly contradicts all her work and her life. . . . In the name of the collective and editorial staff of the journal *Lef*—Brik, Mayakovsky, Aseev—in the name of the members of the Constructivists' group—Rodchenko, Stepanova—in the name of the Association of Constructors of Working Cells—Zhemchuzhny—in the name of the Communist collective of organizers of the studio of the Revolution—Senkin, Klutsis—in the name of the executive office of the professional section of Vkhutemas and the Worker Faculty—Bykov—in the name of the Institute of Artistic Culture—B. Kushner, Lavinsky. [145]

The people who united around this letter to Mossovet represented various detachments of the left Constructivist arts front. They were fighting for their ideas in art and life, and their version of Liubov Popova's art and personality was firmly bound to their ideological struggle and their convictions during that period.

Liubov Popova's place in the history of art does not coincide with that formulated by the leftists in 1924, which contemporaries echoed for decades until a period of silence ensued.

In resurrecting Liubov Popova's name nearly four decades later, we have begun where the leftists left off: with production, the theater, printing—with the image of the passionate "Productivist," the fighter for the ideas of life-building, the consistent supporter of Constructivist aesthetics.

Gradually, however, it becomes clear that this sharply delineated image, devoid of nuance, complexity, or contradiction, does not at all correspond to Liubov Popova's actual image. Now we understand that what was important in her art were not the dogmas of ideological directives but vital creativity itself, its ever-pulsating energy lashing through all consciously and compulsorily erected obstacles and restrictions. Most important of all was the spirit of creative progress, of renewal and inquiry. Popova was a true representative of that glorious tribe of turn-of-the-century Russian artists, artist-discoverers, pioneers, inventors, who passionately bared their art to the upheavals of the era, ardently, and at times tragically, experiencing through their art the drama and dynamics of their revolutionary era.

NOTES TO PART TWO

1. One of the self-portrait paintings of Samuil Adlivankin, *Plenipotentiary of the Samara Vkhutemas*, done in 1922 and ironically demonstrating the artist in his social role, is characteristic.

2. Aleksandr Rodchenko, *Stati, vospominaniia, avtobiograficheskie zapiski, pisma* (Essays, Reminiscences, Autobiographical Notes, Letters) (Moscow, 1982), p. 85.

3. *Katalog desyatoi Gosudarstvennoi vystavki. Bespredmetnoe tvorchestvo i suprematizm* (Catalog of the Tenth State Exhibition: Nonobjective Art and Suprematism) (Fine Arts Department of the People's Commissariat of Enlightenment) (Moscow, 1919), p. 29.

4. See S. O. Khan-Magomedov, "V. Kandinskii o vospriiatii i vozdeistvii sredstv khudozhestvennoi vyrazitelnosti (Iz materialov arkhiva Sektsii Monumentalnogo iskusstva Inkhuka)" (W. Kandinsky on the Perception and Influence of Means of Artistic Expression). From materials in the archive of the Section on Monumental Art of Inkhuk, in *Problemy obraznogo myshleniia i dizain* (Problems in Thought about Images and Design), Works of VNIITE, "Technical Aesthetics" series, no. 17 (Moscow, 1978).

5. Inkhuk, under the Department of Fine Arts in the People's Commissariat of Enlightenment, Section on Monumental Art. (This is followed by the unpaginated text of an unlabeled questionnaire.)

6. Cited in Khan-Magomedov, "Kandinskii," p. 83.

7. Cited in L[arissa A.] Shadova, "Tsvetovaia sistema M. Matiushina" (The Color System of M. Matiushin), *Iskusstvo* (Art), no. 8 (1974): 40.

8. TsGALI (Central State Archive of Literature and Art), fund 2010, op. 1, unit 101.

9. See Larissa A. Shadova, *Malevich: Suprematism and Revolution in Russian Art 1910-1930* (London and New York, 1982), p. 51. Originally published as *Suche und Experiment* (Dresden, 1978).

10. Manuscript Department, Tretiakov Gallery, fund 148, unit 74, sheet 1.

11. Institute of Artistic Culture, *Russkoe iskusstvo* (Russian Art), no. 2-3 (1923): 85.

12. On the "parallel" Inkhuk, see S. O. Khan-Magomedov, "INKhUK: vozniknovenie, formirovanie, i pervyi period raboty. 1920" (Inkhuk: Appearance, Formation, and First Period of Work, 1920), in *Sovetskoe iskusstvoznanie 80-2* (Soviet Art Criticism 80-82) (Moscow: Sovetskii khudozhnik, 1981).

13. Among Popova's papers we find an elaboration of one version of the "Programma Sektsii otdelnykh iskusstv Instituta khudozhestvennoi kulturoi" (Program of the Section on Individual Arts of the Institute of Artistic Culture). This program is a good example of the "objective" treatment of the painting form.

There is also a typescript in Popova's archive with her comments and corrections and signed: "Working Group of Objective Analysis of the S[ection] on M[onumental] A[rt] of Inkhuk" (Manuscript Department, Tretiakov Gallery, fund 148, unti 86, sheet 1). For versions of the program's text, see S. O. Khan-Magomedov, "Rabochaia gruppa obektivnogo analiza Inkhuka" (Working Group of Objective Analysis of Inkhuk), in *Problemy istorii sovetskoi arkhitektury* (Problems in the History of Soviet Architecture), no. 4 (Moscow, 1978), p. 54; and D. V. Sarabianov, *Babichev. Khudozhnik, teoretik, pedagog* (Babichev: Artist, Theoretician, Pedagogue) (Moscow: Sovetskii khudozhnik, 1974), p. 89. An analysis of the materials shows that Popova collaborated with Babichev on the very earliest versions of the program.

14. Wassily Kandinsky, "Muzei zhivopisnoi kultury" (The Museum of Artistic Culture), *Khudozhestvennaia zhizn* (Art Life) no. 2 (1920): 20.

15. See Appendix III.

16. Private archive, Moscow.

17. See Khan-Magomedov, "Inkhuk: Appearance, Formation," p. 350.

18. Archive materials make it clear that apart from the scientific-methodological work, the group to which Popova belonged and which she may have headed was also involved with the housekeeping activities of the museum (putting together the finances and staff for 1922).

19. Private archive, Moscow.

20. Manuscript Department, Tretiakov Gallery, fund 148, unit 75, sheet 1.

21. Private archive, Moscow. This text is a variant of Appendix V.

22. Ibid.

23. Manuscript Department, Tretiakov Gallery, fund 148, unit 71, sheet 1.

24. Ibid., sheet 2.

25. Private archive, Moscow.

26. N. L. Adaskina, "Liubov Popova. Put stanovleniia khudozhnika-konstruktora" (Liubov Popova: An Artist-Constructor's Formation), *Tekhnicheskaia estetika* (Technical Aesthetics), no. 11 (1978): 19 and passim.

27. Private archive, Moscow.

28. Ibid.

29. Ibid.

30. Ibid.

31. Ibid.

32. Ibid.

33. Ibid.

34. Ibid.

35. Ibid.

36. Ibid.

37. Manuscript Department, Tretiakov Gallery, fund 148, unit 26, sheet 1.

38. Ibid.

39. Ibid.

40. Ibid., unit 76, sheet 1.

41. Ibid., unit 42, sheet 1.

42. The first director of the First or, more precisely, General Painting Department was Vladimir Baranov-Rossiné, who left Vkhutemas in October 1921. After him for a time the department head was Aleksandr Drevin (starting December 1, 1921), who was replaced by Aleksandr Rodchenko (starting February 16, 1922).

43. In Popova's personal archive (Manuscript Department, Tretiakov Gallery, fund 148), apart from her own materials there are typewritten program texts by German Fedorov, Aleksandra Exter, Aleksandr Rodchenko, Ivan Kliun, Aleksandr Osmerkin, Vladimir Baranov-Rossiné, with Popova's handwritten comments, which apparently were written in connection with the work of the Program Commission. On September 6, 1921, the following members of the Painting Faculty were named to the Program Commission: Popova, Sergei Senkin (a student), Ivan Kliun, Aleksandr Drevin, Aleksandr Shevchenko, Aristarkh Lentulov, and Pavel Kuznetsov. The order naming the commission was signed by the dean, Fedorovsky, and the rector, Ravdel. TsGALI, fund 681, op. 2, unit 65, sheet 105-6.

44. Manuscript Department, Tretiakov Gallery, fund 148, unit 34, sheet 1.

45. Ibid.

46. Ibid., unit 48, sheet 1.

47. Ibid.

48. TsGALI SSSR, fund 680, unit 845, sheet 353.

49. Manuscript Department, Tretiakov Gallery, fund 148, unit 23, sheet 3.

50. Ibid., unit 73, sheet 5.

51. See *Arkhitektura VKhUTEMAS* (The Architecture of Vkhutemas) (Moscow: Vkhutemas, 1927); Vladimir Krinsky, "Vozniknovnie i zhizn Assotsiatsii 'novykh arkhitektorov—ASNOVA'" (The Origin and Activity of the Association of New Architects [ASNOVA]), in *Sovetskaia arkhitektura* (Soviet Architecture), no. 18 (Moscow, 1963); S.O. Khan-Magomedov, "Nikolai Aleksandrovich Ladovskii," in *Mastera sovetskoi arkhitektury ob arkhitekture* (Masters of Soviet Architecture on Architecture), vol. 1 (Moscow, 1975), pp. 337-43.

52. S. O. Khan-Magomedov, "A. Lavinskii," *Tekhnicheskaia estetika* (Technical Aesthetics), no. 1 (1980).

53. Manuscript Department, Tretiakov Gallery, fund 148, unit 45, sheet 1.

54. "5 x 5 = 25," typewritten exhibition catalog (Moscow, 1921), p. 3.

55. Manuscript Department, Tretiakov Gallery, fund 148, unit 74, sheet 3.

56. Ibid.

57. Ibid., unit 23, sheet 2.

58. Ibid., unit 21, sheet 1.

59. GVYTM was organized by Meierkhold as an experimental laboratory for the new theatrical aesthetics. Under its original name, GVYRM (State Higher Directors' Workshop), it opened on October 1, 1921. It had begun admitting in the previous summer. Meierkhold was chair of the administration and of the Academic-Productivist Board, director of the entire enterprise. Valery Bebutov headed the Academic Department. Ivan Aksionov was rector. On November 10, 1921, the Theater of the Russian Republic (directed by Meierkhold) gave its last performance. After it closed, a group of young actors formed the Laboratory of Acting Technique, later renamed the Free Studio of Vsevolod Meierkhold. The Free Studio merged with GVYRM in the spring of 1922, and GVYRM was transformed into GVYTM and then joined with five drama schools of more or less similar persuasion. By GVYTM's first

anniversary it was already GITIS (State Institute of Theatrical Art).

60. D. Zolotnitsky, *Budni i prazdniki Teatralnogo Oktiabria* (The Workdays and Holidays of Theatrical October) (Leningrad: Iskusstvo, 1978), p. 17.

61. Popova's *prozodezhda* was also used later in the theater. For example, in *Tiara veka* (The Tiara of the Century), by Paul Claudel, adapted by Ivan Aksionov, staged in 1922 by second-year student German Fedorov; also the peasants in *Earth on End* (Marcel Martinet's play *Night* adapted by Sergei Tretiakov) were dressed in the same costumes in this 1923 Meierkhold production. At the same time we know that Fernand Crommelynck's *The Magnanimous Cuckold* was performed in 1928 in ordinary theatrical costumes. Popova's *prozodezhda* was actually clothing for rehearsals and for demonstrating biomechanics during the studio's graduation exercises.

62. Manuscript Department, Tretiakov Gallery, fund 148, unit 88, sheet 1. I date this program 1921 on the basis of Popova's own remark in the "Programma kursa veshchestvennogo elementa spektaklia" (Program for a Course on the Material Element of the Performance) (ibid., unit 33, sheet 6).

63. Vadim Shershenevich, "Tezisy k diskussii" (Theses for Discussion), *Zrelishcha* (Performances), no. 76 (1924): 9.

64. Manuscript Department, Tretiakov Gallery, fund 148, unit 57, sheet 2.

65. Ivan Aksionov, "L. S. Popova v teatre" (L. S. Popova in the Theater), *Novyi zritel* (The New Audience), no. 23 (1924): 9.

66. On this, see N. Adaskina, "Proekt 'Proizvodstvennoi masterskoi osnovnogo otdeleniia'—pervaia sovetskaia programma dizainerskogo obrazovaniia" (Plan for the Production Studio of the Basic Department—the First Soviet Program in Design Education), in *Problemy istorii sovetskoi arkhitektury*, no. 4 (Moscow, 1978) (under TsNIITIA).

67. Manuscript Department, Tretiakov Gallery, fund 148, unit 134, sheet 1.

68. Manuscript Department, Tretiakov Gallery, fund 148, unit 51, sheet 2. Handwritten by Popova.

69. Manuscript Department, Tretiakov Gallery, fund 148, unit 39, sheet 1.

70. Manuscript Department, Tretiakov Gallery, fund 148, unit 76, sheet 1.

71. Popova's programs for the Basic Department of the Graphics Faculty (Manuscript Department, Tretiakov Gallery, fund 148, units 46, 47), where production problems are posed for graphics, are marked September 1923. However, neither Popova's program nor her candidacy for teacher suited the leadership of the Graphics Faculty, and that spilled over into the famous Inkhuk-Vkhutemas conflict. On this, see S. O. Khan-Magomedov, "VKhUTEMAS i INKhUK (k problematike stanovleniia sfery dizaina v 20-e gody)" (Vkhutemas and Inkhuk: On the Problematics of the Design Sphere's Formation in the 1920s), *Tekhnicheskaia estetika*, no. 12 (1980): esp. 13, n. 23; N. Adaskina, "Favorskii i proizvodstvenniki" (Favorsky and the Productivists), *Tekhnicheskaia estetika*, no. 7 (1980).

72. Manuscript Department, Tretiakov Gallery, fund 148, unit 53, sheet 1.

73. B. Ternovets, *V. I. Mukhina* (Moscow, 1937), p. 24; O. Voronova, *Vera Ignatievna Mukhina* (Moscow, 1977), p. 42. Voronova mistakenly supposes that Mukhina helped Exter design Innokenty Annensky's *Famira Kifared* (Tamira of the Cittern).

74. The studies are held in private collections in Moscow and abroad.

75. John Bowlt, "From Surface to Space: The Art of Liubov Popova," *The Structurist* (Canada), no. 15/16 (1976): 8.

76. A. Efros, *Kamernyi teatr i ego khudozhniki* (The Chamber Theater and Its Artists) (Moscow, 1934), p. xxxiii.

77. I do not think there is any convincing evidence for dating Popova's puppet show 1919, as John Bowlt does in the catalog *Russian Stage Design: Scenic Innovation 1900-1930 from the Collection of Mr. and Mrs. Nikita D. Lobanov-Rostovsky* (Mississippi Museum of Art, 1982), p. 236.

78. Natalia Satz, *Deti prikhodiat v teatr: Stranitsy vospominanii* (Children Come to the Theater: Pages of Reminiscences) (Moscow, 1961), p. 70.

79. Three sketches (the *Chancellor's Study* set and two costumes) are in a Moscow private collection; a variation of the *Chancellor's Study* set is in the Costakis collection (cat. no. 87, S 91); two costumes are listed in the N. Lobanov-Rostovsky collection ("Stage Designs and the Russian Avant-Garde [1911-1929]: A Loan Exhibition of Stage and Costume Designs from the Collection of Mr. and Mrs. Nikita D. Lobanov-Rostovsky 1976-78," no. 74, 76).

80. Following family tradition, Aksionov was a professional soldier. During the 1910s, despite his military service and participation in military actions, he became a

well-known translator and literary and art critic. He also published poems and plays. He was an organizer of Bolshevik action in the army during World War One, an active participant in revolutionary events on the Romanian front, and during the Civil War occupied positions of authority in the Red Army. Simultaneously, he continued his literary work. Beginning in 1921, Aksionov was the rector of GVYTM. While Dneproges was under construction he went to Kinkas and taught mathematics. He was a translator and scholar of Elizabethan English literature, was fond of Lautréamont, wrote brochures on problems of bread baking, and contributed to electric-welding journals.

81. Samuil Margolin, "Massovoe deistvo 'Borba i pobeda'" (The Mass Festival "Struggle and Victory"), *Ekho* (Echo), no. 13 (1923): 11.

82. N. Giliarovskaia, *Teatralno-dekoratsionnoe iskusstvo za 5 let* (Theatrical-Set Art in the Last Five Years) (Kazan, 1923), p. 26.

83. Aksionov, "Popova in the Theater," p. 5.

84. All these works are on the Vesnin-Aksionov list as collaborative, but the catalog for "Theatrical-Set Art of Moscow, 1918-1923," gives Popova as the author of "Stage Adaptation of a Military Parade. Two Maquettes (Vsevolod Meierkhold's Stage Design for the Third Congress of the Comintern)," no. 321-22, p. 59.

85. Aksionov, "Popova in the Theater," p. 5.

86. Ivan Aksionov, "Prostranstvennyi konstruktivizm na stsene" (Spatial Constructivism on the Stage), in *Teatralnyi Oktiabr* (Theatrical October), vol. 1 (Leningrad-Moscow, 1926), p. 32.

87. E. Rakitina, "Liubov Popova. Iskusstvo i manifesty" (Liubov Popova: Art and Manifestos), in *Khudozhnik, stsena, ekran* (Artist, Stage, Screen) (Moscow, 1975), p. 162; Christina Lodder, "Constructivist Theatre as a Laboratory of Architectural Aesthetic," *Architectural Associated Quarterly* 2, no. 2 (1978): 30-31; Alma Law, "A Conversation with Vladimir Stenberg," *Art Journal* (Fall 1981): 225-26.

88. John Bowlt explains: Popova is obligated to ideas already expressed by artists working in Meierkhold's studio, Sergei Eisenstein and Vladimir Liutse ("Russkii konstruktivizm i khudozhestvennoe oformlenie stseny" [Russian Constructivism and Artistic Stage Design], *Novyi zhurnal* [New Journal], no. 126 [1977]: 124). Vladimir Stenberg was convinced of the individuality and independence of Popova's plastic resolution (see Law, "Conversation," p. 226).

89. *Teatr im. Vs. Meierkholda. Katalog vystavki "5 let" (1920-1925)* (The Vsevolod Meierkhold Theater: Exhibition catalog for "Five Years" [1920-1925]) (Moscow, *Teatralnyi Oktiabr*, 1926), p. 10. It is curious that in the literature the "type" of mill is constantly changing: having just read "wooden water mill," we read in Camilla Gray "the blades of the windmill" (see *Art in Revolution: Soviet Art and Design Since 1917*, Hayward Gallery, London, 1971, p. 69), as we do in Mark Etkind's article "O diapazone prostranstvenno-vremennykh reshenii v iskusstve oformleniia stseny (Opyt analiza tvorcheskogo naslediia sovetskoi teatralnoi dekoratsii)" (On the Range of Spatial-Temporal Resolutions in the Art of Stage Design [Experiment in Analyzing the Creative Legacy of Soviet Stage Sets]), in *Ritm, prostranstvo i vremia v literature i iskusstve* (Rhythm, Space, and Time in Literature and in Art) (Leningrad, 1974), p. 217.

90. For example, S. Vakhtangov's model for Vsevolod Meierkhold's production of Vladimir Mayakovsky's *Bania* (The Bathhouse) in 1930 strikingly resembles in its outlines the stage for *The Magnanimous Cuckold* while at the same time retaining the elements of the proscenium structure. See the photo in *Russian Art of the Revolution*, Andrew Dickson White Museum of Art (February-March, 1971); Brooklyn Museum of Art (June-July, 1971), p. 10.

91. Aksionov, "Popova in the Theater," p. 6. "Popova's Trial at Inkhuk" is discussed in the biography by T. M. Pakhomova. In the early 1920s there were extremely widespread disputes of every possible sort in the form of trials against historical figures, literary heroes, theatrical characters, and so on. For all their spontaneity, they often possessed a vividly theatricalized stage form. By calling the discussion at Inkhuk a "trial" (the idea most likely came from the "trial's" actual participants), Aksionov and other authors pointed out the abstract, alienated, idealist, and irrelevant—in a sense—practical basis of the debates. We know that at that moment the majority of Constructivists making the accusations were themselves dreaming of the theater and were eager to get into theater work (Rodchenko, Stepanova, and others).

92. Manuscript Department, Tretiakov Gallery, fund 148, unit 56, sheet 1.

93. Ibid.

94. Ibid.

95. Ibid.

96. I. A. Aksionov, "Posmertnaia vystavka L. S. Popovoi" (Posthumous Exhibition of L. S. Popova), *Zhizn iskusstva* (Life of Art), no. 5 (February 3, 1925): 5.

97. Boris Arvatov, "Teatr kak proizvodstvo" (Theater as Production), in *O teatre* (On Theater) (Tver, 1922), p. 115.

98. Manuscript Department, Tretiakov Gallery, fund 148, unit 64, sheet 1.

99. Sergei Tretiakov, "Velikodushnii rogonosets" (The Magnanimous Cuckold), *Zrelishcha*, no. 8 (1922): 12.

100. Minutes of the Inkhuk meeting of April 27, 1922 (private collection, Moscow). See S. O. Khan-Magomedov, *Alexandre Vesnin et le Constructivisme* (Paris 1988), where the minutes are reprinted.

101. "Materialnoe oformlenie zrelishcha" (The Material Design of the Performance), *Zrelishcha*, no. 9 (1922): 9.

102. Ibid., no. 67 (1923): 8.

103. Nadezhda Krupskaia, wife of V. I. Lenin, sent Meierkhold the text of the play with a request to look it over with a view to possible production (Vsevolod Meierkhold, *Perepiska* [Correspondence] [Moscow, 1976], p. 214). John Bowlt noted this fact in attributing the studies from the Lobanov-Rostovsky collection.

104. The studies are mostly concentrated in a private collection in Moscow. They all depict characters. They are executed in various techniques: pencil, watercolor, gouache, India ink.

105. The manuscript is dated July 25, 1922. It was published in *Zrelishcha*, no. 1 (1922): 5.

106. Quoted from the essay manuscript (Manuscript Department, Tretiakov Gallery, fund 148, unit 24, sheet 3).

107. *Zrelishcha*, no. 57 (1923): 7.

108. One of Popova's sketches for *Earth on End* (Bakhrushin Central Theatrical Museum) is inscribed: "To Com. Erdman I. Immediately begin building Liub. Serg. Popova's sets for *La Nuit*, which is to be prepared as the show for the October festivities (1922). (In accordance with this draft and L. S. Popova's personal explanations) Vs. Meierkhold, October 1, 1922."

109. On May 31, 1923, in Kharkov, the performance was given in the garden of the Central Party Club (a real crane was installed); that same year in Ekaterinoslav, instead of a crane, they used a festival building (a light wooden structure), in Rostov-on-the-Don the gazebo in the city garden; on September 2 the performance was given in the Palace Meadow of Neskuchny Garden in Moscow (with more than 10,000 people in attendance); on June 29, 1924, it was included in a mass festival for a workers' holiday in the Lenin Hills in honor of the Fifth Congress of the Comintern.

110. *Lef*, no. 4 (1923): 44.

111. Manuscript Department, Tretiakov Gallery, fund 148, unit 32, sheet 2.

112. Emmanuel Beskin, "Teatr Meierkholda. 'Zemlia dybom'" (Meierkhold's theater: *Earth on End*, *Ekho* (Echo), no. 9 (1923): 13.

113. Aksionov, "Spatial Constructivism," p. 33.

114. Aksionov, "Popova in the Theater," p. 7.

115. *Zrelishcha*, no. 27 (1923): 7.

116. *Teatr im. Vs. Meierkholda. Katalog vystavki "5 let" (1920-1925)* (The Meierkhold Theater: Exhibition Catalog of "5 Years" [1920-1925]), p. 15.

117. On Davydova, see "Krestianskoe tvorchestvo Ukrainy" (Peasant Art of the Ukraine), signed "P.," *Russkoe iskusstvo*, no. 2-3 (1923): 115; Shadova, *Malevich*, pp. 33-34 and p. 121, n. 55.

118. After the artist's death there were fifty-six watercolors and color collages for Verbovka in her studio. At present we know fifteen (private collection, Moscow) that we can positively identify.

119. *The George Costakis Collection: Russian Avant-Garde Art* (New York, 1981), no. 919 and 918.

120. John Bowlt has said that at the "Modern Decorative Art" exhibition in 1916 and 1917, in Moscow, Popova showed designs for purses, belts, and pillows (John E. Bowlt, "Liubov Popova, Painter," in *Zapiski russkoi akademicheskoi gruppy v SShA* [Notes of the Russian Academic Group in the U.S.A.], vol. 15, On Russian Art [New York, 1982], p. 237) This information is incorrect. The catalog for "Modern Decora-

tive Art" (Moscow, [Galerie Lermercier, November 1915, p. 6) lists works by Vera Popova (Liubov Popova's cousin): no. 93-94, tablecloths, sketches; no. 95, dress; no. 96-97, pillows; no. 98-100, binding; no. 101, embroidery; no. 102, tablecloth. Neither Liubov nor Vera Popova participated in the subsequent exhibits at the Galerie Lermercier in 1916-17 and 1917-18, which were then called "Decorative-Industrial."

121. Aksionov, "Popova in the Theater," p. 5.

122. See A. Raikhenshtein, "1 maia i 7 noiabria 1918 goda v Moskve (Iz istorii oformleniia pervykh proletarskikh prazdnikov)" (May 1 and November 7, 1918, in Moscow [From the History of the Design of the First Proletarian Holidays], in *Agitatsionno-massovoe iskusstvo pervykh let Oktiabria* (Agitational-Mass Art from the First Years of October) (Moscow, 1971), pp. 707-72.

123. Vasilii Rakitin, "Liubov Popova," in *Künstlerinnen der russische Avantgarde 1910-1930/Women-Artists of the Russian Avantgarde 1910-1930* (Cologne: Galerie Gmurzynska, 1979), p. 200.

124. Nine sketches were left in Popova's studio. At present we know: La Boetie, Ind. (exhibition catalogue *The Avant-Garde in Russia, 1910-1930*, Los Angeles County Museum of Art, 1980); cat. no. 252; Mr. and Mrs. Roald Collection (ibid.), cat. no. 253; *The George Costakis Collection*, figs. 864 and 965); Tretiakov Gallery, no. P. 47030.

125. Ternovets, *Mukhina*, p. 34.

126. There are several versions: the exhibition catalog *Tatlin's Dream: Russian Suprematist and Constructivist Art, 1910-1923* (Dr. Andrei Nakov 1973-74, no. 66, dated 1922-23; *The George Costakis Collection*, no. 824, dated 1917-18; Tretiakov Gallery, p. 47195 (dated by the author October 1921).

127. See *The George Costakis Collection*, p. 370.

128. Ibid., p. 400.

129. Vladimir A. Favorsky, *Literaturno-Teoreticheskoe Nasledie* (Literary-Theoretical Legacy) (Moscow, 1988), p. 8.

130. Beskin, "Meierkhold's theater," p. 15.

131. David Arkin, "Veshchnoe iskusstvo" (Material Art), *Zhizn iskusstva*, no. 4-5 (1920): 4.

132. Manuscript Department, Tretiakov Gallery, fund 148, unit 17, sheet 3.

133. For example, Bowlt, "Liubov Popova," p. 227.

134. The biography of Popova compiled by T.M. Pakhomova says that, in addition to the First Department of Vkhutemas, the artist taught also in the Print and Textile faculties. There is no information about Popova's having taught in the Texile Faculty in the Vkhutemas archive; in all likelihood this collaboration never actually happened. One of the sketches for *The Magnanimous Cuckold* (Tretiakov Gallery, [p. 47235) was done on the back of a letter that said the following: "Dear Liubov Serveevna, since you are a colleague on the Textile Faculty, said faculty appeals to you with a request not to refuse the bearer of this . . . ."

135. D.M. Aranovich, "Iskusstvo v tkani" (Art in Fabric), *Iskusstvo odevatsia* (The Art of Dressing), no. 1 (1928): 11.

136. Ibid.

137. Ivan Aksionov, "Posmertnaia vystavka Popovoï" (posthumous exhibition of L.S. Popova), p. 5.

138. Yakov Tugendkhold, "Po vystavkam" (From Exhibit to Exhibit), *Izvestiia VTSIK* (News of the [illegible]), no. 26 (235) (February 1, 1925).

139. Aranovich, "Art in Fabric," p. 11.

140. "Pamiati L. S. Popovoi" (In Memory of L. S. Popova), *Lef*, no. 2 (1924): 4.

141. Elena Murina, "Tkani Liubovi Popovoi" (The Fabrics of Liubov Popova), *Dekorativnoe iskusstvo SSSR* (Decorative Art of the USSR), no. 8 (1967): 27.

142. Vasilii Rakitin, "Liubov Popova," in *Künstlerinnen der russischen Avantgarde*, p. 204.

143. John Bowlt, "From Pictures to Textile Prints," *Print Collector's Newsletter* (New York) (March/April 1976): 16.

144. In 1928, Sonia Delaunay published an article in the Soviet magazine *Iskusstvo odevatsia*, no. 2 (2 pp., cover), propagandizing the production of suit-length fabrics.

145. *Vecherniaia Moskva* (Evening Moscow), no. 119, May 26, 1924.

Design for a suit. 1923–24. India ink and gouache on paper, 8⅛ × 5⅞″
(20.6 × 15 cm.). Private collection, Moscow

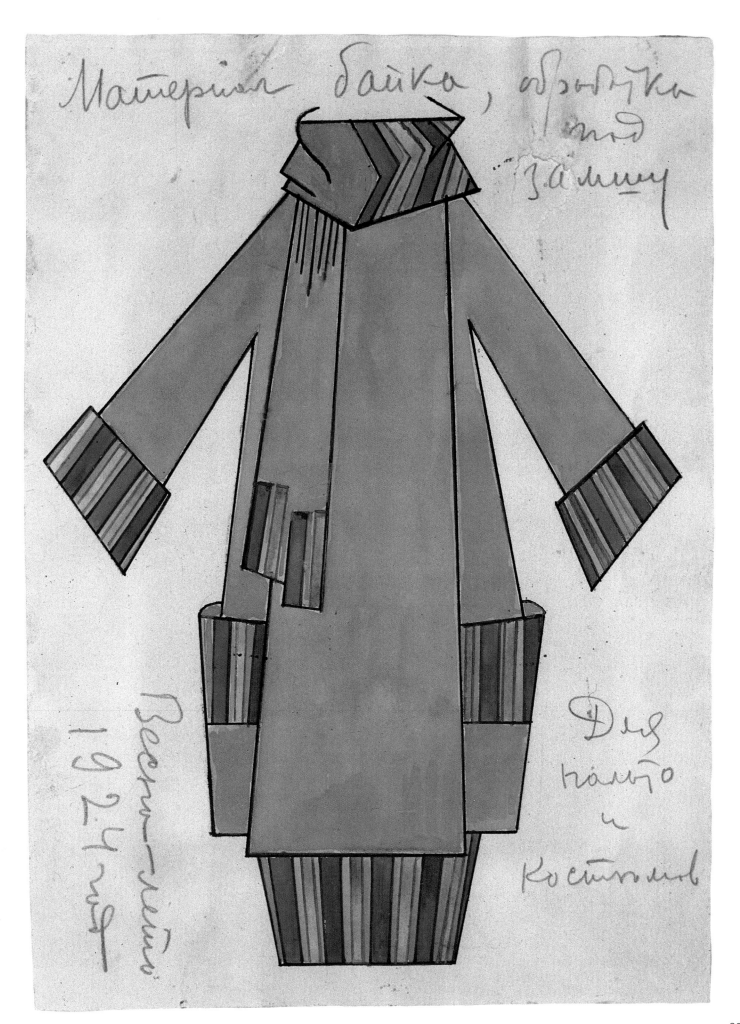

Материал байка, обработка под замшу

Весенний
1924 год

Для пальто и костюмов

Dress design. 1923–24. India ink and gouache on paper, 9½ × 4⅛″ (24 × 10.4 cm.).
Private collection, Moscow

Dress design. 1923–24. India ink and gouache on paper, 8⅝ × 3¾″
(22.1 × 9.6 cm.). Museum of Decorative and Applied Art, Moscow

Textile design. 1923–24. India ink and gouache on paper, 9¾ × 14″ (24.8 × 35.7 cm.).
Museum of Decorative and Applied Art, Moscow

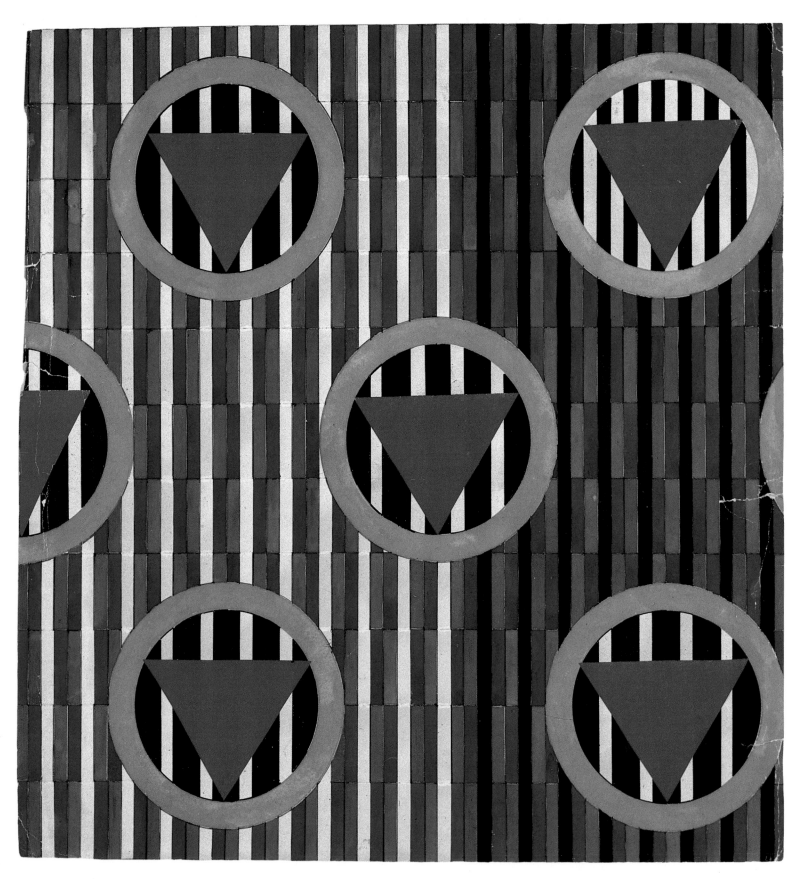

Textile design. 1923–24. Gouache and collage on cardboard, 15⅛ × 14⅝″ (38.5 × 37.2 cm.). Private collection, Moscow

ИЗ ПОДСЛУШАННЫХ РАЗГОВОРОВ

АНТОН: Куда ты уезжаешь, Любочка?
ЛЮБОВЬ: Я везу к Циндель недельную
    продукцию ситчиков.

_____

АНТОН: Что ты, Варвара, сегодня
    налегке идешь?
ВАРВАРА: А я Цинделю 2 ситчика не-
    су, чтобы не зазнались!

Manuscript page for a humor magazine. *Top:* Liubov Popova pushes a wheelbarrow of new fabric designs on her way to the textile factory. *Bottom:* Varvara Stepanova carries her designs in a small bag. The typescript reads:

FROM A CONVERSATION OVERHEARD

ANTON: Where are you going, Liubovka?
LIUBOV: I am taking my week's output of cotton designs to Tsindel.

ANTON: And you, Varvara? It's a light day for you today.
VARVARA: I'm not a showoff! I'm just bringing two designs to the factory.

Textile design. 1923–24. India ink on paper, 2⅞ × 2⅛″ (7.2 × 5.3 cm.).
Museum of Decorative and Applied Art, Moscow

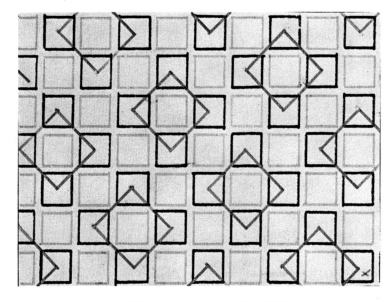

Textile design. 1923–24. India ink on paper, 2¼ × 2″ (5.7 × 5.2 cm.).
Museum of Decorative and Applied Art, Moscow

Dress design. 1923–24. India ink and gouache on paper, 8⅜ × 3⅞"
(21.2 × 9.9 cm.). Museum of Decorative and Applied Art, Moscow

Dress design. 1923–24. India ink and gouache on paper, 8⅞ × 4¾"
(22.5 × 12 cm.). Museum of Decorative and Applied Art, Moscow

Opposite, bottom left: Fabric design. 1923–24. Gouache on paper,
4⅜ × 3⅜" (11 × 8.7 cm.). Private collection, Moscow

Design for a child's dress. 1923–24. India ink and gouache on paper, 8⅞ × 5¾" (22.7 × 14.5 cm.). Tretiakov Gallery. Gift of George Costakis

Textile design. 1923–24. India ink and gouache on paper, 3¼ × 2½" (8.2 × 6.3 cm.). Museum of Decorative and Applied Art, Moscow

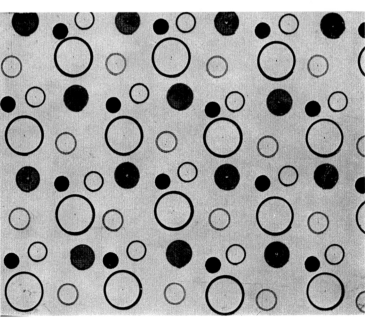

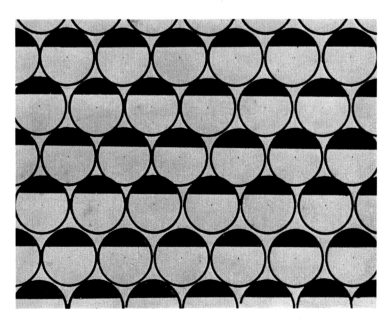

Dress design. 1923—24. India ink and gouache on paper, 8⅝ × 4⅜" (22 × 11 cm.).
Private collection, Moscow

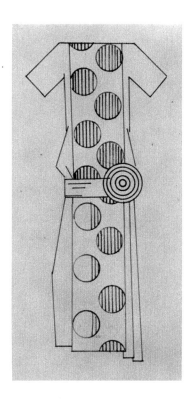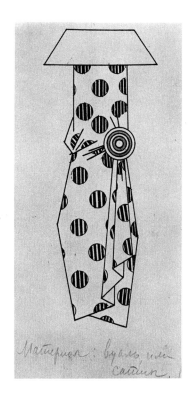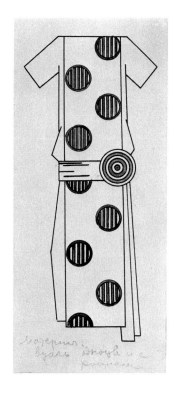

Three dress designs. 1923–24. India ink and gouache on paper. *Left to right:* 8⅛ × 4¾" (20.6 × 12.2 cm.); 10¼ × 4¾"
(26.1 × 12.2 cm.); 9⅛ × 4" (23.2 × 10.1 cm.). Museum of Decorative and Applied Art, Moscow

Textile design. 1923. India ink and gouache on paper, 14½ × 9⅞"
(36.8 × 25.2 cm.). Design used as cover for the review *Lef*, no. 2, 1923.
Private collection, Moscow

Two textile designs. 1923–24. India ink and gouache on paper, 10⅞ × 7⅞" (27.5 × 20 cm.);
10 ⅛ × 7¾" (25.8 × 19.7 cm.). Museum of Decorative and Applied Art, Moscow

Design for a shop window. 1924. Gouache and collage on paper, 14¼ × 9½"
(36.3 × 24.2 cm.). Museum of Decorative and Applied Art, Moscow

Design for a shop window. 1924. Gouache and collage on paper, 16⅝ × 11⅛"
(42.3 × 28.3 cm.). Private collection, Moscow

Dress and textile design. 1923–24. India ink and gouache on paper, textile: 10½ × 7⅛″ (26.8 × 18 cm.); dress: 8⅞ × 4¼″ (22.6 × 10.7 cm.).
Museum of Decorative and Applied Art, Moscow

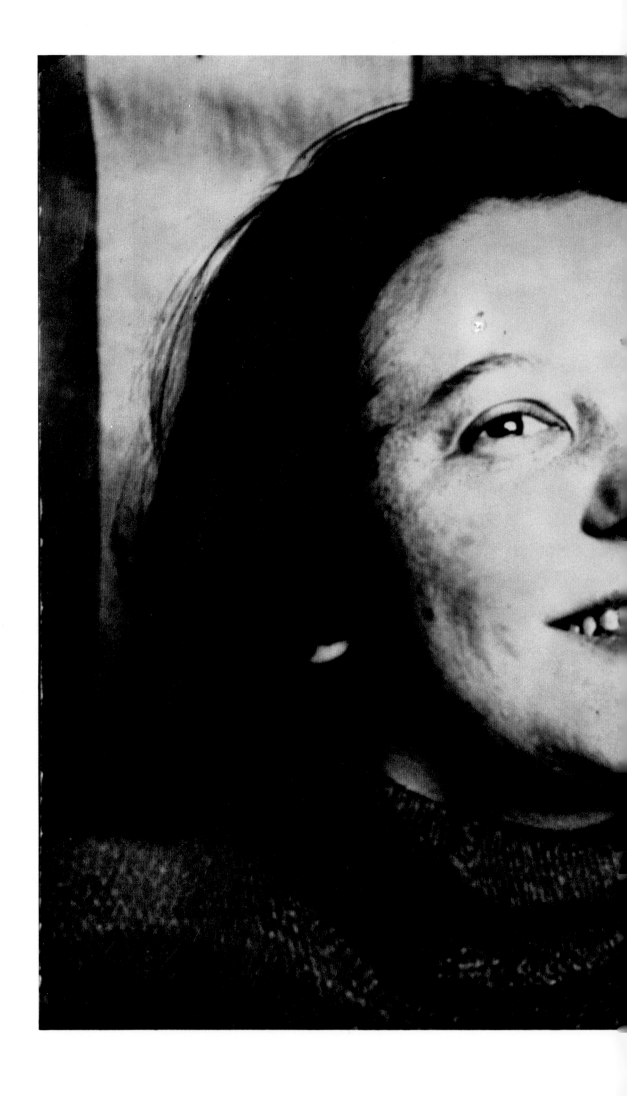

Varvara Stepanova and Liubov Popova. 1924. Photograph by Aleksandr Rodchenko

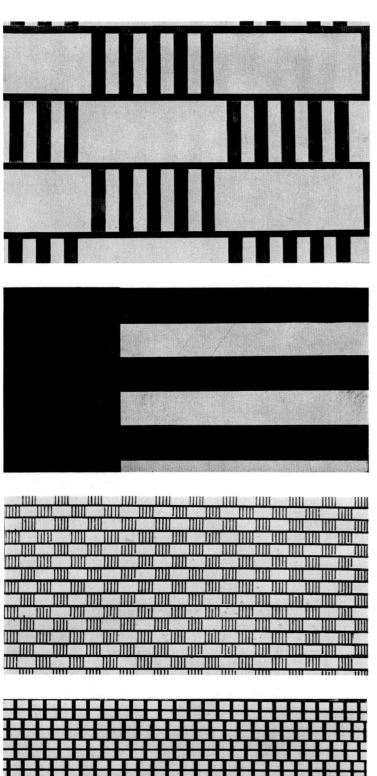

Textile design. Scarf (?). 1923–24. Gouache on paper, 4¾ × 4⅜″ (12 × 11.2 cm.).
Museum of Decorative and Applied Art, Moscow

Four textile designs. 1923–24. *Top to bottom:* India ink and gouache on paper, 11 × 7″
(28 × 17.8 cm.); gouache on cardboard, 7½ × 3¾″ (19 × 9.6 cm.), private collection; India
ink on paper, 5⅜ × 2½″ (13.6 × 6.5 cm.); India ink on paper, 4⅜ × 2⅝″ (11.2 × 6.7 cm.).
Museum of Decorative and Applied Art, Moscow

Textile design. 1923–24. India ink and gouache on paper, 7¾ × 7⅛″
(19.6 × 18 cm.). Private collection, Moscow

Textile design. 1923–24. India ink and gouache on paper, 4¾ × 4⅛″ (12 × 10.5 cm.).
Private collection, Moscow

Textile design. 1923–24. India ink and gouache on paper,
5¼ × 3¼″ (13.5 × 8.2 cm.). Private collection, Moscow

Three textile designs. 1923–24. *Top to bottom:* India ink and goauche on paper,
3¼ × 1⅞″ (8.4 × 4.7 cm.); 2¼ × 1¾″ (5.8 × 4.6 cm.); India ink on paper, 12⅝ × 5¾″
(32 × 14.7 cm.). Museum of Decorative and Applied Art, Moscow

Dress design. 1923–24. India ink and gouache on paper, 8⅝ × 3¾″
(22 × 9.7 cm.). Museum of Decorative and Applied Art, Moscow

Dress design. 1923–24. India ink and gouache on paper, 8½ × 4⅛″ (21.5 × 10.5 cm.).
Museum of Decorative and Applied Art, Moscow

Dress design. 1923–24. India ink and gouache on paper, 8¾ × 3⅜"
(22.1 × 8.6 cm.). Museum of Decorative and Applied Art, Moscow

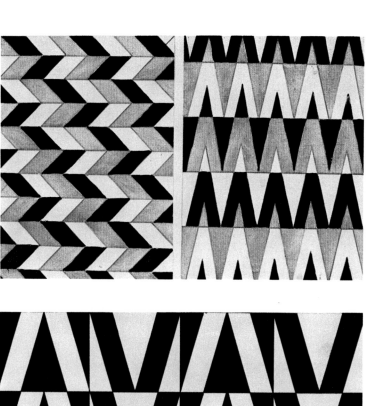

Four textile designs. 1923–24. *Top left*: gouache on paper, 4 × 5⅛" (10 × 13 cm.); *top
right*: gouache on paper, 5¼ × 4" (13.5 × 10 cm.); both, private collection, Moscow;
center: India ink on paper, 9½ × 5⅞" (24 × 15 cm.); *bottom*: gouache on paper, 3½ × 2"
(8.8 × 5.2 cm.); both Museum of Decorative and Applied Art, Moscow

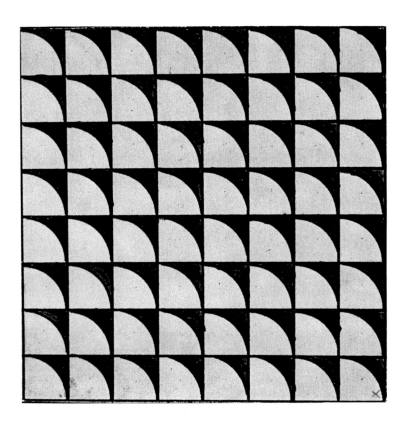

Textile design. 1923–24. India ink and gouache on paper, 2½ × 2½″ (6.3 × 6.3 cm.).
Museum of Decorative and Applied Art, Moscow

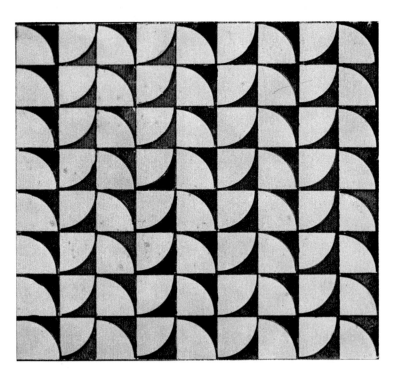

Textile design. 1923–24. Gouache on paper, 3¾ × 3¼″ (9.4 × 8.4 cm.).
Museum of Decorative and Applied Art, Moscow

Three textile designs. 1923–24. *Top to bottom:* gouache on paper, 9⅝ × 6⅜″
(24.3 × 16.3 cm.). Private collection, Moscow; India ink and gouache on paper, 7 × 5″
(17.8 × 12.8 cm.). Private collection, Moscow; India ink on paper, 2⅜ × 1⅞″
(5.9 × 4.7 cm.). Museum of Decorative and Applied Art, Moscow

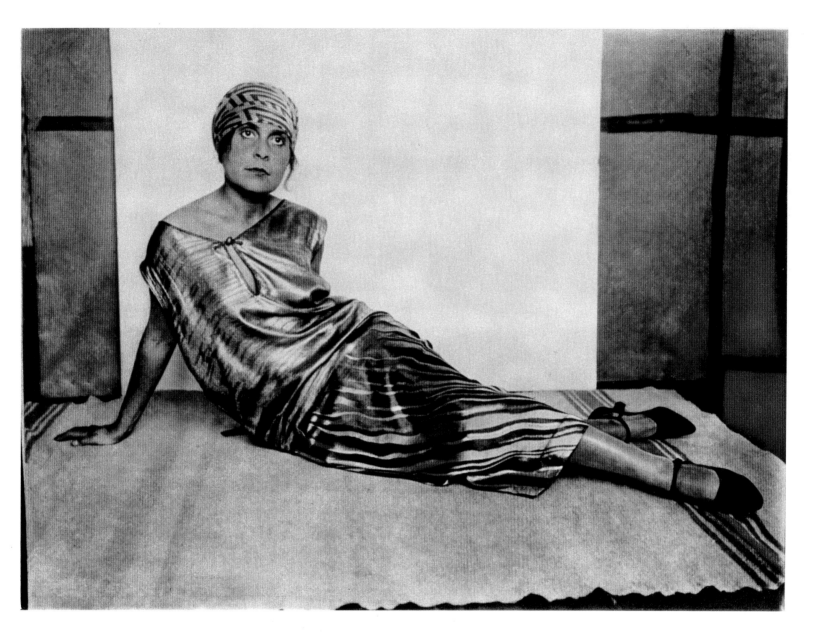

Lily Brik wearing a silk scarf on her head adapted from a motif by Popova. ca. 1924. Photograph by Aleksandr Rodchenko

Two fabric samples. 1920s. Tretiakov Gallery. Gift of George Costakis

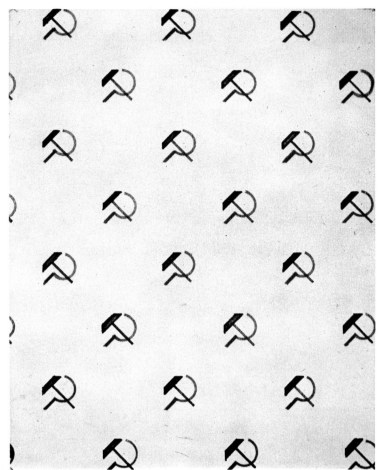

Textile design. 1923–24. Gouache on paper, 4½ × 3¼″ (11.3 × 9.3 cm.).
Private collection, Moscow

Textile designs. 1923–24. India ink on paper. *Top:* 2⅝ × 4⅝″ (6.7 × 11.8 cm.); *bottom:*
3⅞ × 4⅞″ (9.8 × 12.4 cm.). Museum of Decorative and Applied Art, Moscow

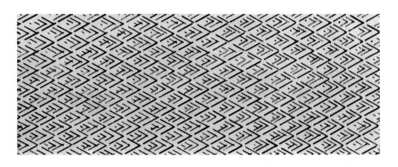

Textile design. 1923–24. India ink on paper, 4⅜ × 1¾″ (11.2 × 4.3 cm.) Museum of
Decorative and Applied Art, Moscow

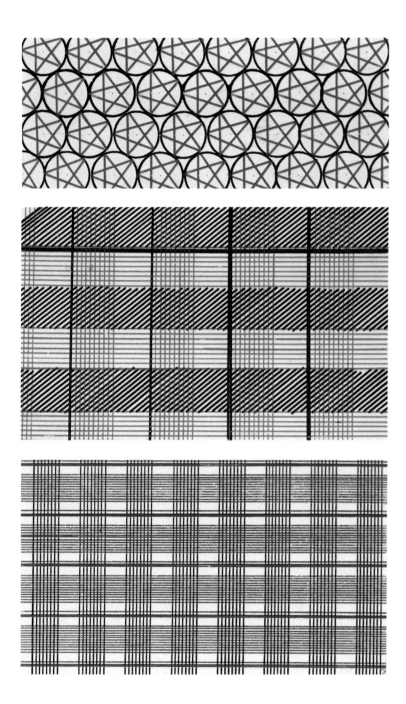

Three textile designs. 1923–24. India ink on paper. *Top to bottom:* 4 × 1⅝″ (10.2 × 4.2 cm.); 2⅞ × 4¾″ (7.3 × 12.1 cm.); 2⅝ × 1½″ (6.7 × 3.9 cm.). Museum of Decorative and Applied Art, Moscow

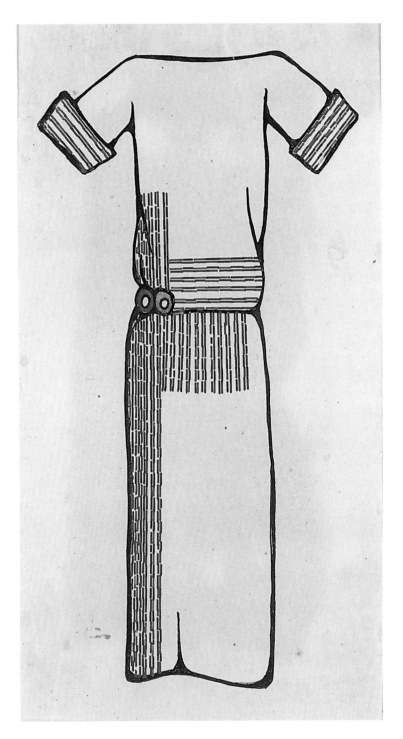

Dress design. 1923–24. India ink and gouache on paper, 9⅛ × 5″ (23.3 × 12.8 cm.).
Private collection, Moscow

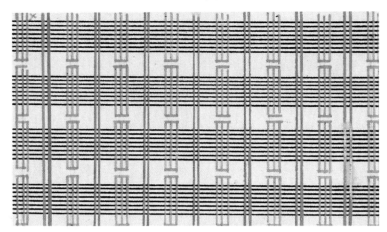

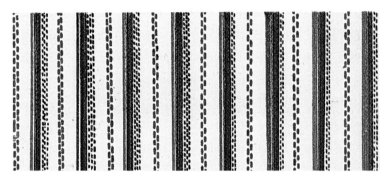

Two textile designs after a traditional motif. 1923–24. *Top*: India ink on paper,
1⅞ × 1¾″ (4.7 × 4.6 cm.); *bottom*: 3⅞ × 1⅝″ (9.7 × 4.1 cm.).
Museum of Decorative and Applied Art, Moscow

Dress design. 1923–24. India ink and gouache on paper, 9⅜ × 4⅛″
(23.8 × 10.5 cm.). Private collection, Moscow

Textile design. 1923–24. Gouache on cardboard, 13⅞ × 9⅞" (35.3 × 25 cm.).
Private collection, Moscow

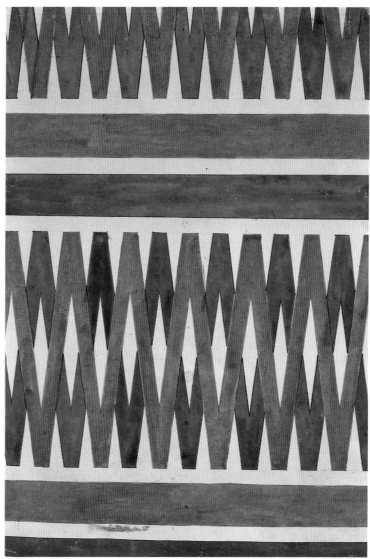

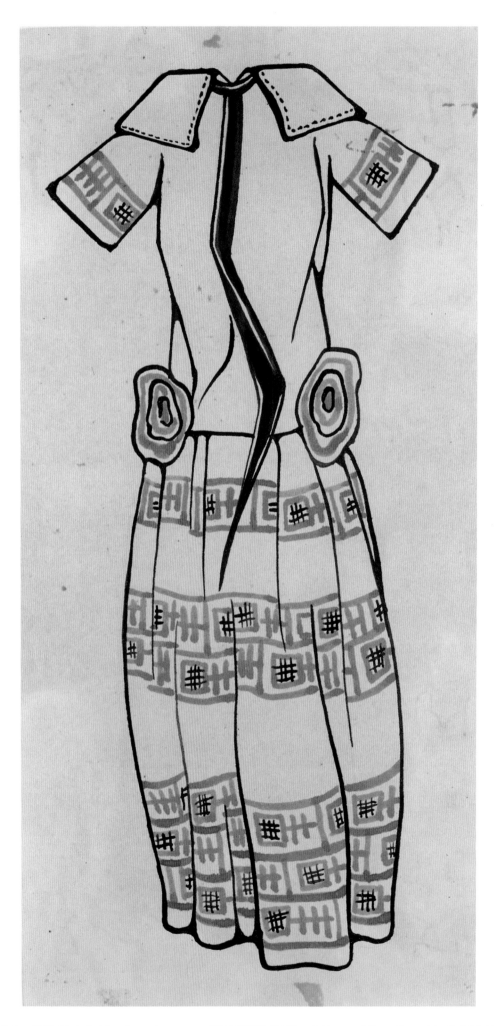

Dress design. 1923–24. India ink and gouache on paper, 9¼ × 4¾″ (23.5 × 12 cm.). Museum of Decorative and Applied Art, Moscow

Textile design. 1923–24. Gouache on cardboard, 8⅜ × 14″ (21.4 × 35.6 cm.). Museum of Decorative and Applied Art, Moscow

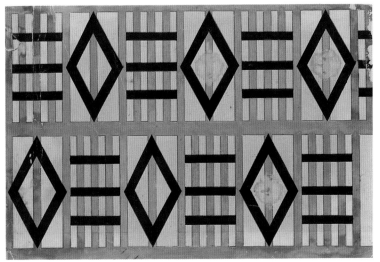

Textile design. 1923–24. India ink and gouache on paper, 12 × 8⅛″ (30.5 × 20.7 cm.). Museum of Decorative and Applied Art, Moscow

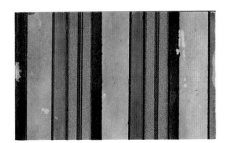

Four textile designs. 1923–24. *Left, top to bottom:* gouache on paper, 8¼ × 7″ (21 × 17.8 cm.), private collection; India ink and gouache on paper, 2⅝ × 1⅝″ (6.6 × 4.2 cm.). *Right:* India ink and gouache on paper, 9 × 3⅛″ (22.9 × 8 cm.); 9¾ × 6¾″ (24.7 × 17.2 cm.). Museum of Decorative and Applied Art, Moscow

Two textile designs. 1923–24. *Top to bottom:* gouache on paper, 4⅜ × 3⅜″ (11 × 8.7 cm.).
Museum of Decorative and Applied Art, Moscow; India ink on paper, 2⅛ × 1⅝″
(5.5 × 4.1 cm.). Private collection, Moscow

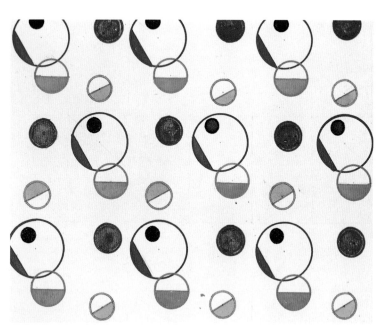

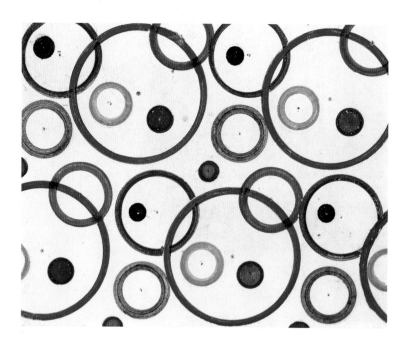

Textile design. 1923–24. India ink and gouache on paper, 5 × 3⅞″ (12.6 × 10
Museum of Decorative and Applied Art, Moscow

Textile design. 1923–24. Gouache on paper, 3⅞ × 3⅛″ (9.7 × 8 cm.).
Museum of Decorative and Applied Art, Moscow

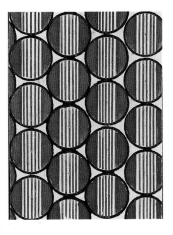 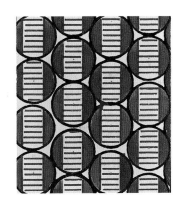

Two textile designs. 1923–24. India ink and gouache on paper, *left*: 2¼ × 1⅝″ (5.8 × 4.3 cm.); *right*: 2 × 1¾″ (5 × 4.5 cm.). Museum of Decorative and Applied Art, Moscow

Textile design. 1923–24. Gouache on cardboard, 13⅞ × 9½″ (35.3 × 24.2 cm.). Private collection, Moscow

Dress design. 1923–24. India ink and gouache on paper, 10 × 5½″ (25.3 × 14.1 cm.). Museum of Decorative and Applied Art, Moscow

335

Textile design. 1923–24. Gouache and collage on paper, 7⅝ × 5¼″ (19.4 × 13.4 cm.).
Museum of Decorative and Applied Art, Moscow

Funeral of Liubov Popova. 1924. Photograph by Aleksandr Rodchenko

ОТДЕЛ ПО ДЕЛАМ МУЗЕЕВ ГЛАВНАУКИ НАРКОМПРОСА

МУЗЕЙ ЖИВОПИСНОЙ КУЛЬТУРЫ /Рождественка 11/

Настоящим приглашает Вас, на открытие посмертной выставки художницы

-конструктора Л. с. Поповой, имеющей быть в воскресенье 21-го декабря

1924 года в помещении Музея, в 12 час.дня.

ОТДЕЛ ПО ДЕЛАМ МУЗЕЕВ :-

Invitation to the opening of Popova's posthumous exhibition, December 21, 1924, at the Museum of Artistic Culture (No. 11 Rozhdestvenko Street), Moscow

Cover for the catalog to Popova's posthumous exhibition, 1924

Cover of the magazine *Novyi zritel* (New Viewer), no. 23, 1924,
with a portrait of Popova

Self-Portrait. 1910s. Pencil on paper, dimensions unknown. Collection Mr. and Mrs. Nikita D. Lobanov-Rostovsky, London

APPENDIXES

Lists of books compiled by Popova. Mid-1910s (?). Among them are: Goethe, "only the volume with *Elective Affinities*"; Shelley, translated by [Konstantin] Balmont; *Logos* magazine; [Valerii] Briussov, *The Great Orator, The School Poems of Pushkin*, letters by Pushkin and letters to Pushkin; French poets of the nineteenth century, "translations and characteristics"; Paul Deussen, *Vedanta, Plato, and Kant: Culture and Wisdom of the Ancient Indians*. Private collection, Moscow

WRITINGS BY POPOVA

ЛЮБОВЬ ПОПОВА.

Москва, Новинский бульвар, 117, 9.

(+)   (—)

Живопись.

(+)	(—)
I. Архитектоника.	Не живопись, а изображение действительности.
а) Живописное пространство (кубизм).	
б) Линия.	
в) Цвет (супрематизм).	**I. Аконструктивность.**
г) Энергитика (футуризм).	а) Иллюзионизм.
д) Фактура.	б) Литературность.
II. Необходимость трансформации путем пропуска частей формы (начало в кубизме).	в) Эмоции.
	г) Узнавание.

Построение в живописи = сумме энергии частей.

Поверхность сохранена, а формы об'емны.

I: STATEMENT FROM THE CATALOG FOR THE "TENTH STATE EXHIBITION: NONOBJECTIVE ART AND SUPREMATISM"

LIUBOV POPOVA
Moscow, Novinsky Boulevard, 117, 9

(+)	(−)
Painting	Not painting but the depiction of reality.
I. Architectonics	
a) Painterly space (Cubism)	
b) Line	1. Aconstructiveness
c) Color (Suprematism)	a) Illusionism
d) Energetics (Futurism)	b) Literariness
e) Texture	c) Emotion
	d) Recognition
II. The need to transform by omitting parts of the form (the start of Cubism)	

Construction in painting = the sum of the energy of the parts
The surface is maintained, but the form is volumetric

Moscow, 1919, p. 22. See Part Two, note 3.

II: POPOVA'S RESPONSE TO KANDINSKY'S QUESTIONNAIRE ON COLOR

The first half of the spectrum—*red, orange, yellow*—shares a sense of shape, even if their forms, for example, the circle and the triangle, have utterly different connotations.

This may be explained by the smaller difference in the number of vibrations of color waves among them than between them and other colors. The closeness goes so far that a circle can be colored yellow (an association with the sun?) and a triangle (with difficulty, it is true) orange.

Red has the curved line of the circle, not a closed circle but, if that is possible, an "obtuse circle."

The second half of the spectrum, whose colors are even closer to one another, and the line of the angle cuts from the edge of the circle first to the obtuse angle *(green),* then through the right angle (of the *blue* square), and turns into an acute-angled violet.

Black has no definite form and changes according to its shading or proximity to other colors; thus, in the order of the spectrum, placed after violet, it forms a very sharp, falling angle, whereas with respect to orange or yellow it is very narrow. It has no curved lines whatsoever.

White, on the contrary, has no angles but only curved lines. Nor does it have any determinate form.

Manuscript Department, Tretiakov Gallery, fund 148, unit 13, sheet 1–2. Handwritten, 1920.
See Part Two, notes 4–6 and pages 210–11.

III: ON THE CONSTRUCTION OF NEW OBJECTIVE AND NONOBJECTIVE FORMS

The outstanding element in our creative consciousness in this era of great organizations is the replacement of the principle of the art of painting as a means of representation by the principle of organization or *construction*. No historical moment can ever be repeated. The past is for history. The present and the future are for the organization of life, for the organization of consciousness, which means both will and creative necessity.

We are breaking with the past because we do not believe it anymore, because its hypotheses are unacceptable. We ourselves are creating them anew, our own hypotheses, we are creating them anew, and on the basis of them alone, on our own invention, can we build our new life and our new worldview.... This working process of the creative consciousness, progressing from representation to organization, is characterized by two basic points:

1. First point: The analysis of the concept of the object, unlike the meaning of its picture and representation, lies at the base of the approach to reality: the object begins to be distorted in order to reveal its essence, which is the concretization of the given consciousness in the given forms and the beginning of the organization of the means of art. There is nothing new in its intention; there is no important era in art when the object was not distorted for the sake of the outward energy of expression or reconstructed in line with the need to make a worldview concrete.

But inasmuch as the given conjunction of historical conditions for the formation of the known consciousness is unique, this condition of consciousness with respect to its past, present, and future is extraordinary and unique. That is the first point.

2. The second point is more important. This is the opportune moment to create. Out of the constant old elements—old only because in the end we have just the same concrete matter—a new organization for these elements is created.

Thus, through the transformation and abstraction of reality, the artist is freed from all conventions of hitherto existing worldviews. The principle of constructiveness renders a work not a means but an end in itself; it objectifies it, thereby making it really existing, *necessary,* and therefore *utilitarian.* But once the goal of an intellectual creative work changes, so does its means.

So the demonstration laboratory and research into these new means is our exhibit. These works are investigations into the elements and means with which we operate in order to operate with them as definite, concrete, researched material (just as in technology, supporting material must also be carefully and thoroughly researched, formalized, without which no construction of any kind is possible).

And the work on each element, such as line, plane, volume, space, color, texture, material, already goes beyond abstract exercise in the elements and as a result forces this research to set itself a definite goal—making a given element concrete, that is, bringing it to a formulated concrete form so that it can be freely and confidently operated with for general constructive tasks.

And our fanaticism in achieving our goals is conscious and convinced. After all, the scale of experience has taught us to take a positive view of the place all that is going on is to occupy in history.

Private collection, Moscow. Handwritten. 1920–21.

Varvara Stepanova. *The Constructor Liubov Popova.* Date unknown. India ink, 9½ × 6¾″ (24.2 × 17 cm.)

IV: FROM MATERIALS FOR A SPEECH ON STYLE

I would like to set as a goal for today's inquiry by this Museum of Artistic Culture into the latest Russian painting the clarification of the concept "new style," of which this museum might serve as an example. Of what does this new style consist? What is its subjective artistic consciousness, composed of the nature of perception and the artistic necessity of design?

Manuscript Department, Tretiakov Gallery, fund 148, unit 74, sheet 4. Handwritten. 1921. See Part Two, note 18.

V: ABSTRACT FOR A SPEECH ON STYLE. VARIATION

1. The theme of my speech is the question of the new style in the history of art, especially in painting, and therefore the question of the form of this objective and nonobjective style.

For me the issue is perfectly and decisively clear, but so difficult that I beg you (1) to forgive me for my mistakes in view of the utter newness of a question about which I have never read but have only contemplated privately, and (2) to help me work through several difficult questions, especially since the speech is constructed around a series of theses.

I am proud to live in the age that has created this new style. New not only with respect to preceding styles but also to everything else that has ever existed in the sense of the style of artistic form.

2. There have, of course, been styles when abstraction and distortion have also been artistically essential for the creation of a form, for example, the art of island cultures, Egyptians, Romans, the Gothic.

But those were periods when, according to Worringer's theory, art was being created by means of abstraction rather than insight (*Einfühlung*, according to W.) into our surroundings. Nonetheless, never before have we encountered any such law necessitating construction of such an entirely new approach, such a new attitude toward the visible world, especially one so compatible with the new historical norm and sociopolitical catastrophe.

Just as a break occurred in all areas of practical and theoretical life, catastrophes have come about after which the forms and images of lives past were no longer possible, so a break or overthrow occurred in the sphere of artistic style. (What do we mean by style.) We clearly see style as the formal expression of the condition of consciousness, be it in painting, sculpture, architecture, music, and so on. It is the form that clearly points out the sense of belonging and place in the historical course of art, and the more intense the era, the stronger and more expressive the style.

I should make one qualification: the highest appreciation of form does not always coincide with intensity and expression in style; there can be periods powerful in style but lower in their absolute appraisal of form. (1) Style and form are not synonyms. Perhaps the most difficult birth of a style occurred in our era, because never before has there been such a break between styles of the past and the new, such an utterly different form, such a different consciousness of form and a different state of consciousness as in our era. (But that should not surprise us since in other spheres as well, for example, politics and public life, science, technology, and so on, we have also seen just such colossal changes that draw an unambiguous boundary between "before" and "after.")

The most characteristic feature of our style in this sense is abstraction, that important abstraction of the artistic form from the form visible in reality. The issue of nonobjectiveness, despite all its naturalness and necessity for the new style, has for some reason provoked a whole series of protests and questions, but those clearly lie wholly within another order of artistic necessities in no way connected with the newborn style—epigones of the century past.

After all, nothing could be clearer than the birth of this style through the necessity for abstraction: (1) the necessity for distortion and omitting parts of the form for the necessity of the new construction of the form, (2) the transformation of visible parts of an image for the construction of the form, (3) the construction of the form, which in the process of distortion and transformation has already become abstract.

Thus, the degree of abstraction indicates the stage in the process of the style's formation, although the basic characteristic "forms" began to become clarified at the very first step of distortion—historically, we can recognize the new style in Cézanne!

Crossing into the area of the "objective"-"nonobjective" debate, any painterly form is an object, regardless of whether it exists in reality.

Private collection, Moscow. Handwritten. 1921.

VI: ABSTRACT FOR A SPEECH ON STYLE.
VARIATION (FRAGMENT)

To relate in words exactly what a sense of style is would be, of course, impossible. For instance, when we used to speak of the "Baroque" style, we certainly did not mean the Baroque facade of the Jesu or of any other Baroque church, or the swirling clouds and impetuously winding folds of Tintoretto or El Greco; what we meant was a tension of spirit agonizing and overplaying its tension. Similarly, the word "Gothic" does not bring to mind the acute angles of Gothic sculpture or the pointed arch but, once again, the tension of spirit later expressed in those forms. And it is this arrangement of tension that is a style with the nature of that tension.

Therefore the question of which object expresses this tension, or, in other words, what a work in this style represents, is secondary. I get an identical feeling from the formal tension that expresses the style in the sharply bent leg of a saint on the portal of some church in southern France—or a portion of the sharply delineated folds of his clothing, and taken as fragments they mean nothing at all, there is nothing objective from reality instilled in them, you would not even guess that these are folds of clothing and not merely fluid, acute, and sharp sculptural lines and forms. Meanwhile, in this nonobjective fragment, as in the entire figure taken as a whole, we definitely feel the whole condensed focus on a single goal, the artist's effort to express that tension in the form [illegible].

And since he thereby expresses his *own* necessity (I stress the word "own"), then it will be identical with nature, that is, it may or may not be objective.

Private collection, Moscow. Handwritten. 1921.

And Now? What Next?

This is the eternal question that, consciously or unconsciously, but continually and mercilessly, hovers in the artist's consciousness and that he hears constantly from all sides.

The difference is only that the questions of the viewer are searching and curious, whereas the question of one's own consciousness is, after all, the principle of one's whole life, one's whole work. "Revolution" is always "revolution"…is always onward, more, even if it is sad and hard to part with the immense labor of one's achievements. But after all, once they are achieved, what else can you do with them? Of course onward, to new struggle, new labor, but always with the revolutionary banner in the front rows of the human assault. And so they fight, they break through to new levels so that mankind can follow, at first rejecting, of course, but then accepting (after all, you have to go somewhere, and they cannot find the way themselves).

Along this path, laid out with such difficulty, but also with such ecstasy of discovery. And this principle of revolution is already a token of the fact that, regardless of whether or not it is true or complete, from the historical point of view, what is important is that it was created by "necessity" (*Notwendigkeit*, in Worringer), and since this is so, then this is already a token of the necessity of this step for the logical progression of mankind.

A revolution can be different: slow and logical, not producing fundamental devastations, not completely sweeping away the meaning of everything created before it in order to create its own "necessities" freely on the wreckage. Logically, like nature, this kind of revolution, gradually replacing one form of living being with another better adapted, transforms the form part by part, adapting it to the evolved understanding. Another form of artistic revolution drastically overturns an entire worldview: no compromises, no evolution is acceptable here, only revolution. This kind of consciousness must at first wholeheartedly reject every form, especially one close in time, in order to feel the newly borning form more vividly and purely. Even if this form is still stagnant, crude, primitive, often one-sided—especially in comparison with the old form, which as it approached its end arrived at dead refinement, academicism, or naturalism. It is, after all, still a child with nothing but possibilities, but the main thing is that it is "new life" because it is "new form."

Thus ancient art's degeneration was evolutionary and gradual, and the art of Christianity was just as revolutionary with respect to it. And onward again the evolution, through the Middle Ages to the Renaissance, and then through the Baroque, academicism, and naturalism to the revolution of our time, to our form.

Our form. Many say it is an end: "You've come to the end, you're at an impasse, you have no way out, you've reached full formal impoverishment," and so on and so forth. I think this is completely wrong. This is not an end but a beginning. It is simply a new look at form, it is the new form itself, although perhaps only in its disparate elements.

Thus Cézanne and the Cubists taught volumetric form on the plane, the Futurists, movement in time on the plane; the Simultaneists and Orphists, color. Of course, these are all still elements of the new understanding of form; the synthesis lies ahead, the whole joyous work lies ahead, the hardest part has been done. But another element has been introduced into the construction of the new form—the element of abstraction or nonobjectiveness. This may in fact be the most important. After all, volume as an idea, if we abstract it from form, is found in the Egyptians, and the intrinsic value of color is clear to us in the Novgorod icons of the fourteenth and fifteenth centuries.

Nonetheless, until now we have not encountered in all world painting a single example where any illusion, any literary emotion, or any recognition was tossed out completely as irrelevant to the painting act.

We do know instances of distortion for formal and painterly achievements—Russian and Byzantine icon painting, the art of primitive peoples, Romanesque Gothic, Cézanne, and other examples. But transformation for the sake of painterly or sculptural construction—that is the revelation of our artistic revolution.

All that is important is the part of the form, line, color, or texture that directly contributes to the painterly construction (Picasso). Hence we can see the irrelevance of all objective form as a whole, which inevitably bears parts that are aconstructive to the whole structure and in this way harm and destroy the construction. From here it is only one step to nonobjective form in general as a more independent form; here then is the fully cleansed and satisfied demand of artistic necessity.

The transformed form is already abstract and fully subordinated to architectonic necessity and the author's intention, but it still acquires complete freedom in absolute nonobjectiveness, in directing and constructing lines, planes, volumetric parts, and the weight of color.

Private collection, Moscow. Handwritten. 1921.

Manuscript for Popova's "Explanation of My Work" (For the Museum of Artistic Culture). December 1922. Tretiakov Gallery, Manuscript Division (Translation on facing page)

Popova's drawings accompanying the manuscript. India ink and pen on paper, *top*: 2⅜ × 2⅜" (6 × 6 cm.); *bottom*: 3 × 2⅜" (7.5 × 6 cm.). Tretiakov Gallery, Manuscript Division

VIII: FOR THE MUSEUM OF ARTISTIC CULTURE

Works of 1920–21
    5 numbers (oil on plywood)
    6 drawings
    1 sketch for a stage set
    3 photographs *(The Magnanimous Cuckold)*

Explanation of the works
From an analysis of the volume and space of objects (Cubism) to the *organization of the elements*, not as means of representation but as integral constructions (whether color-planar, volumetric-spatial, or other material constructions).

The significance of each of these elements (line, plane, volume, color, material) of the means of representation is made the concrete work of the given material, determining the function of the thing itself (be it utilitarian or abstract).

Other than hands-on mechanically visible work, construction involves ideological work, inasmuch as, in its forms, it is the reflection of its time, and by baring the principle of organization, it replaces this principle with criteria of an aesthetic order.

L. Popova, Moscow, December 1922

Manuscript Department, Tretiakov Gallery,
fund 148, unit 26, sheet 1.
(Manuscript on facing page)

IX: FROM MATERIALS FOR A SPEECH AT INKHUK (FRAGMENT)

2 paths to organization as a principle: on the one hand, historically, from analysis of the forms of elements, through distortion, to transformation, to the construction rather than the depiction of a concept, to the organization of the concept, the organization of the thing.

On the other hand—an ideological progress in connection with the principle of organization as the principle of any intellectual production.

Manuscript Department, Tretiakov Gallery, fund 148, unit 60, sheet 1 (reverse). Handwritten. 1922.

Signatures of those present at an Inkhuk meeting February 16, 1922. *From top to bottom:* Viktor Kieselev, Vladimir Khrakovsky, Anton Lavinsky, Nikolai Dokuchaev, Vladimir Krinsky, Osip Brik, Liubov Popova, Aleksandr Vesnin, Aleksei Babichev, Karel Ioganson

X: A CRITIQUE OF THINGS FROM PHOTOGRAPHS

Portrait. [*Portrait of a Lady (Plastic Drawing). Relief.* 1915. Page 83]

In the course of distorting the parts of the object in order to influence merely by the painterly concept of the thing and not by its visual impression, artistic necessity crosses into transformation of the object and its individual parts.

The composition must exert influence on many fronts, constructively. Space is interleaved; forms are volumetric. Color does not paint an object but influences through its own essence.

Still Life. [*Still Life with Tray.* 1915. Page 74]

The thing exerts influence through color [illegible]. The object is almost totally deprived of its concept; all that remains are the forms necessary for the linear building of the color construction. Volumes play more of a textural role.

Lady with a Guitar. Portrait no. 1. Oil, work of 1915. [Tambov Regional Picture Gallery]

Volume and space are arranged sculpturally, but the volumetric form is filled with planar forms. Line is introduced to contrast with the volumetric form. Polychrome is intentionally absent for the sake of a more powerful effect of volumes in their pure form. The composition is conceived as the weight of a sculptural mass. The space of the given painting plane is built on the edges of planes and the sequence of their interleaving.

Violin. No. 2. Work of 1915. Oil. [*Violin.* Page 79]

The composition is built on the rhythm of curved lines and right angles speeding toward spiral movement around the center. The volumetric form is almost abandoned in favor of the overlayering construction of space. Color is material and textural. Letters and graphic forms are introduced to produce the impression of a precise location in counterbalance to the abstract planes of the layers.

Portrait No. 4 and the drawing for it. Oil, work of 1916. [*Portrait of a Philosopher,* 1915, page 92; drawing for the portrait, 1915, page 93, left]

In the course of distorting the parts of the object in order to influence merely by the painterly concept of the thing and not by its visual impression, by means of moving the parts of the form around, artistic necessity crosses into the transformation of the object and its individual parts. The composition is built monumentally-constructively; space is interleaved; forms are volumetric; color does not paint the object but exerts influence through its essence and relationships.

Still Life (Shop). Work of 1916. Oil. [*Grocery*, 1916, page 87]
The thing exerts constructive influence through its color form. The object is almost totally deprived of its concept; all that remains are the forms necessary for the linear building of the color construction. Volumes play more of a textural role. The composition is not central, but built on the space of the painting plane.

1916. The Jug on the Table. No. 6. Wood, cardboard, oil, and size paint. Painting relief. [*The Jug on the Table*, 1915, painting relief, page 82]
The desire to structure the distorted sculptural [several words crossed out] abstract volume more powerfully necessitates that the painted volumetric form be replaced by real volume and also that its sculptural expressiveness be strengthened through the use of subdued color. The composition is the rhythm of volumetric spirals and planes.

Painting Relief. No. 7. Materials: wood, cardboard, oil, and distemper. Work of 1916. [*Volumetric-Spatial Relief*, 1915, page 86]
A laboratory experiment at resolving painterly-volumetric space—a problem parallel to the resolution of the issue of theatrical space. A unified painterly impression is built through real sculptural volume and real layers, nuanced in color, as is the painting surface.

Painterly Architectonics. No. 8 and No. 9. Works of 1917. Oil.*
The painting space is built on the interleaved interrelationships of the

---

*Inasmuch as in the selection of postcards on which Popova commented we know only one composition of a nonobjective nature (*Spatial Force Construction*, 1921), it is difficult to say which works she intended in the given instances.

planes. Line is introduced independently of volume in its pure form, like a graphic outline. Color plays a textural role and is determined by the tension of the space.

Painterly Architectonics. No. 10 and No. 11. Oil, work of 1918, dim. ¾ × ¾ arshins [21 × 21 inches, or 53.5 × 53.5 cm.]. Colors: black, lemon yellow, white, and gray. No. 11. Oil, work of 1918. Colors: red, black, white, and dark blue.*

Comprises three constructions: chromatic, volumetric, and linear. The volumetric is built on the intersection of planes and their extension in space. Space does not have perspective; therefore the color composition and gradation of tone may not coincide with it but build their relationships on the weight of color. Drawn form, like volumetric form, is independent of color and sometimes coincides with the volumetric, since it is created from the lines of intersection of the planes and their extension in space, but it can also be constructed independently of it. All three compositions are united in a single effort expressed in the overall dynamic composition.

Manuscript Department, Tretiakov Gallery, fund 148, unit 15, sheet 1-2; unit 12, sheet 1-8; unit 14, sheet 1, 1921.

XI: ON DRAWINGS

Drawings for Popova's manuscript "On Drawings." Early 1920s. India ink and pen
on paper, 6¼ × 6¼" (16 × 16 cm.). Tretiakov Gallery, Manuscript Division

1. Representation, as a product of artistic production, was a goal that satisfied the utilitarian needs of the era of the Renaissance and the ages that followed it, right down to recent times (easel representation, portrait, icon, fresco, mural, the sculpture of courtyards, squares, palaces, and churches, architecture as a visual object, and so on).

2. The analysis of the formal elements of art, which became the goal of artistic production in recent decades, presents a crisis for representational art.

3. The current artistic moment must be a synthesis and result of existing formal analyses: in Germany and similar countries it has degenerated into emotional and psychometaphysical approaches to the goal of art; in France synthesis is merely the acquired skill of treating material as a result of analytical study.

4. Here in Russia, in connection with the sociopolitical moment in which we are living, the goal of the new synthesis has become *organization* as a principle for any creative activity, including artistic design.

5. The era into which modern mankind has entered is one of the flowering of industry, and therefore the organization of the elements of artistic production must address the design of the material elements of life, that is, for industry, so-called production.

6. The new industrial production in which artistic creativity is supposed to take part will be fundamentally distinct from the previous aesthetic approach to the object in that attention will be directed chiefly not at adorning the object with artistic devices (applied art) but at introducing the artistic moment of the object's organization into the principle of creating the utilitarian object itself.

7. Thus the role of the "fine arts" — painting, sculpture, and even architecture (inasmuch as in this latter until now the principle of the expedient

construction of space has been replaced by the visual image of the object of architecture)—has come to an end because it is irrelevant for the consciousness of our era, and all these arts can therefore simply be relegated to the category of atavisms.

8. Hence too all types of representational disciplines, such as easel painting, drawings, engravings, sculpture, and so forth, if they are still able to maintain a certain expediency, then (1) for now they are still in a laboratory phase of searching for the necessary new means, (2) inasmuch as they are auxiliary projections and schemes of the constructions and utilitarian production objects that are likely to arise.

L. Popova, Moscow. December 1921

Manuscript Department, Tretiakov Gallery, fund 148, unit 17, sheet 3–4. (We can assume that this text was written for Inkhuk as the artist's "credo.")

XII: DISCIPLINE NO. 1—"COLOR." LIUBOV POPOVA AND ALEKSANDR VESNIN

1. The task of Discipline No. 1 is to reveal color as an independent organizing principle rather than as a depiction of optical decoration, and to take it as an element leading to complete concreteness.

2. As an independent element, color can be understood through the following critical analysis of its properties and relationships: (1) The study of the spectrum (Michel-Eugène Chevreul's disk). The law of complementary colors. (2) Tone as a quality of color. (3) The study of the weight of color, its qualitative importance separately and with respect to other colors. (4) The intensity or inner energy of color relative to its kinetic state. (5) The development of painting material for making color concrete.

3. The given properties of color must be adjusted with the help of other elements that enter into painting: (1) *Line* enters as an independent graphic element and also as the boundary of the form or its extension in space. (2) With the help of varyingly intense color planes it constructs the pictorial colored space. (3) Construction is the principle of organization to which the given task subordinates itself. (4) Texture materializes the color levels.

TsGALI, fund 681, [inv. 2, unit 46, sheet 26.
Handwritten by L. Popova. Manuscript Department,
Tretiakov Gallery, fund 148, unit 42, sheet 1. 1921.

XIII: THE ESSENCE OF THE DISCIPLINES

Discipline No. 1 establishes the painterly conception of the object. What is depicted is not the impression of the object but its essence, the essence of its color, volume, characteristic construction, materiality; everything incidental to, uncharacteristic of, the given painterly image of the object is omitted. The emotions emanating from the object are purely formal.

The surface of the painting is subordinated to the given known rhythm of the composition. It is not accidental, as it was intentionally accidental with the Impressionists, but subordinated to the known logic of the given volume, color. Volume and color build the mass of the object, although color does independently resolve its own color problem and does not merely decorate the object. The materiality is accentuated by the object. The materiality is accentuated by the texture.

Further, the painterly conception of the object sharpens; its distortion now follows individual spheres of painting, each of its elements abstracted separately; thus:

Discipline No. 2 constructs form through volume in its pure element. Space and volume are constructed by means of delineating the volumes and space with planes. The object unfolds in its planes, filling the strata of the painting space. Volumetric distortion has already been completed, and the work moves on to transform the painting space with planes. The object is no longer needed for the construction as a whole, with all its parts of volume, mass, and drawing form; the pure form of the object is selected out in its painterly elements without respect to its representational structure but with an internal connection to its artistic structure.

(From here it is but one more step to total liberation from the representation of the object.)

Discipline No. 3. Constructing the form in color, replacing and translating the forms of the object from its linear and volumetric forms to its color form while observing the constructive imperative. The fourth dimension, which is expressed in volumetric construction through the simultaneity of perception of all aspects of the object, is expressed here in the temporal consecutiveness of the color structure. Color is revealed in its tonal expressiveness, which follows simultaneously or not with the textural development according to the rhythmic construction.

Discipline No. 4 specially researches the laws of organization of disjointed elements and the system of their organization.

Discipline No. 6. *Comparison*. The interrelationships of form and its construction with other elements (color, texture, material, movement).

(a) The execution and sketching from nature (on the plane and in volume), (b) The comparison of examples on a given theme and freely (in real volumes and on the plane).

Manuscript Department, Tretiakov Gallery, fund 148, unit 148, sheet 1. 1921.

Manuscript for Popova's essay "Sushchnost distsiplin" (The Essence of the Disciplines). 1921. Tretiakov Gallery, Manuscript Division

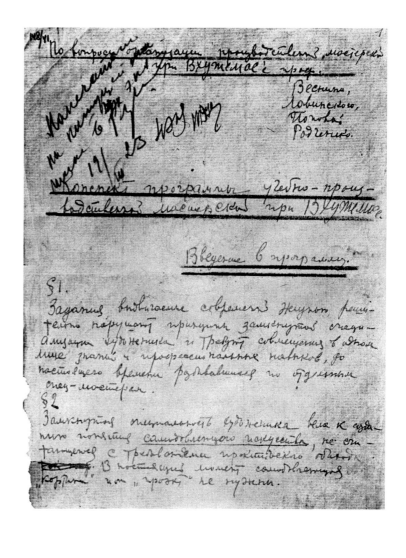

Summary of the program of the Training-Production Studio of Vkhutemas. February 1923. Signed by Popova
with the resolution of Vladimir Favorsky of March 12, 1923. Tretiakov Gallery, Manuscript Division

371

XIV: ON THE QUESTION OF THE NEW METHODS
IN OUR ARTISTIC SCHOOL

A question that is directly connected to the ideological revolution in the sphere of artistic production is that of the new methods in our artistic school, as a place where active cadres of workers in this field are to be trained.

It is perfectly obvious that the revolution that has occurred in the sphere of artistic goals, issues, means, and forms and that has set as our goal of artistic production the "expedient organization of the material elements of a given production" in place of "representation," as a goal leading our traditions from the age of the Renaissance, has clearly posed for us the question of the superfluousness of representational art as such, of its absolute irrelevance today, given the new social conditions, even as an object of production and not just as a product of psychometaphysical necessity.

This is why the matter of creating new active people in this area is such a great responsibility for the modern art school, where this new urgently needed worker is trained, and especially for those programs and methods with the help of which the apprentice should train and be led inside this circle of concepts and creative work.

If we were now to attempt from this point of view to approach those methods that now exist in our art school, this is what we would find in the best of cases: in the very best case, even the new objective method of analysis of the formal elements of each given "art,"* although in its essence constructed according to the analytic method, ultimately is still a matter of the same representational formal elements; their formal side, true, is accentuated, as if that made it (that is, the form as such) into a *means* that would help find the new object, but in essence this accentuation of the formal element serves only as a transitional moment filling in the gap between two worldviews, the bridge for the timid and indecisive attempt to cross to the other side, the brakes for those who already have a clear sense of the necessary goal. It is obvious that the approach to the element should not be started from this side but from that of the element as a material of the given production, and the goal should be not the synthesis of abstractly treated elements but the actual concrete object of that production to which this technology will relate.

And if this is how things stand with the "disciplines"—that objective analytical method of studying art that to this day seems to some immeasur-

*What are known as "disciplines" in our Moscow school.

ably revolutionary—then what is there to say about the programs and methods of other tendencies, for example, the individualists? Here the artist strives without any methodological assumptions whatsoever simply to impose on his pupil his view of the object, his view of the method and manner of its reproduction, without even trying to analyze, on the one hand, the phenomena of the art school in general, in connection with socioeconomic phenomena and, on the other, its specific problems, goals, and means. Therefore the whole result of this kind of attitude seems to be a monstrous anachronism, and the whole school turns into dead academics thrown overboard, an archive of dead canons, completely parallel to the modern museum, with the difference that the museum is an archive of objects and a school always has a tendency to turn into an archive of ideas and methods.

In order to sidestep this danger, in order for life, finding in school none of the necessary vital forces, not to start to shape them somewhere on the side and apart from the school (as has been the case in the majority of instances up till now), the entire school as a whole must be not a dead tradition but a vital organism reacting to and facilitating the positive demands of life. In this instance it should try to seek hand in hand with the creating intellectual consciousness those paths and means that lead from the dead ends of representation, through a knowledge of the technology of its production, to a method of creating those production objects, products of organized material design whose birth we await tomorrow.

L. Popova. Moscow. December 1921

Manuscript Department, Tretiakov Gallery, fund 148, unit 21, sheet 1–2. Handwritten. Evidently Inkhuk requested this essay from Popova for its unpublished collection "Ot izobrazheniia k konstruktsii" (From Representation to Construction).

XV: OUTLINE FOR A SPEECH BY L. POPOVA-EDING: "THE QUESTION OF THE NEW METHODOLOGY OF INSTRUCTION (FIRST DISCIPLINE OF THE BASIC DEPARTMENT OF THE VKHUTEMAS PAINTING FACULTY)"

1. From the history of the methods of instruction: The methods of the masters of the Renaissance. The artistry of craft. The school of the master. The canonization of the methods of representation.

2. The destruction of the academic method. The history of French painting of the last few decades. The ability to "depict" correctly does not make an artist.

3. The Parisian *académies*: individual methods (Maurice Denis, Antoine Bourdelle, Henri Matisse). The *académie* of the Cubists (Fernand Léger, Henri Le Fauconnier). The method of formal analysis. The concept of becoming instead of imagining-depicting. The moment of the idea's distortion for the purpose of revealing the concepts of the objects in the individual element. Transformation as a method leading to nonobjectiveness.

5. The methods of "trends" instead of analytic methods (Free Art Studios, Vkhutemas). The disjointedness of the program, the consequences of this.

6. The problems of color. An analysis of the concept of color among the Impressionists—right through to Matisse.

7. The question is posed at Vkhutemas in 1920-21. The disciplines of "original and maximal" revelation of color. The discipline of the "revelation of color" as discipline no. 1 of the Basic Department.

8. The experiment with the method of abstract construction through the concept of "color" independent of form (Simultaneists, Orphists, Delaunay-Picabia). Rhythmic constructions, the translation of form into color; the spectrum.

9. Fall 1921. Color as a part of the construction of the object. The method of materialization of the concept of color (texture, materials, moments of concretization in the Cubists). The replacement of the real object in the laboratory by an object that is not utilitarian but is ideologically similar. The necessity of concrete production for the materialization of color according to the demand of the object's expediency.

10. Experiment in the expedient study of the element on utilitarian examples.

Moscow. February 2, 1922

Manuscript Department, Tretiakov Gallery,
fund 148, unit 23, sheet 1. Handwritten.

XVI: FROM THE ABSTRACT FOR THE SPEECH "THE QUESTION OF THE NEW METHODOLOGY OF INSTRUCTION (FIRST DISCIPLINE OF THE BASIC DEPARTMENT OF THE VKHUTEMAS PAINTING FACULTY)" (FRAGMENTS)

…The artist no longer teaches his pupil the abstract principle of "representation"; representation is no longer either his or his work's goal. He tries to reveal to his pupil his new approach to the question, his solution of what is already a formal problem, the resolution of one or another formal issue; what do we take from representation, how, in what form, in what perception of form—these are the questions that have taken the place of the old one: simply to depict faithfully something self-sufficient. At Bourdelle's such "representationalists" as Innokentii Zhukov or Nadezhda Krandievskaia meet with protest, and today he sends them off to study "form." In his method Matisse takes another step forward: (1) he already starts to differentiate form: his contour of form is absolutely conditional: it is planar, (2)—deformed. Matisse speaks with his pupils about color as an element, he has already started down the path of analytical study, he has separated out form from color, line from plane.

So we already have the start of the new analytical method which is developing by leaps and bounds the further it proceeds. The Cubists' schools are the best examples of the analytic method. Le Fauconnier poses the question of abstract volume as such; an object that existed for Bourdelle and Matisse here no longer exists: they study the extreme qualities of volume, apart from the object, apart from color, apart from contour (line). Metzinger says outright: learn how to conceive of form independent of color, express it only in volumetric or graphic form, partly in only one color.

The object as such is no longer studied and depicted, only the separate formal elements on which it can be laid out and from which it is composed; only that which defines the concept of the object and not all the elements in order of their existence in the object. The artist has gone from an imagination-depiction of the object to an analysis of the concepts comprising the object's essence.

He differentiates concepts, culls the essential from the coincidental—and you don't need the object with all its coincidental parts and markings, it is distorted according to what the artist takes, what is essential, which element he seeks in it. But if we are free in choosing elements from the object and in the new construction of the object's concept as a new object, if it is not the depiction but the conception of its elements that is our ultimate goal, then clearly the sequence of the parts or elements of the object can be modified according to the tasks of revelation. Here is the beginning of the new method, the method of transformation, as distinct from the previous method of distortion. This is Picasso's method of construction in his latest periods, and from them it is only one step to what has happened with this last method with us in Russia—to the nonobjective method, when freedom from construction of the parts of the object or objects shifts in general to the construction of forms in general, irrespective of their representational significance or link to one object or another....

This principle of teaching only according to a personal method, individualistic teaching or teaching of a "trend" has passed (not into a program, it is true) merely into the practical implementation of the Vkhutemas program. Here in brief is how I see the imminent history of the work for which we at present are responsible. I shall now move in earnest to the question that since last year, since the time I began as a director at Vkhutemas, has faced me. I shall try, insofar as I am able, to approach the question concretely and illuminate it from the aspect that in the given instance seems to me most important.

The problem of color. The problem of color in painting—and not only in painting but more broadly—is in the products of material design.

The analytical element in solving the problem was already clear to the Impressionists and completely clear to the man who synthesized the analysis of the Impressionists' works—Matisse. That is the aspect this question has taken on in the new Vkhutemas program.

Therefore, since the fall of 1921, the method has been changed. Having been an abstract concept like the abstract element of the spectrum and subjugated to all the laws of the spectrum, color has begun to be considered as a *quality of the organizing material*. Once abstract, it has been made real; once laboratory-nonobjective, nonutilitarian, it has been made essential and utilitarian because without it material is inconceivable; consequently the whole construction as well is unthinkable.

In practical terms the matter was not clear: in practical terms at the school we still have all the same atavistic materials: canvas, oil paints, and so forth. The material is obviously not appropriate, having functioned and been devised for the purposes of representation, so that today it is inappropriate for implementing the newly posed task....

The solution I have used, of course, is not an answer to the question; the only obviously clear answer is a new, concrete object, a production object, with its requirements, concrete material, and, hence, concrete materialized color.

There was no such object, there was not even a hint of it. The matter had to be remedied and solely through experiments. I proposed that participants utilize not only oil paints but all possible kinds of other material they could obtain and work with as concrete color in production experiments. The experiments were conducted as abstract works possessing, unfortunately, no utilitarian or practical importance whatsoever other than that of analytic experiment; nonetheless, the necessary condition was set that the exploited forms have a vital relationship with reality, that is, that they be modern, just like the materials experimented upon, in order to facilitate the transition to the practical object, not in utilitarian, abstract form yet, but that it start being prepared, researched, and confirmed.

Manuscript Department, Tretiakov Gallery, fund 148, unit 49, sheet 1–8. Handwritten.

XVII: INTRODUCTION TO THE INKHUK DISCUSSION OF *THE MAGNANIMOUS CUCKOLD*

POPOVA: The task of this short introduction to our discussion today is a brief clarification of those fundamental positions that I would like to note in the process of work on the production of *The Magnanimous Cuckold*. I do not pretend to any final or even generally positive resolution of the problems posed in the given production. In this case my desire is to translate the problem from the aesthetic to the production plane, to deal with the question differently from its usual aesthetic resolution, completely on another plane, with the goal of resolving the tasks exclusively with respect to the given production and its means and aims. For me at the present moment this work is a concretization and realization of my personal theoretical and practical professional work and may be formulated as follows: to equip the theatrical action with its material elements.

I want to subdivide all these questions in general into three basic problems.

1. The organization of the production's material elements, its equipment, a set or prop for the given action. In this, one criterion should be utilitarian adaptability and not the resolution of any formal-aesthetic problems such as the question of color or volume, or the organization of the theatrical space, and so on. These and other formal material elements may have entered into and contributed to the resolution but not as formal elements per se but merely as necessary material parts, for example, the painting of parts of the set, or the size of flats, the platforms, the distribution of parts of the set, and so forth. In this case, of course, the pure resolution of the issue did not work out because (1) it was hard for me at the start to reject outmoded aesthetic customs and criteria, and (2) I was hindered by a condition of an aesthetic order, that the action bore a farcical, visual character and made it impossible for me to consider the action merely as an ongoing work process, and this to a significant degree lent everything an aesthetic character [here the typescript breaks off; from here on the text is handwritten] of the visual action.

2. My second concern was to introduce material elements into the ongoing work not only of a scenic or similar nature but also actively, kinetically, linking their work with that of the whole action; in like manner, it introduced for this purpose into the general score of the action the movement of doors and windows, the turning of wheels, which with their movements and speeds

378

were supposed to accentuate and raise the kinetic meaning of each moment of the action.

This was actually realized only in makeshift fashion due to the absence of the necessary technical means, and thus the first time it was possible to try out the movement of wheels was in the first performance, moving according to a score composed theoretically.

Under the best conditions there was a door that could be used in rehearsal both as a utilitarian prop for the action and as an independent material kinetic element.

3. The third question is the question of the work uniform, turning aside once again, and so on. The elements of analysis had to be sought intuitively; thus there were the modern elements of the acrobat, athlete, sailor, military worker, agitator, and so forth. In addition, the costume was intended for the actor's daily, ordinary life and work and therefore had to be utilitarian both for this purpose and to replace all other clothing, so that it was necessary to add, for example, an overcoat, and so forth.

In all, the costume was intended for seven or eight sorts or types of work. There was a fundamental disinclination to making any distinction between the men's and women's costumes; it just came down to changing the pants to a skirt or culottes.

Here in brief are the fundamental points I would like to set off in this work of mine and submit in their principle and execution for your analysis and criticism.

Manuscript Department, Tretiakov Gallery,
fund 148, unit 56, sheet 1. Typescript.
Unit 57, sheet 1-2. Handwritten.

XVIII: ON A PRECISE CRITERION, ON BALLET STEPS, ON DECK EQUIPMENT FOR WARSHIPS, ON PICASSO'S LATEST PORTRAITS, AND ON THE OBSERVATION TOWER AT THE MILITARY CAMOUFLAGE SCHOOL AT KUNTSEVO
(A FEW THOUGHTS THAT CAME TO MIND DURING THE VOCAL AND BALLET NUMBERS AT THE KRIVOI DZHIMMI SUMMER THEATER IN MOSCOW IN THE SUMMER OF 1922)

Seemingly it should be clear from the heading what this is about. True, the theme is very new, and there is nothing really to get excited about, to tell the truth. That *an aesthetic criterion for evaluating an artistic object has not been established* is well known to absolutely everyone and has been for quite some time; moreover, it was already brilliantly discredited long ago by Tolstoy. . . . Nevertheless, it obviously *has not been enough,* the dose has been insufficient, if it still has not *worked,* if it has to be proved ten times a day in our artistic life and the same aesthetic criterion, or rather the absence of any criterion, reigns as before from remote, godforsaken places in the provinces over the offices of our administrative centers.

Oh, why has there to this day not been a precise formula that might cut short at once the possibility of all these senseless arguments and like the best construction of a saw prune all the aesthetic garbage from life, having assigned it to preserving the monuments of antiquity and luxury. Let it be *infallible,* like the formula for a chemical compound, like the calculation for the pressure on the walls of a steam boiler, like the confidence of an American advertisement, like 2 X 2 = 4. Neither do the poor vocal and ballet numbers of KRIVOI DZHIMMI have any relevance here in the final analysis. They are no better and no worse than any others exactly like them in Moscow and all over.

O EXPEDIENCY! If only YOU could be our criterion for a while. All life in the person of sociology, chemistry, physics, mathematics, engineering, technology, and so on advances thousands of necessities upon us, dictates to us a unified and unitary approach to evaluating vital facts.

Beginning with the simplest clumps of protoplasm in the organic world and ending with the most complex inventions of the human mind, all the vital factors of our world are directed toward expediency and change, according to their will—and are sometimes engendered by them. If that is so, then how, in the name of everything on earth and in heaven, can the most *subjective* and shaky of all subjective judgments, the notorious *aesthetic* judgment, serve as the criterion? After all, how much truer in absolutely all respects is the equipment and deck work of the crew of a warship than any aesthetic-theatrical movements of actors on POINTLESS "stage sets"!

That a podium has to be built for the orator is clear, but why do the Pierrots gesticulate and pose under red lamps (as in Goleizovsky's set) and why does Juliet read her monologue on love from the lining of her collar? After all, this is done in all seriousness: this is not the tribe of Vampuki or some distorting mirror altering the sequence of history; to the present day this has been the most honest morality worthy of the most serious discussion by every sort of newspaper, magazine, and book.

The Institute of Labor and Meierkhold's biomechanics exist only as a lost, lonely oasis.... Let *these formulas of work for the given materials* be found as quickly as possible, be it in two, three, or four dimensions, by precise calculation according to which only work in the area of so-called artistic material design was thinkable, until that happy moment when this same principle of "artisticness," as opposed, evidently, to something "unartistic," is studied solely within the history of superstitions and prejudices.

It is to no avail that the aesthetes try to hide behind representational, poetic, musical, and theatrical art with FORMALLY AESTHETIC "INQUIRIES AND ACCOMPLISHMENTS" (such as "the problems of form and color in easel painting" or "the construction of theatrical space"). The days of their "art for art's sake" have long been numbered, but they persist with their "formal-aesthetic point of view" in DISCUSSING PICASSO: as if he had turned realist and betrayed the Dardanelles of his "formal inquiries"! Whereas Picasso, in the name of what if not "expediency," has started making *portraits like photographs* (what does Ingres have to do with this?!). Honestly, photographically, *in the name of representation* as a goal that is anything but aesthetic: that is what the photographers are doing now. In the meantime, this modest OBSERVATION TOWER OF THE KUNTSEVO CAM-OUFLAGE SCHOOL will be dedicated to everyone who builds, who plans to and will build "constructive" sets for theaters, little theaters, cabarets, music halls, and so on and so on and so on, sites scenically equipped FOR EDIFICA-TION.

Moscow. July 25, 1922

Manuscript Department, Tretiakov Gallery,
fund 148, unit 24, sheet 4.
Typescript. See Part Two, note 105.

XIX: AN EXPOSITION OF THE FUNDAMENTAL ELEMENTS OF THE MATERIAL DESIGN FOR *LA NUIT* (*EARTH ON END*)

1. Treatment of the production's design as it relates to life and not its aesthetic influence, with the center of attention on the propaganda side of the presentation.

2. In fulfillment of this: (a) rejection of any aesthetic aims in planning the sets, both in the area of visual effect and in that of meaning—the costuming and light effects serve as accessories to the propaganda and not to the self-sufficient acting of the actors; (b) objects forming the material side of the production are not changed for any scenic purpose but are taken from the surrounding reality and introduced to the stage in their natural form, insofar as the arrangement of the theater permits.

3. Objects are selected in order to connect the exposition of the play with the successive tasks of the republic's construction and to create the conditions for agitational commentary on the drama.

4. The Red Army, electrification. Heavy industry in the hands of the proletariat, the mechanization of agriculture, the development of transportation—these provide the elements for the props. Propaganda in the present. The old slogans of our Revolution in the commentary to the text of the drama mark the stages completed. Cinematic projection supplements the task, emphasizing the crucial details of the action.

5. The artist's work is in selecting and uniting the material elements of the production with the goal of the most agitational action possible.

Manuscript Department, Tretiakov Gallery, fund 148, unit 139. Handwritten.

XX: ON THE PRODUCTION WORK OF INKHUK. COLLECTION NO. 3. THEATRICAL PERFORMANCES. SYNOPSIS OF THE BOOK

1. Purpose of the book. At the present moment the constructive element of the theatrical performance makes this sphere convenient for bringing the production works of Inkhuk's members to life. The purpose of the book is to acquaint the readers with the theses and slogans posed by Inkhuk's members about the theater and also as a result of their theatrical work.

2. Material of the book. The book's materials are: (a) theoretical investigations, critical essays, theses and slogans on the theater and theater work; (b) reproductions from sketches, maquettes, studies, details, and costumes of productions, from the sets done from them, the flats, and the general scenes and details designed by Inkhuk members; (c) a summary of the materials of each production proposed to theaters by Inkhuk members, with sketches of individual objects and the treatment and use envisioned by the authors.

3. Distribution of the material. All the material enumerated in the second part breaks down ideologically into three sections.

a) The production resolution of the abstract formal problem of plastic methods (for example, the construction of theatrical volumes, of theatrical space, of color space, and so forth, the coordination of costume, the planar and spatial resolution of the propaganda poster).

b) An ideological shift from abstract constructing to constructing the expedient thing and the consequences thereof: the replacement of the formal-aesthetic criterion by an appraisal of the expediency of the functions of what is constructed. The application of this new method to theatrical work: the replacement of formal construction with the equipping of the scenic work (the sets), of the formal-individual costume by work uniforms, of representational or formal properties by the scenic thing as a material of the acting.

c) An experiment in replacing the abstract aesthetics of self-sufficient theatrical production with theatrical work such as designing immediate organizational-productive or agitational-political edifices.

4. Contents of the collection:

a) A[leksandr] Vesnin, "The Statics and Dynamics of Volume on the Stage (Sets and Costume)." Illustrated by reproductions from Paul Claudel's *L'Annonce faite à Marie* (maquette, costume designs, photos of individual scenes).

b) A[nton] Lavinsky, "Stage Depth and Stage Height" (sketches and photos from a maquette and costumes for Vladimir Mayakovsky's *Misteriia buff (Mystery-bouffe)*.

c) N[atan] Altman, "Color as a Material of the Stage" (reproductions: *Uriel Acosta* or *Romeo and Juliet*).

d) O[sip] Brik, "The Theater of the Agitational Poster" (reproductions: 1921, *Mystery-bouffe*—Viktor Kieselev, Lavinsky, Khrakovsky; 1921, Khodinskoe Field—Popova and Vesnin; 1922, *Earth on End*—Popova).

e) Yu[ri] Ekk, "The Formal Costume and the Work Uniform" (illustrations of the author's choice).

f) V[arvara] Stepanova, "The Problem of Special Clothes" (reproductions from Stepanova's drawings and sketches.

g) B[oris] Kushner, "The Problems of Theatrical Staging" (reproductions: *The Magnanimous Cuckold* by Popova; *Tarelkin's Death* by Stepanova; *The Man Who Was Thursday* by Vesnin).

h) V[arvara] Stepanova, "The Actor and the Special Object" (illustrations of the author's choice).

i) S[ergei] Eisenstein, "The Eccentric Object on Stage" (illustrations of the authors'choice).

j) V[asilii] Zaichikov, "From the Decorative Pose to Material Motion, from Distribution to Organization, from Composition to Construction" (illustrations: details from *L'Annonce faite à Marie, Phaedre, Romeo and Juliet*, details from Zaichikov's acting).

k) L[iubov] Popova, "The Material Montage as a Visual Scenario" (reproductions of the author's choice and a summary of stage materials).

l) B[oris] Arvatov, "Aesthetic and Agitational Realism" (reproductions of the author's choice).

m) O[sip] Brik, "The Fruits of [*Princess*] *Brambilla* and a model from *Paken*" (illustrations of the author's choice).

n) A[leksandr] Rodchenko, "The Artist's Place in Staging Technique" (illustrations of the author's choice).

o) L[iubov] Popova, "Experiment with the Directors of GVYTM (illustrations of the author's choice).

Liubov Popova. Moscow. March 1923

Manuscript Department, Tretiakov Gallery,
fund 148, unit 37, sheet 1-7.
The book was never published.
On the publication plans, see *Lef*, no. 2 (1923): 173.

XXI: GENERAL PLAN FOR THE PROGRAM OF THE OCCASIONAL SEMINAR ON "THE MATERIAL DESIGN OF THE PERFORMANCE," FOR MOSCOW PROLETKULT, 1924

1. Methodological section: works out the ideological approach to the subject and the method of its implementation.

2. Production section: fulfills concrete design objects.

1. The fundamental element of the methodological section of the course is the principle of the approach to the question of the performance's material design. This principle is the construction of the object, or the search for its form proceeding from the function of the object itself. In our age of industry the thesis of "functional form" is the principle that lies at the base of every material design.

From this fundamental position flow all the elements of "equipping" the performance, which are organized with the goal of the most expedient and agitational useful action possible.

Manuscript Department, Tretiakov Gallery,
fund 148, unit 153, sheet 1. Handwritten.

Liubov Popova. Date unknown

CHRONOLOGY

1889

April 24 Liubov Sergeevna Popova is born at Krasnovidovo, near the village of Ivanovskoe, Zvenigorodsky District, Moscow Province. Her father—Sergei Maksimovich Popov—owns textile factories and is a philanthropist and devotee of music and theater. Her mother, Liubov Vasilievna, is the daughter of a serf, but her family, the Zubovs, quickly enter the educated classes. The Popovs have four children, of whom Liubov Sergeevna is the second. She has two brothers, Sergei and Pavel, and a sister, Olga.

1889–1901

She receives her initial education at home. Her first drawing teacher is the painter K. M. Orlov.

1902

The family moves to Yalta, where she begins to attend Gymnasium.

1906

The family returns to Moscow, and she graduates from Arseneva's Gymnasium. She enters the two-year general-education course of A. S. Alferov.

1907

She studies in the studio of Stanislav Zhukovsky, a landscape painter.

1908–9

She transfers to the School of Drawing and Painting run by Konstantin Yuon and Ivan Dudin. During her studies she meets Aleksandr Vesnin, Liudmila Prudkovskaia (the sister of Nadezhda Udaltsova), and Vera Mukhina. She spends the summers of 1908 and 1909 painting with Prudkovskaia at the family home in Krasnovidovo. She works on landscape-genre paintings.

1909

Summer On a family trip to Kiev, she sees ancient frescoes in the cathedral and works by Mikhail Vrubel, the Symbolist.

1910

Spring Short family trip to Italy, where she sees works by masters of the fourteenth to sixteenth centuries, especially Giotto and Pinturicchio.

June Travels to Pskov and Novgorod to look at icons.

1911

Summer On a trip to Saint Petersburg, she visits the Hermitage and the environs of the city.

Fall She makes trips around Russia: Rostov the Great, Yaroslavl, Suzdal, Yuriev Polsky, Pereslavl, and Kiev.

Late Fall She and Prudkovskaia set up a studio on Antipievsky Street in Moscow. She concentrates on drawings and copies of frescoes and icons.

1911–12

She paints numerous male models and studies of trees. Her fascination with Vrubel continues.

1912

Summer She spends the summer in Yaroslavl with Prudkovskaia.

Fall Joins artists in the Tower studio on Kuznetsky Bridge, in Moscow, working with Vladimir Tatlin, Viktor Bart, Anna Troianovskaia, Kirill Zdanevich, Ivan Aksionov, Aleksei Grishchenko, and others. Popova visits Sergei Shchukin's collection and is fascinated by the new French art of Braque and Picasso. Goes to Paris with her old governess, Adelaide Dege, and Udaltsova and begins studies in the studio La Palette, where Henri Le Fauconnier, Jean Metzinger, and André Dunoyer de Segonzac teach.

1913

Popova lives in a pension run by Madame Jeanne; Udaltsova, Aleksandra Exter, and Vera Pestel are fellow guests. She visits the studios of Ossip Zadkine and Aleksandr Archipenko, and meets several other Russian artists in Paris.

May Together with Vera Mukhina and Boris Ternovets she goes to Brittany.

Summer She returns to Moscow and works in Tatlin's studio at 37 Ostozhenka Street. With Aleksandr Vesnin, Robert Falk, and Udaltsova, she does several experimental works, particularly still lifes and nudes.

1914

March She exhibits two paintings—*Composition with Figures* and *Still Life with Tin Dish* (both page 56)—with the "Jack of Diamonds."

Mid-April She travels from Paris to Italy via Menton, accompanied by Mukhina and Iza Burmeister. They make a grand tour of the country: from Genoa to Naples, from Paestum to Venice, lingering two weeks in Rome.

1914–1915

A weekly gathering is held in her home on Novinsky Boulevard, where artists read and discuss papers on theories of art. She paints still lifes with musical instruments.

1915

March 3 "Tramway V: The First Futurist Exhibition of Paintings" opens in Petrograd. Kazimir Malevich, Tatlin, Ivan Puni, Ivan Kliun, Olga Rozanova, Udaltsova, and Exter show along with Popova.

December 17, 1915–January 19, 1916 "The Last Futurist Exhibition of Paintings: 0.10" is on view in Petrograd. Organized by Puni, it includes many of the artists in the previous Futurist show. Popova's submissions are pictorial reliefs: *Portrait of a Lady (Plastic Drawing)* (page 83), *The Jug on the Table* (page 82), and *Compote with Fruit (Plastic Painting)* (page 85). She paints portraits and compositions with figures.

1916

She travels to Samarkand, where she sees the great buildings erected by Tamerlane and his successors. She is strongly impressed by the Islamic architecture.

March She participates in the "Store" exhibition, organized by Tatlin, with Aleksandr Rodchenko and Lev Bruni and others. Popova shows *The Card Party* and *Violin* (page 79, left).

Summer She goes to Birsk to visit her former governess, Adda Dege. She does her first *Painterly Architectonics* (which she continues until 1918).

November She participates in a "Jack of Diamonds" exhibition, at which Malevich, Marc Chagall, Ivan Kliun, Rozanova, Puni, Ksenia Boguslavskaia, and Udaltsova also exhibit.

December At the exhibition "Contemporary Russian Art," held at the gallery of Nadezhda Dobychina, Popova shows nonobjective work, including some derived from her trip to Samarkand.

1916–17

Malevich forms *Supremus*, a society of artists, to which Popova and Rozanova belong. It meets at Udaltsova's studio. A journal is projected, for which Popova does many sketches, but the publication never appears.

1917

She makes several collages to serve as designs for embroidery in an enterprise Natalia Davydova establishes in the town of Verbovka. She designs May Day decorations for Mossovet.

1918

March She marries the art historian Boris von Eding, whose specialty is ancient Russian art.

April She collaborates with Aleksandr Vesnin in decorating Mossovet for the May Day celebrations. With Pestel, Karetnikova, and Udaltsova, she designs decorations for the Left Federation of the Union of Moscow Artists. She works on the decor for the Café Pittoresque.

November A son is born to Popova and von Eding.

1919

January In the catalog for the "Tenth State Exhibition: Nonobjective Art and Suprematism," in Moscow, Popova sets down her theories of art (page 347). Others in the show include Stepanova, Rodchenko, Vesnin, Kliun, and Malevich.

Summer She travels to Rostov on the Don with her husband and son. Von Eding contracts typhoid fever and dies. Popova, gravely ill with typhus and typhoid fever, is nursed by Adda Dege.

November Popova returns to Moscow with her son; she is extremely fatigued. She sells some of her work to obtain badly needed money.

December She takes part in the activities of the Sovet Masterov, a precursor of Inkhuk. From 1919 to 1921, she paints *Painterly Constructions*.

1920

There is little work from this year; she continues the *Painterly Constructions*. She begins her first work for the theater, designing the sets and costumes for *Romeo and Juliet*, for Tairov at his Chamber Theater. However, they are not used, and the final designs are those of Exter. She designs book covers and illustrates *Tales of Wonder* by Diez. She designs marionettes for a Children's Theater production: *The Tale of the Priest and Balda, His Helper*, by Pushkin. She collaborates (until 1921) on the sets and costumes for *The Locksmith and the Chancellor*, by Anatoly Lunacharsky.

Spring She organizes the program for the course on "color discipline" of the Basic Department of Vkhutemas, along with Vesnin.

May–December She attends meeting of Inkhuk's Section on Monumental Art, directed by Wassily Kandinsky.

Autumn At Vkhutemas (until the fall of 1923) she teaches "color discipline" along with Vesnin (page 368).

December She participates in the organization of the Museum of Artistic Culture and in the section on new Russian painting.

1921

Spring She uses wood, sand, and metallic and marble powders in her *Spatial-Force Constructions*. She teaches at GVYTM, where Sergei Eisenstein is one of her students. For the meeting of the Third Congress of the Comintern, she collaborates with Vesnin on the mass spectacle *Struggle and Victory*, to be produced by Meierkhold on Khodinskoe Field. Funds are lacking to execute the plans.

September At the Poets Club in Moscow, Popova shows in the "5 × 5 = 25" exhibition, along with Rodchenko, Stepanova, Exter, and Vesnin. Popova designs the banner for the Poets Club.

Autumn For the students in the Basic Department of Vkhutemas, she writes "The Essence of the Disciplines" (pages 369-70).
November She signs a proclamation of artists who renounce easel painting; her last easel work is completed in 1922.

End of 1921–22
She joins in debates on the analysis of notions of Construction and composition at Inkhuk. She writes "On the Construction of New Objective and Nonobjective Forms" (page 349).

1921–24
She continues to design book covers and typographical designs for various periodicals.

1922
April She designs the entire production of Fernand Crommelynck's *The Magnanimous Cuckold* for Meierkhold. It opens April 25 and is a great success.
April 27 There is a debate at Inkhuk on Popova's design of this production (see pages 378-79). She makes sketches for *The Priest of Tarquinia*; the production is not mounted.
Summer She writes an article: "On a Precise Criterion . . ."

(pages 380-81); published in *Zrelishcha*, no. 1 (1922), page 5.
Autumn She begins to work on the designs for the production of *Earth on End*, for Meierkhold. She designs a teacup for a competition sponsored by Glavsilikat.

1923
March 4 Premiere of *Earth on End*.
Spring Popova devotes herself completely to production work.
Autumn She works with Stepanova designing fabric and clothes for the First Textile Print Factory in Moscow. She makes poster designs for Dvigatel.

1924
She organizes a course in "The Material Design of the Performance" for Proletkult (page 385). Creates a series of posters for the Society for the Struggle Against Illiteracy. She falls ill of scarlatina contracted from her son, who dies.
May 23 She loses consciousness.
May 25 She dies.
December 21 A large posthumous exhibition of her work opens.

GLOSSARY

ASNOVA: Association of New Architects (Assotsiatsiya novykh arkhitektorov)

GAKhN: State Academy of Artistic Sciences (Gosudarstvennaia akademiya khudozhestvennykh nauk)

GITIS: A. V. Lunacharsky State Institute of Theatrical Art of the Order of the Labor Red Banner (Gosudarstvennyi ordena Trudovogo Krasnogo Znameni institut teatralnogo iskusstva imeni A. V. Lunarcheskogo)

Glavsilikat: Main Silicate Administration (Glavnoe upravlenie silikat)

GUVUZ: Main Administration of Higher and Secondary Pedagogical Institutions (Glavnoe upravlenie vysshikh i srednykh pedagogicheskikh uchebnykh zavedenii)

GVYRM: State Higher Directors' Workshop (Gosudarstvennye vysshie rezhisserskie masterskie)

GVYTM: State Higher Theater Workshop (Gosudarstvennye vysshie teatralnye masterskie)

Inkhuk: Institute of Artistic Culture (Institut khudozhestvennoi kultury)

Narkompros: People's Commissariat for Enlightenment (Narodnyi komissariat prosveshcheniya)

NEP: New Economic Policy (Novaya ekonomicheskaya politika)

OBMAS: United Leftist Studios (Obedinennye levye masterskie)

Proletkult: Proletarian Cultural and Educational Organizations (Proletarskie Kulturnoprosvetitelnye organizatsii)

TsGALI: Central State Archive of Literature and Art (Tsentralnyi gosudarstvennyi arkhiv literatury i iskusstva)

TsNIITA: Central Scientific-Research Institute of Heating Apparatus (Tsentralnyi naukhno-issledovatelskii institut toplivnoi apparatury)

Vkhutemas: Higher State Art-Technical Studios (Vysshie gosudarstvennye khudozhestvenno-teknicheskie masterskie)

Vseobuch: General Education (Vseobshchee obuchenie)

VsTIK: All-Russian Central Executive Committee (Vserossiiskii tsentralnyi ispolnitelnyi komitet)

INDEX

Italic page numbers refer to illustrations.

Abramtsevo artists, 273
Abstract Expressionism, 109
"Abstract for a Speech on Style" (Apps. V, VI), 195, 353–54, 355
Académie de la Grande Chaumière, 41
Actor's Theater, 254, 255. See also *Magnanimous Cuckold, The; Priest of Tarquinia, The*
Adalmina's Pearl (Zhemchuzhina Adalminy), 219, 255
Adlivankin, Samuil Yakovlevich: *Plenipotentiary of the Samara Vkhutemas,* 305 n. 1
"Against Prostitution" (poster design), 276; *287*
Agricultural Exhibition (1923), 254
Airplane over Train (Goncharova), 58
Aksionov, Ivan Aleksandrovich, 12, 14, 15, 41, 44, 135, 140, 145 nn. 3, 10; 213, 216, 249, 250, 252, 256, 257, 274, 275, 300, 305 n. 59, 306 nn. 61, 80; 306 n. 91, 388. *See also* Vesnin-Aksionov list
Alferov, A. S., 12, 388
Aliagrov [Roman Jakobson], 109
All-Russian Union of Poets Club (VSP), 213; banner designs for, 274, 307 n. 124, 389; *290. See also* "5 × 5 = 25" exhibition
Altman, Natan Isaievich, 41, 57, 384
"Analysis of the Concepts of Construction and Composition . . . , An" (Analiz poniatii konstruktsii i kompozitsii . . .), 193–94
"And Now? What Next?" (App. VII), 196, 356–57
Annensky, Innokenty, 306 n. 73
Annonce faite à Marie, L' (Annunciation) (Claudel), 217, 218, 219, 384
Annunciation (L'Annonce faite à Marie) (Claudel), 217, 218, 219, 384
Apples and Drapery, 15; *32*
Aranovich, D. M., 300
Archipenko, Aleksandr Porfirievich, 41, 388
Architectonic Composition with Orange, Dark Blue, White, and Black, 147 n. 71
architectonics, 42, 44, 133. *See also Painterly Architectonics*
architecture, 43, 133–34, 200, 249–50
Arkhangelsky, Aleksandr, 299
Arkin, David Efimovich, 299
artist-constructor, 212, 213, 216–17
Arvatov, Boris Ignatievich, 191, 273, 384
Aseev, Nikolai Nikolaevich, 275, 276, 304
Association of Constructors of Working Cells, 304
Astrologer (costume design), 254, 275; *262*
"Avant-Garde in Russia 1910–1930: New Perspectives" exhibition (Los Angeles, 1980), 146 nn. 51, 52

Babichev, Aleksei Vasilievich, 138, 193, 305 n. 13; *361*
Bakhrushin Central Theatrical Museum, 215, 219, 250
Bakst, Leon Samuilovich, 273, 303
Balda (puppet design), 219; *236*
Bania (The Bathhouse) (Mayakovsky), 306 n. 90
banner designs, 274, 307 n. 124; *290*
Baranov-Rossiné, Vladimir Davidovich, 41, 64, 305 nn. 42, 43
Baroque style, 218, 219, 354
Bart, Viktor, 15, 388
Bathhouse, The (Bania) (Mayakovsky), 306 n. 90
Bebutov, Valery, 305 n. 59
Bernheim-Jeune Gallery (Paris), 57
Bicyclist (Goncharova), 58
Bilibin, Ivan Yakovlevich, 273
biomechanics, 214, 215, 253, 306 n. 61, 381
Birsk, 69, 137, 146 nn. 52, 53, 54; 218; *104;* studies, 99, *100*
Black Square (Malevich), 109, 110
Blok, Aleksandr Aleksandrovich, 217
Blue Rose artists, 13, 41, 59
Bobrov, Sergei Pavlovich, 44, 274
Boccioni, Umberto, 58
Boguslavskaia, Ksenia Leonidovna, 57, 273, 389
Bomba (Bomb) (Aseev), book cover design, 275, 276; *277*

book designs, 274–76, 277; *277, 283, 284, 285, 292, 293*
Borisov-Musatov, Viktor Elpidiforovich, 41, 273
Boulanger, Marcel, *57*
Bourdelle, Antoine, 41, 199, 374, 375
Bowlt, John, 218, 303, 306 nn. 77, 88; 307 nn. 103, 120
Box Factory, 69, 146 nn. 52, 53; 218; *98;* study, *98*
Braque, Georges, 59, 60, 61, 63, 388; *Large Nude, 59*
Brik, Lily, 327
Brik, Osip Maximovich, 304, 384; *361*
Briussov, Valerii, *344*
"Brother worker, keep your sister from prostitution" (poster design), 276; *289*
Bruni, Lev Aleksandrovich, 57, 389
Burliuk, David, 57
Burliuk, Vladimir, 57
Burmeister, Iza, 41, 43, 388
Bykov, Zakhar Nikolaevich, 304; *201*

Café Pittoresque, 274, 389
Card Game (Painterly-Plastic Balance), 64, 67
Card Party, The, 389
Carpaccio, Vittore, 44
Centrifuge (Tsentrifuga) cooperative, poster for, 274; *290*
Cézanne, Paul, 13, 15–16, 59, 63, 145 n. 9, 194, 196, 199, 354, 357
Cézannism, 15, 16, 58
Chagall, Marc Zakharovich, 57, 389
Chamber (Kamernyi) Theater, 217–19, 220, 250, 255, 389. *See also Romeo and Juliet*
Chancellor's Study, The (The Study) (set design) 219, 306 n. 79; *244*
Chelpanov, Georgii Ivanovich, 12
Chesterton, G. K., 252
Chevreul, Michel-Eugène, 368
Chicherin, Georgii Vasilievich, 257
Children's Theater, 219, 255, 389. *See also Tale of the Priest and Balda, His Helper, The*
china designs, 299; *298*
circle motif, 140, 143, 144, 147 n. 82, 250
city landscape drawings, 41–42, 68, 145 n. 14; *50, 51, 52, 53*
City of the Future (set design), 249, 250, 256; *245, 258*
Cityscape, 41–42; *53*
Cityscape with Smokestack (two drawings), 41–42; *50, 51*
Claudel, Paul, 217, 383–84
Clock (three 1914 works), 60, 62, 146 nn. 31, 34, 44; *73*
clothing designs, 215, 303–4. *See also* costumes; dress designs; work uniform designs
collages, 60, 110, 111, 112, 147 n. 67, 218; *107, 297. See also* Verbovka, embroidery designs for
color, 14, 44, 66, 68, 110–11, 138, 192
color discipline (Vkhutemas), 193, 212, 368, 389
Comedy Theater, 219–20, 250. *See also Locksmith and the Chancellor, The*
Composition (series of 1920–21 works), 141; *156, 162, 165, 166*
Composition with a Half-Moon, 181
Composition with a White Half-Moon (Spatial Construction), 138–39, 147 n. 72; *180*
Composition with Figures (Two Figures), 42, 43, 44, 145 nn. 4, 17; 388; *56*
Composition with White Crescent Moons (Construction), 138, 141, 147 n. 71; *156*
compote motif, 63, 137, 146 n. 37
Compote with Fruit (Plastic Painting), 63, 64, 389; *85*
construction-composition debate, 138, 193–94
constructions in space, studies for, 214; *223*
Construction Sketches, 139
Constructive Drawings, 139
Constructivism/construction, 12, 43, 64, 139, 140, 141, 143, 144, 191, 193–94, 195, 196–98, 212, 214–15, 217, 249, 250, 251, 252, 253–54, 255, 257, 273, 274, 275, 276–77, 299, 300, 301, 302, 303, 304, 306 n. 91; *201*
"Constructivists' Declaration" (Selvinsky et al.), 140

Constructor Liubov Popova, The (Stepanova), *351*
"Contemporary Russian Art" exhibition (1916), 389
"Cooperation . . . " (poster design), 274; *290*
Costakis, George, 139, 145 n. 1
Costakis collection, 15, 66, 67, 111, 135, 136, 137, 141, 142, 143, 146 n. 53, 257. *See also George Costakis Collection: Russian Avant-Garde Art, The*
"Costume as an Element of Material Formation" (course), 215, 306 n. 62
costume designs for: *The Locksmith and the Chancellor,* 220, 254, 306 n. 79; *235, 242; The Priest of Tarquinia,* 254, 275, 303, 307 n. 104; *243, 262, 263, 264, 265, 266, 267, 268, 269; Romeo and Juliet,* 218, 219, 220, 254; *230, 231, 232, 233, 240, 241. See also* work uniform designs
Council of Masters (Soviet Masterov), 192, 389
crafts, 273, 299
Cranach, Lukas, 145 n. 17
crescent moon motif, 138–39
"Critique of Things from Photographs, A" (App. X), 135, 362–64
Crommelynck, Fernand, 250, 306 n. 61, 390
Csáky, József, 41
Cubism/Cubist works, 13, 16, 41, 42–43, 57–58, 59–60, 61, 62, 63, 64, 67, 68, 69, 109, 135, 145 nn. 9, 13, 18; 146 n. 33, 191, 196, 197, 199, 200, 218, 219–20, 273, 357, 359, 374, 375. *See also* Cubo-Futurism
Cubist Cityscape. See Kremlin: Tsar-Cannon, The
Cubo-Futurism, 57–68, 109, 111, 133, 135, 136, 137, 140, 144, 193, 217, 219, 274, 277, 299
cup and saucer design, 299; *298*

Dahl, Mr. and Mrs. Roald, 141
Dallas Museum of Fine Arts, 134, 136
Dancer (costume designs), 254, 275; *268, 269*
Davydova, Natalia Mikhailovna, 109, 110, 273, 299, 301, 389
Dege, Adelaide (Adda) Robertovna, 41, 69, 137, 146 n. 53, 388, 389; *23, 25*
Delaunay, Robert, 41, 42
Delaunay, Sonia, 301, 302, 304, 307 n. 144, 374
Delta (Bobrov), cover design, 274, 307 n. 126; *292*
Demoiselles d'Avignon, Les (Picasso), 59
Denis, Maurice, 199, 374
Deussen, Paul, 12; *344*
Diaghilev, Sergei Pavlovich, 217, 303
Diez [Gavriil Dobrzhinsky], 254, 275, 389
"Discipline No. 1—Color" (with Vesnin; App. XII), 193, 368
Dobrzhinsky, Gavriil. *See* Diez
Dobuzhinsky, Mstislav Valerianovich, 13
Dobychina, Nadezhda, 57, 389
Dokuchaev, Nikolai Vasilievich, 200; *361*
"Donkey's Tail" exhibitions, 44
dress designs, 303–4; *310, 311, 314, 315, 316, 317, 318, 319, 324, 325, 330, 331, 332, 335*
Drevin, Aleksandr Davidovich, 305 nn. 42, 43
Duchamp, Marcel, 57
Du Cubisme (On Cubism) (Gleizes and Metzinger), 43, 63, 145 n. 18
Dudin, Ivan Osipovich, 13, 15, 41, 388
Dunoyer de Segonzac, André, 41, 388
Dvigatel (Engine) society, posters for, 276, 300, 390; *287, 289*
Dynamic Suprematism, 110
Dynamo Machine (Goncharova), 60

Early Morning. See Objects from a Dye Works
Earth on End (Zemlia dybom; adapted from Martinet's *La Nuit* by Tretiakov), designs for, 217, 250, 254, 255–57, 274, 275, 277, 302, 306 n. 61, 307 nn. 108, 109; *382, 384, 390; 270, 271*
easel painting, rejection of, 12, 137, 139, 197, 198, 213, 390
Eding, Boris Nikolaevich von, 44, 137, 389
Efimov, Ivan Semenovich, 219
Eiffeleia: 39 od (Eiffeleia: 30 Odes) (Aksionov): cover design, 275; *284*

Eisenstein, Sergei Mikhailovich, 216, 217, 306 n. 88, 384, 389
Ekk, Yuri, 216, 384
embroidery designs. See Verbovka, embroidery designs for
energetics, 136, 143–44, 347
Engine (Dvigatel) society, posters for, 276, 300, 390; 287, 289
Escher, M. C., 61
"Essence of the Disciplines, The" (Sushchnost distsiplin; App. XIII), 199, 369–70, 390; 370
Etkind, Mark, 306 n. 89
expediency, 213, 214, 216, 255, 380
"Explanation of My Work" (App. VIII), 197, 359; 358
Exposition Internationale des Arts Décoratifs (Paris, 1925), 300
"Exposition of the Fundamental Elements of the Material Design for La Nuit (Earth on End), An" (Tezisy; App. XIX), 256, 382
Expressionism, 57, 255, 276
Exter, Aleksandra Aleksandrovna, 41, 57, 58, 68, 146 n. 45, 147 n. 73, 217, 218, 219, 255, 303, 305 n. 43, 306 n. 73, 388, 389

fabric samples, 300; 327
Factory. See Box Factory
Factory (Goncharova), 58
Factory at Horta de Ebro (Picasso), 41
Falk, Robert Rafailovich, 57, 58, 388
Famira Kifared (Tamira of the Cittern) (Annensky), 218, 306 n. 73
Fauvism, 57
Favorsky, Vladimir Andreevich, 276; 371
Fedorov, German Vasilievich, 216, 305 n. 43, 306 n. 61
Fedorovsky, Fedor Fedorovich, 305 n. 43
Female Model (post-Paris works), 41, 42–43, 68, 111, 145 n. 17, 218; 46, 47, 48, 54, 55
Female Model (pre-Paris drawing), 15; 38
Female Model (Seated), 42; 48
Female Model (Standing), 42; 47
Female Model with Still Life, 145 n. 19
Figure + House + Space, 145 n. 17
Filonov, Pavel Nikolaevich, 276
"First Russian Art Exhibition" (Berlin, 1922), 147 n. 72
First State Textile Print Factory, designs for, 273, 299–303, 304, 390; 311, 312, 313, 315, 317, 319, 322, 323, 325, 326, 328, 329, 330, 331, 333, 334, 335, 337
First State Theater for Children of the People's Commissariat for Enlightenment. See Children's Theater
"5 × 5 = 25" exhibition (Moscow, 1921), 139, 191, 197, 198, 213, 274, 389; catalog cover, 143, 191; 187, 207
Florensky, Pavel Aleksandrovich, 44
Flower (prop design), 253, 256; 261
Forest, 12
Forest, The (Ostrovsky), 216
formovariator, 214
"For physical fitness" (poster design), 276; 287
"Fortress of the Capital, The" (monumental set), 249, 256
Four Studies for a Composition, 209
fourth dimension, 63, 133, 134
Free Studio of Vsevolod Meierkhold, 305–6 n. 59. See also work uniform designs
Free Theater Studios, 216
French Cubism, 13, 41, 42, 57, 58, 59, 60, 61, 62, 67, 68. See also Cubism; Cubo-Futurism
Friar Laurence (costume design), 218, 254; 233
Friar Laurence's Cell (set design), 218; 241
From Cubism to Suprematism (Ot kubizma k suprematizmu) (Malevich), 109
"From Representation to Construction" (Ot izobrazheniia k konstruktsii) (Inkhuk), Popova's essay for, 372–73
"Fundamental Elements of Painting . . . , The" (Osnovnye elementy zhivopisi . . .) (Kandinsky), 192
Futurism, 14, 57–58, 109, 191, 196, 199, 215, 217, 274–5, 277, 357. See also "Tramway V"; "Last Futurist Exhibition of Paintings"

GAKhN (State Academy of Artistic Sciences), 274
Galerie Gmurzynska (Cologne), 112
Galerie Lemercier, 307 n. 120
Garden in Front of the House, The (set design), 218; 240
Gauguin, Paul, 13, 15, 41
"General Plan for the Program of the Occasional Seminar on 'The Material Design of the Performance' for Moscow Proletkult" (App. XXI), 385
genre paintings, 59
geometric abstractionism, 109
George Costakis Collection: Russian Avant-Garde Art, The, 15, 138, 139, 140, 141, 145 n. 5, 146 nn. 50, 52; 147 n. 69, 273, 274, 275. See also Costakis collection
Geranium in a Pot (prop design), 253, 256; 248
Giotto, 14, 44, 388
Girl at the Piano (Villon), 67
Girl with a Mandolin (Picasso), 67
GITIS (State Institute of Theatrical Art), 216, 306 n. 59. See also Priest of Tarquinia, The
Glavsilikat, teacup for, 299, 390; 298
Gleizes, Albert, 41, 43, 57, 59, 63, 66, 145 n. 18; Woman at the Piano, 67
Goethe, 12; 344
Gogh, Vincent van, 13, 41
Golden Fleece (Zolotoe runo) (journal), 13
Goleizovsky, 381
Golovin, Aleksandr, 59
Goncharova, Natalia Sergeevna, 13, 14, 41, 57, 58, 60, 141; Airplane over Train, 58; Bicyclist, 58; Dynamo Machine, 60; Factory, 58; Laundry, 62; Mirror, 62; Petrovsky Park, 13; Weaver, 60
Gorky Museum of Art, 136
Gothic style, 14, 15, 16, 43, 61, 137, 140, 141, 218; 354
Grabar, Igor Emmanuilovich, 13, 14, 59
graphic design, 274–77
Gray, Camilla, 306 n. 89
Great Orator, The (Briussov), 344
Greco, El, 355
Gris, Juan, 59, 60, 61, 62, 63, 66, 146 n. 33; Le Lavabo, 59; The Man in the Café, 66; Smoker, 67; Still Life in Front of an Open Window (Place Ravignon), 146 n. 37; The Watch (The Sherry Bottle), 146 n. 33
Grishchenko, Aleksei, 14, 44, 388
Grocery, 63–64, 363; 87
Guido da Siena, 44, 145 n. 20
Guitar (series of 1914–15 works), 60, 61–62, 109, 146 nn. 31, 34; 71, 77, 78
guitar motif, 59, 60
GUVEZ (Main Administration of Higher and Secondary Pedagogical Institutions), 249
GVYRM (State Higher Directors' Workshops), 220, 305–6 n. 59
GVYTM (State Higher Theater Workshops), 191, 197, 213–16, 220, 250, 251, 256, 305 n. 59, 306 n. 80, 389. See also work uniform designs

Hack collection, 135
Hairdresser's (Rozanova), 62
Haystacks, 13; 35
Head of a Woman. See Birsk
Higher State Art-Technical Studios. See Vkhutemas
Hinton, Charles Howard, 63, 133
Horse (puppet designs), 219; 236
Houses (two 1912 drawings), 41–42; 52, 53
human figure, 14–15, 59
Hungarian masters, 41

iconography, of Cubism, 59, 60, 61, 62. See also Russian icons
Impressionism, 13, 14, 58–59, 194, 195, 199, 374
Inber, Vera, 140
industry, and art, 140, 214–15, 299. See also Productivism
Inkhuk (Institute of Artistic Culture), 12, 138, 145 nn. 1, 3; 190, 191, 192–94, 196, 198, 199, 200, 213, 215, 251–52, 253, 299, 304, 306 nn. 71, 91; 360, 365–67, 372–73, 378–79, 383–84, 389, 390; 361;

Objective Analysis Group (Section on Individual Arts), 193, 194, 195, 305 n. 13; Section on Monumental Art, 192, 194, 305 n. 13, 389
inscriptions, 60, 65
Institute of Artistic Culture. See Inkhuk
Institute of Labor, 381
Instruments, 111, 119
interleaving, 60, 110
"Introduction to the Inkhuk Discussion of The Magnanimous Cuckold" (App. XVII), 215, 251–52, 378–79
Ioganson, Karel Valdemarovich, 138, 214, 273; 361
Irkutsk Regional Museum of Art, 15, 111
Italian Futurism, 42, 57, 58, 65, 68, 69. See also Futurism; Cubo-Futurism
Italian Still Life, 60–61, 145 n. 28; 79
Ivanovskoe, Bridge, 13; 29
Izdebsky, Vladimir, 41

"Jack of Diamonds" exhibitions (Moscow, 1910–12), 41; (1914), 44, 388; (1916), 57, 68, 389
Jack of Diamonds group, 15, 41, 58, 59, 66, 145 n. 10
Jakobson, Roman [Aliagrov], 109
jazz, 303
Jeanne, Madame, 41, 42, 388
Joint Studios of the Left (OBMAS), 200
Jug on the Table, The (Relief), 64–65, 146 n. 42, 363, 389; 82

Kandinsky, Wassily Wassilievich, 57, 109, 139, 192–93, 389; artists' questionnaire, 192, 193, 348; 210, 211
Kantsler i slesar. See Locksmith and the Chancellor, The
Karetnikova, S., 15, 41, 274, 389
Khlebnikov, Velimir Vladimirovich, 57
Khodinskoe Field, 249–50, 256, 384. See also Struggle and Victory of the Soviets, The
Khrakovsky, Vladimir Lvovich, 384; 361
Kieselev, Viktor Petrovich, 274, 384; 361
Kipling, Rudyard, 219
Kitchen (Udaltsova), 62
Kliun, Ivan Vasilievich, 57, 58, 62, 64, 67, 109, 191, 305 n. 43, 389; Landscape Running Past, 58
Klutsis, Gustav Gustavovich, 273, 304
Knife Sharpener (Malevich), 43, 58
K novym beregam muzykalnago iskusstva. See Toward the New Shores of Musical Art
Konchalovsky, Piotr Petrovich, 41, 58, 59, 66
Korovin, Konstantin Alekseevich, 13, 14, 59
Krandievskaia, Nadezhda, 375
Krasnoiarsk Museum, 135
Krasnovidovo (country home), 12, 13; 18–19, 22
Kremlin: Tsar-Cannon, The, 68–69, 146 nn. 51, 52; 98
Krimov, Nikolai Petrovich, 13
Krinsky, Vladimir Fedorovich, 200; 361
Kruchenykh, Aleksei Eliseevich, 57, 109
Krupskaia, Nadezhda K., 307 n. 103
Kulbin, Nikolai Ivanovich, 57, 58
Kuntsevo Military Camouflage School, Observation Tower, 381
Kuprin, Aleksandr Vasilievich, 59
Kushner, Boris Anisimovich, 191, 253, 273, 304, 384
Kuznetsov, Pavel Varfolomeevich, 14, 59, 305 n. 43

Laboratory of Acting Technique, 305 n. 59
Ladovsky, Nikolai Aleksandrovich, 138, 200
Lady with Guitar, 67, 362; 95; studies, 146 n. 50; 95
La Fresnaye, Roger de, 41, 57, 59
Lamanova, Nadezhda Petrovna, 303
Lamp (prop design), 218; 234
Landscape Running Past (Kliun), 58
landscapes, 13, 14, 42, 58, 68–69
Landscape with a Red House and a Woman Washing, 13; 30
Landscape with Female Figures, 13; 31
Large Nude (Braque), 59
Larionov, Mikhail Fedorovich, 14, 41, 57, 109, 141
"Last Futurist Exhibition of Paintings: 0.10, The" (Petrograd, 1915–16), 57, 63, 64, 109, 146 n. 46, 389

Laundry (Goncharova), 62
Lautréamont, Comte de, 306 n. 80
Lavabo, Le (Gris), 59
Lavinsky, Anton Mikhailovich, 200, 216, 304, 384; 201, 361
Le Corbusier, 133
LEF (Left Front of the Arts; journal), 256, 304
Le Fauconnier, Henri, 41, 59, 109, 145 n. 13, 374, 375, 388
Left Federation of the Union of Moscow Artists, 389
Left Federation of the Union of Moscow Painters, 274
Léger, Fernand, 57, 59, 199, 374
Lenin, V. I., 256
Leningrad Pravda, Moscow office, 250
Lentulov, Aristarkh Vasilievich, 41, 57, 58, 59, 66, 68, 217, 305 n. 43; Ringing: The Kremlin Bell Tower, 68; Saint Basil's Cathedral, 68; Strastnoi Monastery, 68
Leonardo da Vinci, 44
life-building, 141, 144, 193, 194, 195, 197, 213, 255, 273, 304
life drawing, 14–15
light, problem of, 136
"Link" exhibition (Kiev, 1908), 13
linocuts, 110–11, 138, 191
Lipps, Theodor, 196
Lissitzky, El (Lazar Markovich), 196
Liutse, Vladimir Vladimirovich, 216, 251, 306 n. 88
Locksmith and the Chancellor, The (Kantsler i slesar) (Lunacharsky), Comedy Theater production, 219–20, 253, 389; costume designs, 220, 254, 306 n. 79; 235, 242; set designs, 219–20, 306 n. 79; 244
Logos (journal), 12; 344
L'Oiseau bleu (Metzinger), 44
Lunacharsky, Anatolii Vasilievich, 219, 220, 389

magazines, graphic designs for, 275, 276, 277; 278, 279, 280, 281, 282, 284
Magnanimous Cuckold, The (Velikodushnyi rogonosets) (Crommelynck), Actor's Theater production: prop design, 253, 256; 248, 261; rehearsal clothing, 306 n. 61 (see also work uniform designs); set designs, 140, 215, 219, 250–54, 256, 257, 302, 306 nn. 61, 90; 307 n. 134; 378–79, 384, 390; 248, 259, 260, 261
Ma Jolie (Picasso), 60–61
Male Model (Semi-Reclining Old Man), 15; 32
Male Model (series of ca. 1911 drawings), 15; 33
Male Models (1913 works), 42
Malevich, Kazimir Severinovich, 14, 43, 57, 58, 59, 67, 109, 110–11, 133, 134, 135, 142, 190, 191, 192, 196, 199, 217, 274, 299, 389; Black Square, 109, 110; Knife Sharpener, 43, 58
Man in a Crown (costume design), 254, 275; 262
Man in the Café, The (Gris), 66
Man Who Was Thursday, The (Chesterton), 252, 384
Man with a Fan (costume design), 254, 275; 263
Man with a Pipe (costume design), 220, 254; 235
Man with a Sheep (book illustration), 275; 283
Man with a Small Bowl (book illustration), 275; 283
Margolin, Samuil, 249
Marinetti, Filippo, 57
Martinet, Marcel, 256, 306 n. 61
Mashkov, Ilya Ivanovich, 58, 59, 66, 145 n. 10
mass festivals, 249, 256–57. See also Earth on End; Struggle and Victory of the Soviets, The
"Material Design of the Performance, The" (Moscow Proletkult course), 217, 300, 385, 390
"Material Element of the Performance, The" (GVYTM syllabus), 216
mathematics, 196
Matisse, Henri, 194, 199, 374, 375, 376
Matiushin, Mikhail Vasilievich, 63, 67, 145 n. 18, 192, 273
Mayakovsky, Vladimir Vladimirovich, 57, 304, 306 n. 90, 384
mechanistic motifs, 60, 62, 140
Medunetsky, Konstantin Konstantinovich, 250–51
Meierkhold, Vsevolod Emilievich, 198, 213–14, 215, 216, 217, 219, 249–54, 255–56, 277, 305 n. 59,

306 n. 90, 307 nn. 103, 108; 381, 389, 390
"Memorandum to the Vkhutemas Administration on an Organization Plan for the Studio of Vkhutemas Professors Vesnin, Lavinsky, Popova, Rodchenko," 216
Menkov, Mikhail, 57, 109
Merry Wives of Windsor, The (Shakespeare), 217
Metronome (Rozanova), 60
Metzinger, Jean, 41, 43, 44, 57, 59, 63, 66, 109, 145 nn. 13, 18; 199, 375, 388; L'Oiseau bleu, 44
Michelangelo, 44
Mirror (Goncharova), 62
Misteriia buff (Mystery-bouffe) (Mayakovsky), 384
"Modern Decorative Art" exhibition (Moscow, 1916–17), 307 n. 120
Modernism, 13, 59, 254, 273, 303
modern (new) style, 194–96, 199, 216, 254, 352, 353–54, 355, 356–57
"Modern Russian Painting" exhibition (Petrograd, 1916), 57
"Modern Trends" exhibition (Saint Petersburg, 1908), 13
Moi vospominaniia (My Reminiscences) (Udaltsova), 44
Monet, Claude, 194
montage style, 277
monumental design, 274. See also Earth on End; Struggle and Victory of the Soviets, The
Monument to the Third International (Tatlin), 249
Morgunov, Aleksei Alekseevich, 41, 44, 57
Morozov, Ivan Abramovich, 15
Moscow Association of Artists exhibition (1908), 13
Moscow Chamber Theater. See Chamber Theater
Moscow Children's Theater. See Children's Theater
"Moscow-Paris"/"Paris-Moscow" exhibitions (1979), 134
Moscow Proletkult, 217, 300, 385, 390
Mossovet (Moscow Soviet), 219, 274, 304, 389
Mowgli (Kipling), 219
Mukhina, Vera Ignatievna, 41, 42, 43, 44, 145 n. 10, 217, 274, 303, 306 n. 73, 388
Murina, Elena, 301
Museum of Artistic Culture, 193, 194, 197, 305 n. 18, 352, 358–59, 389
Museum of Modern Art (New York), 134
Museum of Modern Western Painting, 194
Musical Instruments (ca. 1914), 60, 61; 72
Musical Instruments (alt. title for a Painterly Architectonics of 1916), 111; 119
Musical Instruments (series of ca. 1914 works), 60–62, 111, 146 n. 29; 72, 79. See also Guitar
musical score, cover design, 275–76; 281
Musical Virgin Soil (Muzykalnaia Nov; journal), graphic designs for, 276; 280, 281, 282
Music and Revolution (Muzyka i revoliutsiia; journal), cover design, 276
Musician (costume design), 254, 275; 268
Muzyka i revoliutsiia. See Music and Revolution
Muzykalnaia Nov. See Musical Virgin Soil
Mystery-bouffe (Misteriia buff) (Mayakovsky), 384

Nabis group, 41
Narkompros (People's Commissariat for Enlightenment), 219, 220
Neoprimitivism, 13, 66
neo-Romanticism, 273
New Economic Policy (NEP), 256, 301
new style. See modern style
New Viewer (Novyi zritel; magazine), cover with Popova's portrait, 341
Neznakomka (The Unknown Woman) (Blok), 217
Night, The (La Nuit) (Martinet), 256, 306 n. 61, 307 n. 108, 382. See also Earth on End
Nikolskaia, Varvara Andreevna, 40
nonobjectivism, 62, 63–64, 66, 68, 69, 109–12, 134–37, 141, 143, 193, 194–96, 198–99, 212, 374, 375–77. See also "Tenth State Exhibition"
Norton Simon collection, 67
Novalis, 196
Novyi zritel. See New Viewer
Nuit, La (The Night) (Martinet), 256, 306 n. 61, 307 n. 108, 382. See also Earth on End
No. 8, 141; 157

Objective Analysis Group (Inkhuk), 192, 194, 195
objectivism, 195
objects: Cubists, 59, 63, 64; abstract, 213, 375–76
Objects, 63
Objects from a Dyeworks (Early Morning), 62, 146 nn. 32, 33; 218; 80
OBMAS (Joint Studios of the Left), 200
"O konstruktsii novoi formy predmetnoi i bespredmetnoi" (On the Construction of New Objective and Nonobjective Forms; App. III), 194, 197, 349–50, 390; 205
Old Devil, The (puppet design), 219; 236
Old Man (costume design), 254; 264
Omsk Regional Museum of Art, 15
"On a Precise Criterion . . ." (O tochnom kriterii . . . ; App. XVIII), 255, 307 n. 105, 380–81, 390
On Cubism (Du Cubisme) (Gleizes and Metzinger), 43, 63, 145 n. 18
"On Drawings" (App. XI), 365–67; 365
"On the Construction of New Objective and Nonobjective Forms" (O konstruktsii novoi formy predmetnoi i bespredmetnoi; App. III), 194, 197, 349–50, 390; 205
"On the Production Work of Inkhuk . . ." (App. XX), 383–84
"On the Question of New Methods in Our Artistic Schools" (App. XIV), 198, 213, 372–73
Orange Painterly Architectonics, 136; 177
Orientalism, 254, 255
Orlov, K. M., 12, 388
ornamental style, 275
Orphists, 196, 357, 374
Osmerkin, Aleksandr Aleksandrovich, 305 n. 43
"Osnovnye elementy zhivopisi . . ." (The Fundamental Elements of Painting . . .) (Kandinsky), 192
"Ot izobrazheniia k konstruktsii" (From Representation to Construction) (Inkhuk), Popova's essay for, 373
Ot kubizma k suprematizmu (From Cubism to Suprematism) (Malevich), 109
"O tochnom kriterii . . . " (On a Precise Criterion . . . ; App. XVIII), 255, 307 n. 105, 380–81, 390

Painterly Architectonics series, 16, 63, 111, 112, 133–37, 142, 144, 302, 389
—1915 work, 109, 133, 147 n. 56
—1916–17 works, 69, 109–10, 111–12, 134–35, 136, 138, 147 nn. 58, 59, 60, 65, 66; 363–64, 389; 106, 114, 117, 118, 119, 120, 127, 130, 131, 132, 150, 151, 153; studies, 110, 111, 112, 135, 147 n. 68; 113, 114, 118, 120, 121, 128, 150, 294
—1918 works, 134, 135–36, 137, 138, 140, 141, 147 nn. 69, 70; 191, 218, 364; 129, 153, 154, 155, 174, 175, 176, 177; studies, 135; 152, 173
—"1919" work, 147 nn. 69, 70; 154
Painterly Architectonics: Orange, Black, Gray, 110, 147 n. 60; 106
Painterly Architectonics (Still Life: Instruments), 111, 147 n. 65; 119
Painterly Architectonics with a Black Quadrangle, 134–35; 130
Painterly Architectonics with a Pink Semicircle, 135–36; 129
Painterly Architectonics with a Saw, 112; 114
Painterly Architectonics with Black Board (study), 112; 118
Painterly Architectonics with Black Rectangle, 109–10; 120; studies, 147 n. 58, 120
Painterly Architectonics with Three Stripes, 134; 117
Painterly Architectonics with Turquoise Rear Plane, 135, 136; 131
Painterly Architectonics with Yellow Board, 112, 147 n. 66; 118
Painterly Construction (series of 1920 works), 137–38, 139, 389; 158, 179; studies, 138; 159, 178
Painterly Synthesis of the Town of Prato (Soffici), 68
Painting Relief. See Volumetric-Spatial Relief
Pakhomova, Tatiana Mikhailovna, 13, 145 n. 1, 147 n. 69, 274, 307 n. 134
Palace of Labor, 250

Palette studio, La, 41, 388
Paris académies, 199–200, 374
"Paris-Moscow"/"Moscow-Paris" exhibitions (1979), 134
Pavlov, Evgenii, 275
Pearl of Adalmina. See Adalmina's Pearl
Peck, George, 142
Perm Picture Gallery, 111, 143
Person + Air + Space (Seated Female Model), 43, 58, 145 n. 17; 49
Pestel, Vera Efimovna, 15, 41, 57, 109, 274, 388, 389
Petrovsky Park (Goncharova), 13
Petrov-Vodkin, Kuzma Sergeevich, 14, 192, 199
Phaedra (Racine), 384
photography, 255
Pianist, 67, 146 n. 49
Picabia, Francis, 374
Picasso, Pablo, 41, 59, 60, 61, 63, 64, 65, 255, 357, 376, 381, 388; Factory at Horta de Ebro, 41; Girl with a Mandolin, 67; Demoiselles d'Avignon, Les, 59; Ma Jolie, 60; Portrait of Daniel-Henry Kahnweiler (The Aficionado; Toreador), 65
Pinturicchio, 14, 388
plastic dynamism, 57, 58
plastic paintings, 64. See also sculpto-paintings
Plenipotentiary of the Samara Vkhutemas (Adlivankin), 305 n. 1
Pobeda nad solntsem. See Victory over the Sun
poets, 57
Poets Club. See All-Russian Union of Poets Club
Pointillism, 194
Polivanov, S. [Naum Iosifovich Sheinfeld], 254
Popov, Pavel Sergeevich (brother), 12, 66, 145 n. 3; 21, 23, 25, 27, 221
Popov, Sergei Maksimovich (father), 12, 388; 20, 27
Popov, Sergei Sergeevich (brother), 12; 21, 25, 27
Popova, Anna Ilinichna (sister-in-law), 12
Popova, Liubov Sergeevna:
—biographical data: birth and family background, 12; education, 12–13; marriage, 137, 190; birth of son, 137, 190; husband's death, 137, 190; typhus bout, 137; mother's death, 257; final illness and death, 304; funeral, 338. See also Chronology, pp. 388–89.
—influences on, 13–14, 15, 42, 43–44, 60, 65, 66, 67, 133, 137, 146 n. 33, 192
—nature of, 44, 190; as a teacher, 212–13
—photographs of, 5, 26, 149, 341, 386; with family members, 17, 21, 22, 23, 24, 25, 27; with colleagues, 40, 201, 203, 321
—portraits of, 341, 351; caricature, 313; self-portraits, 66–67, 146 nn. 46, 47; 101, 342
—posthumous exhibition, 14, 58, 62, 64, 68, 133, 137, 139, 140, 143, 145 nn. 6, 17; 146 nn. 29, 30, 31, 32, 35, 51, 52; 147 n. 56, 61, 68, 82; 198, 274; invitation to, 339; catalog cover, 340
—travels: Birsk, 69, 146 n. 53; Brittany, 42; Italy, 14 43–45, 58, 133; Kiev, 14; Novgorod, 14; Paris, 41–42, 43; Rostov-on-the-Don, 137; Saint Petersburg, 14; Samarkand and Central Asia, 111, 133, 254
—"trial" of, 251–52, 253, 306 n. 91
Popova, Liubov Vasilievna Zubova (mother), 12, 257, 388; 20
Popova, Olga Sergeevna (sister), 12; 23
Popova, Vera Aleksandrovna (cousin), 12, 307 n. 120
Portrait (two 1916 works), 111, 112; 115, 116
Portrait No. 4. See Portrait of a Philosopher
Portrait of a Girl Against a Tile Stove, 14; 34
Portrait of a Lady (Plastic Drawing), 64, 65, 146 n. 46, 362, 389; 83
Portrait of a Philosopher, 42, 65, 66, 67, 146 nn. 46, 50; 362–63; 92; drawing for, 66, 146 n. 46, 362–63; 93; model for, 66, 221; preliminary drawings, 93, 94
Portrait of Daniel-Henry Kahnweiler (The Aficionado; Toreador) (Picasso), 65
portraits, 14, 58, 59, 64–68
Ports and Factories (Rozanova), 58
Post-Cubism, 109
poster designs, 257, 275, 276–77; 271, 284, 286, 287, 288, 289, 290, 291

Post-Impressionism, 59, 199
Pozdneev, A., 253
Pre-Constructivism, 43
Pribylskaia, Evgeniia, 303
Priest (costume design), 254, 275; 264, 265
Priest of Tarquinia, The (Zhrets Tarkvinii) (Polivanov), unstaged Actor's Theater production, 254–55, 307 n. 103, 390; costume designs, 254, 275, 303, 307 n. 104; 243, 262, 263, 264, 265, 266, 267, 268, 269
Priest's Daughter (puppet design), 219; 239
Primitivism, 57, 219, 274
Primorsk Art Gallery, 141
Princess Brambilla (Hoffmann), 384
Problems of Stenography (Voprosy stenografii), cover design, 277; 284
Productivism/Production Art, 140, 141, 191, 193, 196, 197, 198, 213–14, 217, 250, 257, 273, 274, 275, 299, 300
"Program for the Color Discipline of the Basic Department" (Programma distsipliny tsveta Osnovnogo otdeleniia), 212
Proletarian Culture Movement. See Moscow Proletkult
prozodezhda. See work uniform designs
Prudkovskaia, Liudmila Andreevna, 13, 15, 41, 145 n. 13, 388
Puni, Ivan Albertovich, 57, 58, 62, 64, 111, 389
Punin, Nikolai, 139
puppet show, designs for, 219; 236, 237, 238, 239
Puppet Show Booth, The, 219; 238
Pushkin, Aleksandr Sergeevich, 12, 219, 389; 344

"Question of the New Methodology of Instruction (First Discipline of the Basic Department of the Vkhutemas Painting Faculty), The" (Apps. XV, XVI), 64, 374, 375–77

Rakitin, Vasilii, 274
Rakitina, Elena, 252
Raphael, 44
Ravdel, Efim Vladimirovich, 305 n. 43
rayic system, 141, 142–43, 220, 302
Rayism, 57, 109, 141
realism, turn back to, 212, 301
Rebellion of Misanthropes (Vosstanie mizantropov) (Bobrov), cover design, 285
Relief. See Jug on the Table, The
reliefs. See sculpto-paintings
Renaissance art, 43–44, 133
representational style, 199, 276–77
Riegl, Alois, 196
Ringing: The Kremlin Bell Tower (Lentulov), 68
Rodchenko, Aleksandr Mikhailovich, 44, 57, 143, 190, 191, 198, 214, 215, 216, 250, 273, 277, 299, 300, 301, 304, 305 nn. 42, 43; 306 n. 91, 384, 389; photographs by, 5, 201, 221, 321, 327
Rodchenko, Madame, 201
Rogovin, N. E., 15
Romeo and Juliet (Shakespeare), Moscow Chamber Theater production, 217–19, 255, 303, 384, 389; costume designs, 218, 220, 254; 230, 231, 232, 233, 240, 241; lamp, 234; set designs, 218; 226, 227, 228, 229, 240, 241
Romeo in a Mask (costume design), 218, 254; 230, 240
Rossiiskaia pochtovo-telegrafnaia statistika (Russian Postal-Telegraph Statistics), cover design, 275; 293
Rostov-Yaroslavl Museum-Archive of Architecture and Art, 137
Rozanova, Olga Vladimirovna, 41, 57, 58, 60, 109, 111, 273, 389; Hairdresser's, 62; Metronome, 60; Ports and Factories, 58; Sewing Box, 62
Russian icons, 14, 137, 139, 357
Russian Museum, 135
Russian Postal-Telegraph Statistics (Rossiiskaia pochtovo-telegrafnaia statistika), cover design, 275; 293
Russian Revolution, 190, 214, 249, 255–56, 274, 299
Ryazan Museum, 111

Saint Basil's Cathedral (Lentulov), 68
"Salon" exhibition (Saint Petersburg, 1908), 13

"Salon of the Golden Fleece" exhibition (Moscow, 1908), 13
Salt of the Earth (Sol zemli) (Tserukavsky), cover design, 277
Sapunov, Nikolai Nikolaevich, 13, 59
Saryan, Martiros Sergeevich, 59
Satz, Natalia, 219
School Poems of Pushkin, 344
sculpto-paintings (reliefs), 43, 64–65, 134
sculptors, 41
sculpture, 193
Seated Female Model (Person + Air + Space), 43, 58, 145 n. 17; 49
Seated Male Model, 15
Second Free State Studios, 199
Second Notebook of Lyrics. For Piano (Vtoraia tetrad lirika. Dlia fortepiano) (Pavlov), cover design, 275–76; 281
Section d'Or, 57
Sections on Individual Arts and Monumental Art. See under Inkhuk
Self-Portrait (1910s), 67; 342
Self-Portrait (1915), 66–67, 68, 146 n. 46; 101
Selvinsky, Ilia, 140
Senkin, Sergei Yakovlevich, 304, 305 n. 43
Sergeev, M. S., 44
Serov, Valentin Aleksandrovich, 13
Servant with Tray (costume design), 218, 254; 231
set designs. See Earth on End; Locksmith and the Chancellor, The; Magnanimous Cuckold, The; Romeo and Juliet; Struggle and Victory of the Soviets, The
Sewing Box (Rozanova), 62
Shah-i-Zinda works, 68, 111, 147 n. 64
Shamshina, Varvava, 145 n. 3
Shchukin, Sergei Ivanovich, 15, 41, 388
Shechtel, Fedor, 12
Sheinfeld, Naum Iosifovich [S. Polivanov], 254
Shelley, Percy Bysshe, 12; 344
Shevchenko, Aleksandr Vasilievich, 14, 305 n. 43
Shklovksy, Viktor Borisovich, 191
shop window, design for, 318
Shterenberg, David Petrovich, 41
Shusev Museum of Architecture, 274
Signac, Paul, 194
Simonovich-Efimova, Nina, 219
Simultaneists, 196, 357, 374
6 Prints, linocut plates, 110–11, 147 nn. 61, 63; 136, 191; 108, 122, 123, 124, 125, 126
Skozka o pope i rabotnike ego Balde. See Tale of the Priest and His Helper, Balda, The
Sketch for a Portrait, 221
Slap in the Face of Public Taste, A (Burliuk et al.), 57
slogan texts, 254; 271
Smert Tarelkina. See Tarelkin's Death
Smoker, 67; 88
Smoker (Gris), 67
Sobolyev, N., 201
Society for the Struggle Against Illiteracy, poster designs for, 276, 390; 284, 286, 291
Soffici, Ardengo, 65, 146 n. 45; Painterly Synthesis of the Town of Prato, 68
Sofronova, Antonina, 276
Soldier (costume design for The Priest of Tarquinia), 254, 275; 243, 265
Soldier (costume design for Romeo and Juliet), 218; 241
Sol zemli (Salt of the Earth) (Tserukavsky), cover design, 277
Sotheby's, 138
Soviet Masterov (Council of Masters), 192, 389
Spatial Construction. See Composition with a White Half Moon
Spatial Force Construction (series of 1921 works), 138, 139–44, 147 nn. 79, 82, 83, 85, 389; 160, 166, 167, 172, 183, 184, 185, 186, 221; studies, 141–42, 143, 147 n. 80, 363 n.; 161, 163, 164, 168, 169, 170, 171, 182
Spatial Force Construction (Composition), 141; 166
Spring, 111
Square, The (set design), 218; 226, 227

State Academy of Artistic Sciences. *See* GAKhN
State Higher Directors' Workshops. *See* GVYRM
State Higher Theater Workshops. *See* GVYTM
State Institute of Theatrical Art. *See* GITIS
State Museum of Art of the Uzbek S.S.R., 136
Stenberg, Georgii Avgustovich, 250–51, 273
Stenberg, Vladimir Avgustovich, 250–51, 273, 306 n. 88
Stepanova, Varvara Fedorovna, 44, 191, 273, 299, 300, 304, 306 n. 91, 384, 389, 390; *201, 313, 320–21; The Constructor Liubov Popova, 351*
Still Life (two ca. 1914 works), 60; *70, 71*
Still Life (1915), 63, 146 n. 35; *86*
Still Life in Front of an Open Window (Place Ravignon) (Gris), 146 n. 37
Still Life Interiors (series), 64
Still Life. Milk Pitcher. Plein Air, 13–14; *35*
still lifes, 13–14, 15, 58–59, 60–64, 198–99, 212
Still Life (Shop). See Grocery
Still Life with Carafe (study), 62; *76*
Still Life with Compote, 62, 63, 146 n. 36; *84*; study, *86*
Still Life with Kitchen Utensils, 76
Still Life with Lamp, 62; *74*
Still Life with Mask, 63, 146 n. 39; *81*
Still Life with Stove (study), 62; *76*
Still Life with Tin Dish, 43, 44, 60, 64, 145 n. 17, 388; *56*
Still Life with Tray (two 1915 works), 59, 62–63, 362; *74, 75*
"Store, The" exhibition (Moscow, 1916), 57, 64, 146 n. 30, 190, 389
Strastnoi Monastery (Lentulov), 68
Stroganov Art School, 198
Struggle and Victory of the Soviets, The (proposed mass festival), set designs, 249–50, 256, 389; *245, 258*
Study, The (The Chancellor's Study) (set design), 219, 306 n. 79; *244*
Study for a Composition (series of 1921 works), 204, 206, 208, 209
Study for a Portrait (series of 1915–16 works), 65–66, 67, 137, 146 nn. 34, 44; *91, 94, 102, 103*; preliminary drawings, 66; *90, 91*
Study for a Rejoinder to a 1915 Work, 146 n. 36
Study for a Two-Figure Composition, 89
Study for Female Model (series of 1913 works), 145 n. 17
Sudeikin, Sergei Yurievich, 13, 59
suit design, 309
Suprematism, 64, 67, 109–11, 135, 191, 192, 199, 273, 274, 277, 302, 303. *See also* "Tenth State Exhibition"
Supremus (projected journal), 109, 139, 273, 389
Supremus society, 109, 273, 389; logo for, 109, 135, 147 n. 68, 273, 274; *107*
"Sushchnost distsiplin" (The Essence of the Disciplines; App. XIII), 199, 369–70, 390; *370*
Svomas Free State Art Studios, 191
Symbolism, 13, 14, 145 n. 9, 273

Tairov, Aleksandr Yakovlevich, 217, 218, 219, 252, 389
Talashkino artists, 273
Tale of the Priest and Balda, His Helper, The (Skazka o pope i rabotnike ego Balde) (Pushkin), designs for Moscow Children's Theater puppet production, 219, 254, 306 n. 77, 389; *236, 237, 238, 239*
Tales of Wonder (Volshebnye skazki) (Diez), designs for, 275, 389; *283, 293*
Tamerlane, 389
Tamira of the Cittern (Famira Kifared) (Annensky), 218, 306 n. 73
Tarelkin's Death (Smert Tarelkina) (Sukhovo-Kobylin), 384
Tatlin, Vladimir Evgrafovich, 14, 15, 41, 42, 43, 44, 57, 58, 61, 64, 109, 139, 143, 145 n. 17, 190,

212, 301, 388, 389; *Monument to the Third International*, 249
Tatlinism, 139
teacup and saucer design, 299; *298*
"Tenth State Exhibition: Nonobjective Art and Suprematism" (Moscow, 1919), 136, 191, 389; catalog, 191, 192, 347; *346*
Ternovets, Boris Nikolaevich, 41, 42, 388
textile designs. *See* First State Textile Print Factory
"Tezisy" (Theses; An Exposition of the Fundamental Elements of the Material Design for *La Nuit* [Earth on End]; App. XIX), 256, 382
Theater of the Russian Republic, 305 n. 59
theatrical October, 214, 249
"Theatrical-Set Art of Moscow, 1918–1923" exhibition, 306 n. 84
Theodoric, 43
"Theses." *See* "Tezisy"
Third Congress of the Communist International, 249, 389
Thyssen-Bornemisza collection, 111
Tiara of the Century, The (Tiara veka) (Claudel), 306 n. 61
Tintoretto, 44, 355
Toward the New Shores of Musical Art (K novym beregam muzykalnago iskusstva; journal), designs for, 276; *278, 279*
Tower studio, 15, 41, 44, 388
"Tramway V: The First Futurist Exhibition of Paintings" (Petrograd, 1915), 57, 145 n. 17, 389
Traveling Woman (two 1915 works), 42, 65, 67–68; *96, 97*
tray motif, 59
Tree (drawings), 15; *39*
Tree (stage design), 218; *234*
Trees (drawings), 16; *36, 37, 38*
Trees (painting), 16; *45*
Tretiakov, Sergei Mikhailovich, 206 n. 61, 253, 256
Tretiakov Gallery, 135, 136, 139, 140, 142, 143, 251, 274, 275
Troianovskaia, Anna, 15, 388
Tsentrifuga (Centrifuge) cooperative, poster for, 274; *290*
Tsindel, Emil, 384
Tugendkhold, Yakov Aleksandrovich, 274, 300–301
Two Figures. See Composition with Figures

Udaltsova, Nadezhda Andreevna, 13, 15, 41, 44, 57, 58, 59, 109, 111, 145 n. 13, 273, 274, 388, 389; *40; Kitchen*, 62; *Violin*, 59, 61
Union of Russian Artists, 13, 14; exhibition (1908), 13
"Union of Youth" exhibitions, 44
Unknown Woman, The (Neznakomka) (Blok), 217
Uriel Acosta, 384
Uspensky, Piotr Demyanovich, 63, 133
utopianism, 133–34

Vakhtangov, S., 306 n. 90
Vasilieva, Maria Mikhailovna, 41, 57
Vedanta, Plato, and Kant: Culture and Wisdom of the Ancient Indians (Deussen), 12; *344*
Velikodushnyi rogonosets. See Magnanimous Cuckold, The
Verbovka, embroidery designs for, 110, 111, 147 n. 62, 273, 274, 299, 300, 303, 307 n. 118, 389; *272, 294, 295, 296, 297*
Vern 34, 141–42
Vertepov, Aleksandr, 41
Vertov, Dziga, 257
Vesnin, Alexsandr Aleksandrovich, 12, 15, 44, 145 n. 3, 146 n. 39, 191, 193, 212, 216, 217, 218–19, 250, 252, 255, 274, 368, 383, 384, 388, 389; *105, 201, 203, 221, 361*
Vesnin-Aksionov list, 12, 13, 14, 41, 63, 65, 66, 109, 110, 111, 112, 133, 135, 137, 139, 143, 145 nn. 3, 6, 17, 19, 146 nn. 29, 31, 32, 36, 44, 51, 52;

147 nn. 58, 60, 61, 62, 66, 71, 74, 79, 82; 219, 274, 306 n. 84
Victory over the Sun (Pobeda nad solntsem) (Kruchenykh), 217
Victory from My Window onto Houses, 13; *28*
Viktorov, Petr N., 299
Villon, Jacques, 57, 59; *Girl at the Piano*, 67
Violin, 59, 61, 146 n. 30, 362, 389; *79*
Violin (Udaltsova), 59, 61
violin motif, 59, 60
Violins and Cannons, 145–46 n. 28
Vipper, Boris Robertovich, 44
Vkhutemas (Higher State Art-Technical Studios), 190, 191, 192, 193, 198–200, 212–13, 214, 215, 216–17, 299, 301, 304, 305 nn. 42, 43; 306 n. 71, 307 n. 134, 374, 375–77, 389, 390; *202–3, 371*
Volshebnye skazki. See Tales of Wonder
Volumetric-Spatial Relief, 64, 65, 146 n. 43, 363; *86*
Voprosy stenografii (Problems of Stenography), cover design, 277; *284*
Voronovna, O. I., 306 n. 73
Vosstanie mizantropov. See Rebellion of Misanthropes
Vrubel, Mikhail Aleksandrovich, 14, 15, 145 n. 9, 273, 388
Vseobuch (General Education), 249
Vtoraia tetrad liriki. Dlia fortepiano (Second Notebook of Lyrics. For Piano) (Pavlov), cover design, 275–76; *281*

Watch, The (The Sherry Bottle) (Gris), 146 n. 33
Weaver (Goncharova), 60
Wei, Lilly, 142
Woman (costume design for *The Priest of Tarquinia*), 254, 275; *267*
Woman (costume design for *Romeo and Juliet*), 218, 254; *232*
Woman and Child, 218; *55*
Woman at the Piano (Gleizes), 67
Woman in a Yashmak (costume design), 254, 275; *266*
Woman with a Briefcase (costume design), 220, 254; *242*
Women (costume designs), 254, 275; *266, 267*
Work in Oil (four works), 139, 147 n. 82
work uniform *(prozodezhda)* designs, 215, 250, 253, 254, 256, 306 n. 61, 379; *224, 225, 246, 247*
World of Art, 13, 41, 59, 217, 273
Worringer, Wilhelm, 195, 196, 353, 356
"Wreath" exhibition (Saint Petersburg, 1908), 13
"Wreath-Stephanos" exhibition (Moscow, 1908), 13

Yakulov, Georgii Bogdanovich, 41, 66, 251
Yaroslavl Museum of Art, 136, 137
Young Devil, The (puppet design), 219; *237*
Youth (costume design), 218, 254; *230*
Youth in a Cape (costume design), 218, 254; *231*
Yuon, Konstantin Fedorovich, 13, 15, 41, 388

Zadkine, Ossip, 388
Zaichikov, Vasilii Fedorovich, 384
Zdanevich, Kirill, 388
Zelinsky, Kornelii, 140
Zemlia dybom. See Earth on End
"0.10" exhibition. *See* "Last Futurist Exhibition of Painting: 0.10, The"
Zhegin, Lev, 12
Zhemchuzhina Adalminy. See Adalmina's Pearl
Zhemchuzhny, 304
Zhrets Tarkvinii. See Priest of Tarquinia, The
Zhukov, Innokentii, 375
Zhukovsky, Stanislav Yulianovich, 13, 388
Zolotnitsky, David Iosefovich, 214
Zolotoe runo (Golden Fleece; journal), 13
Zrelishcha (Performances; journal), 253, 254, 390
Zubov, Vasilii Pavlovich, 12
Zubova, Liubov Vasilievna. *See* Popova, Liubov Vasilievna Zubova